Beyond the Fire and the Rain

My Journey

An intimate story of the struggle of an African-American youth to become a medical doctor, as he overcomes racism and the resistance of the establishment.

Wilbert Williams Jr., M.D.

Wilbert Williams Jr., M.D.
40 Underhill Road
Middletown, New York 10940

www.trafford.com

North America & international
toll-free: 1 888 232 4444 (USA & Canada)
phone: 250 383 6864 ♦ fax: 812 355 4082

ALSO BY WILBERT WILLIAMS JR., M.D.

Petals

Dancing in Fire

Shouting at the Rain

The Secret Place

In Memory Of

Dr. Robert V. Vaughn

FOR

My father, who was born in Chesson, in Macon County, Alabama, I remember your long quiet moments looking through our living room windows at the people. I admired your indulgence with God's Creation. I am proud that in the midst of racism, which you encountered almost everywhere, you did not allow it to destroy you. Because of your strength, I am the man-child who will always respect, honor, and adore you. I am proud that you were my earthly father.

My mother, who was born in Baltimore, Maryland, I am indebted to you for telling me about life. I will always remember you're sharing with me the story of Harriet Tubman and the Underground Railroad. Thank you also for sharing with me the beauty of Baltimore. I am grateful that you exposed me to what you felt would benefit me the greatest. When I think of Baltimore, I see your beautiful soft brown face smiling at me.

My beautiful and faithful wife, you have always loved me dearly and honestly. I thank you for giving me you. I am blessed and rich that you are my wife. You gave me seven beautiful children who fascinate me and whom I adore. Thank you for allowing me the time to work on and finish our story.

My only two sisters whom, I have always loved, and thank God that I have. Thank you for encouraging me to aspire toward greater heights. I pray that this memoir will reflect an expression of your love for our parents, who raised us well.

My late friend Dr. Robert Vaughn, thank you for your determination to be my stepfather. Thank you for the many hours you labored with me to complete my manuscript from the inception of this body of work. Thank you for the many hours you shared with me in your beautiful warm home as you encouraged me to hold on to my faith in God. I learned many things from you that will last me a lifetime. Enjoy your fellowship with God. I love you.

My kind and intelligent friend Beryl Shaw, who is my wise confidant. Thank you for taking your precious time while you studied in college to help me with the manuscript. You raised it to a higher level of acceptance and professionalism. Your soft spoken words to me encouraged me to hold on to my dreams and goals and move forward.

Thanks to my children for tolerating my absence while I labored over my writing. Thank you for allowing me to speak to you for long periods of time even when you had things to do. Thank you for showing me your Agape love, mercy and forgiveness.

Thank you Shoshanna for putting up with my need to ask constantly for your help correcting many of the mistakes in the manuscript.

Many thanks to Mildred who read the full manuscript and gave me important critical advice.

Thank you Domitilia for listening to why I had to publish my manuscript. I am indebted to you for giving me endless hours to review, edit and discuss my life.

Thank you Charlotte for your advice about the manuscript and always telling me how you feel about my behavior.

Thank you Amelia for your ability to search and find what needed important attention and correction when I thought I was finished with the manuscript.

"Men do not live by bread alone; so with nations, they are not saved by art, but by honesty; not by the gilded splendors of wealth but by the hidden treasure of manly virtue; not by the multitudinous gratification of the flesh, but by the celestial guidance of the spirit."

Frederick Douglas

Contents

Forward

Some stories need telling. *"Beyond the Fire and the Rain"* is such a story. It is a story of success, and of overcoming challenges and prejudices from without and from within. Herein we follow the trials in the life of a young man whose father was a barber, and his mother a domestic worker. They lived where gangs notoriously spawned, an area from which this author "graduated," or perhaps better stated, "Escaped."

This is the inspirational story of a young African-American man. With the dedicated assistance and support of his parents, and his ever-loving wife, he has achieved a major goal in his life. It is the story of a young man who left the "safety" of his birthplace to seek an education in the "foreign" areas of long-established schooling systems. He often experienced hostile racial attitudes.

Inspiration should be the cornerstone of those who are privileged to read this intimate and very personal account. I hope many of these readers will be young people of different colors, cultures, religious beliefs, locales, etc. It is a lesson in overcoming the development of hatred and fear, which result from illogical discrimination; especially that of racial prejudice.

This book, too, should be an inspiration to those who have been engendered with prejudice as young people, and who have grown to adulthood, carrying those prejudices with them. It is another chance to look at ourselves, and to see others in light of our similarities, rather than our differences. This work is a message of hope in a "minefield" of racial prejudice, fear, and hatred.

Dr. Wilbert Williams Jr., M.D. is a role model for young people of all hues. He is a dedicated physician who alleviates the illnesses of people in the Virgin Islands and wherever he goes, including the poor and the disadvantaged. He is living proof that one can make it "Beyond the Fire and the Rain."

Robert V. Vaughn, Ed. D.
Christiansted, St. Croix, VI

Introduction

Beyond the Fire and the Rain is a fascinating and compelling story of a young African-American who grew up in a South Brooklyn, New York public housing project. He beat overwhelming odds to become a medical doctor. His story will take one meandering through valleys and mountaintop experiences. He will journey from the streets of New York, and a housing project called Red Hook in South Brooklyn, to the beautiful Caribbean island of St. Croix in the United States, Virgin Islands. He will share his joy, and his pain and agony to overcome anxiety, depression, and a near nervous breakdown. He struggled to deal with racism, lost and broken relationships, and trying to become a physician. His journey through medical school will at times exhaust you. His revealing hurt when he faced racism, and the forces behind it, which threatened his life, may bring you to tears. *Beyond the Fire and the Rain* speaks to all of us. It gives us a mirrored reflection of our strengths and weaknesses in the presence of our challenges. It tells us that in spite of everything short of death, we can overcome anything in our lives by faith, hope and trust in God and in ourselves. Dr. Williams proclaims that perseverance and commitment are keys to conquering our tallest and most rugged mountains, and still grow. *Beyond the Fire and the Rain* is not only a success story of an African American youth from Brooklyn, New York. It is the story of a person's refusal to give up his dream to become a medical doctor, while facing tremendous odds. It is a statement to all of us that we do not have to let the existing society mandate or dictate our destiny. We can soar like eagles, to conquer our goals and dreams.

Robert V. Vaughn. Ed. D
Christiansted, St. Croix, VI

Preface

I have changed some names in this journey. I have not altered the situations and places, however, except to express them in my own conceptualization. Some names, on the other hand, have not been altered, since they are a matter of a public record.

The audience for which this memoir has been written is the public, Blacks and whites, medical and non-medical persons, traditional and non-traditional religions and philosophy. This memoir is intended to portray the feelings and experiences of a Black person from childhood to adulthood, college, medical school and actual medical practice. It illustrates the revelations of prejudice and discrimination exerted on Blacks and whites, by the establishment.

Faced with the dilemma concerning terms used, such as African American, Black, Negro, white, Caucasian, etc., I have taken poetic license and have used the term "Black" for it was generally in use at the time of this memoir. African American, while perhaps more definitive and politically correct, was too cumbersome, just as the word "Caucasian" was cumbersome.

Both of those terms, Black and African American, would have been capitalized. "Black" as a common noun capitalized and "white" lowercase are being used here, as it appears as "standard" in similar contemporary literature.

Capitalization, which was a dilemma in relation to "Black," was also a problem in relation to other words, such as academic and medical areas of study, such as Philosophy, Chemistry, Obstetrics, Gynecology, Hematology, Cardiology, and for acronyms such as OB/Gyn, IV, ICU, etc. Titles and positions, such as Chief of Obstetrics, Assistant Chief, Administrator, etc., have been generally capitalized. Capitalizations in all of the cases do not imply greater or lesser importance than if it were un-capitalized.

This is my personal account of my family and me, and as such, it is an ongoing saga. There is no logical ending, except that this account ends upon a happy note at this stage in the life of my family and my life.

Wilbert Williams Jr., M.D.
Middletown, New York

Praise For Beyond the Fire and the Rain

"Dr. Williams' inspiring story...takes the reader with him from boyhood and youth in a housing project to the rigors of medical school and early practice...We are with him in every step of his journey. I highly recommend this uplifting autobiography."
Susan Thornton, Ph.D., Binghamton, NY

The author survived racism before, during and after medical school as well as threats on his life and that of his family. He lived with his wife and family in the Virgin Islands on the island of St. Croix for 28 years where he had a successful medical practice. His story is one of a person's refusals to give up his dreams while facing tremendous odds. You will experience his tears and joys and discover how his faith in God and mankind triumphed over tremendous odds.
Robert V. Vaughn, Ed.D., USVI

Dr. Williams' style is riveting — forthright and in your face. His first volume [Dancing in Fire] traced his years of dancing in the flames of America's social fires from Red Hook Housing Projects in Brooklyn, New York to St. Croix as a Christian physician. This page-turner will draw you into the fires as Dr. Williams unflinchingly confronts his insecurities and misgivings until a timely visit to relatives has him shouting at the rain.
Mr. Mario Moorehead, Historian

"Dr. Williams speaks the language of his people with an intent that is supernatural, his soft voice, his humble attitude and loving action dripping wet in compassion with a message of hope from "Beyond the Fire and the Rain." He is a highly skilled achiever who has hurdled over the same difficulties you and I may be experiencing or someone we know. Personally, I saw his heart of honesty, asking can I help, I saw personal collateral damage to his sincerest intentions as he went through the fire and shouted at the rain, he offers you a soaking wet view into the interiors of his life.
Raymond Scott, Th.B., Th.M., New Jersey

Nebuchadnezzar the King made an image of gold,
whose height was three score cubits,
and the breadth thereof six cubits:
he set it up in the plain of Dura,
in the province of Babylon.

Daniel 3

Part I

The Fumes of Babylon

Chapter 1
Danger

Nebuchadnezzar the king made an image of gold, whose
Height was threescore cubits, and the breath thereof six cubits:
He set it up in the plain of Dura, in the province of Babylon.

Daniel 3:1

It was July 13, 1978. I was standing on Seventy-Eighth Street between
Fourth and Fifth Avenues in Brooklyn, New York, afraid for my life. It
had not been three months since I was awarded the Doctor of Medicine
and Surgery degree at the prestigious Albany Medical College in upstate
New York. Some angry white people were yelling racial slurs at me. They
were sitting on cars, standing, and some were walking in my direction. The
police were guarding me from their fury. I wondered if their hatred for me,
because I was Black, was real. Racism had affected my life at times, but not
like this. I heard someone say, "We don't want that black nigger living here;
we'll kill him and his family. He can go back where he came from."

The New York City Assistant Commissioner of Human Rights was
standing by my side, as he encouraged me to take this duplex apartment in
that racist white neighborhood. "They're only bluffing," the commissioner
said. "Don't worry, you'll get the apartment and they won't hurt you or
your family." I stood next to a police officer who had a gun strapped to his
ankle, as he protected me from the crowd. I thought when the people saw
me in my intern clothes they would realize that I was a medical doctor
and calm down.

A casually dressed white man grabbed his penis and shook it at me.
A white woman named O' Keefe, with red hair, stood in my presence

3

and told the commissioner that they did not guarantee my safety. She said if my family or I got hurt, our blood would be on the hands of the Commissioner of Human Rights and the police. I feared for my wife Iris, and two children Shoshanna and Taina, as the commissioner begged me to walk up the stairs to the duplex apartment.

When the crowd got out of control, the police officer stood closer to me. The other police officers pushed the crowd back. I told the commissioner that I didn't want the apartment, and he got upset. "What do you mean you don't want the apartment, we've come too far to turn around now?"

I replied, "It's not worth the destruction of my family, to live in a neighborhood with people who hate me for being Black."

He put his hand on my shoulder and nudged me forward. I resisted. "I am telling you," he said, "it will be OK. They're just bluffing."

I gave in and walked up the stairs, which lead to the apartment. I thought that someone was going to kill me. I braced my body in anticipation of being shot. When we got inside the apartment, wires were hanging from the ceiling and walls and the light fixtures were not in place. The sliding glass doors were broken and a brick was on the new carpet floor. Those racist white people outside, who were full of prejudice and hatred for Black people, were serious. They were willing to kill my family and me.

The contractor, Mr. Hansen, was with me. The Assistant Commissioner of Human Rights asked Mr. Hansen, "When are you going to have this apartment ready for Dr. Williams?"

"If you want it finished," he said, "I'll give you the money and you can finish it yourself. I'm not gonna get killed." The police officer who was standing by my side looked at Mr. Hansen.

We learned that Mr. Hansen sent his thirteen-year-old daughter to Norway because they threatened her life. Someone phoned his house and told him if he finished the apartment for those "niggers," they would rape his daughter. They informed him of his daughter's panty and bra size over the telephone.

If those racists had handed me the keys to the apartment on a golden platter, I would not have taken them. The commissioner was disappointed with me, but I didn't care how he felt. They humiliated and emotionally broke me.

The Fishing Trip

I was angry with the Swift Real Estate Company in the Bay Ridge section of Brooklyn for being racist. Mr. Swift claimed to be a Christian. He had deceived me. He had a real estate agent take me to two roach-infested apartments, one in Brooklyn, and the other in Staten Island, as he tried to get me to rent one. He didn't want me to rent the apartment on 78th Street. I was angry and hurt.

Seemingly as a gesture of friendship, Mr. Swift invited me on a fishing trip off the coast of Staten Island, New York on a late afternoon with his friend. They took me out in their boat and then stopped it. I thought that they were going to throw me overboard. They scared me. When we returned ashore, it was by then already dark, and they drove me to a dark dreary isolated street on Second Avenue in Brooklyn. Mr. Swift yelled at me in an uncontrollable rage while his pale face turned red, saying over and again, "You better not take that apartment." He had foam forming at the sides of his mouth and as he opened it, his saliva sprinkled my face. He wouldn't let me out of his car until I said, "OK, I won't take it." When I finally got out of that car, I thanked God for my life. I was mad but still scared.

Iris was in upstate New York camping with her family and when she came home, I told her what happened and she begged me to forget the apartment. She said that we could find another apartment in a neighborhood where people did not care about our color and race. I understood her fear because I was frightened for our family. I questioned my self-worth and my pride was ripping at me while I was struggling with my manhood. I tried to go on with my life. I was ashamed that at this point in my life, after I had proven myself, having struggled so hard to become a medical doctor, that anyone in his right mind would make my color and my race a focal point. They called me a "black nigger." I never felt so low and broken in all of my life.

Running

Chesson, Alabama could not have been more than eight hundred miles from Brooklyn, New York. Both states swelled like a dead animal on a hot day with racial prejudice and hatred for Black people. It was so bad in Chesson that some white people gave the only Black doctor in town twenty-four hours to get out, for attending to a white woman.

My father, Wilbert Williams, was a little boy growing up in Chesson, when they ran the Black doctor out of town. He told me,

"Them white bastards got up early in the morning and threatened to hang the doctor." The Blacks in Chesson didn't do a thing about it. They had to be careful not to get out of line around white people. Some white "cracker" might just shoot them or hang them from a tree like a slaughtered raccoon.

When my father was a teenager, he hunted raccoons and squirrels in the woods. He enjoyed the outdoors because it helped him feel free around all the oppression Black people suffered in Alabama. They clouded his memories of his hometown with racial slurs, discrimination, lynching and mobs of hateful white people threatening the existence of Blacks. When he spoke of Chesson, Alabama his face twisted and his eyes fixed in one area. He would not divert his eyes unless another subject was mentioned. I asked my father if he would ever return to Chesson to visit. He said, "What the goddamn hell for? Those white crackers were no damn good, and if I had stayed in that goddamn place, those racist white bastards would have to kill me. I was not going to let them treat me like a lowdown no-good nigger." He told me that the armed services were just as racist as the white "sons of bitches" in Alabama. They drafted him into the United States Army and put him in a segregated barracks, and treated the white soldiers with respect while they ridiculed the Blacks. When his superior officer (who was white) told him to stand guard duty at night, he replied, "If you want this place guarded, you better guard it your own Goddamn self, because I am not doing it." My father felt slighted by the United States government because of the way they allowed Black soldiers to be treated in an inferior manner as compared with the white soldiers. He wanted to get out of the military because he believed that the United States did not care about him or any other Black citizen. He rebelled against white authority whenever he had a chance. He refused to put his life on the line for America, because Black people in Chesson, and throughout the country, were discriminated against and treated worse than animals. He wrapped it all up in telling me that the people in Chesson, and all of those damn racist "white cracker bastards," could have the whole goddamn country and go to hell with it.

The Other Side

My mother, LaVerne Smith Williams, did not have the kind of racial scar my father had. Her memories of her childhood while growing up in

Baltimore, Maryland was pleasant. Racial prejudice and hatred were in Baltimore, but it did not change the way she felt about life and people.

She spoke to me about a place called "Pig Town," in the southeast section of Baltimore, where her grandfather had horses and sold its droppings for fertilizer. The horses all mysteriously died one by one, and my mother believed that he was killing them. Some horses' legs got broken and my grandfather put them to sleep. Whenever someone questioned him about the horses, he would make some excuse for why they were dying. She believed that he got tired of that business.

My mother loved Baltimore. She told me about the beautiful white marble steps in front of almost every house in her neighborhood and how the people cleaned it meticulously. My mother told me about great Black people whom she learned about in school like Harriet Tubman and Sojourner Truth, how Harriet ran the Underground Railroad, and took many slaves to freedom from the South to the North. She told me that Sojourner was the first Black woman to speak out against slavery. My mother never spoke to me about anything negative without showing me the positive side of it. Even the time that she had to eat horsemeat during the 1920s Depression was told to me. She often told me of people standing on line to get a cup of soup. When I asked her how she dealt with it, especially eating horse meat, she said, "That's just the way it was."

Desire

When my father met my mother in Brooklyn, New York, he liked her at first sight. She told me that he was handsome and aggressive. He frequently roamed her block and asked for the girl with the big legs. When she saw him, she didn't think much about romance; although she liked the way, he looked physically. He carried himself high class, while he paraded around as if he owned the world. Her mother, Queen Victoria Smith, had a few negative words for my mother, about my father, but my father pursued my mother regardless whenever and wherever he could. I don't know what it was that my grandmother didn't like about my father, but she was not happy about my mother being with him. My mother told me that she didn't want to be bothered by him, but he insisted in making contact with her. He sported fancy clothes, wore expensive shoes, and kept money in his pocket. After World War II, he opened a barbershop business in the Bedford Stuyvesant section of Brooklyn, near Fulton and Nostrand

Avenues. My mother named it "Tonsorial Studios." My grandmother continued to warn my mother about seeing him, but my mother fell in love with him. My parents got married, and they moved into a one-bedroom "flat" on Pacific Street in Brooklyn. They shared the bathroom that was in the hallway with other people in the building.

Moving On

Less than ten months after her marriage, my mother gave birth to my sister Janice by C-section, because she couldn't advance in labor. When it was time for my sister to be delivered, the doctor had to cut into my mother's abdomen and womb, and pull my sister out. It was one of three C-sections my mother would have. She showed strength, and ability to face odds and survive just as she did while she was growing up during the Depression. My parents needed more room after my sister's birth, and couldn't stomach the one-bathroom deal anymore. They moved to Canarsie, New York, in Brooklyn, into an old World War II army barracks, which the government converted to public housing.

My father was a long way from Chesson, Alabama, but the memories of it still haunted him. Although opportunities were better for him in New York and he could make a decent living cutting hair, he still faced racial challenges. He was just another Black man in America struggling to take care of his family, and survive the racist system. He still was not going to allow any "white cracker" to treat him like a "low-down no-good nigger," anywhere. My father was determined to be a free Black man, in spite of racism. He understood if he returned to Alabama with such an attitude, his life would be in danger.

Negro

Sometimes the only thing that gave a Black man any kind of control that satisfied him was to love his woman and raise his family. My father was no different, and my mother was both the object of his love and the target of his frustration. In his mind, to be a man while challenging the white man's system was consuming, but he knew he had to feed, clothe, house, and protect his family. Many Black men have fared well trying to overcome the racist system, and my father did the best that he could. Every Black man understands this dilemma and what it costs to be a strong Black man in America.

My mother and my father loved each other and they continued to share their affection in the center of things that challenged them. Fair housing, good jobs, and respect from whites and Blacks were challenges that faced most Black people.

When I Was Born

My mother was pregnant with me and on February 11, 1948 entered Kings County Hospital in Brooklyn, to deliver me by C-section. While she lay on the operating room table, the nurses and doctors were preparing to open her up with a scalpel (knife). It was all planned due to her first C-section when she had my sister Janice. No labor was involved, just the anesthesia, the nurses, the doctors and the knife.

I was born healthy. My mother named me after my father and I became a junior, but one of my cousins said, "Let's call him Buddy." They wrote on my birth certificate "male Negro." I don't know who told the vital statistics employees at Kings County Hospital that I was a "Negro." My father's father looked white that they called him "pecker wood," and we have Native American Indian in our family. My father's sister had light skin with freckles and had long straight hair, which extended to her waist. I don't pretend to be anything other than what I am, a creation of God. It was not my choice to be called a "Negro" baby boy; it was the decision of the people who failed to find out who my mother and father really were.

When my mother took me home, she knew her brand new healthy "Negro" baby boy would face challenges, being male and being "Negro."

My father and my two-year-old sister Janice waited anxiously at our house to greet us. Our house in Canarsie was comfortable. We had a back yard and a porch. My father was living in an Army barrack for the second time in his life. This time he did not have to kiss up to any white person in a uniform with authority spouting words to him that he resented. He didn't have to stand in the cold while guarding and cursing America for being racist. He was in a rented home, owned by the federal government, protected, and he felt good about it.

My mother told me about a white family who lived next door to us and the children frequently had head lice. This was my first encounter with white people (other than the doctor that delivered me, and the hospital staff). My father was furious concerning those children with head lice. He did not want me or my sister to be infested as well. Once, my father

9

cut off the hair of two children in the family next door to us in order to get rid of lice.

The only thing I remember about Canarsie, New York, is a picture of me in my father's arms. He stood on the back porch and held me proudly, like a precious gift. I had on a little one-piece top and bottom with straps coursing over my shoulders. My hair was bushy and thick, and it looked like a mini-Afro. My father stood like a king on his throne holding me, surveying his wealth. My mother stood to the left of him. She had a sweet smile on her face and her hair was full, just like mine.

Polio Virus

My father worked hard in his barber's business. He understood the responsibility of taking care of us. He did well financially cutting hair, until he caught the poliovirus that crippled him in his right leg. He stayed in the hospital for months. My mother took care of us while he recuperated, and she had enough money saved to take care of our financial needs until my father came home from the hospital. When he got better and came home, he had problems bathing in the shower. It was trying for my mother to take care of my sister Janice and me after my father's paralysis. It was a full-time job for her, but she handled it well.

Two years after I was born, my mother got pregnant with my sister Shelly. She had her third C-section and the doctor told her that she could not have any more children. She did not particularly want more. I never heard her comment that she was disappointed with the doctor's decision.

Red Hook Projects

We moved to Red Hook housing projects in South Brooklyn, because my father could not stand in the shower and he needed a bathtub. That was the only reason we moved to Red Hook projects.

They built Red Hook many years before I was born, sometime after the Great Depression, when my mother ate horsemeat. Most of the people who lived there were white. It looked like a colony of skyscrapers. The buildings numbered more than one hundred. They were six stories tall, in that little corner of Brooklyn near the famous Brooklyn Battery Tunnel, which connects Brooklyn with lower Manhattan. It really was a unique place to live because it had almost everything the people who lived there needed. Red Hook projects even had its own theater, and an Olympic-size swimming pool. One pool was sixteen feet deep and had a ten-foot diving board. Red Hook had a beautiful manicured lawn with a chain link fence and tall trees spaced on each side of it.

The community respected the police, and they walked their beats day and night doing their job. If someone, was caught riding a bike on the sidewalk, climbing a tree, or walking on the grass, the police notified your parents, and they gave the people a fine for breaking Red Hook projects' laws. Blacks and whites lived there without regard to racial lines, ethnic background, or religious beliefs. Racial prejudice was not an issue then, and people spent their energy and time being neighbors and helping each other. We borrowed bread, milk, sugar and eggs from each other. I remember my father bringing home a fifty-pound bag of potatoes. He would tell my mother to round up the neighbors in the building and let them know that they could have some. Watching my mother's response was funny. She just looked at me, then at the ceiling, in disapproval of his suggestion. It wasn't that she didn't want to share, but my father did this each time he brought some extra food home to us.

Gangs

Red Hook had a gang called the "Kovons." They would walk in the middle of the street singing some dumb gang song, marching like soldiers, putting their weight on their left leg, (which gave them the "bee bob" walk), "doing the bad walk," and literally stopped traffic. The power, which they had was amazing. I knew a guy in it named "Nero," his real name was Neal Wooden. He was a hefty-looking guy who scared me if he made an ugly face. He had a big square head, a wide mouth, and big lips. Neal told me often to behave, because he knew that I was a terror on the block. When he came to my house, he saw me in action creating confusion and would look at me and shake his head. Red Hook's elevated train station at Smith and Ninth Streets had his name written on the wall with paint, in bold letters, "Nero." It remained there for many years, along with the names of other devious kids. I never looked up to Neal because I knew he was wayward in his behavior. I did enjoy watching him write script because he had a beautiful handwriting.

The only rival gang in Red Hook the "Kovons" had to deal with the "Black Diamonds," a Puerto Rican gang full of delinquents. Hearing of anyone being killed was rare. Occasionally someone was shot with a homemade zip gun. The guys made the guns by using a car antenna for a barrel, and a deadbolt door latch as a hammer, with fifty million rubber bands as a spring. This gadget, made on a piece of wood, could fire a .22-caliber bullet. Their other weapons were knives, bats, chains, rocks, and anything else that they could find. The "Kovons" never bothered children in any way. Some of them told us kids to stay in line and do well in school.

Chapter 2
Affection and Protection

O Lord, thou hast searched me, and know me.

Psalm 139: 1

My father made lots of money cutting hair in his barbershop. When he came home on Saturday night from work, he prepared himself to cut hair in our apartment on Sunday morning. We had constant traffic through our small living room into my parents' bedroom. He used our dining room table chair for his customers. Many people sat in that chair, while he reached for his barber tools that were in a cardboard box on his dresser.

He stood for hours cutting hair. The hair piled up in bunches on the floor, and sometimes hair was along the floor leading to the entrance door. My mother complained about the dirty hair in our apartment. My father would not let anything stop him from cutting hair unless he got sick (which was not often). He worked long hours in his barbershop. His paralysis didn't stop him from making a living for us. He stood all day. When he was at home, he would drag his right leg in an attempt to keep it above the carpet. His right hand was strong, because he used it to support his weight on his right side. I watched his hands, especially when he used them to cut hair; the veins bulged and it made them look muscular. My father cut my hair almost every two weeks. I did not enjoy the haircuts, because he would twist my head when I was not paying attention to his commands to turn it. After he close-cropped my hair, he washed it. He massaged my scalp with his strong muscular hands, and it made me feel protected by him. I especially liked watching him wring out a washcloth with one hand, because the muscles in his arm bulged. He washed my

13

hair with Ivory soap, then took the soiled washcloth and squeezed it with one hand. My father flipped the washcloth in his hand until it was almost dry.

My mother took us to the Baptist church every Sunday. Often when we arrived home, my father was sitting on the couch in our living room as he looked out the window at the people in the courtyard. He liked watching people and followed a person's every movement if he could. My father was a no-nonsense kind of guy who spoke very pleasantly and calmly. If crossed, he would curse while the veins in his forehead and neck bulged. If he liked a person, but something they did annoyed him, he would not tell them unless he believed that they gave him a reason. Even then, he would be very quiet until he could not take it anymore, and he would tell us about it as he sprinkled his feelings with "choice" curse words. I never understood his attitude about his family. He would not talk to me about them except to say that they were "no damn good." He had ten brothers who were older than he and one sister who lived in Indiana. Once, his brother Louis came to our house in an old 1920s Model-T Ford with the skinny tires and the crank handle in front of the radiator. My uncle impressed me, but I could not figure out how that thing made it hundreds of miles on the roadway from Alabama. He came walking toward our apartment building with a guitar under his arm, dressed in a black suit. My uncle looked like he just came off a long journey. I never remembered seeing my father's brother before. When he saw me, he gave me a big hug. I didn't see any great reception between him and my father. After he settled down in our living room, he lit up a filter less cigarette.

Those cigarettes and all the smoke that they made in our little apartment made me sick. Every time I turned around, cigarette butts were everywhere. One day our uncle took us to Coney Island in his 'Roaring' 20s car. It was great riding on the Brooklyn Belt Parkway, watching "all them people" in faster cars looking at us Black folk rolling to Coney Island. I never did get to know him well, although he was friendly. Respecting and loving my Uncle Louis was easy because he was family. When he went to Alabama, I stood on our sidewalk and warmly waved him off. My father's relationship with his brother did not seem very close, though they talked seriously about life. I'm sure my father loved his brother, but a gulf was between them. My father's life never seemed exciting unless he called a guy whom he knew, named Mr. George Washington. Mr. Washington had a Cadillac to take him out for a drive. My father didn't have the desire to buy his own car, although he had the money. I think he was afraid to drive. It was probably due to his paralysis, but a neighbor of ours who was paralyzed in both legs drove his own car by hand controls. Mr. Washington was this fat guy with a big belly who strutted around as if he was worth a million dollars. I am sure he was worth that, and even more, to my father. Occasionally he asked me to go along for the ride. I enjoyed sitting in that big car.

During the week, my father spent an average of ten to fourteen hours per day working. He stood on his bad leg, taking occasional breaks to rest on a hard wooden chair. His barber chair was in the back of a long storefront. Six other barbers were there. My father chose the chair in the back so he could easily get to the bathroom when he needed. Sometimes during the winter, when it snowed and was slippery, he stayed in the barbershop all night, sleeping on a dull-looking cot in the back. I missed my father when he didn't come home. I wanted him to be home with us, though he never wanted to talk much. The times he did come home, he was so tired dealing with people and exhausted from standing all day that he just wanted some peace and quiet. He liked to lie in bed and listen to religious stations all night until the morning. His radio would hardly ever go off from 9:30 p.m. until he went to work, which was usually at 5:15 a.m. Sometimes I watched him walk slowly on his bad leg with that brown scratched up cane of his, as he tried not to slip on the snow. I knew that I would not see him again for many hours.

Once, my father asked a neighbor to take me to his barbershop. My father wanted to give me affection. When I walked into the shop, all eyes were on me. The other barbers greeted me as if I were special. I had never seen them before. I'm sure that my father told them that I was coming. I know that he was proud of me. He told my neighbor to take me across the street to the toy store and buy me anything that I wanted. My father loved me special that day. I forget what I picked out, but it was a red toy; maybe a fire truck. Fire trucks fascinated me.

My father was working hard for us. He appeared strong, as he stood at his barber chair, and he had the most customers waiting for him.

Finding Trouble

My mother had her hands full with us because we were constantly asking for something, and she never refused us. She cooked some great meals, and she enjoyed watching us gulp them down. Sometimes my father's absence was a burden for her because I, in particular, gave her a hard time. She endured my father's absence as a strong soldier. I never heard her complain, although sometimes I knew, she was lonely, when he stayed in the barbershop if it snowed heavily. She sat with us at times and told us stories in order to amuse us and make us laugh. My mother loved to see us laughing and enjoying each other's company. I remember her telling us always to be pleasant to each other. Her love was healing to our souls and she hugged us a lot and made sure we never wanted for anything. The foundation for my love began to grow in my mother's arms. It wasn't that my father didn't love us; he did, but my mother expressed it more openly, and as children, we received it just as freely as it came. When I went outside to play, my father sat at the window, on our French provincial couch, which my mother cherished. If I did something he didn't like, he would yell at the top of his voice from three stories high, and many yards away, in order to get my attention. Whenever he did, my heart pounded and I shook because he usually called me upstairs and cursed me out. He would say, "What the hell is wrong with you, didn't you hear me calling you?" Face to face, I stood before him, and listened to anything he wanted to lay on my mind or my behind. When he finished with me, he would roll his eyes and say, "You can go."

When I went downstairs to play again, I found a spot where he could not see me creating confusion. I was a bad little boy (in the sense of the word) and I learned how to curse a person's ears right off his head. I didn't care who the person was; I spoke my mind. The neighbors were always complaining to my mother about my foul mouth. Once my mother washed my mouth out with a bar of Ivory soap. She told me each time she caught me cursing, that she would do the same thing.

The Psychiatrist

My mother took me to a psychiatrist at the county health clinic when I was four years old. I was devious. She couldn't control me, and she thought that some psychiatrists could. My mother thought that I was crazy. She told the doctor that I wouldn't sit still and every moment I was doing something upsetting. My mother was at the end of her rope with me, but I had no idea that she was in torment. The psychiatrist looked at me. I looked at him. I thought that he just wanted to talk to me. I had no idea that he wanted to pick my brain and control my behavior. When he saw me, he made direct eye contact and didn't deviate. When he finished speaking with me, he told my mother that I had too much energy. He suggested that she put me to bed at 6:00 p.m. and awaken me at 6:00 a.m. in order to calm me down. It only helped for a few weeks, and it was just a matter of time before I acted up again.

I remember the first time my mother took me to school. I saw all these books and things. The first thing that I picked up was a wooden block with a red letter on it. As I held it in my hand, I felt like throwing it. I wasn't upset about being there. I just didn't want my mother to leave me alone. I stood in the middle of the floor, while my mother spoke to the kindergarten teacher.

While the kids sat on the floor and played with the books and things, I figured out how to sneak out with my mother. When she left the classroom, I felt abandoned and lonely. I didn't want to play with the other children. When noontime arrived, my beautiful mother was waiting to take me home. I couldn't wait to get out of there and forget much about kindergarten, books, and things. Nevertheless, I do remember when I didn't have to go there anymore.

When my mother got her first job working in Jewish homes, she had my cousin Leray child-sit. Leray didn't put up with any foolishness. I gave her a hard time. We sat in the dark all evening when Leray came to sit with us. She watched TV, and I hated it. She, however, kept me in line. Her eyes and harsh voice intimidated me. I was frightened of her.

When my mother came home, I gave her the hard time that I couldn't give Leray. My mother stayed home with us when she didn't have any houses to clean in the Jewish neighborhoods. I enjoyed myself by jumping on my mother's bed from the shaky wooden headboard. "Buddy," she would say, "Is that you jumping on the bed?" I wouldn't answer. Most of the time my mother would continue whatever she was doing. Once I was practicing swan dives on her bed. After two good dives, she yelled, "Buddy, is that you jumping on the bed again?" I didn't answer. Bang, the box spring hit the floor. "Buddy, I know you're jumping on the bed, I'm going to come in there and whip you." I ignored her, and did another dive on the bed. She dashed in my direction with a shoe in her hand and started swinging it at me, hitting me on my arms, shoulders, and butt. I tried to guard my head, but she found everything else without much effort. She never hit me on my head with anything unless it was soft. She must have believed I was missing enough brains. I rarely cried when she beat me, but I knew not to ask for any more.

When my mother was at work, after school, I roamed our little two-bedroom apartment and looked for anything to take apart or destroy. We had the family's favorite fish with big eyes in a fish tank in our living room. It was a bad fish. It killed every fish in the tank. I was determined to kill that joker. I went into our kitchen cupboard and found vinegar and food coloring. Then, I went to the bathroom cabinet and got some iodine and alcohol. I put all of the ingredients in the tank, and I stood with my nose and forehead pressed against the glass, as I watched the skin peel from its eyes. It wouldn't die and float to the top. I pulled it out and stabbed it with a kitchen knife; then, I flushed it down the toilet bowl. When my mother asked about the fish, I told her it died and I threw it away.

My mother took us to many places. I remember the time that she took my sisters and me to the neighborhood theater (Clinton Movie House) in order to see a picture called "Hi Lilly." We sat in the movie theater; proud to be with our mother. When she spent recreational time with us, I felt very special. We sat in the balcony eating popcorn and candy, and the big screen was larger than life. Each spring she even took us to the Barnum and Bailey Ringling Brothers' Circus at Madison Square Garden. I always asked her to buy me a light that the circus ringmaster asked that everybody twirl when the high-wire act came on. The lion act was my favorite. I liked to see the lion tamer snap his whip and command those big beasts to roll over and jump over barrels. The high-wire act always tensed me. I believed each year that someone was going to plunge to his death. What really thrilled me was when a man was shot from the cannon into a net. Anything that could fly excited me. I wouldn't have let anybody put me in a tube with gunpowder, light it, and propel me through the air. The clowns were great. They had a tall skinny one every year that uncurled out of a little car.

I laughed hard when the clowns ran around and hit each other on the head with fake bats. They had an act where a clown picked up a bucket of fake water that was confetti paper, and tossed it on the crowd. I always wished that I were sitting in the path of it. The circus was great and my mother knew I loved it. One year at the circus, my mother bought a white cowboy hat for me, and I was proud to wear it. We did more than most of the kids on my block. My mother tried to expose us to as many things as she believed would stimulate healthy growth. She was always talking to us about loving people, and caring about each other.

Stealing

My father showed his affection for my sisters and me when he walked into our apartment after working a full ten to thirteen hours in his barber shop. He would bring us Chinese food, ice cream, or chocolate candy. My mother sometimes got upset with him for doing it, because often she spent hours getting us to calm down, take a bath, and go to sleep. Often we were in the bed when he came. He would stand at our dining room table, rest the goodies down, and call our names. I was the first one to jump up. It was great when he brought old-fashioned vanilla ice cream for us. It was hard like a rock, and he would beat it until it got soft. I would watch those veins pop up in his strong hands while he whipped it. After we had our treat, my mother had a job getting us back to sleep. My father did this about once every week, and I loved it. He called during the day from his barbershop and asked me what I wanted him to bring home. Usually, whatever I told him, he walked into our apartment with it. (I should have told him once to bring me a real car so we could go out together as a family, as my father did with Mr. George Washington), He never made me a promise that he did not keep, and this was one of many things that I respected about him.

My father understood the importance of being truthful with me. That is why it upset him when I stole some of his money. My sister Janice asked me to steal some of it in order to go to the movies. He usually allowed me to count his money on Friday nights. He would throw some cash on his bed and call me in to count it. This time I stuffed quarters in my pockets, shoes, and under my belt. He let me walk out of his room and did not say a word to me; then, he called me back while I was showing Janice some loot. My father asked me if he had more money than what was left on the bed. I told him "No." He said, "Empty your pockets." Tons of quarters came out. "Is that all you have?" he said. I replied, "Yes." He told me to take off my belt and tons of quarters dropped on the floor. He told me to take off my shoes, and I had more quarters.

He was infuriated, and called me a little lying nigger. He said, "I hate a lying nigger. Go and get my goddamn razor strap, lying black nigger, I'm gonna beat your black ass." While I went for his weapon, I was afraid. He beat me like his arm needed exercise, and while he was beating me, he kept calling me a lying nigger. If I had a quarter for each time he called me a lying nigger, I could have taken the whole family to the movie theater. I didn't mind the beating nearly as much as my father calling me a "nigger." I knew I hurt him and pushed a raw nerve. He believed that stealing was taboo, and he was right. I just got caught and had to pay the price. My sister Janice denied the whole thing. My father didn't say whether he believed her or me, but I paid for being a thief.

After a couple of days, my father apologized for beating me, and told me that I was never to lie again. It was rare when he beat me and didn't call the following day to apologize. It hurt my father to chastise me, but he knew I needed it. He understood my being a Black boy would make life hard enough for me, and I didn't need the added burden of getting locked up or killed for stealing. Christmas in my house was wonderful. I got almost everything that I asked for, unless I told my parents too late what I wanted Santa Claus to bring me. It was exciting hunting for a Christmas tree. I loved the evening my mother and my sisters got together and dressed the tree with lights, bulbs, icicles, and angel hair. When the angel hair touched my skin, I would itch all night. I especially liked placing the main ornament on the top of the tree. When we turned the lights on, the tree looked pretty in our living room. My father never spent time decorating the Christmas tree with us. I missed him. He spent so much time making a living in his barbershop and doing whatever else, that all of us suffered from not doing important things together. I don't know how much he thought about his absence from us because he never spoke about it.

The things I missed doing with my father were substituted with plenty of things I did with my friends. Many things I did with my friends I would have never done in my father's presence. I don't know why, but I never spoke to my father about his staying in the barbershop so many times and believe it affected me in a negative way. Every child, especially every Black male child, needs his father to interact with him other than the times he gets a beating by him. Black males need their fathers to be their greatest friend, and their greatest role model. Therefore, my father's greatest influence on me was when I was in his presence.

Friends

My friends of my age were full of energy. I was not interested in girls except to laugh at them and pick fights. They had no purpose or interest to me. My friends were different races and it never dawned on me that it made any difference to either of us. We never talked about how we looked, about race or color.

One of my friends was Jewish, Herman. He lived across the hall from me. Herman was a rude boy, always cursing at his parents. His mother was constantly calling his name, and Herman ignored her. If I had done that, I would have been set on fire by my father's razor strap. My father had a big fat leather strap that he used to sharpen his straight razors, and if I were bad, he made me fetch it. He beat me with it often, until he got tired. I don't think Herman's parents ever beat him. He was out of control. I was not much better than he was, because often I was also out of control.

My father did not allow my sisters or me to do certain things that he believed would set a bad trend. My parents did not allow me to play marbles, because my father believed it would encourage me to gamble when I got older. Nevertheless, when the marble season came, my friends got their marbles, and I wanted some. My mother told me that I could not have any, because my father had forbidden it. I bought some anyway. A friend of mine named Eric was skilled at playing marbles and he won all of mine. I started a fight with him because I wanted them back, and he refused. He held me in a headlock and would not let go until I gave up. When my mother heard about it, she made me throw all my marbles in the incinerator of our building. I nevertheless purchased more marbles, and I won a lot. When she heard about that, she made me get rid of my marbles again. No matter what she did with my marbles, I kept buying more, because I often had money to buy candy. I didn't fight with Eric again over marbles for two reasons: he was bigger than I was, and it would only get back to my mother.

I had lots of fun with my friends. Richard was my white friend, who wore thick glasses. Richard's father was paralyzed like mine, but his father was paralyzed in both legs. Richard was funny. When something was done, which he did not like, he would just stand in one spot and look at you. I constantly disturbed Richard's life, poking fun at his thick glasses. He never seemed bothered by my actions. Most of the time Richard would laugh when I joked about him. We spent much time together and our color was never an issue between us.

One incident between our parents almost put a wedge in our friendship. One day Richard was teasing my little sister Shelly. My mother yelled at his mother, "You better tell Richard to leave my Shelly alone." Richard's mom yelled back at her, "Ah, shut up."

My mother dashed down the stairs like a football star. Without breaking her pace, she grabbed a paddle bat from a little girl and went to beat Richard's mother on her head, saying, "Ah, shut up?! Ah, shut up?"

I was in a state of shock. I could not believe my sweet little mother had assaulted and battered my friend's mother. That catastrophe took a back seat in my relationship with Richard, and we went on with our lives.

Steven was my best friend. He was chubby, light-skinned, and had curly hair. I liked Steven's family because they were always laughing, especially his father, whom they called "Danny Boy." Steven and I were prone to misbehaving. Steven's father thought I was the troublemaker. I encouraged some foul behavior, but Steven was not exactly an angel. Once I gave Steven a wrench to open the water hydrant. I ran and hid in the bushes, while Steven slowly turned the nut. A police car rolled up, and a police officer caught him. I laughed at what happened, not taking seriously the consequence of the crime. Steven's father forbid him to be with me, because I cursed too much and was a bad influence. The separation hurt us. Steven obeyed his father's wishes. I continued mischief wherever I went. I fought with girls on the block. I was constantly teasing my neighbors, Brenda, Patty, Sherlina, Gloria, and Sheila. Most of my fights with these girls were with Sheila. She was bold enough to fight me if I bothered her. Our fights ended with my face scratched and her ears hurting, and some of her hair would be gone. Sometimes we locked like two horned goats with my right hand in full contact with her left ear, while she scratched my face, neck, and arms.

Once I punched Brenda in her chest for butting in while I was bothering her sister Patty. Brenda and Patty came to my house and complained to my mother. While they were leaving the building, I tossed dirty kitchen water down on them from my third-floor kitchen window. They hollered and ran next door where they lived.

I started turning on all my neighbors, and no one knew what to expect from me at any moment. My neighbors branded me as a terror, and most people believed I was either crazy, or possessed by the devil.

One day I was in my apartment with some firecrackers that I purchased with some money that my father gave me. I tossed a lighted one into a baby carriage under my kitchen window. It blew up before it hit the carriage. No baby was in it, and it was not my intention to hurt one. I was just bad.

When my mother found out about the firecracker incident and the baby carriage, she scolded me verbally and asked me if I were crazy. She knew I wasn't crazy. It was her way of communicating to me. She reminded me that she had already taken me to a psychiatrist once and would do it again. It never bothered me when she called me crazy, because I thought a crazy person was someone who did whatever he wanted.

I even roamed the streets looking for cigarette butts to straighten out and smoke in order to pass time. I even tried smoking a mini-cigar one day and almost choked to death. One of my wildest adventures was when I went off with some guys whom I didn't know and scaled a large fence. We went into the famous Todd Shipyard, where lumber was kept. They had some bad dogs in there, and we all knew it. Halfway into the yard these dirty-looking dogs charged us. I barely grabbed onto the galvanized fence before one of those dirty dogs tried to rip into my behind.

I took many chances and put my life on the line. My life was in danger of extinction until I almost lost my left eye. I was in Coffee Park, the neighborhood park, clowning around as usual. I grabbed my friend Tyrone's hat from his head and ran into an occupied swing heading toward my face. The swing struck me above my right eyebrow and exposed my skull, and the blood gushed out like a fountain everywhere. A person took me to the first aid building. When my mother arrived, she screamed when she saw me. It hurt me to see her frightened and crying. After they took me to the hospital, they stitched me. I vowed never to hurt my mother again.

I behaved on holidays when the little family we had in New York got together. Thanksgiving was one of those times. My aunt Doris, Leray, Leray's husband Louie, my cousin Sarah, her husband Douglas, and all their children with a host of other relatives flooded our little project apartment. The men would sit with my father and discuss all kinds of things. The women would talk between themselves and serve the men food and drink. It was the only time my parents allowed me to drink alcohol (12% grape wine). Once I drank a whole 8-oz. glassful as if I were drinking milk, got drunk, and fell in the clothes closet. My cousins who were my age loved to joke and have fun. We got along well. I forgot if I fought with any of them, although I probably did. I enjoyed Thanksgiving almost as much as Christmas because I felt secured by being with my relatives. When the evening ended and everyone got restless and started going home, I wanted them to stay. I will never forget these special times that we stayed together.

Chapter 3
Books and Things

Thou knowest my down sitting and mine uprising,
Thou understandest my thoughts afar off

Psalm 139:2

I was in love with my fourth grade teacher, Mrs. Aronawitz. She was Jewish. When she gave us our assignments on the blackboard, she tiptoed in order to reach the top and the muscles in her legs bulged. She was short like my mother. Her hair was dusky brown and neatly styled to her neck. Her nose was long and fat and her eyes and lips were large. Except for her skin, she looked like a Black person to me. She could not have been more than four and one-half feet tall. I thought that she was beautiful, but most of the kids in my class thought that she was ugly. I spent more time looking at her than I did in learning my lessons. Mrs. Aronawitz never gave me any reason to believe that I was special to her, but that did not matter.

The first girl to come into my life and cause me pain was Francis, and she was Black. Francis was not bad looking. Much of her beauty was hidden beneath her evil, lying nature, which she practiced on me. She turned my world upside-down emotionally, and Mrs. Aronawitz became allies with her. Francis sought my attention. I was, however, much too in love with the teacher to think about Francis.

Francis was quiet. She had large eyes like Mrs. Aronawitz, but she turned me off and I did not know why. It wasn't anything she had done that caused me to feel this way. I just didn't like her. It wasn't because she was Black, her eyes being big, or her hair not being straight. My mother and sisters were Black and female, just like Francis, and I loved them. At my age the only female I liked, other than my mother and sisters, was Mrs. Aronawitz. She was the first female I thought of romantically, and I don't know why. I cannot say I didn't fall in love with her because she was white. One thing I know for sure, I had the capacity to love her, and I convinced myself that I was special to her.

We had mock fire drills. One day Francis had a brand new white wool hat that her mother bought her. During the drill, her hat fell on the floor and she accused me of deliberately stepping on it. Francis knew I didn't step on her hat, but she wanted to blame me with hopes of getting my attention. When she told Mrs. Aronawitz, Mrs. Aronawitz demanded that my mother take me to Francis's house to apologize.

I told my mother I didn't do it, but she wouldn't believe me. She knew that I could do anything, and she made herself allies with Francis, but this time Francis was framing me. "Nevertheless, Ma," I said, "I didn't do anything."

"Buddy," she said, "You're always doing something."

I pleaded with her to believe me, but she carted me down the beautiful manicured lawn in Red Hook Project to Francis' apartment. My mother had no idea that she had picked up the wrong banner, believing Francis' lie. She didn't know that what she was going to make me do would create a hate in me for Francis for many years. When we got to Francis' apartment, Francis was waiting as if someone was bringing her a prize for winning a contest. They were shuffling me like a pawn. Francis repeated in front of both of our mothers the same lie that she told my teacher. "He knocked my hat off my head and got it dirty," she said.

I yelled, "I did not dirty your white hat, Francis."

"You did too dirty my white hat," Francis yelled back. She was lying.

I wanted to choke her until her eyeballs rolled down her cheeks past her lying mouth. I even wanted to wash her mouth out with Ivory soap like my mother did to me once, and beat her like my father did to me, when I stole his money and lied. My mother made me apologize to Francis for something I did not do, and I decided never to speak to Francis again. I hated her. Not even the lie that my sister told on me about not telling me to steal my father's money was worse than Francis' jumbo lie.

Mrs. Aronawitz gave me less attention after the incident with Francis. Her lack of attention caused double jeopardy between Francis and me.

The secret romance, which I had with my teacher, all vanished away after that lie. I wouldn't look at Francis unless she showed up unannounced before my eyes. My behavior became more aggressive because I felt abused. My studies were less important to me and I became a problem in school.

I don't mean to suggest that anyone was responsible for my early rebellion or lack of interest in school. What happened with Francis and I served to distract me from the important issues of life for a nine-year-old.

When I finished the fourth grade, I didn't care much for school. It wasn't Francis' fault (although she gave me a reason to be angry), Mrs. Aronawitz's belief of Francis, or my mother playing with the wrong team; it was rebellion against what I believed was dishonest and wrong in this life.

I spent much time at the Clinton Street movie house. Every Saturday I went to the movies, especially if Tarzan or Superman was playing. Superman influenced my behavior. I imagined myself being Superman, by putting a red cape around my neck. I fantasized that I could run faster than a locomotive, fly faster than a speeding bullet, and leap tall buildings in a single bound. When I came home from school, I'd put the red cape around my neck and would walk outside my window three stories high. My mother was at work, but sometimes the neighbors saw me and told my mother when she came home. I knew that I couldn't fly, but I imagined that I could, as I was three stories from the ground. My mother asked me often if I were crazy. I tried flying all the time in my parents' bedroom. Standing on the top of the headboard, I'd launch myself in the air and plunge to the mattress, wishing to fly.

My mother quickly got tired of my acting out my fantasy about Superman, and bought an authentic Superman costume for me. After another few hundred dives to the mattress, Superman finally fell to his death. I imagined that someone killed me with krypton, because that was the only way Superman could die. The fact that Superman was white and had all the power, which he did, caused me to believe that I could never be him. I could never have the strengths that he had, because he was white, and I was Black. I felt that the reason Superman wasn't Black was because Black people lived in a different world from white people, concerning power.

When Superman died, Tarzan came to life in my house. I would sit in the movie house and watch Tarzan command the animals, and those Africans with bones in their noses, and paint on their bodies, to behave. I saw Tarzan as being one lonely white man in a loincloth as he overpowered all of those strong-looking vicious Africans and spoke in their language. I wanted to be like him. Then, when I saw Jane, Tarzan's white wife with muscles, I wanted a woman like her. Tarzan was swinging through the jungle on a tree vine hollering some stupid sounds that I didn't understand, being a hero. He fascinated me.

When I took a bath, which was only every Saturday (because I didn't feel any more frequent was necessary because I didn't smell), I would put on my bathing suit, strap a rubber knife to my side, and imagine myself fighting alligators and snakes. Splashing water all on the floor and on the walls, I imagined that I had an alligator in a headlock, stabbing it with my knife, just like Tarzan. My mother would come to the door and ask me why I was taking so long to bathe. I couldn't tell her that I was killing alligators. I always gave her another excuse; other than that, I was playing Tarzan.

I imagined myself trapped by vicious black Africans, with bones pierced through their noses, who tried to hurt me. They had large wooden spears, and I was telling them in the African language to "Get back, get back," while holding them at bay with my knife.

The more I went to the movies, the more I understood that all of the people who were strong, beautiful, or rich were white and had power. I didn't know that this was the way Hollywood made them, and it wasn't the way it really was. When I saw a romantic picture, I never saw any display of affection between people who looked like me. It was always some white people, and some of them talked with different accents and languages. Their white skin bonded them more than anything else did. It was Hollywood's way of telling Blacks, "You are not a part of our group." It offended me to believe this. However, I continued to frequent the movies, like the rest of my Black friends.

Hollywood

By now, I was sensitive about my color. I didn't know anyone who was Black like me who was strong and in a position of power. I did see Black people sometimes in the movies and on television. They were cast as servants, maids, and butlers. Hollywood was playing a game on Black folks, and we were buying it. My color became a burden to me. I wondered what it would be like to be white. All of my wondering and wishing couldn't change what I was; a Black boy.

The Colored Mask

The picture "Imitation of Life" damaged me racially. It was a story about a woman who looked white, but was Black. Hollywood was slick. They picked a delightful-looking white woman to play the part, and picked a

27

woman who was fat and dark with heavy "Negroid" features to play her mother. The white woman was ashamed of her Black blood and she crossed the color line into the white world. She rejected everything about herself that was Black in any way, including her mother who loved her dearly. She escaped the bitterness of bigotry, racism and racial hatred by just being a white woman, living in a white world. I didn't know it was so easy to be treated like a human being, by just being white.

I felt rejected as I watched that picture. It had a lasting negative effect in my mind. It was at this point that I became angry about being Black. It felt as if I had on a "colored mask," because inside my soul I did not feel Black.

My friend Richard left Red Hook projects without giving me his address. It did not dawn on me that Red Hook projects were changing. The whole country, for that matter, was changing; concerning the races. Life had begun polarizing; one white world and one Black. White people, like my friend Richard, were moving from the inner city while more Black and Hispanic people were moving in. One by one, white people started moving out of Red Hook projects. Within no time, very few white people were living in Red Hook. The color and race issues had fully invaded my life; I had an aversion to anything Black, and that included Black people.

Mrs. Aronawitz, my fourth grade teacher, was still fresh in my mind and Francis, a Black female, destroyed the romantic fantasy fling that I had with her. I still hated Francis and anyone who looked like her. My mother, sisters, and a host of relatives, and some people I cared about, were spared my emotion. I didn't dislike Black women. I just wanted to feel free and not locked into a race color mode. I wanted to remove my "colored mask."

My fantasy world became larger and so did all the lies about most of the things that I thought were true. I continued to frequent the movies and all those white people that I saw as heroes, who were not true heroes at all. They were Hollywood's fabricated heroes, and they were nothing like me. The fact that Hollywood did not portray Black people as heroic, strong role models hurt me, and the lie continued to get bigger. My fantasies were out of control and I became hostage to being Black. The movies engrossed me and I fed on Hollywood's cancerous "junk food" almost every weekend. When I went to the movies, I watched the picture about one and one-half times, and then created confusion. I ran up and down the aisles to be noticed. If the usher didn't catch me and throw me out, I would dash to the staircase that led to the balcony bathroom. After that, I would grab a roll of toilet paper, wet it, roll it up in pieces, and throw it into the projector movie light in order to watch it glitter.

I slid down the huge wooden staircase banister from the second floor, and when I reached the bottom, tumbled onto the carpeted floor. Then, I would run around the theater smacking people on the back of their heads, or throwing paper balls or emptying candy boxes at them. I never got caught by the ushers and would exhaust myself clowning around until it was time to go home.

My First Girlfriend

Major events were taking place in the world, but I had no idea what was happening. Red Hook projects were my worlds. Except a few outings, visits to the movies, and The Ringling Brothers' Barnum and Baily Circus with my mother, all was well around me. It was 1957. Two years after Emmett Till, a 14-year-old Black boy from Chicago, Illinois was murdered in Mississippi for saying, "Hey Baby" to a white woman in a grocery store. Emmett didn't know his life was in danger of extinction for just being a Black boy like me, growing up in America. He had no idea that racist white people would torture and murder him, and throw him into a river. I, like Emmett, acted out my romantic fantasies with Hollywood's best white women on the screen and fell in love with my white Jewish teacher, Mrs. Aronawitz. I also had a thing about Tarzan's white wife, Jane, and even wanted that "white/Black woman" in "Imitation of Life."

I had no idea what it would cost me to act out my greatest fantasies in certain parts of the United States. For romance, there was innocence in me. I never thought of the opposite sex with any sexual intimacy until I was about nine years old, sitting in the white man's movie house, looking at all those white women.

My first attraction to a Black female was Beverly. She was a fair-skinned nine-year-old who had fine hair and a big dimple in her chin. She was much lighter than I in complexion. It was an immediate attraction and Beverly felt the same way about me. I walked home from school with her often when my friends were not around (because I was teased if seen with any girl by the guys). Beverly lived across the street from me, and before we reached our block, we had to separate, because she lived with her aunt, who was strict. Her mother and father lived in Germany because her father was in the Army. Beverly was leaving for Germany the summer of 1957, but the date was not exact. I wanted to take her to the Clinton Theater to be alone with her. My friends and I were close and it was hard getting away from them, especially on Saturdays, without their asking a whole bunch of questions. I finally worked it out with Beverly to meet during the Saturday show. When I got in the movie house, I sat next to her and did not say a word. I looked at her and smiled. For over an hour, I didn't have the nerve to place my arm on her shoulder. I sat there thinking of the big dimple in her chin and her pink lips and wanted to kiss them. I was marveling at her beauty, looking at her long hair. She was the prettiest girl that I ever saw; even prettier than Tarzan's wife was, Mrs. Aronawitz was, or any woman who I saw on the silver screen, and she was, surprisingly, Black. As I pulled her closer to me, she didn't resist, and I knew that I had her approval. Leaning over to her, I put a closed-mouth kiss on her lips. I instantly fell in love with her. I stayed with Beverly through the entire picture and even remained after, in order to watch it again. I didn't think about running around the theater or throwing wet toilet paper on people, or smacking anyone on the back of his head. The world was a safer place in which to live because I was in love.

When the school year ended, so did my relationship with Beverly. She left Red Hook and went to Germany. She never said goodbye, and it hurt me. I couldn't believe what she did and I don't know why. I wanted to believe that her aunt did not give her a chance to say goodbye. My heart was broken and I felt cheated and lost. I knew that I would never see her again. It was a kind of hurt, which I had never experienced. Beverly was on my mind every day, for more days than I care to remember. I hurt so badly. It took me a long time to heal.

School had become an issue in my life. I just wanted to have a good time. It wasn't anything in particular that finally turned me away from school. I just didn't care. The lost relationship with Beverly may have had something to do with my hurt. All I wanted was to draw attention to me. It was as if I needed something or someone special in my life, other than my parents, sisters and a host of relatives. I needed someone to help make me feel special.

I was the class clown, who made my classmates laugh. My last name, Williams, rendered me last at many things. I got the last seat in the back of the class. I was the last one to get my test paper returned, the last one to walk out of the classroom at the end of the day, and the last one noticed if I needed something. Sometimes I would misbehave in class just to change my seat. Most of the time when I was bad in class, my teacher put me under her desk. Sometimes while under the desk, I tried to look under her dress. Once we had a substitute teacher. The teacher asked me to stop talking and I refused. The teacher came toward me, and I got up and ran around the classroom. Students were in an uproar. I was having a ball, by not letting her catch me. She had her handbag with a long strap dangling from it in her hand. It was caught on some clothes hangers in the student closet. She continued to run and fell backward. She lay on the floor and played, dead. When I walked to her, she grabbed me by my collar and smacked me in my face a few times.

The principal called my mother to the school and told her. It was the decision of a few faculty members to leave me in the fourth grade. My mother looked at me, then at him and said, "If you are going to leave him back, then leave him back." I stood spellbound, while my mother changed the course of my life with just a few simple words. I was angry with her for letting those people do that to me, but she didn't care. She knew that she was doing the right thing. She knew that it was for my own good. My mother was just tired of my foolishness.

Before the school year was over, a "gorilla" named Ronald beat me. For no reason known to me, he punched me in my stomach and I fell on the school yard ground. When I hit the ground, he stomped on me, and hurt me badly. While I was on the ground, having surrendered, he continued to beat me. Some kids came to my aid and picked me up. It was the first time anyone hurt me viciously. Emotionally it created a fear in me because I didn't fight him back, and I knew how to fight. Ronald was the second person whom I hated, besides Francis. I hated him for violating me, and I vowed to hurt him one day, even if I had to do it from a distance.

Desire

My mother decided to put me in the Cub Scouts. That blue uniform with the yellow and blue scarf made me feel special. I enjoyed the Cub Scouts' meetings because I had a chance to be noticed. I memorized the Cub Scouts' slogan and motto and found pride in reciting them. I didn't grasp fine tasks like the rest of the boys, and that challenged me to do better, because I wanted to do as well as all of them. I didn't like reading the booklet and the text, but I enjoyed listening to our scout master, Mr. Skipper. He was a tall, light-skinned, thin man who was very gentle. I liked him, and he and his wife took a special interest in me. They held our meetings in the Police Athletic League building in the projects (they held many community activities there). Every week I learned what it meant to be a good Cub Scout and it helped discipline me. The Cub Scouts gave me a different direction and created positive motivation in me.

The most memorable thing I remember about the Cub Scouts was meeting a guy named Raymond who was the Boy Scout leader, who took a liking to me. I was the only Cub Scout whom they allowed to go on an overnight camping trip in New Jersey. We all slept in a huge cabin in the woods and it was the first time I was ever without electricity or heat from a radiator. The cabin had a massive fireplace and we burned wood in it and used Coleman lanterns for light. We slept in a "bunk," which was a piece of canvas stretched between two steel pipes. I couldn't get comfortable in that thing for any thing, the pipes were freezing cold, and the canvas sagged in the middle. They teased me because I was the youngest among them and the smallest of all the guys. It was a great experience, but at the end, I was glad to go home.

Doing Wrong

I had a fascination with fire alarm boxes and always wanted to pull the little red handle to see the fire trucks come screaming down the street. The guys in the black rubber suits with the yellow broad stripes on their pant legs and arm sleeves were great. The fire truck that came to Red Hook had one of those white dogs with the black dots who was supposed to be brave in fires. We called it a "fire engine dog." The fire alarm box kept enticing me, and one day I slowly walked to it and pulled down the huge red handle. It started making this clicking sound and my heart raced as fast as I ran to hide behind a car. Within moments, I could hear the fire trucks with the sirens coming closer and closer to my block. I stood in excitement while the trucks pulled up and the firefighters searched for the fire. It was a big joke to me. I felt bad about it later when I realized that someone may have needed those firefighters to save his life in a real fire.

I looked for anything to keep me busy. Sometimes I walked the streets, picked up cigarette butts and smoked it. When I got tired of that, I would find old peach nuts in the street, break open the shell with a red hammer, which I stole from a fire alarm box, and eat the fruity center. I had become a bad little guy and my biggest problem was me.

The Hard Way

The summer of 1958, I spent much time at the Red Hook swimming pool. I clowned around with my friends, and tried to look at the girls' breasts. My interest in the opposite sex became more focused on intimate body parts and I enjoyed looking at all the different shapes, sizes, and colors. Once I saw a guy and a girl doing some funny things in the water, they pushed against each other back and forth. The guy had a serious look on his face. The girl had her eyes closed. It didn't take me many more visits to the pool in order to figure out what they were doing, because many people were doing it. After the summer was over, I was convinced that people had sex in the water at Red Hook's public swimming pool.

When I got back to school that September, I had to repeat the fifth grade again. My parents, as usual, bought brand-new clothes for my sisters and me. Going back to school, very sharp, was customary for the kids in my neighborhood. I had a thick tan wool sweater with a pair of dark corduroy pants and new black shoes. The first day of school was always great. I got to see people whom I had not seen all summer, because many went on vacations to relatives ;sometimes down South. We would gather in the school yard with our new notebooks with our names neatly written on them. Only a few unfortunate kids would be without any new book or new clothes. It all started well for me. The first day of school, big Black "gorilla" Ronald didn't jump on me and give me a few kicks to my stomach. I'm sure I would not have laid on the ground and taken a beating from him again. I would have tried to stomp him as he did to me. I still hated him and I would have fought him with hate in my heart.

For the first couple of weeks all was well for my studies. I really wasn't up to being left behind my class a second time. They didn't place me in the back of the classroom again, nor was I considered last at everything. They knew I had a strong deviant history behind me and they were watchful of my behavior.

Chapter 4
Stealing Again

Whither shall I go from thy Spirit?
Or whiter shall I flee from thy presence?

Psalm 139:7

I knew that stealing was wrong. I got beat by my father when I stole his money. Ossie was a friend. He came to my house almost every Saturday and we would, on occasion, go to the downtown shopping district. We weren't going to buy anything, but just look around. My mother told me often not to steal. She would say, "Buddy, watch your hands, do you hear me?" I didn't understand why she wouldn't just tell me not to steal.

I was in the habit of picking things up, which weren't mine. Once I shaved down some pennies on the asphalt street until it had the shape and size of a dime, and used it to make telephone calls. I was caught putting one in a soda machine at a gas station. The owner shook me up a bit and told me never to come back to his place again. When Ossie did something wrong, people blamed me, and when I did something, wrong they thought that it was he. Many people thought we resembled each other. Ossie became one of my best friends, and every weekend we roamed the projects and shopping districts together.

Marvin was another strange guy. He was cocky. He looked older than he really was and he was my age and grew hair on his face. Most people respected him because he had a deep voice and walked around as if he owned the world. One Saturday he came to my apartment and asked me if I wanted to go to the Brooklyn downtown shopping district and steal. He didn't say what we were to steal, and I jumped to it. I don't know why

34

I was in a stealing mood because my parents gave me almost everything for which I asked. We went to a department store called Abraham & Strauss. It was an exclusive store where many wealthy people shopped. My mother frequently shopped there, and I could easily have asked her to give me some money in order to buy things. I chose to steal instead. When we got in the store, security guards were everywhere. We caught the elevator to the famous 8th floor toy level. When we got off the elevator, I saw toys stacked up on counters and the bright lights made it enticing. They really didn't have to entice me, because like most kids, I loved any kind of toy. Marvin went behind the toy counter and lifted a large shopping bag. We walked around the store picked up things and dropped it into the bag. I took a Remco science kit and a small radio. Marvin lifted a baseball glove. We walked out of the store as honored shoppers with our stolen goods. We were fortunate not to be caught. One day I was sitting at the dining room table in my apartment listening to the stolen radio, and my mother was cooking in the kitchen. A friend of mine named Donald said, "Ain't that the radio you stole?" My mother's head spun on its axis and she said, "What?" I didn't say a word. I acted as if I never heard him. My mother asked me later if I stole anything and I told her no.

My relationship with Ossie ended without any fanfare. I forgot why, but maybe we grew out of our reasons to be together. I never had a relationship with Marvin and didn't care; I was glad that we never crossed stealing paths again. All the time I was being a thief, I remembered that my father hated thieves. To this day, I am not sure why my father hated a thief.

Being Bad

Once I caught a scalp infection early in the school year. I had to wear a female stocking on my head because I had sores that ran with pus that was very contagious. My father cut all my hair off, as he did our neighbors in Canarsie, and I was embarrassed and didn't want to go to school. The kids teased me and told me that I stunk like something dead. I could smell the mess myself, steaming from my head like a heating blanket. Sometimes those scabs would cause the stocking to stick to my scalp. When my father pulled it off my head, I felt as if my scalp was on fire. I suffered with the infection for weeks, until my father, in his barber's wisdom, could clean it up with scalp medication and continuous washing.

I became a rebellious terror in school after my scalp cleared up. I don't know if it were because they teased me without mercy or if it was just my time to create confusion on earth again. One time the teacher put me out of the classroom into the hallway for misbehaving. It was cold outside with ice and snow on the ground and the school's heat was piping hot from the large radiator. It dawned on me how I could make some urine smoke and stink up the whole hallway. I pulled out my penis and "pissed" on the radiator. It smelled so bad that I had a hard time staying out there. My teacher made me stay in that hallway until the school day had ended. She got tired of my foolishness.

One day while I was clowning around in class and being disruptive, the teacher called my mother to the school. I have no idea how my teacher engineered notifying my mother to come to the school. I never remember my teacher leaving the classroom. I was creating so much confusion that I didn't realize when she left the classroom it was in order to call my mother at home. When I saw my mother's face, I was shocked. I almost died. She motioned to me to leave the classroom and beat me so bad I cried real tears. When I went back into the class, no one teased me that I had tears streaming down my face. I believe that for the first time, my classmates felt sorry for me.

Academically I was not doing up to standard and I was facing being left back again. My mother kept telling me that I had to do well in school, and she begged me to take my school work seriously. When she talked to me, I would promise her that I would do better. I had a rebellious streak running through me as big as a superhighway, and it seemed to control me. I know now that I was angry and hurt, and had not recovered from Hollywood's assault on my mind, and from the lost and broken relationships. The whole thing did something to me, and twisted me. I wanted to react as most of the people I knew and hung out with, but I was sensitive, super-reacting to the world around me. Everybody else did not seem bothered by it. I wondered why no one that I hung around with questioned why they were Black, who they were, or why the world worked the way it did. I felt as if the world around me was on fire, and its fumes were smothering me. My mother repeatedly told me that she had her education and if I wanted to get mine, I would have to work for it.

My father never knew about most of the things, which I did because my mother would not tell him. She knew he would beat me bad, so she saved me from his sting often. She did threaten me often and say, "Buddy, I'm going to tell your father about you." I never took her seriously because she usually never did tell him. She had watched my father beat me and my sister Janice often, like a wild man, not stopping his hard hits with his razor strap on my behind. Once she had to stop him because he accidentally hit my sister Janice in her face with the belt. He was so engaged in tearing her hefty frame up that he didn't realize it. My mother got between them and said, "No more, Wilbert!" It was rare when my mother could stop him from doing anything. When he chastised, it was without mercy. So either he would tell us to get the goddamn hell out of his face or he would say, "Go get my goddamn razor strap." Sometimes he would get angry with my mother for what appeared to me to be something stupid on his part. As an example, if she brought him a plate of food, and it had a hair in it, he would tell her about it and then throw the plate of food against the wall or onto the floor. Without saying any thing, she would rush to clean it up, and he would continue to curse her out, calling her, "a no-good low-down damn spiteful nigger." My grandmother, in her wisdom, tried to warn my mother by giving her a hard time. My mother followed her heart, and married my father. I guess that's what we're supposed to do in this life. Whatever my mother received from my father, in a sense, was hers to bear, because she "fixed her own bed" and was lying in it. Whenever he got angry, he accused her of doing something vicious against him. If she were vicious, I never saw it, and I felt she was a victim of his mental cruelty. I never understood why he treated my mother this way. I know that he was angry and sometimes in a rage. Nevertheless, I believe that he truly loved my mother.

My father suffered from what most Black men suffer in America: a feeling of wilted strength and lean authority, and anger and rages are expressions of most Black men's deep pain. Black men swallow a bitter pill in order to provide for their families, because of added pressure of dealing with the white system. The white system does not gear Blacks for survival. Sometimes my father talked to me about how some damn "white crackers" were no good. He still wouldn't talk to me about his family. He would, however, speak about his sister in a warm and passionate way. I'm sure she was his favorite because when I asked him about her, he never frowned or cursed.

He never talked about his paralyzed leg. I never saw him cry, and I think he was the strongest man, Black or white, whom I knew. He worked long hard hours in his barbershop that was doing well. I was getting to the point of not wanting him at home, so we could have more peace. A few times, I saw him in such an uncontrollable anger and rage that he took his brown cane in order to strike my mother, and each time she would grab a big black iron frying pan and would tell him to come on and hit her so she could tear his head up. Though my mother was short, she stood tall emotionally when my father backed her against a wall. I never saw him take her up on her offer. He would stand motionless, breathing hard, with his eyes fixed on her. I'd look at him frightened, and stare at him while he contemplated his move. I hated when he was this way, but I loved my father. When the eye game was over, he would put his stick down and walk away. He was so predictable after a crisis, no matter how bad it was. When he came home from work, he tried to compensate for his behavior. He brought us Chinese food, ice cream or chocolate candy, and on occasion flowers for my mother. I loved my father, and though I felt our house at times was more peaceful without him, I wanted him by our side.

Raymond

In the summer of 1960, I joined the Boy Scouts of America. Raymond Scott became a major player in my life. He became my role model. Raymond loved kids and was the only adult that I knew who played with us at our level. He graduated from Fort Hamilton High School in Brooklyn. From the first time I met him as a Cub Scout, Raymond worked at least two jobs. He loved electronic things such as short-wave radios and stereo component sets. Swimming and bicycles were his two favorite sports. He could swim like a fish and you would have believed he had been born on a bicycle. He had a bike made from aluminum and I could pick it up with one hand. It had ten speeds, which was a big thing in 1960.It had a "Compenolla" gear changer that was one of the best made. Once, Raymond rode his bike to Philadelphia, Pennsylvania from Brooklyn, New York. He took some of us on a bike trip to a Boy Scout camp to Alpine, New Jersey. We rode over the famous Brooklyn Bridge to lower Manhattan, New York, past Central Park, through Harlem, across the famous George Washington Bridge, then ten miles to the camp. It was great until we had to ride back to Brooklyn. Half of us struggled to make it back, but Raymond and his light-frame bike eased on home. It wasn't only his bike that gave him an edge over us. It was those strong muscles in his skinny legs. Raymond had a way of teasing us when he knew he had challenged us. We struggled to meet the challenge, and he won. He would start laughing and telling us that we were tough and "out of sight" (that we were very good). It was his way of embracing us and giving his approval. Approval from Raymond was important. We wanted him to be proud of us.

The first camping trip that I had with him is still fresh in my mind. I made some new friends, which included Clinton, Randy, Butch, Sam, Abney and Philip. Each week we met and had our Scout meeting. Steven was in my sixth grade class. Though his father split us up because of my cursing when we were younger, his father allowed him to be a friend with me again.

My language had improved and my mother didn't have to use Ivory soap to wash out my mouth anymore. I decided to change my attitude in sixth grade. I was embarrassed over having to repeat the fifth grade, and now and then "gorilla" Ronald reminded me how stupid I was. He was still as black as ebony, and looked even more like a gorilla now that he was older. I hated him with a passion and I wanted to hurt him.

Being Special

I admired and was jealous of a class that had academically gifted kids in it. They were some smart kids, and the teachers and faculties were noticing them. I wanted to be recognized as they were, but I had not done anything academically special to earn it. My mother told me in many ways that I could be just as special as those kids, but I never took her seriously. I believed that I didn't have what it took to be special at anything. Besides my mother's "pep" talks and my father's "razor strap," I was determined to change the course of my life.

Steven was also an encouragement to me, for although he liked to have fun, he was a good student and I admired him and his handwriting. On our first math test, I struggled with it because I didn't know my times tables and counted on my fingers. I didn't have enough fingers or toes to do the computations and I was doing terribly. Division was a block in my mind. I just couldn't do the stuff. My parents even asked a friend of theirs to come to the house and help me. That man was so frustrated trying to help me understand the simple rules of division that he had to take coffee breaks and smoke tons of cigarettes. Week after week, he tutored me free of charge until I was finally able to do the problems alone. Learning fractions was another part of math with which I had trouble. I didn't understand proportions. I hated math because I couldn't count fast enough in order to do as well as my classmates.

I enjoyed being with my friends. It was a serious break from my studies. When I was with them, I concentrated on having fun and tried not to think about school. Ronald was still teasing me. I wanted to fight him. Nevertheless, I knew that I couldn't beat him unless I first kicked him in his balls, but then I would have been considered a punk. If it didn't kill him, he would only knock me down and stomp on me another time. I knew that my day would come. I would hurt him, and I looked forward to it.

Boy scouting was exciting. Raymond had taken a special liking to me and made sure that I matured in it. Raymond was in his twenties and lived at home with his mother. Many Scouts didn't know it, but Raymond was having problems at home. His mother, Angelina, was a strong devout born-again Christian, who lived by the rules and teachings of the Holy Bible. She wouldn't even allow Raymond to play checkers in his bedroom. Once I was in their apartment in Red Hook. She nagged him so much that he in frustration hurled the checker board (with the checkers in their respective places) against the wall. His mother had a way of riding him when she believed that he was in error. She didn't mean any harm to him. She loved Raymond very much. Raymond needed to feel free in order to follow his best talents. He was gifted. He knew how to soothe a broken heart and ease a person out of depression. He opened himself to people and he needed the latitude to do it. Raymond disciplined himself around his mother and always tried to respect her, so Raymond surprised and shocked me when he did that with the checkers.

He had an edge with me because he realized that I felt I had an inferiority complex and my anger was due to my hidden anxiety about me. He never let me get away with displaying fear, anxiety, or rage without confronting me. When I was frustrated and creating an atmosphere of confusion, Raymond would stare at me until I noticed him and say, "What's wrong with you, bonehead?" He made me laugh, and then he would deal with me and make my problem look petty. I loved Raymond. I hardly ever ignored his words.

I loved airplanes and Raymond liked to tease me about my attachment to them. Anytime an aircraft flew above me I looked at the sky, and Raymond would motion to whoever was around to notice me. He encouraged me concerning the good things I liked. He frequently took me and other boys to Kennedy International Airport to watch the planes take off and land. He was a help to me in many areas where I was weak. Raymond always tried to elevate me above my inferiority complex and fears. I did not completely know what it was that made me feel inferior to others. I didn't understand it.

Though Raymond had problems, he always found time for us guys and we soaked it in like a sponge. Most of the time, when Raymond wasn't with us, he was riding that bike of his or swimming. He encouraged me concerning bicycling. He talked to Steven, Butch (who was a friend of mine) and me about buying a new bicycle with four speeds. Each week he took us to a bicycle store near Coney Island Amusement Park that had many bicycles. An Italian guy who was very pleasant with us owned the store. Raymond acted as if he were a friend with him, but Raymond wasn't a friend with him, he just had a respectful attitude and took care of business well. I liked this about Raymond. When I was with Raymond, I felt protected and safe. Raymond had a beautiful way with people, white or Black.

We paid money down on three brand new blue four-speed bikes. My parents gave me money each week to pay down on my bike. After many weeks, we had our bikes and it was a good feeling being one of three boys in Red Hook with four-speed bikes.

One day Raymond was busy fixing a boy's bike when I was trying to fix my front brake. I asked him for help, and he told me to wait a while because he was busy. I acted out my frustration, grumbling and panting to myself, and Raymond called me a "bonehead" and asked me to wait. I was mad and continued to be upset and accidentally broke my brake in frustration trying to fix it. When Raymond realized what, I had done, he didn't get upset. He looked at me and said, "That's what you get for being a bonehead." I wanted to curse him out. He never did help me that day, and I was angry. It was a day I never forgot, because Raymond taught me a lesson in patience. In spite of Raymond's toughness, he showed me lots of love and compassion and I wanted all of it. He made sure that I learned the basic rudiments of drumming in the Drum and Bugle Corps. Though I wasn't as good as the other boys playing, I had a spot to play. He also tried to teach me how to fence, but I would get angry because I couldn't tag him with my foil. So I quickly gave it up without a fight, but never stopped admiring how graceful Raymond looked when he fenced. He took a group of us to Washington, D.C., including my friend Randy. Randy was my neighbor and I especially liked him because he made me laugh a lot. He enjoyed cracking jokes about almost anything. Raymond piled us into his Plymouth car that had push-button controls. We hit the New Jersey Turnpike to Delaware, then Baltimore, and into Washington, D.C. He even pushed that Plymouth to one hundred miles per hour.

I liked Washington, D.C. I marveled at the Lincoln Memorial and Washington Monument. My favorite site was the United States Capitol building, where we rode the underground train. When I returned home, everyone had an earful about my trip.

Raymond continued to do many things with my friends and me. My most exciting time with him in the Boy Scouts was when he took me to an old armory in Harlem, where he was in charge of the artillery room. I saw huge bullets and mortar shells. He even let me hold and play with a walkie-talkie. I adored Raymond; he was my role model, and I always wanted to please him.

Bothering My Neighbor

I still had a mean streak in me and occasionally it came out. When I felt things had gotten too orderly in our courtyard, I devised ways to disturb people without their ever knowing I was doing it. If my neighbors were sitting on the benches having a good time, laughing and discussing everyday life after dark, I would sneak into the building (which was seven stories high), go up on the roof, and throw gravel onto them. They would jump up hollering and cursing about being hit with gravel. Someone would usually say, "Who the hell is throwing those gravel again?" When it played out for the week, I would make a match launcher out of a thread spool with rubber bands. While sitting in my bedroom, I would set up my attack, then kneel at the window ledge where no one could see me, and take straight wooden matches and launch them against the red brick building next to ours. The matches would burst into flames. People would be jumping. A few times I heard someone say, "That's that Buddy again," and I would burst with laughter. I never got tired of surprising my neighbors, but when I ran out of matches or my hands hurt from picking up so many rocks, I'd quit. This was my little secret and I never let onto any grownup what I did to disturb them at night.

Chapter 5
Challenges

Yea the darkness hideth not from thee; but the night sineth
Like the day, the darkness and the light are both alike to thee.

Psalm 139:12

I tried to overcome my math problem in school and stop counting on my fingers, but I continued to struggle with it. I knew that I was as smart as anyone was in my class. It bothered me being thought of as stupid or dumb. In the fifth grade, it never mattered because it drew attention. Now I was tired of being looked down upon academically. I had to show my friends and Ronald that I was just as good as they were in school. Throughout my sixth grade, my performance was marginal and my writing and reading skills were below average; math was never mastered and I still didn't know the times table. However, they promoted me to the seventh grade and sent me to Junior High School 142.

Junior High School 142 was not located in Red Hook projects. It was across a highway that separates Red Hook from an Italian neighborhood, in Carroll Gardens. Most of the homes in that area were brownstones. No Blacks were living there that I knew of and no Hispanics. Racial prejudice was definitely a part of the neighborhood's makeup. The Baptist church that I attended was all Black, and it was in that neighborhood. We constantly had problems with some residents. A few times, I saw references to us as "black niggers" telling us to get out of the neighborhood, written on the ground in front of our church. I recall a couple of times when they got more aggressive. They threw a dead dog at the front gate. Another time a dead fish was placed on the steps. I didn't like going into that neighborhood even when I had church, because of the way some white people looked at me. I never looked anyone straight in their face. I was too scared.

Camping

The summer of 1961, I went away to camp with the Boy Scouts. We went to Pauling, New York to a camp called Sanita Hills Boy Scout Camp. It was for three weeks; the longest camping trip we ever took. My friends, Butch, Sam, Clinton, Steven, and Philip went also. In the first few days at camp, Steven got hurt on his bicycle and had to go to the hospital. His parents came for him and took him home. Clinton got homesick after a few days and decided to call his parents to pick him up. I remember watching him look out of his father's car through the rear window. I was upset with him because he wouldn't stick it out like a tough Scout, and secondly because he was smiling, and really I wanted to go with him.

That trip started with a bang. First, one Scout, named Estrada, stomped a big bullfrog to death for no apparent reason except to watch its brown gut come out. Raymond was very upset. He didn't believe that it was necessary, and it was done in the cabin. A few days later a guy named Johnny found some baby rabbits in the woods and neither him or Raymond would let any of us play with them. Seeing all the wild animals was fascinating because Red Hook only had a few squirrels and some pigeons, and a few stray dogs here and there.

A mile-wide lake was in the center of the camp. Some older Scouts were going to do a mile swim, including our scoutmaster, Raymond. They told me from the beginning that they excluded me and had me take a swimming test in order to get in a canoe or a rowboat. I took the swimming test and passed it successfully.

One morning I got up early while most of the other Scouts were sleeping and walked around the camp, as I marveled at the beauty of the woods. We had our regular Boy Scouts' duties and tests for our merit badges. I didn't like going through all the details for the awards, but I did earn three little round colorful patches on my sash: the cooking, swimming, and hiking merit badges. Raymond encouraged me and looked forward to the day I would even become an Eagle Scout. One day Butch and I went down to the lake and saw some Scouts boating and we threw rocks at them. The word got back to Raymond. He summoned us into the cabin. "What is the matter with you two guys?" Don't you know you could have hurt someone with those rocks?"

Butch said, "Yeah, thanks, Buddy, to your big ideas."

"Hey Butch," I said, "It wasn't only my idea."

Raymond said, "You two boneheads are gonna do kitchen duty."

"We have to do duty for a whole week? Hey Raymond," I said, "That ain't fair."

"Was it fair when you guys decided to throw rocks?" he replied.

For a whole week, we did kitchen duty. We didn't do it without mouthing off. We had to wait until all the other Scouts went to the lake, before we could go and check out a canoe or rowboat.

The following week Raymond had to discipline me strongly. He was playing with me, put a big roach in a plastic bag, and dangled it in my face. I was afraid of insects and he knew it. I cursed him out and said something bad about his mother. I don't know why I said anything about his mother, but he went into a rage and grabbed my T-shirt collar and got close to my face with his, and literally told me that he would waste me if I ever said anything about his mother again. I was frightened to death because Raymond never spoke to me that way. I knew I had pushed his panic button. He pushed me around a bit and pinned me against the sleep bunk,;then, he let me go. He kept telling me that I had better never try that again. It was a day that I would never forget. I respected and loved Raymond and knew that he felt the same way about me, although he was ready to tear me up. The most memorable thing about my camping trip was going to the lake by my self with a fishing pole and some bread to catch fish. I stayed at the lake for hours. I enjoyed putting soggy bread on the hook. I would throw the line into the water and wait until the little round red and white float went under. When a fish was hooked, I would become excited. Most of the times I caught small fishes and threw them back into the lake.

When we arrived back in Red Hook, I went to the swimming pool to show off on the ten foot-high board and look at the girls in their bathing suits. Not much more happened that summer, but I was grateful to Raymond for taking me away from Red Hook in order to enjoy a different kind of life. I wished that I could have taken Ronald to camp and left him there with all the other animals. Ronald was still showing me his ugly black face and teasing me about going into a dumb class. Junior High School 142 had, at each level from 7th to 9th grade, a number designations. They started from 7-SP (special students academically) to

7-21 for students who didn't care to study or work hard. I was in 7-15 and Ronald was in 7-2. He asked me if I were so smart why was I in a dumb class like 7-15. Ronald was smart, but that didn't give him the right to make me feel small. He was my nightmare in living color. He was an evil black kid.

As usual, my parents bought brand new clothes for my sister and me to attend school. On the first day in seventh grade, I wore sharkskin pants, pointed-tip shoes and a knit sweater. I was not interested in entering one of the dumbest classes in the school and I didn't want to go. When I arrived, Ronald's "gorilla" face was in the schoolyard smiling at me. He didn't say a word and he knew that I could read his mind. He was calling me stupid, with that smile.

My courses were basic and general. They were not challenging and I did my share of not paying attention in class. Although I liked science, I had difficulty remembering facts. Math wasn't much better than it was in the sixth grade because I was still counting on my fingers. After years of being harassed by Ronald, he convinced me that I was not intelligent. He made me feel dumb. I didn't know how to handle having low self-esteem, an inferiority complex, and being dumb. The fact that I could not boast of great grades in school only reinforced in me how dumb I must have been. No one ever told me I was smart, so I had no reason to believe that I was.

My defense against the negative feelings of Ronald was to plot to hurt him any way I could. It was a difficult time for me emotionally. It was the first time that I had to struggle with myself and I believed I was losing. I wanted to go somewhere and hide.

On weekends, I got bored and left Red Hook, even if it were only for a couple of hours. Most times, I went to downtown Brooklyn, where the big stores were, in order to look in the electronic store windows at the walkie-talkies and cameras. On occasion, I went to 42nd Street, and walked to 59thStreet at Central Park, looking in the electronic store windows. Sometimes I would stop by a pornographic store to look through the window at the nude pictures. I would go inside and slowly walk to the back where the nudist camp books were. I saw pictures of people who were old and young, fat and skinny, short and tall, and pretty and ugly. They were all white. I believed that white people thought they were the standards of beauty in America. It was white America flexing her racial muscles again. I didn't expect to see any Black people in those books, because it wasn't a Black thing.

American Racism

I didn't know that the United States was in racial turmoil. Blacks all over the country were demanding equal rights and protection under the law. Horrible crimes were committed against many Black people in the South and in the North. Red Hook was in some ways a protective zone where I didn't have to worry about my life being threatened by hateful, racist people. I began listening to the news on TV and reading the newspapers.

It was 1961; however, in 1955, on August 28, Emmett Till, a 14-year-old Black boy from Chicago, Illinois, was murdered in Mississippi. Black people were shocked, knowing that the United States did not protect children from hate crimes.

In 1960, John Fitzgerald Kennedy had become the President of the United States. Many Blacks thought that it would change the climate of racial prejudice and hatred in America. It didn't. It made things worse. The President had his hands full with the whole mess. He was expected to pass the Civil Rights Bill in order to help Black people gain their full rights in the United States. The first Civil Rights Bill to pass through Congress since 1875 occurred on August 29, 1957. It would be a challenge for Kennedy to convince Congress to pass another. The fact that Black people were suffering under the arm of racism made the passing of a new Civil Rights Bill critical. In some places in the South, Black people still didn't have the right to vote.

Martin Luther King, Jr. was putting the heat on President Kennedy to pass another Civil Rights Bill, and the President was dragging his feet. King, a pioneer of the civil rights movement, was caught in the midst of its early violence. Some whites bombed his home on January 30, 1956 in Alabama. An organization called the White Citizens Council used its racial strong arm against him and his family for exercising their rights to protest injustice in America.

In 1954, the Brown versus the Board of Education decision was passed, which overruled the "separate but equal" laws in school segregation. Only one school in Texas and two schools in Arkansas complied. In the rest of the South, not one classroom was racially mixed.

Daisy Bates, who was president of the NAACP in Little Rock, Arkansas, fought in the struggle to have integration fully started in the United States schools in the South. In her book, *The Long Shadow of Little Rock*, she recounts the night that a stone was thrown through her living room window and said, "I threw myself to the floor. The glass covered me.

I reached for the rock lying in the middle of the floor. They tied a note to it. I cut the string and unfolded the soiled piece of paper. Scrawled in bold print were the words: 'Stone this time, dynamite next."

On September 23, 1957, nine Black students called the "Little Rock Nine" gathered at Daisy Bates's house in order to integrate Little Rock's Central High School. Shortly after, they notified Daisy that at 8:00 a.m. police would escort the nine students to school. Four Black journalists waited at the school. Someone had a brick in his hand and he hit reporter Alex Wilson on the side of his head. Wilson was more than six feet tall and an ex-Marine, but he went down like a tree. Time magazine reported, "A cop stood on a car bumper to get a better view of the fighting."

The South had boycotts. Blacks were demanding what was their right to have, the same opportunities as any other United States citizen. They denied Blacks equal protection guaranteed under the United States Constitution by local laws. Many Blacks were under the strong arm of their white neighbors. They had tortured, or murdered some and raped. Even the right to vote had become a part of the agenda by some whites in order to commit genocide against Black people.

If anyone had tried to hold a discussion with me on racism and Blacks in America, I would not have known where to start or end my views. Being a Black boy in Brooklyn, New York did not make me any less a target for racism, it just came in a concealed package. As for me, I was a Black boy growing up in a racist country. I didn't know that since racism existed that it would have a hold on me. As a Black person, I did not know how I fit into the scheme of things.

It was during the time in my life, when I was thirteen years old; I truly focused in on the race question. I hated that race and color permeated my life.

When I looked at the few white students in my Junior High School, I felt isolated. I didn't see many Black teachers in the school; the two whom we had taught typing and band. I identified with the Black students, and my friends were special to me. Nevertheless, I didn't want to share in the ugly racism that we as Blacks were facing, but Hollywood, television and the system kept racial prejudice and racism alive before me.

I'm No Punk

The following year I was placed in class 8-11 and I told my mother that I wanted a smarter class. She went to the school and demanded that they give me courses that are more challenging. They transferred me to class 8-5. I couldn't believe my mother pulled it off. I was in science class learning about jet engines, electricity, and animal kingdoms. My English teacher had us reading Walt Whitman, Robert Frost, poetry, and writing essays.

Most of the people in my class were smart. One guy named Douney sat next to me almost every day and counted down to the second when the period bell would ring. He was bright and played basketball well. I admired him because he was always pleasant to me and liked to laugh. He would enter a basketball game, calmly walk onto the court, and score high points and it never seemed to go to his head.

I joined the school band and learned to play the clarinet. I didn't like playing the clarinet because it looked stupid to me. I only did it because I wanted to go home with an instrument. I really wanted to blow a trumpet but they did not offer it to me and they had no empty spots. My friend Herman played it and I admired him.

My interest in education and learning became short-lived and I did the least requirements. It wasn't because I didn't like school, but I got bored. I was placed on the last clarinet row blowing the thing. Sometimes I would miss notes and just fake it. I did the same thing in typing class. We had to memorize the keys. I never did. Each time the teacher told me not to look at the keys I did and never learned to type. Anyway, I hated typing. The only enjoyable thing about my typing class was my teacher, who was a beautiful Black woman. I loved when she came to my desk in order to help me because she smelled sweet and had beautiful hands with red nail polish on her fingernails.

Slam-Dunk Time

I become a regular at the Police Athletic League Center and ironically, I felt very insecure being there, because every night while the guys played basketball the girls were their greatest audience and I didn't know how to play. These guys were working up sweats and sporting their jockstrap strings above their shorts, looking sexy and heroic. People cheered after hoops were shot with accuracy or someone slam-dunked a ball. Only a few guys could go that high to slam it in, and Downey was one. Guys like Clinton and Myra, who were brothers, who were also good-looking, were favorites. Lawrence Hannahan was the shortest one on the team, but he survived. Often people poked fun at his height, but it didn't seem to bother him much.

I was still in the Boy Scouts and I was hearing comments about tin soldiers (Boy Scouts). It didn't bother me until it became aggressive. I'd have on my uniform and someone would yell out, "Look at the tin soldier." At first, I didn't understand what it meant, until they called me a punk a few times in relationship to it. The Boy Scouts was considered in my neighborhood by a few Red Hook bad guys a "sissy" organization, full of punks.

I kept leaving Red Hook when I was bored or felt like I was missing something. I made a ritual of going to automobile and air shows. Airplanes and helicopters fascinated me. Once, I bet my friends Butch and Sam that I could beat them to Kennedy International Airport traveling by helicopter, and they would travel by the subway train. I had to catch the train from Red Hook to lower Manhattan, and then get on the helicopter at a heliport. I could fly in the helicopter because my parents gave me the money. My parents knew that I loved airplanes and helicopters. I beat them by one half-hour. Flying in that helicopter was greater than beating them at the bet. I did things like that, and my friends dared not follow me. Ever since ,I can remember, whenever my parents gave me some rope to venture out of Red Hook, I pushed my limits. Sometimes I just went to a museum and would spend half a day there. If I had enough energy, and I usually did, I went to Central Park in order to visit the zoo.

I still frequented the Police Athletic League. Butch, Sam, and the Boy Scouts were still a part of my activities. One night while at the Police Athletic League, a tough guy named Lacey, who was considered one of Red Hook's bad boys, kicked me. I was sitting on the gym floor watching a basketball game. He called me a punk and invited me to the boys' bathroom to fight. I hadn't fought anyone in at least two years and I knew that he would beat me, but I said, "Let's go." As we were on our way out of the gym, a couple of his friends told him to forget it. He called me a "jive-ass punk," and walked away. I was thankful to his friends because I didn't believe I could beat Lacey. He was a good street fighter, and I never took well bleeding from my mouth or nose (I suffered nosebleeds when I was younger). I didn't want to lose any teeth and besides, it would hurt. I saw people who lost their teeth due to fights. I wasn't ready to look like a teenage Michael Spinks with no front teeth.

Another guy named Willie grabbed me by the collar when I walked out of my building. While he tried to choke me to death, he asked me why I was messing with his woman. I told him that I wasn't, and his friends had to pull him off me. I was afraid of Willie because he was massive, had big muscles, and looked mean. I was grateful just to get away from him.

I could not understand why suddenly Red Hook's bad boys were troubling me but they felt I was a punk tin soldier. So I figured I should change my image. I quit the Boy Scouts, went to my friends Butch and Sam, and told them I would not be hanging out with them anymore. Both stood motionless, looking at me. It wasn't that they were the source of my trouble with the Red Hook bad guys, but we clowned around a lot and it drew too much attention. Butch said okay. That was it. The following morning, while I was going to school, Butch's sister Gloria grabbed me by the collar and said, "Who the hell do you think you are?" " Do you think you're better than my brother?" I didn't say a word to her because she was much bigger than I was. From that day on, Butch and Sam didn't speak with me or I with them. The decision to abandon my friends was difficult, but I didn't enjoy being thought of as silly anymore. Being a target for the Red Hook bad guys wasn't healthy.

My Sisters

My sister Janice was one of the craziest people whom I knew. She loved to laugh and joke. She could make some ugly faces and steal the hearts of even strangers around her. As my sister, however, she sometimes created confusion in my life. I'm not implying that I never gave her a reason in order to attack me, but sometimes she did it with a smile on her face. Out of all the people, I created hell with, I could unleash some wicked power on her, and I did it while loving her also.

When my mother was away at work, she would ask my sister Janice to cook for us. Janice had a favorite dish that she liked to fix; white potatoes, onions, and hot dogs. She would mix it together in a black frying pan and some burned potatoes would stick to the bottom of it. She always made enough for us to eat. Once, I would put ketchup all over mine until I hardly saw the stuff, and then thoroughly enjoy it. She made that potato mix so often I developed an aversion to it. It was so bad that while it was cooking I got a slight headache. Nevertheless, what is a kid supposed to do when his sister says, "You better eat it, or else." My sister Janice was special to me and I loved her very much. She wasn't a perfect sister, and I was definitely a challenging brother.

Shelly

My sister Shelly never cared about much, except sitting around looking innocent. She was chubby and my father constantly spoke to my mother about her weight. My mother would mumble under her breath because she believed that he contributed to Shelly's heaviness. He constantly brought home sweets (chocolates) for us all, and he would parade the box before Shelly. She would play shy and hesitate, knowing that my father would encourage her on until she took some. I watched my mother look serious at him for pumping Shelly with candy. She knew that he would mention Shelly's weight in a negative way when he wanted to blame her for something.

I remember when Shelly was small; she sucked a baby bottle like it was going out of style. When she was about five years old, she was still sucking the thing. When she wasn't sucking it, she held it in her hand like a football. I think that she was afraid to put it down, thinking someone wanted to suck it or make a pass for it. Shelly was the only one in my house, I believed, who thought that I was a good boy whenever I had a problem as far as I can remember, but I may have blocked some things out. I always viewed her as being in need of my protection, maybe because she kept sucking that baby bottle.

I often fought with Janice and sometimes they were punch, knock down, and get up fights. Once we were fighting over my not wanting to listen to her and she beat me up. Doing it wasn't hard for her because she was muscular and much bigger than I was. Even when she walked, she looked strong because she bounced on her toes. I got angry because I couldn't win. Then it was snowing outside. I tied T-shirts around my feet and went out in the snow without a shirt on. I hollered and screamed at her from the ground level and refused to go upstairs; however, when my feet got cold enough, I did. I may have been stupid, but I wasn't crazy, even if my mother took me to a psychiatrist when she thought that I was.

I loved my two sisters. Being the only boy in my house and full of terror, made me special, and I wanted to be special. If I couldn't be special in school, I could surely be special at home. They had to watch me, always.

My sister Janice got caught drinking alcohol in the girls' bathroom in school and got suspended for a few days. That was a big event in my house. It even overshadowed my stealing my father's money and my mother's having taken me to a psychiatrist. I felt Janice was stupid for doing that, but especially for being caught. I was angry with her for making herself look bad, and I also felt sorry for her, because I knew that she was embarrassed and hurt.

Shelly was still fat and quiet. She remained the benign one in the house. My father was just as angry as ever. My mother was beginning to fight back the tears and raise her voice at him. As for me, it was long overdue. I had seen her pick up many plates of food and put it into the garbage, which he threw against the wall. I never heard him say he loved her or thanks for being here. I felt more for my mother's emotional state than I did for my father's. Although I didn't think that he had his life under control, everyone was afraid of him, and I felt he could take care of himself.

Chapter 6
Raw Life

If I say, surely the darkness shall cover me:
even the night shall be light about me.

Psalm 139:11

When the school year ended, I believed that I had accomplished something, I knew how to play a clarinet without anyone telling me to shut up. I passed all of my courses though I still couldn't type well.

That summer I met a beautiful girl at the Red Hook pool. She had long wavy brown hair and a light soft brown complexion. I saw her sitting on the concrete deck. She was leaning back on her hands and her legs were crossed. I saw her often before in Red Hook. She was sitting with a couple of girls and I walked over to her. "Hello. I'm Buddy." She ignored me. I sat in front of her and she smiled. I didn't know what to say so I talked about how enjoyable the pool water was. I saw her a few times and we started dating. She was a Jehovah's Witness and I didn't know her mother was going to ask me to become one. She told me that her mother wouldn't allow me to date her unless I converted from being a Baptist to Jehovah Witness. When I failed to convert, her mother made her end our relationship. I didn't feel too bad about it because I realized I only liked her for the way she looked sexually.

Puerto Rican girls looked very sexy to me. It was the way they fixed their faces, putting on makeup. Most of the Black girls didn't wear makeup at an early age. I believe that Black parents were stricter concerning it, and most of the Black girls didn't look like they needed any. I viewed Puerto Ricans as a "Safe Race," probably because of the mixture of races (Taino

Indians, Africans, and Spaniard) in some cases. The fact that they ranged from a white complexion to black, spoke the same language, and was from a little island in the sea was exciting to me. I sensed a oneness in them and I could visibly see some of their culture.

I realize what I am saying might offend some Black women, but this is how I felt at the time. I know that many beautiful Black women can stand next to any woman and not feel lacking. This whole Black/Hispanic thing is some "crap," and it has served to separate our peoples. If we realize the system benefits from our strife at any level, we will be the wiser and richer for it. I believe my attraction to Puerto Rican girls was something in me trying to discover who I was, without boundaries, being free, like I was born. The system wanted to convince me that my birth certificate said who I was, a "Negro" boy. A Negro was far from who I was. I am a human being.

I didn't know at the time that some Puerto Ricans felt the same way about me and each other about color, as some whites feel about Blacks. When I heard some Puerto Ricans talking about the "bad hair" versus the "good hair" and all that foolishness, I knew that there were serious problems among them.

None of the Black girls ever seemed interested in me. I did feel that my neighbor Patty was attractive, but she too had no interest in me. Once I tried to kiss her. She stuffed her mouth full of potato chips, and then she opened it for me to see the slimy yellow stuff. That cooled me out. Then, Donna was another girl who I felt was pretty, but she was more interested in guys with athletic ability and intelligence. I had neither, so I imagined being a Black was hard no matter on which side of the fence I sat. If I couldn't get a Black girl to take an interest in me, then I would look else where, and that is exactly what I did.

Clowning Around

I had another year before completing junior high school. They promoted me to class 9-5 and it was loaded with challenges for me. My teacher was a Black man who taught the school band and orchestra. Butch was in my class, which was not one of the best situations for either of us. We were in competition together for attention and we both made fools of ourselves. To top it off, 9-5 was not considered one of the smarter classes. The students in my class were not considered to have much academic promise. I had not proven that I was smart enough to be in a more challenging class. A guy in my class read at the third-grade level. My reading score was sixth grade and I needed at least a seventh-grade level in order to get a diploma at graduation in ten months instead of a certificate.

A quiet olive-skinned Puerto Rican girl in my class named Rosa had my attention. I took an immediate liking to her. Rosa could have cared less about me, but I made sure that she noticed me by teasing her about how beautiful she was. Butch was in competition with me for her attention. I clowned around a lot with Butch and it irritated my teacher. Once before going home, with my books weighing heavy on my arms, my teacher stopped me. "Why don't you stop being a clown?" he said. He had a frustrated look on his face and I believed he was embarrassed, being a Black teacher, seeing how terribly most of us Black kids behaved. His words stung me because I knew that he was right. I think that if he had called me a "Stupid black nigger" and beat me, I would have listened to him. The problem was, I did not respect him. He had a weak streak in him. I really wanted him to tell the whole lot of us to shut up and sit before he beat all our asses. He never did and he paid for it, because one-third of us aggravated him to death.

My most exciting class was English. My teacher was in love with poetry and she demanded that we learn at least two hundred lines of poetry. I loved the poem "Oh Captain, My Captain," by Walt Whitman. I learned my lines well. I always did my homework, but did average in class. I tried to get higher grades, but it just didn't happen. The problem was I couldn't read well. I could repeat the words on the page but my comprehension of the information was slow. I had to read one page over about three times in order to get all the information and even then, I would retrieve only 70% for a test. It was frustrating and it angered me. When the film "West Side Story" came out, I caught a bus and went to Ridgewood in Brooklyn to see it. I sat in the movie house all alone, mesmerized by Natalie Wood, who was playing Maria, a Puerto Rican. My fantasy with Hollywood started again, but this time I was old enough fully to understand it was a plaything. "West Side Story" had such a great impact on me that I visited the site where they filmed it. The writing in the street, "Jets," the name of the white gang, was still there in dull yellow paint. Then, I found the name "Sharks," the name of the Puerto Rican gang. Rita Moreno, who is a Puerto Rican, was also in the film, and I became more attracted to Puerto Rican women than ever after seeing her.

When I saw Rosa at school, I started singing a song from the movie to her. When Butch realized that I was getting Rosa's attention, he butted in and robbed me of time with her. My teacher saw me in Rosa's face often, and this irritated him because besides my disrespect for him, I was not respecting others with my harassment. A few times, I tried to follow Rosa home, but was distracted by my friends. I didn't want them to catch on that I really liked Rosa. The fact was, I felt that I loved her. By this time in my life, I knew that I was a set-up to get hurt by any girl. When I loved someone, it was very serious and real to me.

One day Rosa approached me and told me not to follow her around the class and she wanted me to leave her alone. Because she said it with a smile, I didn't take her seriously. I continued to sing love songs to her in class, and she just smiled. One day Rosa caught me following her home. The next day she told me that her parents were very strict and not to follow her. She didn't explain how they were strict or why. How they felt really was not any of my business, but I was offended. I believed that Rosa did not want me to follow her home because her family wouldn't want her with a Black boy. My color and race kept surfacing on me. I felt inferior as a person. Though Rosa never made any mention about Blacks or Puerto Ricans, I attached this to her. I did stop following Rosa home, but never stopped singing to her or loving her.

Betty

Betty was the second Black girlfriend whom I had. It was love at first sight. Betty had the prettiest teeth that I ever saw and a smile to go with it. She reminded me of Dionne Warwick, the singer. I had to watch out, for when she didn't have a smile, she could be vicious. I don't really know what attracted us because we were as different as peas and rice. Our relationship was fine for a few weeks, and then she broke off with me because she said I was too childish. We went back together until she was aggravated again with me and called it quits. Each time she vowed never to date me again. The third time around Betty decided to renew our relationship because I literally begged her, but it was under her terms. Betty felt that I was not serious about her and she asked me to grow up. After my split with my friends, I thought that I had grown up, but she had a different opinion. She told me that the relationship was going to be done her way and if I didn't like it, it was too bad. I never did appreciate her gross arrogance and this time was no exception. Nevertheless, I liked Betty so I let her have her way. One day after school, I said something that she didn't like; she scratched my arm, and some of my skin was under her long beautiful fingernails. I told her that if she ever did it, again I would cut them off with scissors. A few days later, she did it again and I chased her home after school. While she was running up the stairs, I was at the bottom and she accused me of looking under her dress.

The following day I asked a boy in my class to put a note in her violin case asking if I could see her legs again. My home room teacher, Mr. Harris, who felt that I acted like a clown, was also my band teacher. He intercepted the note and sent me to the guidance counselor, Mr. Fitzpatrick.

Mr. Fitzpatrick was a stern Irish man who spoke bluntly. He said what he meant. "Wilbert," he said, "what do you think this girl would feel knowing you wrote a note like this and put it in her music case?" If you do not stop your foolishness, you're never going to see high school."

That was it for me; no high school for messing around with Betty or any girl was crazy. I decided at that point I would never clown around in school again. As the school year was nearing an end, they gave me an opportunity to bring my reading score up to seventh-grade level. Each day I had to stay after school and read, read, read, and then answer questions about what I read. I worked at it very hard, and could bring it up to seventh grade. They informed me that if I graduated to high school, I would get a diploma.

Betty and I called it quits for all time, but still stayed friends. Being only friends was better for both of us.

During my last week of school, one afternoon I was with Betty. We stayed late getting some of our last remains for the school year from our classrooms. As we walked across the street from the school, Betty went ahead of me, turned the corner, and was out of my sight. Three white men called me to them. At first, I hesitated and when they realized it, they got verbally aggressive. One guy said, "Ain't you the guy who's been starting trouble around here?"

"Come on, let's pull him into the hallway," another said. One grabbed me by my arm while the others coaxed him on. I told them that if they wanted to mess with someone, I would get someone to mess with them. One of them took a bucket of dirty water from a car wash and tossed it on me. He told me to walk straight and don't say a word or they would bust my head open. I was frightened.

I went to a gang member of the "Kovons" in Red Hook and told him that these three white men messed me up. He said, "Man, if you were one of us we'd fight for you, but you ain't one of us." Being Black, I felt like one of them, but they didn't consider me a part of their family. I found out later that those three white men belonged to a gang of five brothers called the "Sumner Brothers." That was the first incident that ever happened in my life, which I felt, was totally racial.

Farewell

Graduation from junior high school was great. The graduation ceremony was in a movie theater in the Bay Ridge section of Brooklyn, not too far from 78th Street near 5th Avenue. The traditional graduation song almost made me cry. It was beautiful. The only award I got was for 100% attendance during my time there. I especially remember my friend Herman, who blew the trumpet in the school band with me. He looked so silly with his graduation hat on his head, tilted to the side. I will never forget the smile on his face.

Some of our parents got together and decided to have a graduation dinner for us at the Police Athletic League Center. I remember how they arranged the food neatly on the tables; the center used for games. The record player was hooked up to large black speakers in the front of the room. The lights were dim and we played 45-r.p.m. records (the ones that you have to put the plastic piece in the center to make it fit the other phonograph). We were having a great time until one of Red Hook's deviant kids urinated at the open window where the food was. To this day, I forget what happened to the food on the table. We had to close the windows for the rest of the party. Closing the windows didn't disturb us. We continued the graduation party until late in the night. I had a chance to dance with some girls who wouldn't give me the time of day during my three years at Junior High School 142. My mother had her first glance at watching me dance. When the party was over, I felt a bit sad. I knew that my life was moving into a different arena, and I was going to enter a different world. I would have to be more responsible concerning my actions and decisions about my life. I hugged some of my classmates and bid them farewell, and told some, "I'll see you later."

Going South

I enjoyed my summer before high school. I went to Virginia with my friend Clinton with his brother, father and mother in order to visit his grandmother on her farm. The drive from New York seemed endless. It was 1963, and finding a place to rest in a motel was not easy for Blacks. We drove straight through, only stopping to get gas. We even parked on the Chesapeake Bridge to eat fried chicken, potato salad, and collard greens that Clinton's mother cooked.

Clinton was learning how to drive. His father allowed him to take the wheel, and he drove the car well. I sat in the back seat, envious of what was going on. I was thinking that my father could have done the same thing with me if he wanted. He still refused to learn to drive. He wasn't going to buy us a car, no matter how much money he had; and he wasn't cheap. Maybe it was the Polio, or he didn't feel we needed it. Nevertheless, he wouldn't buy one.

I enjoyed staying on that farm eating fresh corn, collard greens, corn bread and fresh fried chicken. We stayed in a wooden house. I still recall how old the wood appeared. When I stood on the porch, I looked out and saw a huge field and my heart was beating fast. I was excited and I didn't know why. I believe it was my fascination with open space and nature. I said to myself, "You're gonna have one of these one day." Clinton's grandmother looked just like his mother. She was pleasant to me and welcomed me into her beautiful home.

My mind shifted to Ronald. I was more than 300 miles from Brooklyn, New York where he was. I had my thoughts on a BB gun to shoot him. BB guns were illegal in New York City (and still are). I decided to break the law and finally finish him off after six full years of total harassment. He was still bothering me and I wanted to light him up with a few pieces of metal. I went into a hardware store and purchased a high-powered CO_2 cartridge pistol that was semiautomatic. I tucked it into my luggage and checked it every day to see if it was still there.

When I got back to Brooklyn, I secretly hid my gun away, high up in my closet. I had figured out the line of fire. All I needed was the monster, Ronald, to walk in the path of it.

That summer of 1963, I reflected on my life and how dissatisfied I was with myself. I realized how much precious time I had wasted in school because I did not feel like I learned anything. I was still counting on my fingers. I felt inferior to all of my peers, more than any time. Giving up my friends Butch and Sam didn't help me to feel any better about myself, because I had no new friends at the time. I looked at the Black race and didn't want anything to do with it. Being Black was tough. I felt twisted like a pretzel, and some racist bigots and Hollywood did not help. Knowing I was confused about my place in the world made me feel terrible. Everything my father said to me about racism and racial prejudice had raised its ugly head, and I wanted to kill the thing forever. I was hurting inside and crying out for help.

No where to Hide

Racial prejudice in America was at a high in 1962. The Federal District Court ordered the University of Mississippi to admit its first Black student; James Meredith. Within the next three weeks, a riot broke out and some people died, while some hosts of others were injured. Racial hatred was really brewing all over the country and race caught Black people in the middle.

It was August 28, 1963. I had graduated from Junior High School 142. The civil rights movement was on the line. America had to deal with the complaints of Blacks who believed not enough was being done to protect them against hatred, bigotry and injustice. Martin Luther King Jr. led the march on Washington, D.C. It was one of the historical events to take place in America where Blacks and whites rallied for freedom and justice in America. I didn't fully understand how this event would shape my life. Nevertheless, the marches on Washington become a major event in my life and I would become a part of the civil rights movement in America.

Choices

I had the choice of entering one of two high schools. One was predominantly Black and the other predominantly white. The white school, John Jay High School, was dangerous for Black people. A Black guy named Stanton was beaten badly at the white school. They put him in the hospital. It was in my best interest to attend Boys High School, though it was predominantly full of Blacks and Puerto Ricans, but I didn't want to be there. I felt stigmatized going to school with mostly Black and Hispanic boys. I hated that my color became a major issue to others and me. I wanted to forget the color thing and it refused to go away. My second challenge was surviving the train ride miles from Red Hook into a tough Black neighborhood called "Bedford Stuyvesant." The school was in the heart of the ghetto and it had two gangs: One from Red Hook, the "Kovons," and another from a housing project called the Marcy project, the "Buccaneers."

Butch and Sam went to other schools that were trade schools. Philip went to Aviation High School and Clinton went to Eli Whitney High

School. Steven also entered Boys High School and was placed in the annex building, which was a couple miles from where I was. My first week at school was uneventful. Except a few young men standing in the hallway asking for money, I didn't see any negative behavior-taking place. I did see a couple of young men who might be homosexuals who kept to themselves. The school had a bad reputation for fighting, but I didn't see any activity going on my first few days there. The school had a great athletic program; especially track, football and basketball. I could have cared less because I wasn't efficient at sports or sports-minded. Boys High's scholastic record was low, al though it was an academic school and it offered college preparatory studies. They noted the early years of Boys' High School for the academic program, but that was before, when it was predominately white.

I entered its academic program and my first big challenge was Algebra I. I never had Algebra before, and if I did, I forgot. It was like a foreign language to me. I failed every test that I took. I liked Art and hated American History with a passion because I didn't like memorizing all the dates of events in history. I enjoyed Biology but found it hard memorizing animal kingdoms and families, etc. The written tests were all challenging to me. When the first semester was over, I failed Algebra I and did average work in my other courses.

Ronald was attending Boys High School. He still harassed me and called me stupid. It was very painful for me. Ronald was determined to hurt me emotionally for no-good reason known to me. I guess Ronald felt that he was too old to pick a physical fight, and if he did, I had gained enough weight and could possibly beat him. I would have tried to stomp him to death, as he did to me in the schoolyard when I was in the fourth grade. I was truly sick and tired of him. One day he embarrassed me in English class by challenging me on the word "bison," which I pronounced incorrect. Though it was a simple word, I had never seen it before. He just laughed aloud at me and pronounced the word correctly. My ability to pass basic Algebra I and inability to pronounce words correctly at high school-level made me feel academically inferior to my peers.

School became such an issue that I started studying as if it were the only thing left on earth to do. I cut off all other activities, but I joined the high school glee club. I took Algebra I again and barely passed it. A guy in Red Hook named Lenny Malloy, who was a whiz in math, took a liking to me and he offered to tutor me. I spent late hours in the Red Hook Public Library studying with Lenny. He was very patient and compassionate with me. When the problems were difficult for me to figure out and my face started to twist in frustration, Lenny would encourage me to calm down and think.

I got accustomed to being at Boys High and sported its T-shirt and shorts proudly. I even put its book covers on all of my books. I finally believed Boys High was giving me the academic courses, which I needed to be prepared for college. Though I was struggling through my courses, I was excited about taking them.

I saw Steven infrequently. He was taking a general course of study. I didn't understand why Steven took that road because I believed that he was much brighter than I was. I still admired Steven because I knew he was taking school seriously.

Anna

I didn't have any close friends. I didn't even have a girlfriend. I started to like a girl who lived in my building; her name was Anna. She was a Puerto Rican and she was almost as dark as I was. I admired her from the first day that she moved in. She had long brown hair and she smiled a lot. She never said much to me. We were in the Drum and Bugle Corps together and that's where I got close with her. After a competition meet, we sat on the bus next to each other on the return trip home. We started dating and I liked her a lot.

Her mother was not too happy about the relationship because I was a Black. I did not understand what her mother's problem was because her mother was just as Black as I was. Once her mother referred to me by the Spanish word "negro," and had a terrible look on her face when she said it. I knew that she had not read my birth certificate, so I wondered how she knew that they called me a "Negro" when I was born. I later understood from her daughter that she was calling me "a Black." Anna later told me that her mother didn't want her around me. We continued to see each other without her mother's knowing. My courtship with Anna was never intimate then with sexual intercourse, because I was still a virgin. Anna added excitement to my life on a social level and she made me feel good.

I was taught in the Baptist church that sex before marriage was wrong and I felt that I was a good churchgoing regular and a Christian. One thing my mother never stopped insisting on was my sisters and I going to church.

My relationship with Anna went sour because her mother found out about us, and literally separated us. She was afraid that her mother would make her life unbearable if she didn't stop seeing me, so we stopped seeing each other. That was another bittersweet relationship that ended in rejection because I was Black.

My High School Heroes

Another friend, Alberta, was smart, attractive and witty. She loved to laugh and crack jokes. She got tired of hearing me telling people how terrible I was doing in school. She took notice of the way I spoke about myself and couldn't stomach it anymore. One day she asked me to improve on my vocabulary and that, she would help me. She suggested a book for me to read which had all these big words in it and she spent many hours tutoring me. She told me that I needed to have greater confidence in myself and constantly badgered me about my low self-esteem. She also kept me laughing, while she joked. Her laughing and joking were therapy for me.

I was in and out of depression and Alberta was aware of it. Depression had become a norm with me because no matter how well I did in school, my grades were never better than my peers were, and Ronald continued to harass me.

I admired a guy named Raymond Frost. He was excelling academically and socially, and the girls liked him. Once a guy named Oliver was taunting him, teasing him about his deceased brother, a Harvard University student, who died in a boating accident. I went home with Raymond. He didn't say a word all the way. He put on his dirty sneakers, went back to that guy, and beat him down. Raymond took his time punching him in his face, but my true admiration for Raymond was his coolness and his "smarts" in school.

I also admired William Emerson, who was a whiz in Chemistry. I could not figure William out for he hardly ever studied and still got A's and B's on Chemistry tests. I was studying hard and struggling through Chemistry. While riding the subway train to school, William would go over some chemistry questions with me between stops. I liked William because he was serious and didn't take well to foolishness.

William and Alberta dated a few months, but they seemed like a mismatch to me because Alberta continued to joke around and loved foolishness. I was glad when they broke up because it gave me more time with Alberta.

"Gorilla" Ronald was still around and very intelligent. I even admired his gray matter, but he was still an evil devil. Most of my peers were intelligent and I never believed I belonged in their academic circle. I had settled one issue in my mind. I would never be as smart as they would academically no matter how hard I tried.

Vietnam and Civil Rights

The United States was engaged in the Vietnam War and I started hearing about it in school, seeing it on television and reading about it in the newspapers. I had no idea what it was all about (nor did most Americans Black or white). We had a President, Kennedy, who had promised to help Black people in America get their fair share of opportunities. He was young and full of energy and the whole country seemed to like him. I marveled at the way he spoke and the things he said; especially about the New Frontier and reaching outer space. I became fascinated with rockets and astronauts.

Martin Luther King, Jr. didn't especially appreciate the fact that Kennedy was dragging his feet concerning passing a Civil Rights Bill. Kennedy didn't feel it was the right time to push hard in that direction. Nevertheless, regardless of what was occurring on the high level with his administration and other areas of government in response to civil rights, I viewed the President as my hero and friend and felt intimacy in my acceptance of him.

On November 22, 1963, my friend and hero, President Kennedy was assassinated in Dallas, Texas while I was in the Boys' High School library learning to catalog books. When I heard the broadcast on the radio, I stood silent in one spot, not believing the report. Then I understood that Black people in America had lost a vital player in the saga of racial prejudice and racism in my country. The man who federalized National Guard troops in Mississippi in order to assure that James Meredith could enter the University of Mississippi safely on September 29, 1962, the same man who had met with civil rights leaders on June 20, 1963 about the march on Washington, was dead. He was gone forever. His death affected my life. I hurt with the rest of the country because of his death.

After they buried John Fitzgerald Kennedy, I sent Jacqueline Kennedy a copy of Walt Whitman's poem, "Oh Captain, My Captain," which I had memorized in junior high school. I also sent letters to her in order to let her know that I cared deeply about her husband, and her loss. One evening while watching the news on TV, I heard a news reporter reciting "Oh Captain, My Captain" about the slain president. A few days later, I got a strange call. The person who called asked if I were Wilbert Williams Jr., and I said, "Yes." The caller said okay, and hung up the telephone. I told my mother that I was sure someone from the White House called me. A few weeks later, I received a card from the White House with the slain president's wife's signature stamped on it. I expected her to write me in her handwriting, considering all the letters that I sent her. I guess that would have burdened her further in her sorrow, considering all the mail that she was receiving (and perhaps I was expecting too much).

Low Self-Image

I tried improving my social image. When my peers gave parties, I went, though I didn't know how to dance well. All I could do was stand on the floor, do the grind with a girl, and afterward pray that nobody saw my erection. Most of the time, I would sit in a chair or lean up against a wall as I watched others display their dancing.

I tried basketball and ended up making a fool of myself. Raymond, Lawrence, Hannahan, William, Clinton and Myra played well and I still admired their abilities on the basketball court. I was just as excited as the girls were watching them make baskets, and slam-dunk. The girls stood around cheering them on and I wanted some of their attention. At the time, I didn't have a steady girlfriend and I had not had any sexual relations with any girl. My friends knew it because I continued to talk about it. It wasn't that I was trying to impress anyone, but my firm religious belief had a profound influence on me.

Some of my peers had a good time laughing at me. So my chance to show my friends that I had something going for me was to enter my first basketball game in competition. They didn't even give me a basketball uniform like the other guys. When they put me in the game, I was shaking like a drunk and my head was just as foggy. When they passed the ball to me, I shot it so hard at the rim that it passed the rim and shot cleanly over the backboard and people roared in laughter. I felt like hiding. No one passed the ball to me again and they pulled me from the game. When the guys played softball, I would sit around with the girls watching. As for me, I was athletically inept, and this helped to destroy any confidence in which I could shine like the others. So I decided that my chance to excel was in academics, if I applied myself more. I knew that it would be difficult because even in scholastics, I lagged behind the others, but I was determined to excel in at least something.

Lydia

Lydia was the second girl after Anna to like me romantically. Lydia was Black and had West Indian roots, about which she never talked. One day I was at her apartment and her mother showed me pictures when Lydia was younger and in show business. I never knew Lydia could dance professionally and understood that she was on "The Ed Sullivan Show." Lydia was kind to me and I believe that she was a bit lonely. She wasn't glamorous in appearance and her sweetness made up for it. I didn't like her as much as she did me and responded to her intimately because I needed the affection. I knew one thing about me that probably no other person knew. I needed love other than from a family member. I needed someone to love me because they felt that I was special and valuable. What motivated these emotions is beyond me, because my family loved me dearly, and I was very special to my mother since I was her only son. I just wanted her affection and was not interested in having sex with Lydia.

Emotionally, I had become sensitive and romance clouded my mind. I didn't know what had happened to me, but I was craving to satisfy my sexual feelings. It was probably no more than getting older and "feeling my oats."

Lydia was very open to me. It wasn't anything that she said or did with me; it was the way that she looked at me and held my hand. I was in a sexual war with myself; caught between my own sexual desires and what they told me in church and at home. I believed God understood because He made me and loved me.

I became interested in pornography. When I was in the library I would look for the Art section in order to see naked women, and they were all white. This, usually, was satisfying, not because they were white, but because they were women. I was constantly going to 42nd Street in Manhattan in order to visit pornography book stores. Because of my age, they usually motioned me to leave, but not before, I had a chance to pick up a nudist colony book. I concluded that there were no Black people in those books because no one cared about how beautiful our bodies were.

The war I was fighting concerning sex had become full-scale while I was still attending the same Baptist church where my mother raised me. I felt terrible about what I was going through and had no control over how badly I felt. I was still attending Sunday school regularly and on occasion prayed in church and sang in the choir.

My Friend Randy

Randy became my new friend. He was big for his age, but had muscles in the right places. He loved playing football. I could never understand how he played that brutal game without getting all beat up. Nevertheless, he persevered well. Randy came from a quiet family. Eric, his brother, was much younger than I was, and Randy was very affectionate with him. Their mother Norma was just as affectionate with both of them and she even shared her affection with me. Sometimes I sat and talked with her for hours and unloaded all my problems and she patiently responded. Randy, in my view, was the perfect son; very obedient to his mother. I liked being with him because he always had a good joke to crack or laugh, a lot like Alberta.

One day we decided to horseback ride in Central Park in mid-Manhattan. Neither of us had ever been on a horse's back before. Randy's horse was skittish and kept doing the "inner city waltz" in the streets of Manhattan and my horse seemed to know exactly where I wanted him to go. While we were crossing Fifth Avenue in heavy traffic, Randy's horse threw him in front of a yellow taxi cab. I laughed so hard that I almost fell from my horse. To make Randy's life more complicated, the horse ran back to the stable blocks away. We finally did meet back in Central Park and otherwise thoroughly enjoyed ourselves.

Randy's mother wouldn't let him hang out with the guys staying up late hours. She tried her best to help him stay out of trouble and it worked. I never remember Randy getting in any kind of trouble. I didn't know anyone who didn't like him. Sometimes he would stand around the guys and just keep people laughing. He had a way of rewording a story about some Boy Scout experience or something that happened in the neighborhood. People would stop what they were talking about to listen to him. Randy didn't go to school with most of us. His mother had him in a school called "St.Mary's Star of the Sea." It was a Catholic school. I don't believe that he liked going there because he kept us from knowing it for a couple of years. I don't know who found out where he was going to school, but when he realized that we knew, he was embarrassed. I don't know why he was embarrassed because he was the only one of us who was in a private school. I always liked Randy and always will. I am grateful to his mother for her affection with me and for listening to my problems patiently. I also respect her for the way she raised Randy and Eric. In spite of her paralysis in both legs, she was a great mother to them, and I watched them respect her and give her love and affection.

Loving Mrs. Grudinsky

My homeroom teacher, Mrs. Grudinsky, continued to expose me and the guys in the singing group to all forms of music and I became fond of her. She took us to Broadway plays and music concerts in mid-Manhattan, New York. I studied Beethoven, Bach, Aaron Copeland, and a host of others.

I fell in love with Mrs. Grudinsky. She may have reminded me of my fourth-grade teacher, Mrs. Aronawitz, with whom I was still in love; by the way, both of them were Jewish. A student told me that she was dating a Black man and this showed to me that she didn't have any hang-ups about Blacks. I fantasized being with her. I played up to her, but she never gave me any special attention above the other guys. I told my mother about her, and she cautioned me concerning my romantic thoughts. Once Mrs. Grudinsky invited the singing group to her house and I went. This was the closest I ever got to her.

The All-City High School Chorus

The next fall I tried out for the All-City High School Chorus in Manhattan, at Julia Richmond High School. Only the best voices were picked to represent New York's finest choir at Lincoln Center for The Performing Arts. They asked that I sing a portion of "Just a Song at Twilight." They rejected me. Mrs. Grudinsky told me not to worry about it and to try out again the following year. I wanted her to be proud of me and I felt as if I failed her.

I was now doing well in Geometry and I had an earth science course that I liked, but I still hated History. By the end of the semester, I did so well that I made the honor roll. My name was in big bold white letters on the Dean's list for six months. It had company with the names of Lenny Malloy, Raymond Frost, William Emerson, and Ronald. I felt proud to be at Boys High School and the fact that I was on the honor roll gave me confidence in pursuing an academic course of study.

Ronald was still in my life, and I still hated him even more than ever. I was frustrated because he wouldn't walk close enough to my bedroom window so I could shoot him with my BB gun. Each time that he saw me, he would look at me and smile and say something insulting. I decided to forget him and concentrate on doing well in school. I felt that I could compete with him in my studies. I passed all my courses that year, but I was behind in math so I had to go to summer school. I hated it, but fought the feeling and toughed it out. I soaked my peers of their academic knowledge, and focused on my goal to get an academic diploma that would allow me to attend a four-year college or a university. I realized that the key to success was remaining focused on my studies and goals, and not going to jail for "gorilla" Ronald. While most of my peers were concerned about being popular, I was studying my buns off.

During my third year in high school, I auditioned for the All-City High School Chorus again, and made it this time. I was proud of myself and I knew that Mrs. Grudinsky would be happy. Each Saturday I caught the public train from Brooklyn to Manhattan and met hundreds of other students who sang very well. Every moment that I practiced added to my self-esteem. Sometimes some of us, while riding the train on our way home, would start singing the "Hallelujah Chorus." We knew that we were good because people took notice of us and encouraged us.

That year I became very religious and started taking my Bible to school in order to read it. When I took my test, I would pray to God to help me pass. A guy in my class named Kirk criticized me for doing so. He asked me if I really believed that God helped me to pass and I told him yes. He laughed and said that he didn't think so. We constantly argued about God and His existence and presence in our lives and I never stopped telling him that God was with me.

In gym, we had a track suspended from the ceiling, and sometimes I would take my Bible up there and read it, all alone. That is where I argued and had my greatest discussions with God.

Racism Again

My history teacher planned a trip to Washington, D.C., and I waited anxiously for weeks to go. When we arrived at the Washington hotel, some white girls from the South occupied the hotel. Though there was space in the hotel, they would not let us check in. We had to check into an inferior quality hotel across the street until those white girls checked out the following day. They told us that the management at the hotel refused us because they didn't want a bunch of Black guys in the same hotel with these white female students. That incident offended and hurt me. I tried to enjoy our trip after that, but it was hard. One day I got up early in the morning and took with me an 8mm movie camera, shooting almost every monument and flower garden in sight. I took a short walk behind the Capitol building and was shocked to see Black people living in slums. I could not understand how they could be in the same district that legislated to improve the living conditions of all Americans. Here in the Capital state, Black people were living in poverty.

After my trip to Washington, D. C. I could not stomach my history teacher, because I believe he didn't protect us from those racist white people in the hotel to which they refused us admittance. After I thought about his lack of protecting us, I felt that by him being Jewish he was probably considered a white nigger and was just as vulnerable as we were to racism. After my involvement in the civil rights movement, I understood why they hated him as they did me. Jews were an integral part of the civil rights movement.

That summer I went to summer school in order to take History. I hated it just as much as I hated it during the school year. I suffered through the course and passed it. During my last year in high school, I concentrated on finishing my college preparatory work. I had to take the New York State Regents exams in all of my major academic courses, and the regent's exams were hard. I had to repeat Chemistry; I finally passed the second time around.

I wasn't doing well in school. My life did not have much excitement, and I became very serious about myself concerning the world.

Death

I saw guys wasting away on drugs (heroin) and it scared me. My friend Tyrone got himself drunk, climbed the pool wall, and jumped into the 16-foot-deep pool at night. A guy named Michael saw him struggling to swim and when he went in after Tyrone, Tyrone bit him. Michael let him go, and Tyrone drowned himself. I was a pallbearer and helped to carry Tyrone's casket with some of his other friends. Lawrence Hannahan was there and had beads of sweat pouring down his face and he cried like a baby. I knew that Tyrone had deliberately wasted his life, and I was upset with him. I felt bad that many times I saw Tyrone on 42nd Street in Manhattan, standing on the corner looking like a bum. I never had the nerve to encourage him to go home. Many guys like Tyrone just got lost in the shuffle of life. I knew that I didn't want to get lost like that and lose my life. It scared me, seeing the world around me so unstable. I believed that I was no longer in control of my little world and I was anxiously trying to understand how to survive it.

I continued to socialize with friends, but I made studying my number-one objective. I studied anywhere I could. Sometimes I stopped off at the library and studied before going home from school. Often when I arrived home, it was dark. My peers still did better than Ronald did and I had even stopped taunting me, but I still hated him.

I was afraid and angry and I didn't know why. I believed there were things that were not fair about the world and being a Black. All the racial turmoil going on in the country didn't exactly encourage me to be patriotic. I didn't know it at the time, but I was beginning to hate white people. It happened in little steps, until I found myself thinking and talking just like my father. It wasn't that he and I had exhausted the topic of Black and white relations in America. The situation of race in America seemed hopeless, and I gave up on white people. I just began to see and understand things that continued to affect Black people. I felt that as a Black person they would always confront me with my color in a negative way. I wanted to leave the United States, even if for a moment, as if getting a burst of fresh air. I really wanted any person who didn't see my color to love me. I was looking for a color-blind world and it wasn't there. I was confused and that is what the aftermath of racial prejudice did to me, just as it had done to my father in Alabama and in New York, and many other Black people. I was hurting inside racially, torn apart emotionally, and sometimes I felt like dying. I started writing poetry and all of it spoke of my "Blackness" in relationship either to white America, depression or religion.

My friend Hannahan graduated. He went to Vietnam to fight in the Vietnam conflict. He sent me a picture of himself dressed in Army rags with a monkey on his shoulder. I worried about Lawrence and wanted to go to Vietnam in order to help him when I graduated. I didn't know why the United States was in the war and didn't really care. All I was concerned about was my friend, Lawrence, whose life was in danger.

Graduating High School

When I graduated from high school, I had one of New York's most prestigious diplomas. It was an academic diploma and it signaled that I had done college preparatory work. Although I had achieved my goal, no four-year college accepted me for admission. I thought about going into the Army or Marines in order to fight for my country, but I didn't believe America was worth my dying. I guess I felt like my father about America. It had not proven to me that I was a part of its agenda. My friend Lawrence was still in Vietnam and I worried about him. I wasn't admitted to a four-year college, and I felt terrible about it. This had proven to me that I wasn't as smart as my peers were.

Lenny got a full four-year scholarship to Princeton University. Alberta got a full four-year scholarship to New York University. Raymond was admitted to City College, William decided not to attend college, and Ronald was accepted into college, but I don't know which one. I believed most of my peers were moving on and I couldn't even get off the ground. As I looked back on my four years in high school, I realized how hard it was for me, though I worked very hard. All of my work did pay off, even if I were the least academically gifted of all my peers. I probably might have gotten into a four-year college, but I never thought about moving out of my parents' house, and definitely didn't want to leave New York City. All the colleges I applied to were in New York State.

I got an application from New York City Community College, which was a two-year school. They accepted me into the night college program. They guaranteed me admission to their full-time program during the day if I maintained a 3.0 grade-point average in Trigonometry, Anthropology and Western Civilization. I buried myself in these courses and thoroughly enjoyed Anthropology.

I got a job working in May's Department Store in downtown Brooklyn. Though I made $60 per week working a full forty hours, I didn't feel good about working there. The only job, which they had for me was wrapping packages at the checkout counter with an elderly woman named Mary (who was very pleasant to me). I didn't see anybody with any supervisor role working in the store who was a Black. One Black man stood out in my mind every day, and he operated the elevator. He just seemed to do it out of habit and had no feeling concerning it. He was very polite to people and no one seemed to care much about what he did, but taking them where they demanded to go. I never experienced his being grumpy or hostile.

He sang to himself and ran the elevator as if it belonged to him. I felt as if I had no business there and I saw my father and myself in that man. He was the first Black man (besides my father) whom I felt intimate with, though I only said hello to him daily. He represented what my father and I was running from, losing ourselves in this world. When I left that store, I went straight to school by walking the streets of downtown Brooklyn to Cadman Plaza near the Brooklyn Bridge. After the first semester, I got my 3.0 grade-point average and was admitted into day college.

My Friend Clinton

My friend Clinton attended the same college and we hooked up in the cafeteria many afternoons. Some students hung out in the cafeteria all day instead of going to classes and still got their grant and loan money until they were thrown out. It was such a waste. They created the Affirmative Action program in Congress to help minority students gain a headway in jobs and vocations, which then excluded minorities. It was a way to help bridge the gap between whites, whom they gave preference because of their color while Blacks were discriminated against. Some Black students could attend college and were given tuition. All we had to do was go to school and pass our courses. At this point Affirmative Action had not benefited me because I was in night school paying my way through college without the assistance of Affirmative Action. I was paying for my tuition with my job (May's Department Store) money. I didn't understand why these Black and Puerto Rican students were acting like some fools. It was hard enough just being a Black trying to make it, and they were wasting an excellent opportunity to advance. I couldn't afford to be stupid also.

Clinton introduced me to two young women in the cafeteria one afternoon. They found out I sang and they invited me to sing with them with a guy named Earnest on a Saturday morning radios how. Each Saturday we got together and sang. I shared with them my struggle to get into day college and how hard I had to study in order to get decent grades. On one of our radio programs, Bonnie sang, "You'll Never Walk Alone," and dedicated it to me. When she sang it, I almost cried because I knew that I was not walking alone, God was with me.

I hated my job at the department store. A Black West Indian woman got upset with me because I wouldn't give her a shopping bag free. My boss told me not to give anyone a shopping bag unless they had at least three small packages, and she didn't have at least three. She told me that if I were so smart, I wouldn't be packing bags in a department store. I felt small and I wanted to hide because she did it in front of the public. I was determined from that point on that I wouldn't settle for anything less than getting a Bachelor's Degree from college. I knew being Black, I didn't have a chance at making a good living working in a cheap department store in the house wares section.

I became fond of a Black woman who worked there with me, named Helena. She was much older than I was. I teased her a lot and she was well aware that I liked her romantically. Many of my working hours in May's Department Store were spent looking at her.

At this time in my life, no one really expressed any serious interest in me romantically. I created my own romance by teasing women with whom I worked.

Black Power

Stokely Carmichael, a Black West Indian from Trinidad, coined the phrase "Black Power." I didn't care where he was from and, like many Blacks; I caught onto the phrase quickly. He was an early member of the Black Panther Party. I didn't care too much for them because I believed that they were too militant. I didn't know that their main objective was to protect our communities and help Black people help themselves through force. They were too militant for me. I, however, was at a point in my life where I felt I needed to say that about my African roots and myself.

My burden, being a Black and having to face the fact that Black people were not treated fairly, encouraged me to be bold. My Blackness would evidently not go away. I decided to sport an Afro, Dashiki, and a Black Power button. It made me feel more confident because I was expressing to white people that I didn't care about how they felt about me. I didn't care if white people didn't like what I was doing because they were becoming less important to me; at least that is what I convinced myself. One day, Helena, whom I sought attention from, asked me why I had on the Black Power button. I told her, "It's because I'm tired of white people." She didn't know what to say to me and I walked away.

When I was over the anxiety of wearing my Black Power button, I tried building confidence with young women. I saw a dark-skinned Puerto Rican woman in the department store cafeteria. She was sitting alone eating dinner. I spoke to her politely and said, "Hello." She ignored me. I thought that she did not hear me and I spoke to her again. She still didn't answer me. The third time I spoke to her she acted like I wasn't there. I simply said to her, "I'm only trying to be friendly; I'm not trying to get fresh." She never looked at me. She made me feel like I was a nobody again. This was my last attempt for a long time to consider having a relationship with a Puerto Rican woman. They convinced me that they felt that they were better than Blacks; no matter how black some of them are.

Day College

After admittance into day school, I quit my job in order to study full-time and applied for loans to pay the tuition. I felt very proud of myself; having achieved what others thought was important. Not that I didn't feel that getting good grades were important. It never really proved anything to me I didn't already know, that I could do well at anything at which I tried hard.

All the young women at school were a distraction to me. I still had no one special in my life; at least not of the opposite sex, because Lydia and I had gotten out of touch.

My Grandmother

I'm sure when my Grandmother Queen Victoria Smith was my mother's age she looked just like her. I don't know who thought of her name, but I liked it. My grandmother was plain with her conversation. She was just as plain with me as she was when she told my mother to watch out for my father. She once said to my mother, "La Verne, one day that boy of yours is going to make you cry." She was more than right because I almost drove my mother crazy. I heard my grandmother say often that I was terrible. I respected and loved my grandmother. She was my mother's mother and she cared about all of us.

I remember the times that we went to her house on Pacific Street in Brooklyn. She lived in an old musty damp, dirty wooden three-story building. She didn't live there because she couldn't get out of that place. The fact that it was her own place made it special. A Jew owned the building. The whole neighborhood once was Jewish until the Blacks moved in. The hallway smelled of urine. When I walked up the stairs, I was afraid to hold on to the stair railing because it shook and made noise as if it would fall apart. The stairs squeaked as I walked up. It was a nasty building. My grandmother's apartment was clean, but hundreds of cockroaches were running all around. Cockroaches took over the building and allowed the tenants to live there. Sometimes one would crawl over me and I felt sick. My appetite was usually shot after that and I tried not to eat anything. It was an ordeal if I had to go to the bathroom because cockroaches would run up the walls and jump off inside when I went. I almost never closed the door. Everybody in the house knew when someone used the toilet because it made tons of noise while the water tumbled from the wooden box above your head. I couldn't wait to get out of there.

My grandmother was always hospitable. She liked to serve us what we wanted. I would sit on the old couch and slowly eat whatever she gave me, although sometimes I had to go downstairs and buy something from one of the local stores. I would dash down the staircase into the street because the hall was dark. I never remembered any light in that hallway. I always had to purchase food from a Jewish person. That didn't bother me. The only thing that I knew about Jews was Jesus Christ was one, and some Jews whom I bought things from looked like Jesus. Though I loved my grandmother, I couldn't wait to leave her apartment. Each time that I went there, I wanted to spend less time. Those cockroaches worked on my mind.

My grandmother had diabetes mellitus (high sugar in her blood). She became ill and my Aunt Doris took her into her beautiful apartment on President Street in Brooklyn. Convincing my grandmother that it wasn't in her best interest to stay on Pacific Street wasn't easy for my aunt and my mother. My grandmother was defiant. They forced her against her will. It was the best thing for her. My Aunt Doris took good care of her. After a couple of years, my Aunt Doris needed a break so my mother took my grandmother, Queen Victoria Smith, into our apartment.

My grandmother developed a condition where she needed to clear her throat of excessive mucous. Each time she did, I felt sick. I knew my grandmother was ill. She had a big lump in her neck and I looked at it every day, hoping that it would go away. The last time that I heard my grandmother tell my mother that I was going to make her cry one day, was in our apartment. She was sitting at our dining room table. "La Verne," she said, "that boy is going to make you cry one day, and you just wait and see." My grandmother continued to be right, because while I was growing up, my mother was pulling her hair out over me.

My mother took care of my grandmother for years, until my grandmother got so sick that my mother couldn't help her. She reluctantly put her in a nursing home. I visited my grandmother there often. She was never without us, because we all respected and loved her enough not to abandon her. She got sicker and remained in a coma for weeks at Long Island College Hospital. I believed that if I were a doctor, I could help her get well. I didn't feel the doctors did all that they could for her. I'm sure that they tried to keep her alive, but I believe that I would have tried harder. So I decided at this point in my life to become a medical doctor.

I was so hurt about her illness that I went into Visitation Catholic Church near Coffee Park. I put holy water on my face, lit a candle, and asked God to spare her. Within a few days she died. I received the news of her death while I was in Calvary Baptist Church preparing to march with the choir down the aisle. A neighbor whispered it to me. I burst in tears and marched down the church aisle singing, "We Have Come This Far by Faith Leaning on the Lord."

I will always love my grandmother and know that she loved me. Each time she told my mother that I was going to make my mother cry, she only spoke the truth. She tried even in her old age to prepare my mother for challenges in life. Queen Victoria Smith had no idea that her death would seal in me a hunger that would never cease, namely to become a physician.

The Existence of God

Philosophy at New York City Community College was challenging and I spent a great deal of time studying. It dealt with life on terms with which I could identify. Almost everything in life seemed to me to be abstract and nothing was for sure; not even God. My philosophy teacher was an ex-bishop in the Anglican Church and he challenged us on the existence of God. My religious belief was that God surely existed, but I found the arguments compelling to deal with. I would take some of this knowledge home with me and toss it around and my mother would listen to me as if I were crazy. Noticing the reaction of my family hearing, this new stuff was fun.

Talking About Sex

After leaving my job at May's Department Store, my former attachment to Helena was long past. At times, I visited her just to say hello and she received me well. I still felt that she was attractive, but I understood why she treated me as if I were a plaything, so I gave up that ghost.

I was attracted to a beautiful Black woman in New York City Community College and it took me many weeks to say anything to her. When I finally did, we started talking about sex before marriage. I told her that I didn't believe in it. She looked at me angrily and said, "You're either crazy or a liar," and walked away from me. We never spoke again. It was a confusing part of my life and I didn't know where the acceptable level to approach females was. I felt stupid in revealing that information to her and it cost me. At that moment, I never wanted to talk to a woman again, Puerto Rican or Black.

Gwen and Her Church

I became very unhappy about my life and buried myself into my schoolwork. Philosophy continued to challenge me and I became critical of every aspect of my life and my surroundings. I wanted a female friend; someone whom I could talk to and confide in. I started talking to a young woman named Gwen in my Philosophy class. She was plain looking, a bit on the heavy side, and refused to wear makeup because she was an Orthodox Pentecostal. She invited me to her church in Queens, and I accepted. Her father was the pastor and her mother helped him. She had a sister who looked like her twin.

I sat in that little storefront of a church and sank myself into the music and the praying. I was so vulnerable then,; hurting emotionally, and feeling rejected that I just wanted to feel good about something, anything. Suddenly I started shaking and calling Jesus. I knew that this was what her parents expected of a boy who wanted to be a friend to their Christian daughter so I fell right into the mold. When I thought that, they had seen enough of my struggle with the Lord I gave up the fight and settled into my seat. I could tell that they were happy that I allowed God to bless me. Gwen and her sister sang a song; we prayed some more and went home. I knew my behavior in the service was not for real. When I saw all that Pentecostal energy going forth, I knew if I didn't join in they would single me out as needing salvation. I would not be able to see Gwen again.

I now saw Gwen almost daily in school and we decided to date. I took her to Red Hook in order to meet my mother and friends. I could tell no one was very excited about her and I think that it was her plainness. Ironically, it was one thing that attracted me to her. She was a challenge to me, but I cared for her. She had my respect and I was cautious in how I behaved around her. Once I took her to Prospect Park in Brooklyn and sat on a bench with her, doing little to nothing ,but holding her hand. My relationship with Gwen didn't last long because she claimed that I was depending on her emotionally. Though she could not explain to me what it meant or how it affected her feelings for me, she decided to break off our relationship. Again, I was without a female friend for whom I cared and who I needed.

Depression

School was running neck and neck with my love life and my grades were below a C average. They dropped me as a result from day school. That was another turning point in my life because I had no idea where I was going educationally or what I could do with my life. I fell into depression again and began writing poetry again about everything I could think of; especially those things to which I was sensitive. I wrote about my loneliness as a young Black man and how it was destroying me. Vietnam was still affecting my life and my friend Lawrence was soon to come home. Two other boys I knew who lived in Red Hook projects had died in Vietnam, Pop and Samuel. I felt so bad that I decided to play "taps" on the bugle each evening for a few nights.

I was feeling guilty that I wasn't in the war. Church was as church was, singing in the choir, hearing the preacher sermonize, making noise and praying. I really enjoyed being there every Sunday but it had become a way of life for me and it was definitely a routine. I was even beginning to challenge its importance in my life.

I was very active in the church. I attended every Sunday morning and most evenings. I sang in the choir, prayed during morning service, and read Scripture from the Holy Bible. I didn't like Sunday school except the times that I could debate the Scripture. Sometimes a discussion would break out beyond the prepared lesson and we wouldn't finish the study. I believed the Scriptures to the letter except where it says, "Servants, obey your masters in the Lord." I believed that every Black person in America had a problem understanding what it means for us in particular. I was nineteen years old. I still believed sex before marriage was wrong and I was battling with my sexual urge to fulfill my lust to have a woman in bed.

White people also became a big religious issue to me. Most of them were the enemy of Black people, as for me; yet the Scriptures asked Christians to love our enemy. I didn't want to love someone who hated me and tried to destroy me. To the contrary, I hated them. I didn't feel most of them wanted any Black person to love them. It was a waste of a good prayer and my time; nevertheless, I did pray a lot for white people. I prayed that they would see how wrong they were to hate anybody. Some of them brought us here on slave ships across the middle passage (Atlantic Ocean). We didn't ask to go to any of the places they took us. I knew that they had no right to treat us like animals. Sometimes I prayed to God in my secret closet (my heart), and wished that I were white, only because I believed it was better than being Black. I had mixed feelings in my mind. I didn't know what to do about white people because deep inside my heart, I loved them in spite of what they were doing to me.

Sometimes I went through the motions in church and struggled through a prayer, or stumbled reading Scripture, or sang a song without feeling. I was searching for myself and for God.

The Phony Preacher

I don't know anyone in Calvary Baptist Church who didn't like me. If someone did not, I never heard about it, except the pastor who stole more than $25,000 from the church. He was a thief and a liar. He deceived us and was the only one who I knew didn't like me. He was a real thief.

When our first pastor, Reverend Enoch B. Scott, died in a car accident, our church was devastated. We loved Reverend Scott. He was stern and didn't take to foolishness. He founded the church in 1954 and started having church gathering in a basement dwelling in Red Hook projects. The church moved from Red Hook projects to 120-4th Place, not too far from the project. My mother was one of the original members. They purchased a building that had old stained-glass windows and had an apartment on the third-floor level.

Assassinations

It seemed like the whole country was going mad. Assassinations were taking place. My first reaction to President John Fitzgerald Kennedy's assassination on November 22, 1963 was shock and dismay. When Malcolm X was shot on February 22, 1965, I was confused because Black people killed him.

I watched my mother sit in front of the television and cry during Malcolm's televised funeral. I was more shocked over her tears for Malcolm than I was over his death, because I had no idea that she even cared for Malcolm.

Martin Luther King, Jr. was murdered in Memphis, Tennessee during the time of the sanitation garbage workers' strikes. King was at the forefront of the civil rights movement.

When they assassinated Martin Luther King, Jr., on April 4, 1968, I knew that the world stood still for most Black people. I was frightened because I believed Black people would never find their way to freedom without him. When Robert Francis Kennedy was shot in June 1968, my emotions from assassinations almost stood still. I was saturated with it. I wondered, why was America going mad?

The Poor People's Campaign

In June 1968, I decided to get involved in the civil rights movement. I packed a knapsack and told my parents that I was going to the poor people's campaign in Washington, D.C.

When I told my parents I was leaving, they didn't have much to say to me except to give me some money and tell me to be careful. I flew to the nation's capital and caught a taxi to the Washington Monument mall, where thousands of people were living in little shanty houses in the mud. As I was walking through the camp, my sneakers were sinking in the mud and it was touching the bottom of my pants. A young woman who couldn't have been more than twenty-five years old approached me and asked if I needed a place to stay. She took me to a wooden shanty where I met a young white guy who was very friendly. I stayed with them for a few days.

David Ralph Abernathy, Jessie Jackson, Andrew Young and many civil rights activists were there. We were all waiting for the big day when we had a chance to voice our concerns to the United States government. They planned a march to the Lincoln Memorial. King's wife, Coretta Scott King, was going to be there to speak from the steps of the monument. The first night I was there, the Black Stone Rangers, a gang from Chicago, and a rival gang from California were at each other's throats. They were shooting guns and fighting, and some people got hurt. I was frightened. This went on for two nights of my stay.

I met many people, took many pictures and spent time talking to people of other nationalities. People from varied fields were there in order to speak for the poor and the downtrodden people of the nation. On the day of the rally at the Lincoln Memorial, there were thousands of people. I had my 35-millimeter camera strapped across my left shoulder, which was customary for me. I loved taking pictures. I followed the press past the security guard to the top of the monument and sat at the feet of Coretta Scott King and her children. I snapped as many close pictures of her as I wanted to and no one said a word to me. She was so beautiful, one of the most beautiful women that I had ever seen. News reporters were all around. Newsweek magazine was there with a host of other magazine companies. Newsweek magazine got a picture of me while I was attentively listening to a speech, and put it on the front cover of their magazine.

I saw Dr. King's brother there and walked by him often. He would, within a short period, drown in a swimming pool.

I enjoyed listening to Jessie Jackson. Andrew Young and Ralph David Abernathy aroused the crowd in our camp.

I knew that I had embarked on something historical and great. I was happy with myself for having the courage to do what I felt benefited me the greatest at this time in my life. My mother, when she spoke to me about great Black leaders, shared with me what she believed would benefit me. My father shared with me the story of the great George Washington Carver, and how he made hundreds of different products from the lowly peanut. It was one of the few things that my father never hesitated to share with me. It was as if George Washington Carver were his relative. I guess in many ways all Black people are relatives in one way or another.

I caught a flight back to New York and buried the experience of that historic moment in my life in my heart. I will never forget it.

Disappointments

My mother started sharing with me some of her secret closet emotions and thoughts at this time. Two things she told me: "If white people don't want to teach you anything in school, just sit there and listen to get it." Second, "Italians are black people in whiteface." I believed every bit of what she told me. So when some Italians in the neighborhood raised hell because we were Black, having church service in a building we paid for and owned, I wanted to tell them to go to hell, but that wasn't the proper attitude for a good Christian to have.

After a few months, the members of the church decided that they needed to find a new pastor because the congregation believed that we needed a Shepherd full-time. Having visiting pastors come to preach was not the congregation's desire. They invited a few pastors, but one guy they really liked. A young man named Yarber, who had charisma and could preach, was invited. He had a beautiful wife and a daughter. We didn't know that he was a lying thief and would ultimately take twenty-five thousand dollars of our money for his own use. He even had the guts to send his white German Shepherd dog to obedience school with it. I remember when he first spoke. The people were falling out (getting touched by the Holy Spirit), and clapping their hands and saying "hallelujah" to almost every word that came out of his mouth. He talked a lot about Jesus Christ, and that's what the people needed to hear in order to believe that the minister was sent from God. If he were sent from anywhere, it must have been from hell, in order to confuse and steal hard-earned money from us. It didn't take me long to catch onto him, and when I did, he knew it. He would ride some teenagers in his car coming from a preaching engagement and allow them to smoke cigarettes. He even smoked it, and to do that in our church was considered a sin. He never spoke on that one topic. He also never spoke on stealing other people's hard-earned money. Once I went to his apartment on the third floor of the church. Occasionally he stayed there when he wasn't at his beautiful private home in Queens, New York. Most of the church members lived in the project while he was robbing us blind and living in luxury in a better neighborhood. When I went to the apartment, he came to the door with no shirt on, bare feet, and smoking a cigarette. I was shocked. When I informed my mother, she told me to mind my own business. We had a church business meeting and I went and raised some issues concerning the teenagers in the church. He asked me to put it to rest. They were handling other business. I continued to press him and he asked me to leave. I said, "No." He told the members if I didn't leave, he would not continue the meeting. My sister Janice looked at me and said, "Buddy, you're always starting trouble." (I wonder; who was starting trouble when she told me to steal my father's money and he beat me?). My mother was sitting next to me and she asked me to leave. I told her, "No." She begged me and I would not leave. Yarber told me that he was leaving the church auditorium and if I were there when he came back there was going to be trouble. When he returned, I was still telling my mother that I wasn't going anywhere. She was on her last begging when Yarber looked at me in frustration. That lying stealing preacher closed out the meeting, and everybody was mad with me. They should have been mad with themselves for not standing up to the crook.

A couple of years down the road the congregation found out that he stole our money. My good friend, Raymond, uncovered the dirt for all to see; bounced checks, illegal transactions, and lies. Most of the people decided to ask him to resign. I wanted him thrown in jail. We planned to approach him that Wednesday. The Monday before, he came into the church when no one was there and took with him preaching robes worth thousands of dollars. I understood now why I saw two degrees on his wall in his study. One degree was from some seminary in Pennsylvania, and the other in business management from City College in Manhattan. I felt like a fool being preached to and led by a thief, liar, and a cheat. I was glad to see him leave.

Chapter 7
Roslyn

I will praise thee: for I am fearfully and wonderfully made:
Marvelous are thy works; and that my soul knoweth right well.

Psalm 139: 14

Roslyn was like no other girl I had ever met. She was meticulous about
caring for her body. Sometimes she washed and changed outfits two or
three times a day. I met her at Calvary Baptist Church, she was fourteen
years-old, and I was eighteen. I never thought of her romantically because
she was younger then me. I treated her as if she were my little sister. She
was pretty, witty, smart, and lovable. Roslyn had a charm that enticed me
and a smile that warmed my heart, both of which ultimately turned cold.
If looks were all that mattered in a romantic relationship, ours would have
been near-perfect. She had a golden-brown complexion and long brown
hair that passed her shoulders. I loved the way she styled her hair. Each
style said something about her makeup and attitude. When she wore
the French roll, she looked dignified and kept her head high. When she
dragged her hair to her mid-forehead in a bang, she looked every bit like
a school kid. Sometimes she let it dangle to her shoulders and she looked
sexy. Roslyn could be versatile in appearance and manners.

Roslyn and I spent a great deal of time together and ultimately it was
to our detriment. I'm not saying that we didn't have a good time together;
much to the contrary, we had a ball. I believe that the first time that I
closed mouth kissed her was at the Red Hook pool; she was sixteen. One
day she was like my little sister and the next day she was my girlfriend. I
fell in love with her.

Many people liked Roslyn. She was outgoing and friendly. She had three sisters and a brother and they were very pleasant. Her mother was a faithful member at the Calvary Baptist Church, which we attended, and she loved her children, like most mothers.

Roslyn and I were officially dating and we did not ask our parents what they thought about it. We had our relationship in our hands. They tried steering our relationship and sometimes suggested that we slow down and see other people, but we did not listen. Everything that happened to us was our fault. We were responsible for everything that happened. Both of our parents loved us dearly and showed it even in the midst of the tragedy to come.

On holidays, our church had many outings, and Roslyn and I often went. I especially remember trips to amusement parks, state parks, and the Danbury, Connecticut State Fair. On one of our trips to the Danbury State Fair, Roslyn and I flew in a small aircraft. She was nervous with so much distance between her and the ground; she was afraid of heights. In spite of her fear of flying, she followed me.

She did anything that she could to please me. I enjoyed all the trips to other states; church picnics, and special activities, which the church planned.

Roslyn liked our pastor, Yarber, because he gave her the attention that she wanted. It was important for people to know that the pastor liked them. He was a person whom they thought was sent from God to show us the good Christian way (but I never believed God sent him). Roslyn never had anything ill to say about him, even when he stole our money. I believe that Roslyn needed a father figure because her biological father was dead. She wanted someone who she could confide in and satisfy her longing for love.

We spent considerable time talking to each other about life, our families, and our relationship. Our parents were concerned because they believed that we were spending too much time together. They warned us about it and encouraged us to seek other friends with whom to be. It was not that they wanted us to forget each other, but they wanted us to include other people in our lives.

Once, Roslyn and I were arguing because I wanted to spend time with Alberta. Alberta had a brother named Barry, and Roslyn and Barry were close. When Roslyn felt Alberta was a threat to her, she would greet Barry with a kiss on his lips. Barry did not mind because that is how I saw him greet most females (I did not agree with it). I got upset with both of them each time it occurred, but I never said anything to him. I liked Barry and he was always pleasant to me. He liked teasing me about being a virgin and called me "bareback" (one who didn't use a condom while having sex). I spoke with Roslyn about kissing him in his mouth. She told me since I had a special relationship with Alberta; she would have the same with Barry. My relationship with Roslyn was showing signs of strain from the beginning.

Long Island College Hospital

When they dropped me from day college for poor academic performance, I went to Long Island College Hospital and applied for work. The only job available was working as a corpsman in the operating room. I had to clean the rooms after each operation with a mop and disinfectant. After my first day, I knew that I could not stay there.

My boss was a tough old white woman who told me that I had to work on the weekend, including Sunday. Working Sunday for me was like a Jew working Saturday. It was my Sabbath. It was the day my father gave me hell for thinking about riding my bike or going to the movie theater. They did not allow that I played marbles on that day when I was a little boy; I was not going to work Sunday for anyone. When I told her that I could not work Sunday, she told me that Jesus Christ healed on the Sabbath Day, and it was all right for me to work. I thought, I am not Jesus Christ and I am not working Sunday. I cleaned the operating room floors for about two days and could not take it. The job was way beneath being able to challenge me. It was a dead-end job, and not for an aspiring college student. An employee told me that medical records needed a person in their department. When I spoke with the supervisor of the department, I told her that I was a college student, and they took me in.

The medical records section was loaded with some Black women. One woman in particular took a liking to me, Helena. She was the second woman named Helena that came into my life and made a great impact on me.

Helena was from the West Indies and she was proud of her roots. I liked her a lot. She smiled most of the day, cracked jokes, and always had something pleasant or encouraging to say to me. She teased me about how good-looking she thought I was. Helena looked out for me and helped me around the medical records department. She was very pleased that I was in college and told me often, "You're smart, and if you study hard you're going to do well." She constantly encouraged me to move ahead in life and get all I could educationally.

I did not like the medical records system. I could never find a chart without a hassle; no matter how often the women helped me, there were too many color codes to read. My job was pulling medical records for the outpatient clinic. I was up and down the elevator and stairs with records all day long. I met a West Indian named Steven Welch from Barbados. Steven was a friendly guy who did all that he could in order to make me feel comfortable. We became friends and he helped me out in the clinic. He warned me about being entangled in the gossip and showed me how to get around.

My Friend Paul

Paul worked in the financial aid department of the hospital as a supervisor. It was not until later that Paul became an important part of my life. He was the only white person whom I learned to trust then. He was also the only Italian whoever cared about having a relationship with me. His wife was very pleasant to me and she also was beautiful, and they had two children; a boy and a girl.

A coworker in medical records told me that Paul needed someone to work in his department, and I was tired of medical records, with all the color charts. When I applied for the position, Paul took me. He told me later, "I did not hire you for your good looks or your color; I hired you because I felt good about you from our first meeting."

My working attire went from a neat pair of pants, shirt and tie to a suit. They had me looking like a lawyer or a banker. Many clients in the hospital thought that I was a doctor when I walked into their room, until I asked them for money that they owed. My job was collecting unpaid bills from family members, and they gave me the authority to collect it any way I could. Once I walked into a patient's room and a relative said, "The doctor's here."

I said, "Oh, I am not the doctor." The family member put a sour look on his face when I told him I was there in order to collect an unpaid bill. For the most part, I didn't like collecting money from people in the hospital. I felt that they were burdened enough with their illness and did not need the added pressure, but the hospital hired me for that purpose. I did the job well.

I had the opportunity to help many needy people and put them on medical assistance. This was the highlight of the job, besides working with Paul.

Tumbling Walls

I enrolled in New York City Community College's night school program. They told me I could not get back into Day College unless I pulled my average up to a B level. It was embarrassing telling my mother and father what happened. They encouraged me to push ahead against the odds. I studied hard and spent many weekends at the Brooklyn Public Library.

Roslyn Again

My relationship with Roslyn was not getting any better. We were fighting most of the time. Sometimes it got physical. Once, I smacked her near the Red Hook Pool (I don't remember what we were fighting about), and she tried to tear my head off. Our parents were seeing our frustration and depression. Roslyn's mother told me that she never had me picked out for her daughter, and my mother told me to give up Roslyn if we could not get along. We did not listen to our parents and we paid for it. Once we got physical with each other and the twisted romance took a more dangerous turn downward. Although Roslyn and I loved each other, we were tolerating and enduring each other painfully. I don't know why we put up with each other; maybe we did because we allowed ourselves to think that we couldn't make it without each other. We would not break up and we did not stop arguing and fighting. Ironically, she would type some of my schoolwork. I had a booklet of poetry that she typed for me. It contained a bunch of poems about being a black boy in America, racism, and Vietnam. She took an interest in my hobbies and liked helping me.

I went to my friend Raymond for some answers, but I was not ready for his answer. "Buddy, just break up with Roslyn; it is obvious you two cannot get along, and you guys cannot agree." I wanted Raymond to pamper me and tell me that it would all work out, but he knew differently. So did many people who knew us. We doomed our relationship and we needed to break up.

At work, I talked to Paul about our problem. He spoke with me gently, but firmly. "Buddy, you have to let her go. Look at you, it's destroying you, and it is destroying her also." His suggestion to leave Roslyn was difficult for me. I loved her, and I didn't want to do it.

I worked hard in school and at work. The more people thought that I was a doctor at Long Island College Hospital, the closer I became to believing that I could become one. I did not see one Black doctor in the hospital; most of them were foreign-born and foreign-trained. I wondered where all the Black doctors were. I had never touched a Black doctor's hand. So that role model was out the window. Though I did not see one Black doctor in the hospital, I did know about one; Dr. Evans, at Kings County Hospital (where I was born). My cousin Sarah told me what a wonderful and intelligent doctor he was. I believed that she tried to encourage me to look at medicine as a vocation. She never told me that she thought that I should think about becoming a doctor, but she never stopped talking about Dr. Evans.

A Freaking White Guy

My relationship with Paul was growing and he showed himself trustworthy. I confided in him, and we became close friends. He continued to talk to me about my life and anything that he believed would help me see the world as it is. He even talked to me about some attitudes that he had as a man and told me that I would understand better, when I got older. I believed that he loved me and did not care about my race or color. "Buddy," he said, "I'm a freaking white guy and there is no reason that you should trust or believe me. Nevertheless, I think that you're an honest, respectable guy. If my daughter were old enough to date, I would let you date her." Paul surprised me that those words came out of his mouth, being an Italian. I knew one of the white man's greatest fears is losing his "white princess" to an "oversexed Black man."

Three taboos, not to touch concerning most white men, are their money, their woman, or their daughters. Nevertheless, Paul was not just a freaking white guy. He was a real human being who cared about me; despite my color. He was not only my boss; he was special, and he was my friend.

Looking for Love

I was doing well in school and though my relationship with Roslyn was still challenging, we were going through one of our better periods and our relationship became more intimate. We thought that it would bring us closer to each other, but it only served to put a wedge between us. We did not know what love was and never found out; at least not with each other. After our intimacy, our relationship became bittersweet and even worsened, and we were fighting almost every week. I do not know what had us holding on to each other.

One day my cousin Leray told my mother that she knew what was wrong with me. My mother asked her what. She said, "I know what's wrong with him and he knows what is wrong." She made reference that Roslyn and I were having sex, and she was right. I believed that it was long overdo because I was a virgin at twenty-one-years old. Roslyn was also a virgin. I believe that she had sex with me because she was concerned about the guys teasing me about not having had any sex, and I was in my twenties. She always wanted me to feel good about myself. After I had sex, my sexual life got out of control. I was sowing my oats, and had a number of affairs.

I believe Roslyn and I were convinced that we loved each other. We could not figure out what was wrong and we did not think anyone else knew. That was one of our biggest mistakes. Many people saw our relationship and to them we twisted it, and they did not hesitate to say it. If we loved each other, we were not mature enough to allow our love to keep us together or protect each other.

I was a few months away from graduation from New York City Community College. My job was going well. Roslyn was accepted into Hampton Institute, in Hampton, Virginia. I told her if she went, I would not guarantee our relationship lasting. I wanted to be honest with her. She was disappointed with me and decided not to go. I'm not sure why I told her that, because it was one of the worst mistakes that I ever made in my life. I think that I was afraid of being abandoned like Beverly and Richard abandoned me when I was younger, and like losing relationships with Mrs. Aronawitz and Mrs.Grudinsky. I had no right to complicate Roslyn's life any more than it already was. A friend of hers promised never to speak to me again if I did that to Roslyn. I didn't change my mind. I did not want Roslyn to leave me. Our sexual relationship made me feel more insecure. So I threatened her by telling her that I might not be there for her if she left me in Red Hook.

Seduction

Roslyn and I created hell on earth for each other. I don't know how badly she really wanted to go to Hampton Institute. "Damn it, she should have left me standing in Red Hook, looking anyway I chose to look." " It was her life." Our biggest problem was that we didn't know when to let loose and free each other of the agony.

The world has not changed about people messing up each other's lives. Most young people think that they understand what love is, and how to conduct their own lives and make decisions based on their false ideas of it, and it ruins lives. Roslyn and I were no different. She was depressed and, I thought she was suicidal, but she was crying out for help. There were other conflicts in her life other then me, and although, she tried to hurt herself other times by taking pills, I never thought that she would really try to kill herself. I think that she was crying out for attention. She wanted to tell the world that she was in pain. I didn't understand her agony and didn't know that she needed to be heard. My thoughts were that she was confused and depressed, and I didn't know how to help her. Compassion and protection were very much a part of my relationship with Roslyn because I loved her.

For the first time in my life, a woman who watched me for two years go into my apartment building seduced me. One day Judy, who was a Seventh - day Adventist, approached me about doing a Bible study and I agreed. After the first meeting, she asked me to come back the following week. When I went back, after our meeting, she told me that she loved me and had watched me from her children's bedroom window almost every day. She told me that she and her husband were separated. When I was leaving, she blocked the door, pressed her body against mine, and kissed me. At first, I didn't respond; then, she put her tongue in my mouth and I felt sick, because I had no feeling for her romantically. I didn't go back to her house the next week. When she saw me, she invited me to her house again, and foolishly, I believed that she wanted to try the Bible study stuff again. I was naive. I really didn't think that she would try her stunt again with me. This time she gave me plenty of space during the Bible study, but toward the end started feeling my leg. I got up to leave and she grabbed my waist. When I went toward the door, she blocked it and pressed her heavy body against mine and I could hardly move. She told me that she wanted me and had to have me. She pulled me into her bedroom and took off her clothes. I told her that I didn't have any rubber and she said that I didn't need it; she was on the birth control pill. I had bare sex with her without any rubber (I knew one person who would have been proud of me, Barry, because he called me "bareback"). When we finished having sex, I felt dirty and I still didn't have any feeling for her. She aggressively kissed me and I quickly left.

After a couple of months, I got a call on my job. My sex-crazed Bible tutor told me that she was pregnant by me. She seduced me, lied to me about taking birth control pills, and wanted me to believe that she was carrying my baby. She asked me for $300 in order to get an abortion. I reminded her that she told me that she was on birth control pills. She said, "I lied." I told her that I didn't have the money and she said, "You need to get it." I couldn't believe that she tricked me and I didn't want to believe that she had my child inside her.

I called Roslyn and told her what I did, and pleaded her forgiveness. She was hurt. She boldly called the woman on the telephone. When Roslyn called me back, she told me that it wasn't my baby. The woman got pregnant by a man whom we both knew, and blamed it on me because she believed that I was the more vulnerable of the two. I got far away from that woman.

Oh God, Not Roslyn

I graduated from New York City Community College with an Associate of Arts Degree and had a wonderful graduation at Cadman Plaza near the Brooklyn Bridge. My family was very proud of me. I was accepted into Brooklyn College and decided to major in Chemistry.

Roslyn graduated from high school, decided not to go to Hampton Institute. She enrolled at Staten Island Community College instead. All was going well, so I thought. After her first week at school, she was very excited. I called her on the telephone late one evening, and we had a casual conversation. We were discussing how great school was and she exchanged some hostile words with her mother about telling me the family business. We were not discussing any family business. Roslyn never resumed her conversation with me. The phone was silent. I dialed her number a few times, and no one answered. I told my mother that I had to go to Roslyn's house and dashed out the door. As I ran down the street, a member from our church named Reggie informed me that someone jumped out of a window from five stories high. I ran faster. "Oh God," I said, "I hope it's not Roslyn."

I thought of the times that she told me that she would kill herself when our relationship was on the rocks. When she took some pills and fell over in Coffee Park across the street from her house, I believed that she was serious, and she was crying out for help again. When I arrived at her apartment building, Roslyn was lying in the grass, flexed, looking up, saying, "Let me wake up, let me wake up." I didn't know what to say. Her mother didn't address me, nor I she. A friend of mine named Reverend Charles Hall was there and he tried to console all of us. When I arrived at the hospital, Reverend Hall approached me and said, "I spoke with the doctor and he said she may never walk again." In that instant Roslyn changed the course of her life forever. I stood with Reverend Hall and I didn't want to believe what he had told me.

A news reporter approached me and asked what happened. I told him that I didn't know. He asked me if I thought that it was her mother. I told him that it was possible, but I really didn't know. The following day they broadcast on the radio that I implicated her mother. I tried to defend my statement, but it was too late. I should never have said a word to anyone. I had no proof for what I said. I was wrong for saying it. To this day, I am sorry for the words, which I spoke to that reporter.

My life took a sharp downward turn and I was bewildered, shocked and hurt. I couldn't understand why Roslyn felt life wasn't worth living; no matter how challenging it was. That morning I went to the hospital, and Reverend Yarber (the thief) and her mother were there. Her mother told me that it was my fault for running around with women. I told her mother that I was nowhere around when Roslyn did what she did and it was not my fault. We argued and Yarber broke us up.

When Roslyn came from the emergency spinal surgery, I didn't recognize her. Her face was swollen like a balloon. She was motionless and I felt terrible. I left the hospital and went to school. At work I told Paul what occurred and he was hurt and disappointed with me. He did not tell me, "I told you so." He tried the best he could to console me, I devoted my energy to seeing Roslyn at Kings County Hospital and whatever energy was left for studying. Roslyn wiped me out.

Majoring in Chemistry had fully challenged my mental capacity. The textbook was thick and they gave me multiple chapters each night to read. I couldn't understand the mathematical portion of the course. I could not do the equations to measure moles, milli mole and Avogadro's numbers. It was all confusing. Between Chemistry, my other courses, and Roslyn's tragedy, I didn't know which direction to put more energy in. I went to the college bookstore and bought some cards. I had a book with delightful sayings and wrote one on a card almost each day for her. I visited her in the hospital almost every day. Her mother and I didn't have anything to say to each other. I tried to visit Roslyn when her mother wasn't there. Most of the time, I sat with Roslyn and tried to encourage her emotionally. As the weeks passed, Roslyn was recovering. Her doctors were pleased with her ability to push onto recovery. When she could sit up, I stayed with her for longer periods. Sometimes we argued about whose fault it was that she was paralyzed from her waist down. When she got upset with me, she told me if it were not for me, she wouldn't be paralyzed. Each time she said it, it tore my heart in pieces. I felt guilty. Roslyn wanted me to feel guilty, but I did not know it. I don't blame her for feeling her paralysis was my fault. She had some problems and challenges, and I was not helping her with any of them. I didn't make her life any easier. I'm sorry I never heard her cry for help. If she had told me, she needed help, I'm sure I would have tried to help her. This is a good example of how some young people believe that they make the best choices for their lives and they don't. They mess their lives up.

My parents believed that I was taking on Roslyn's misfortune. They sat with me and tried to help me recover from my guilt. My father asked a friend of his, whom he called a doctor, to speak with me. I went to my father's barbershop, and a neatly dressed middle-age man was waiting for me. I didn't know what kind of doctor he was, or even if he was a doctor at all. All I knew was that my father trusted him to talk some sense into me. He was very gentle and polite. He simply told me what happened to Roslyn was not my fault and she was programmed before she met me to hurt herself. He said no one could make another person do what Roslyn did. I did not agree with him. I believed that I had to be responsible in some way. I wasn't sure how much responsibility I carried.

Leaving Home

I told my parents that I was leaving home and going to my Aunt Doris's house on President Street to live. I felt that they didn't understand my hurt concerning Roslyn's suicide attempt. They were hurt that I did not want to live with them anymore and they knew that they did nothing to hurt me. I knew that they loved me very much. That is why I believe they let me go. When I left, I was not in a good mood. I kissed my mother and may have shaken my father's hand. I forget saying farewell to my sisters. I did not see my mother or my father shed a tear, but I know that I broke their hearts.

I thought that it was going to be great living with my aunt. She gave me a little room in the front of the house to live in. My Uncle Billy, who was my aunt's brother, stayed in the same room when he lived there. Many of his books were still in the room. I felt lonely for my parents the first night, but I was determined to show them that I made the right decision.

My aunt let me settle in, and then gave me a hard time. To make matters worse, I bought a Great Dane puppy, for $250.00, in order to keep me company that had markings like a tiger and called her "Amani," ,which means peace in Swahili. My dog did waste in my aunt's kitchen by a back room where I kept her at night. Aunt Doris awakened me many nights and said, "Buddy, get up and go in that kitchen and get that mess off the floor your dog made." If it were not my dog she complained about, she would say, "Buddy, go take out the garbage." When she told me to take out the garbage there was either snow outside or it was freezing; Alaska like weather. She was showing me that I was not wise to leave "her sister's" apartment, and move into her house. Between her being on my behind, Roslyn blaming me for her paralysis, failing chemistry and a couple of my other courses, and the dog-doo, I was going down,;tumbling like a weak wall.

My aunt wanted me to get off my behind and to start making some good decisions about my life. She loved me and proved it. I remember when I graduated from junior high school; she bought a motorized airplane that operated on gas for me. I never told her that I wanted it, but I had wanted one for a long time. She didn't give me much money, although I believe that she had enough to give some of it away. My aunt was determined to teach me some lessons concerning tough living.

Roslyn's mother and I continued to have contentions. As I previously said, I tried not to be at the hospital when her mother was there. The fights did not end between Roslyn and me. It was a sign to me that Roslyn was getting physically and mentally better, though she still could not walk. Each time I looked at Roslyn, I believed that if I were a doctor I could help her. I could do more for her than what her doctors were doing. I got into a big fantasy thing about helping her to walk again.

One evening I went to the hospital and Roslyn asked me to tell her mother to leave us alone and not interfere in our relationship. When her mother arrived, I sat quietly for about one half-hour. I told her mother that I wanted her not to interfere in our lives. Her mother was furious, and we started fighting verbally in the hospital; making lots of noise. The nurse told us to quiet down or leave. We continued to argue, and the nurse threw us out. I had no idea how her mother must have felt when I told her not to interfere. Her daughter was paralyzed and she believed it was my fault, and I was asking her to get out of Roslyn's life. I do not think that Roslyn really had any idea what she had asked me to do, nor did I. Her mother had every right to protect her, and I should have respected it. I was the intruder. The next night when I visited Roslyn, she told me that I had no right to speak to her mother the way I did. I said, "What way?"

She responded, "The way you talked to her wasn't right."

I was confused, not knowing what Roslyn wanted from me. I believe that Roslyn was confused and she was using me like a puppet on a string, and I was doing the "jig" for her.

Leray's Tactic

My cousin Leray (who has piercing eyes), was at her mother's house (my aunt's house). My aunt went through her usual and told me to take the dog's out the house. I got upset, but not because of what she said to me. My life was just a mess and I started crying when I thought of it and Roslyn's attitude with me. I knew that I did what Roslyn wanted and I did not know what else to do in order to please her. Whatever she wanted from me, I did not feel that I could give. Leray, who never minced words, said, "What the hell is wrong with you? Do you think you're the only damn person who has problems? You better get your damn life together. You want to be a damn doctor but you ain't gonna be no doctor because doctors are born, not made, and you don't have what it takes." She tore into my behind, took a big bite, and opened me up. I continued to cry. The more I cried, the more she verbally tore me to pieces. I left the house that morning depressed. Before going to college, I went to the hospital and told Roslyn what happened and she tried to console me. One moment Roslyn wanted me not to leave her and the next moment, she was beating me emotionally. I forget how often I called on God to rescue me because I was falling apart. I guess God was waiting for me to rescue myself.

Failing Chemistry

Every Chemistry test I took I failed, and I was failing Calculus. A young West Indian woman in my class who befriended me tried to help me through the calculations but it didn't do any good. I did not understand the stuff. My brain was in reverse and I was failing college. Each time I got an F on my Chemistry test, I knew I was moving further away from medicine. I said to myself, "How the hell are you gonna become a doctor when you cannot even pass chemistry."

My cousin Leray's comment to me kept surfacing in my mind. I wanted to believe she was wrong but the facts stated otherwise. When the semester was over, I failed Chemistry; along with other courses.

My relationship with Roslyn cooled down and we were not fighting as much. When we did however, Roslyn reminded me that her tragedy of paralysis was my fault. It hurt when Roslyn blamed me for her tragedy. They scheduled her to leave the hospital in a couple of months, and she was receiving physical therapy, but still could not walk. I was praying and believing that she would suddenly walk. Nevertheless, I lost hope and believed that she would never walk again. I felt terrible and I wanted to be absent from her life, but I could not. I cared too much about her.

In 1969, at Brooklyn College, I changed my major from Chemistry to Biology. I could not remain a Chemistry major because I failed the subject. A student could not keep a major in a subject that he or she failed. I took Chemistry the second time, while the school was in political turmoil. Many colleges and universities were protesting the Vietnam War and unfair government policies. The Vietnam War was winding down and the civil rights movement was trying to find a new direction without Martin Luther King, Jr. The Jesus movement, the flower children, and the Hari-Khrisna religion were going strong. Brooklyn College had its share of the mass confusion. A hosts of people and I who wanted to move ahead educationally were almost at a standstill. In my Chemistry class, they gave us the chance to take an exam. If I passed, it would satisfy Inorganic Chemistry I. We were more than halfway through the course. I took the exam and failed. I could not believe that I failed Inorganic Chemistry twice.

Roslyn came out of the hospital with leg braces, crutches and a wheelchair. Her mother and I had enough sense not to fight openly anymore. I knew that she had the right to help her daughter any way she wanted. I was just feeling so damn guilty and Roslyn was not helping me to feel otherwise; she was still blaming me.

Professor Harmon Finston

Professor Harmon Finston at Brooklyn College was a lifeline for me. He taught Quantitative and Qualitative Chemistry. I went to his office and told him that I did not understand Chemistry and failed it twice. He told me that he was aware of my difficulty and promised to help me. He asked a young Jewish professor to tutor me after school hours.

Up to this point, I never spoke with Professor Finston. I did not think that any of the professors cared if I passed Chemistry. Something was special about him, for he was a fine human being of quality (like Paul Garguilo, my old boss at Long Island College Hospital).

Professor Finston was soft-spoken and calm and liked to talk to me. I told him about my growing up in Red Hook and my difficulty in high school and being left back in the fifth grade. He did not pull away from the things that I talked to him about, but engaged himself with me. He made sure that my tutor was available to help me any time I needed.

I decided to leave my aunt's house and go back home, and I believe my aunt was glad to see me go. My aunt had thoroughly taught me a good lesson. Don't jump out of the frying pan into the fire; especially if your aunt is fanning the flames. My Aunt Doris tried her best to show me that life is full of choices and I could make as many wrong choices I pleased. My cousin Leray's statement to me that doctors are born and not made still hurt me emotionally, but I would understand her role later in my life.

I continued to go to church and was very involved in the programs. I was working with the young people there and they saw some of my struggles, and what they did not see, most of it I shared with them.

At the end of the college semester I finally passed Chemistry and Professor Finston, my tutor, and I were very happy. It was at this juncture that I became determined to become a doctor no matter what. Academically I had not done well and I had a long journey before me. I knew in my heart that I would be a good doctor who cared about people and who would love them. I started telling various people that I was a premedical student majoring in Biology; though I failed Botany, which was in my major. They then dropped me from the Biology Department and I was without any major.

Roslyn was going through her trials with her paralysis. She kept saying that she did not feel like a whole woman. She was about eighteen years old and I tried to convince her that she was. I carried her in my arms where we went. Sometimes people thought that we were joking around; especially when I carried her into the movie theater. She told me that people were looking at us and she was self-conscious about it. I took her many places in my Volkswagen Bug, which I purchased with part of my school loans, and packed her wheelchair in the back seat. I even took her with me to upstate New York that winter when I went hunting and let her shoot my high-powered rifle. When we were intimate, it was a problem for her. She told me that she did not feel like a whole woman. I tried hard to help her, but it was useless. I had mixed feelings. I was trying to convince myself that her paralysis was not my fault, and Roslyn was convinced that it was. I was doing a job on myself and I did not realize it.

My parents were bearing my mistakes and tolerating my dog. Amani, a Great Dane, had grown to a large size. The apartment seemed smaller with her in it. My mother didn't like dogs, but she did more than tolerate Amani. I believed that she actually liked her. She even walked her for me. Sometimes I had Amani packed in my multicolored polka dot Volkswagen with Roslyn and her wheelchair. We were a sight.

Harvard University

Michael Mac Cleoud was a premedical student at Brooklyn College. He told me about a summer program for minority students; he was in at Harvard University. Harvard was interested in helping minorities get into medical school. They gave housing and offered two science courses and a hospital rotation. If a student passed the courses and got a decent evaluation from the hospital, Harvard University gave a recommendation to any medical school in the United States. It was all free, sponsored by the federal government. He completed the program and did well. He suggested that I apply. I knew that I wasn't Harvard University material and I didn't take him seriously. He gave me the address and I applied. Within a few weeks, they accepted me. Harvard accepted ninety students from all over the United States. I could not believe that I was one of them. I told Roslyn that I was going to Harvard and she did not want me to go. I told her that I had to go because it was my chance to show that I could become a doctor. My parents were excited and many who knew me were shocked that I was going to Harvard University. When I went to the airport in order to catch the flight to Boston, Massachusetts, Roslyn was in her wheelchair with my parents and me. When it was time for me to board the aircraft, she started to cry and I felt terrible. I told her everything would be OK. I kissed her. I kissed and hugged my mother and father and walked swiftly away. I needed a break from Roslyn. It was crazy trying to please her and trying to convince myself that she and her mother were not right about Roslyn's tragedy's being my fault. I guess I had some nerve going to Harvard and leaving her in Red Hook projects. I did not want her to do the same thing to me as two years prior, but it was time for me to care for myself.

Harvard and Eleanor

When I arrived at Harvard University and saw the historic campus and the huge courtyard, I thought, how was I ever able to convince anyone to select me for the minority student health careers summer program for ten weeks? I thought it had to be God helping me.

The following day I went to the orientation meeting and met the other students. I met a fast New York-type guy. He was from the Bronx, named Chris. He was checking out some young women from the South. He told me that they were interested in meeting some young men. He asked me to go with him to one of their dorm rooms to meet them. He said that they were waiting for us. When we arrived about five young women were in the room. They giggled when we walked in. Chris said, "What's happening, how yawl doing?"

One young woman was a spokesperson and responded, "How yawl doing?"

I didn't say anything. I was shy and the leader of the pack picked me out. Soon someone dared another to take their clothes off.. The leader said, "If the guys do it first, then we will do it."

Chris said, "Go on, Buddy, take off your clothes."

One young woman said, "We won't look, we'll turn the lights off, but let us blindfold you first." They turned off the lights, and I took my clothes off down to my underwear and one of them turned the lights on. They all burst into laughter. Before I took the blindfold off, I knew what they had done. I scrambled for my pants and shirt, and they screamed in laughter.

One young woman was sitting with a half-smile on her face, looking at the floor. When I looked at her, we made eye contact. She didn't poke fun at me like the other women. When the commotion cooled down, I went and sat by her and introduced myself formally. "Hello," I said, "My name is Buddy."

"My name is Eleanor," she responded. I told her where I was from, and she said she was from Rome, Georgia. She told me she was finishing her last year of college in education. Eleanor impressed me that she was so young and was going to be a teacher. Chris was having a ball with the women and I focused on Eleanor. When the evening was ending, I asked Eleanor if I could see her again. She told me, "Yes."

The next day I was on cloud nine. I saw Chris and he told me what a wild time he had with the women. "Man, that one you were talking to looked really good. I noticed you spent much time with her." He cracked jokes about how funny some women acted and we parted. The next day I was studying Cell Biology and Organic Chemistry I, and was placed at the Boston Lying-in Women's Hospital. The hospital turned me on from the start. The first time I ever saw a baby born was there. It blew my mind and the slimy baby fascinated me when it came out. That woman's vagina opened like the Holland Tunnel, and the baby came out like a Mack truck. A guy by the name of James Lowe from North Carolina was with me and his eyes were bugging out. From that, instant I said to myself, "If this is medicine, I want it."

When I saw Eleanor, my heart beat fast and I did not know what to say to her. Eleanor looked at me and did not say a word. I greeted her and we walked the campus, talking about how crazy the previous night was. When she talked to me about my taking off my clothes, she told me it was an old trick. We laughed about it. After that walk with Eleanor, I thought about her repeatedly.

That evening Roslyn called me. I don't know where she got my dorm phone number, but she tracked me down to the public phone in the hallway, like a Federal Bureau of Investigation agent. From that time on, Roslyn burdened my mind. One evening she called me and I got depressed and went to see Eleanor. I told Eleanor about Roslyn and how Roslyn messed up my life. I stood in the middle of the floor and wept. Eleanor put her arms around me and held me tight. She told me that it would al work out and I would be fine. She helped me forget my guilt for a few moments and free my mind and heart from Roslyn's tragedy. I will never forget how I felt in her arms: while she held me, I felt safe. I was now in love with Eleanor from that night on. When Roslyn called me, I told her about Eleanor. She was furious with me and blamed me again for her paralysis. After that conversation, I didn't feel bad because I was not alone for I had Eleanor.

I studied hard at Harvard and when I had a break from it, I took long walks with Eleanor along the Charles River. We sat most of the time on a bench. She told me about her boyfriend in Georgia named Poncho, whom she was not sure she still wanted. They were having problems and she felt their separation was healthy. We talked about our lives. I did most of the talking and she always listened. Eleanor knew my whole life story because I told it all.

Five weeks passed and the program was half over. Eleanor had three more weeks at Harvard and I didn't want her to leave me there. I knew that I was going to miss her tremendously. Conversations with Roslyn were ongoing and each time we spoke, we fought. Roslyn gave me an ultimatum. She told me to leave Eleanor in Boston when I came home. I told her that Eleanor was coming with me. Eleanor had a sister in the Bronx whom she wanted to see. I had planned to take Eleanor with me to Red Hook. Roslyn told me if I did, our relationship would end. Eleanor came with me and Roslyn "griped with rage." I didn't let Roslyn shake me up because Eleanor helped me by giving me emotional support. She was almost holding me up.

When I took Eleanor to Red Hook projects, she wore pink hot pants and they were tight. I don't think that my mother appreciated the way she was dressed, but as usual, my mother was pleasant. A neighbor in my building who was from Georgia said, 'o you have a Georgia peach; she is beautiful."

After I took Eleanor to her sister's house, I visited Roslyn and she was mad as a wounded rattlesnake, spitting venom. She told me to get rid of Eleanor like one would get rid of a sick dog with mange, and if I did not, our relationship was finally over. I called her bluff; I went back to Boston in a few days and wrapped my arms around Eleanor. I believed that I loved Eleanor, and I knew after I returned to Harvard University, I would separate myself further from Roslyn. Roslyn had beaten me well. I was feeling guilty, sick, and tired of her pulling me down. I didn't really know what love was until I met Eleanor. For the first time in my life, I was intimate with someone whom I really believed loved me. I cherished Eleanor's affection. She made me feel like a man. When Eleanor left for Rome, Georgia, I felt like my strength left with her. I told her that I would never forget her and would go to Georgia to see her. I made love to her the night before, gave her hugs and kisses and said, "I'll see you later."

My last two weeks at Harvard were trying. I kept thinking about Eleanor, and Roslyn kept calling me. Chris was fooling around with a new set of women, trying to encourage me to join him, but I refused. I now wanted to be faithful to Eleanor. A young woman from New York tried to start a romance with me and I turned her down. Chris thought I was crazy. He told me no woman was worth turning down another.

I met a pleasant-looking white woman named Ann who lived in California. Her father was an important employee at a space center in California. A Black guy named Mario was dating her. He was using her for what he could get; he didn't care about her, but she liked him a lot. I didn't get to know her well, but I did give her my address and telephone number in New York. Ann would later visit New York and call me.

After the ten weeks were completed, I passed Cell Biology with a C+ and Organic Chemistry I with a B. I was proud of myself. I enjoyed the hospital rotation and was positive that I wanted to be a doctor.

My parents gave me some money to spend at Harvard, and I had some left at the end of the program. I used some of it to go to Rome, Georgia and visited Eleanor before returning to New York. She picked me up at the airport in her Karmann-Ghia. We drove 90 miles to her home in the country from Atlanta (for the first time in my life, I saw and tasted a yellow watermelon). I met Eleanor's mother and father and they were kind to me. They prepared a room for me to stay in. I had a wonderful time with Eleanor. She told me that she was not sure if she did not want her boyfriend Poncho because things had gotten better between them. I never believed that she would pick him over me. I thought that she loved me. I made love to her before I left for New York. I gave her a ring that Roslyn bought for me and kissed her. I told her that I loved her. She didn't respond. I then realized that she was not sure what direction her life would take concerning Poncho or me.

It's All Your Fault

I was back in New York and still feeling guilty because Roslyn was still blaming me for her paralysis. Roslyn was upset and I couldn't blame her, but she didn't own me. We didn't discuss my affair with Eleanor at length. Roslyn was deciding what direction she wanted her life to take. After a few days, we were corresponding regularly by mail. She decided that she wanted us together again.

I received a package from Eleanor and it had the ring in it. She gave me a "Dear John" letter. She told me that she renewed her relationship with Poncho, and our romance was over. She apologized to me for leading me on. After I received her letter, I lost contact with her. I did not want to believe that Eleanor didn't want me. As much as I loved her, I didn't write her back. I told Roslyn that my relationship with Eleanor was over and Roslyn and I started dating again. I still felt sorry for Roslyn, and still confronted with the reality of her paralysis. She still reminded me that it was my fault that she could not walk. We still were not really getting along. I was still carrying her in my arms when we went out. When we went to church, I carried her down the aisle. Once, a sister in the church approached me and said, "Buddy, I'm so proud of you, you're still with Roslyn, and treating her so well." That sister had no idea the burden

Roslyn added to my life. I was convinced that if I left Roslyn, I would be considered the villain. I did not feel I could leave Roslyn under the pressure. Roslyn's main complaint was not feeling like a whole woman, and I tried to disprove her feeling by my intimacy with her.

I was struggling in school and still failing courses but getting some D's in others. I now wanted to be a doctor more than ever. Michael was accepted into medical school. When he broke the news to me, I was happy for him, but also jealous that I was far from medical school.

I was taking Comparative Anatomy. My professor was British and he was tough. I was failing his course. We were dissecting the nurse shark, exposing the twelve cranial nerves. I liked the lab portion, but hated the written test. He said that his course would separate the men from the boys because he taught the course on the same level as Downstate Medical School's course. He told the students if we couldn't pass his course we probably couldn't get into medical school. If anyone had the luck of getting in, they probably would not get out with a degree. He discouraged and frightened me. I had to be a doctor, whether I passed his course or not. At the close of the semester, I failed Comparative Anatomy.

The only courses in which I did well were English courses. I did not particularly like English, but it was a subject with which I felt comfortable. I had an excess of thirty credits in English. Nevertheless, it was not English that I needed for medical school it was science.

Professor Finston was still encouraging me. Besides him, the only other professor who encouraged me was Professor Williams. Professor Williams was another super guy who taught in the Chemistry Department. He was the only white Anglo person who spoke positively to me about my goal to become a doctor. I admired him highly. He and Professor Finston discussed me. Professor Finston told me if I didn't make it into medical school, not to give up reaching goals.

"Wilbert," he said, "wherever you reach on the ladder of success you're climbing, don't jump off. If you do not make medical school, continue your journey upward." I appreciated him for his words. I loved Professor Finston and he made a big difference in my life.

Dr. Dillard was the only Black Chemistry professor that the school had. When he was a student in the 1950s, he received a full four-year scholarship to a prestigious college to major in Chemistry. When the college found out that he was Black, they rejected him. Racism wounded him and he suffered the trauma of it at the hands of the white establishment. He was still talking about it. In return, he committed himself not only to the field of Chemistry, but also to Black students. I believe that he understood the emotional strain on us being Blacks in a white school. Brooklyn College was white and Jewish. Many Black students felt intimidated and lost at the college. I heard Dr. Dillard was tutoring the Black students after school hours and was doing it with exams. One week before the course exam, he gave a similar exam to the Black students that had the same type of questions on it. Midway through Chemistry-II, I went to a few sessions. At the end of the semester, I passed Chemistry-II. Dr. Dillard became my instant hero and I respected him even more highly. I had seen him on campus walking very dignified with his gray hair and broad shoulders. I wondered what it had cost him to be at Brooklyn College; the price he had paid as an intelligent Black man in America. Dr. Dillard would later become another pillar of hope for me.

Family

All of my family knew that I wanted to be a doctor and none of them discouraged me for they believed that I could make it. Things were well at home. My sister Shelly was married and she got a job working at Long Island College Hospital.

My sister Janice had four children and she was going through some trials with her husband Randy. She was not happy. Janice continued to laugh and crack jokes, but her problems never seemed to get her down to the point where she could not function. I knew her problems were serious and I was furious with her husband who, I think, never did right by her. My mother helped him when he came from North Carolina in the winter with only a thin coat without buttons. He got a job in the bubblegum factory making Bazooka bubble-gum. My mother got him an application from the US Post Office, and encouraged him to apply. The Post Office hired him. He got involved in a stolen car ring based in New Jersey, and served jail time. My sister suffered through his ordeal and it broke her down.

My Life

My life still evolved around Roslyn, school, church, and family. I was still doing terribly in school, still paying for Roslyn's paralysis, crying at the altar in church. My life was a wreck. My life really was not much better than my sister's was and I was not married. I wanted out of the emotional stress. I didn't think that there would ever be an end to my misery, and I didn't know what to do.

In the summer of 1971, I enrolled in Long Island University to take Organic Chemistry-II. Roslyn was enrolled there. She had transferred from Staten Island Community College. They had a special program for the physically disabled. She had a small apartment, which the school provided for her. It was across the street from the university. I visited her often and our relationship continued. Organic Chemistry-II was very difficult. The professor taught it on an accelerated level and I wasn't able to understand the molecular structures. I had four weeks to study and pass it. Sadly, at the end of four weeks I failed. Roslyn went to the professor who taught the course and asked him to pass me. I had no idea she did that. Instead of failing me, he gave me an incomplete in the course. The incomplete saved my grade point average from dropping further. In spite of Roslyn's pain, she cared about my future. I was beginning to believe that I did not consist of the right stuff for medicine; maybe Leray was right after all, "doctors are born, not made."

The Medical College Admission Test

I took the medical college admission test without completing all the premedical requirements. Physics I & II had not been completed. My Chemistry sequence was not complete. I repeated Comparative Anatomy and received a D, and I got a D in Botany. My grade-point average was having a cardiac arrest, 2.1 and dropping. I needed at least a 3.0 grade-point average to get into medical school. They had organized a Black science student organization on campus. One Black student recommended that I attend. I never went to the meetings, and each time he saw me he let me know that I needed to get involved.

The Stanley Kaplan course, a prep course for the medical college admission test was available. It cost $100 per student. They gave it each year throughout the United States. The Black science students at Brooklyn College believed it was another competitive edge for white students. Ten Black students each contributed $10. The plan was to take the course and make photocopies for the rest of us.

Orlando, one of the Black science students, approached me and told me I was making a mistake not getting involved with the organization. He was bright, like many Black students, and I admired him. I never officially joined the Black science student's organization and I suffered because of it.

I was doing what many Black people do, not sticking with other Blacks, the way some white people stick together. I took the medical college admission test and failed. The Black students, who accepted the prep course and studied, passed. My chances of getting into medical school were slim from the start and failing the test put me even further behind, but it was partly my own fault. I was too preoccupied with believing that I was not smart enough to pass the test.

Crying at the Altar

When I went to church, I fell on my knees and again cried at the altar. I wanted to be a doctor, and I was distraught. I didn't understand why me why couldn't I do like most of my peers? What was wrong with my brain? My parents were still encouraging me. My mother told me to hold on, and my father told me that I would make it. At times, believing them was difficult because it seemed a useless journey even to me.

My relationship with Roslyn was as stormy as ever and we were going down for the third count. I tried everything I knew to please her. When things didn't go the way she wanted them to go, she put her paralysis before me. I felt trapped. I kept telling myself that God created me free, but I could not free myself from anything; especially Roslyn. I felt helpless and cried out to God to rescue me. I submerged myself in the Bible and tried to soothe my pain by studying the Bible every day. I read the Book of Psalms; the same way I did when I was lonely in Boys High School.

New Friends

John and Valerie became my new friends in college. We liked each other from the start. We had lunch together often at Brooklyn College. I liked John and Valerie because they were my sincere friends; they cared about how I felt. We could discuss anything. John knew about my relationship with Roslyn even before our friendship because he lived in Red Hook projects. I never said much to John in Red Hook because I believed he was a tough guy who bullied people in the project. Nevertheless, I was wrong. John was gentle if you didn't try to take advantage of him. Even then, he would still be civil. Valerie was always considerate with me. When I talked with her, she always relaxed and listened to me, never taking her eyes off mine. I believed Valerie was a relaxed person who was in touch with herself. She was good for John because he had too much Red Hook in him (like me) and it showed in his actions and mannerisms. Sometimes John and I would crack jokes and laugh, and if Valerie saw a way to join us, she would.

Trying Romance Again

The young women at Brooklyn College for the most part were nicely pleasant. I wasn't attracted to anyone in particular. Two young women liked me romantically. Both of them were from the West Indies, Camille and June. They were very feminine and gentle. I dated them at different times. I tried romancing June, but it didn't work. I really didn't like her romantically. Camille really cared for me, but she wasn't my type, whatever that was. Roslyn's image was always in my mind, though I wanted to forget her. I had allowed her to mentally enslave me, and I had become her prisoner. In spite of how I felt, I still saw Roslyn as much as I could. I took her out in my red, blue, and silver polka dot Volkswagen bug. Sometimes my Great Dane dog, Amani, was in the back seat, blowing smelly hot air on us. Roslyn liked Amani. Wherever Roslyn and I went, I carried Roslyn in my arms, though she had learned to walk with leg braces and crutches. The more she complained about not feeling like a woman, the more I tried to help her feel otherwise. We were still making a mess of each other's lives.

An Exodus of Black Power

In the fall of 1971, there were few Black science students at Brooklyn College. One young woman, Diedra, after not doing well in the sciences, quit college. A guy I knew, who wanted to be a doctor, literally packed his duffel bag, quit college, and went to Africa. Many Black students were victims of the system in more than one way. It caused many exoduses from college. It was like an "exodus of Black minds." If it was not racial prejudice, racism, or apathy for Blacks by the educational system, it was what racist America did to our people as a whole. Slavery was long gone. but the system that operated in its place was alive.

Michael and Orlando were successful educationally and made it through the system, and got into medical school. They did not become statistics and failures. They danced to the tune, went through the fire, and survived.

I finally studied the Kaplan prep course notes that Orlando gave me, and took the medical college admission test over. My score was 50% better, though the score was below the national average. I did my very best and there was no more to give. I decided to reapply to medical school.

Applying to Medical School

I applied to medical school before completing Organic Chemistry-II and Physics II. I had a D in Physics I and decided not to take it over. Physics was hard and painful on my brain. The math part of it drained me. I hated it.

When I took the medical college admission test it didn't seem hard, I just didn't know most of the answers. My score was very low. I had the Harvard University recommendation. I did well in the minority health career's summer program, but my grades at Brooklyn College were horrible and the medical college admission test confirmed my weakness in science.

I went to Professor Finston and he spoke with me plain and simple. "Wilbert," he said, "how am I going to give you a recommendation to medical school with your grades? The only thing I can tell the medical schools is you are a hard worker. If you had greater opportunities educationally, you would probably be one of the best students around. Wilbert, I told you before, if you don't make it into medical school, do not give up. At this point you should not stop on the ladder keep climbing." I respected Prof. Finston for honesty. I did not like what he said to me because I felt he put me down. He was right and I knew it.

I went to the Comparative Anatomy teacher. I had a D in his course. He almost laughed at me when I told him that I was applying to medical school. "Wilbert," he voiced, "how can I give you a recommendation to medical school when you only attained a D in my course? I do not think that you're medical school material. I am sorry. I cannot write you a recommendation." I went to my Botany professor and he told me the same thing, but he didn't have a smirk on his face. I understood why both of my former professors and my friend Prof. Finston did what they believed was right. I had to believe that the Comparative Anatomy professor enjoyed turning me down. I believed that he was a racist from the start. I didn't feel that he was a racist for turning me down because I really agreed with him. He would have looked bad, but I still believed he was a racist.

I believed that he was a racist because he never seemed to want to help me in class. He would not even be friendly with me, but he was all over the white students in the class, laughing and carrying on. Talking to many white people about their behavior toward Blacks is hard because they rarely see it, most times they deny it, and call us paranoid.

I went to Professor Dillard and asked him to write a recommendation for me and he agreed. He asked me how many schools, and I told him about thirty, which turned out to be forty. I waited patiently in the fall of 1970 to hear from the medical schools. Rejection letters started coming back to me after a couple of months.

The Lowest Score in the Whole Country

"Downstate Medical School and Stony Brook Medical School" requested interviews. At Downstate, Dr. Green, who is Black, interviewed me. Dr. Green simply told me that he was sure I was a nice guy, and he believed I could make it through medical school. He said that I needed to show it by getting some A's and B's on my college transcript in the sciences. "Wilbert," he said, "I am sure you got the lowest score in the whole country on the medical college admission test." I was shocked when he told me that. He did not apologize for saying it, and I swallowed it. In my mind, it became a part of my low self-image. He told me if I attained what he suggested, he would personally handle my application favorably the following year. I rode the Long Island Railroad two hours to reach Stony Brook Medical School. It was a new school and they were accepting only twenty-four students in their first-year class. I waited patiently for hours to get an interview. When they finally called me into the interviewer's office, the interviewer continued to tell me that their school interviewed all Black students. After looking at my record, he had no idea why someone asked me for an interview. He said, "Many bright students are applying to medical school and some of them are engineers, and I doubt if you're gonna get in." I sat there wondering, "Then why ask me out here, to tell me I am not good enough?" I was mad. I got a car ride back to Brooklyn and was upset all the way home.

Rejections from medical school were pouring into my mailbox. Downstate medical School and Stony Brook Medical School rejected me. All forty schools turned me down. That crushed me. I broke down and cried in church and no one really knew I was crying because I was afraid I would never become a doctor.

Attending Two Colleges

That spring semester I enrolled at New York City Community College's night school while I still attended Brooklyn College. I didn't let either school know what I was doing, because it was not allowed. I was determined to get the A's and B's Dr. Green talked to me about, even if he was lying.

I took Microbiology, Physics II, and Organic Chemistry-II. I worked hard at these courses. At Brooklyn College, I took a course called "History of the English Language." It had one exam at the end and I thought it was going to be easy. I failed the course. It set me behind six months in college. I changed my major to English in order to get out of Brooklyn College, because I had more than thirty credits in it. At that point, I didn't care what my major course of study was since I got a Bachelor's Degree. Medical schools preferred candidates to have a Bachelor's Degree in anything, and that is what I was going to give them. I bought a ten-speed bike, rode it to Community College at night, and took the subway train to Brooklyn College during the day. I was dealing in the system.

Chapter 8
Romancing Iris

For thou hast possessed my reins:
Thou hast covered me in my mother's womb.

Psalm 139:13

My life was at a strain and I was in and out of depression. I rode my ten-speed bike to pass the time and think about my future. The only relief I had from my troubles was sharing my life with a girl named Barbara, who attended the same church that I did. We were not romantically involved. We were friends. We shared many conversations about Christianity, God, and man. We enjoyed talking and spending time together. Barbara was pleasant. We were involved with the youth group at Calvary Baptist Church.

When I was not with Roslyn, at church, or studying, I rode my bike to pass time. One day I was riding through the project and I saw Barbara. I stopped to talk to her, and Iris passed. She was beautiful. Iris's light brown hair was long to her shoulders. She was wearing blue jeans, sandals and a tank top blouse. I looked away from her for a moment, continuing to speak with Barbara. Suddenly, Iris yelled, "Hi." When I turned in her direction, she was waving her hand in the air looking at me. She had a smile on her face that could have taken the heart of any young man. I wasn't sure that she was talking to me, so I tried to ignore her. Iris's friend, Minerva, was looking out of a window. Minerva yelled to Iris. She said something to her that I thought was about me, and they laughed. These two Puerto Rican girls were talking to each other; one was like an Anglo, Iris, and the other was blacker than I was. Iris's hand was still up in the air waving at me, and

114

I said to me, "No, she's not trying to get my attention." As quickly as she appeared, she was gone. I found out from her dark Puerto Rican friend that her name was Iris.

Iris lived in Red Hook projects and I saw her often, but never gave her much attention because I was older than she was. Nevertheless, now she was grown up and beautiful. I remembered her as a little girl with bushy eyebrows and bright eyes. Once I was with my dog Amani. She walked by and asked me to move my dog so she could pass. I told her Amani would not hurt her. That was the closest I ever remember being near her.

After my conversation with Barbara, I got on my bike and tried to find Iris. I still had this thing about "West Side Story" and Natalie Wood playing the role of a Puerto Rican. The song "Maria" was playing in my soul. I thought of "West Side Story" as I did in the ninth grade. Nevertheless, Iris was more beautiful than Natalie Wood or Rosa. I found Iris by the Red Hook swimming pool sitting on a bench with her cousin Rosaria, who was her same age and her cousin Adelita. My heart was pounding while I slowly stopped my bike in front of her. She looked at me with a smile, but was silent. "Hello," I said, "My name is Buddy." When I asked her what, her name was, she said, "Iris." She introduced me to her cousin. The next words I heard come out of her mouth were, "Aren't you the guy that Roslyn jumped out of the window over?" I wasn't surprised she asked me, but I was shocked that she had the nerve to ask it as if she believed it to be true. I got on the defensive and told her that is not the way it was. I was straddling my bike making conversation with her, feeling like I was defending myself. I resented the position she put me in and she appeared to enjoy the whole fiasco, watching me squirm like an earthworm. While I spoke with her, Adelita fell on her knee and cut it on the concrete. I jumped to the chance to offer limited medical experience. Iris took her home, and I followed. I walked into her apartment as if I lived there, which was not like me. Iris had enticed me, and I liked what I saw. I was looking her up and down as if I had no control of my senses.

When the door closed behind me, the first face I saw was her father, Zacharias. He stood motionless and stared at me. I focused on his frown, then his strong-looking body, and started quivering. Commotion in the house over Adelita's cut gave me some airtime. Her father gave attention to Adelita, and then glanced at me. I tried not looking at him. I said to me, "You better say something or attention will focus on why you are here." While Iris was explaining what took place, Iris's mother, Doris, was looking at the cut. She was short, just like my mother, and I immediately related to her because of it. She looked at me and smiled. I figured; let me play a junior doctor. What the hell, I did apply to medical school, even if I got forty rejections. Therefore, what if they told me I probably got the lowest score in the United States of America on the medical college admission test. It was only a small cut and I knew it would be OK. Her father looked at me as if to say, "Now who the hell is you?"

Iris's mother, Mrs. Santiago, got some antiseptic and I cleaned and bandaged the wound. "There," I said. "She'll be OK." I talked after that until people in the house looked weary. I felt they had enough of me for one exciting day, and I left. I told Iris I would see her around.

A couple of days passed and her cousin Rosaria encouraged her to seek me out so I could take them to Coney Island Amusement Park for a good time. Nevertheless, I had to work. Her cousin must have figured that I had money to throw away.

I had a job working in Larsen's Bakery while I was attending college, which was the neighborhood bakery in the project. They baked the pastry and bread during the day and I washed the dirty baking pans at night and early in the morning. During the day, the aroma of Larsen has filled the air blowing west of it. Just walking by and smelling the air made one want to go in. Some people went in, even if they had no money, just to get a bigger smothering of the aroma. Often I went in with a few cents in my pocket and walked out empty-handed with nothing to eat because I didn't have enough money. I had the privilege of not only cleaning the baking pans with all the remaining pastry left on the bottom; I was also eating as much as I could find in boxes, while working on Fridays from 7:30 p.m. until 5:00 a.m. at $40 per night. I put baking pans on the conveyer belt and took them off all night. I would sit on a stool and listen to preachers like Reverend Ike and Reverend Shambock on the religious stations. Sometimes I was so mad at Rev. Ike with his get-rich-quick religious schemes. I felt like smashing the little cheap radio that I heard him on (which is not the one I stole when I was eleven years old). Rev. Ike would tell people to send him a particular some of money, and God would bless them with a Cadillac Automobile, as God did for him. His favorite line was, "Ain't no pie in the sky; the pie is right here love ones." He begged for money so much that it made me emotionally ill. Rev. Ike needed a whipping for telling all those lies that he told to people. I took it personally. Rev. Shambock was a bit wild with all his hollering, but he was more believable. I enjoyed listening to him. I was extremely religious at the time and I let people know it.

When Iris finally caught up to me, she told me that her friend Minerva thought that I was fine looking. Minerva told her, "Honey, if you don't want him, I'll take him." Minerva was kind to me, but too aggressive and loud, although the few times I was in her company I enjoyed it.

A Stupid Mistake

Roslyn was still a factor in my life and she found out through her sister that I was seeing "a Puerto Rican girl who looked white." Roslyn was very blunt; she told me that I had better stop seeing Iris or she would end our relationship. I continued to see Iris, and Iris did not know I was still dating Roslyn. I liked Iris a lot. I was still feeling guilty about Roslyn's paralysis. She continued to tell me that she didn't feel like a woman and blamed me for her being crippled. She practiced her usual serious game on me, and I was still her prisoner. That is the only reason I made a stupid mistake by continuing to trust her.

I introduced Iris to my family. My mother liked her from the start. My sister Janice was a bit laid-back, wondering why I had to date a Puerto Rican girl. Shelly, as usual, was noncommittal verbally. I believed that she liked Iris. My father was silent on the issue until he realized I was serious about Iris. "Buddy," he said, "why can't you find a Black girl to date? They have plenty of them out there."

I responded, "I like Iris." He never said another word to me about it.

Iris's father was not happy about our relationship either. He told me our cultures were too different. I felt that he did not want me because I was Black. Her mother liked me and kept feeding me rice, beans, steak, and plenty of milk, and that spoke enough about liking me. Iris's sister was going through her rough teen years and was having her own problems and running away; she could have cared less about me. Her younger brother Tibbs was cool with me. He was dating a girl named Nancy with whom he was in love. They were like two peas in a pod. Iris's little baby brother Pito was too busy having Mrs. Santiago do his homework and eating avocados at the dining room table. I watched that boy put away avocados like they were becoming extinct. Our relatives, overall, were quiet about our romance. One in her family and one in mine voiced their negative concerns about our relationship. To my knowledge, everyone else in the families was either accepting or tolerating our being together.

I was doing well at New York City Community College. I finally enjoyed Physics and Microbiology and tolerated Organic Chemistry. I even took an English course called Chaucer at Brooklyn College and it was tough. I underestimated that course. I didn't think that I would do well, but surprisingly I got a B.

Roslyn finally decided that there was nothing she could do to break me away from Iris. She told me I could be with Iris if I told her what went on between us. I fell for it, completely. I foolishly told my mother and Iris I was no longer with Roslyn.

Mr. Santiago Protecting Iris

Iris and I had some great times together. Each time I wanted to take her out during the evening, I had to ask her father. It was an ordeal I had to go through, but I respected Mr. Santiago for his concern for his daughter. Most of the time I had diarrhea before approaching him. I tried waiting until there were no people in the living room before asking to take her out. Iris helped because she tried to clear the conversation zone when I arrived. He never gave me a hard time and I believe that he knew that I was afraid of him. He could put a look on his face and gas would bubble in my stomach. I wanted his daughter and I was willing to do the jig to get her.

I usually took her to Manhattan, New York to see a movie. After the picture, we walked a lot and when we got tired of that, we found a restaurant to eat. Once I took her to a Hawaiian restaurant. She enjoyed it and I felt good showing her a good time. I remember when I went to the bathroom; there was a guy in there who tried to wipe my hands with a towel. I wasn't used to going to fancy places and I didn't know what was on his mind. I left him standing where I met him and walked out. When I told Iris about it, she laughed. Iris saw her first play with me and my family, "Your Arm's Too Short to Box with God." It was a memorable evening. I wanted my family to accept her and I wanted her to like them, and unbelievably it was happening.

Some racial stuff was happening. Some people in the projects believed that I was selling myself out as a Black guy by being with a white Puerto Rican. Some others believed that she should not have been accompanying a Black guy. We didn't care what they wanted because we knew that we were in love. Once I was running for office on the Red Hook Community Board and some Black people didn't want to vote for me because of my being with Iris. I presume people had their reasons for acting the way that they did. It did not give them the right to act out their feelings in the way they did.

Interracial dating to some people was taboo. I wanted to be free to choose my friends and my girlfriend. The fact that she looked white Anglo was nothing for which to apologize. Iris was not a mistake or a freak of nature. She was a beautiful young woman. If she were some misguided creation of God, then we were all freaks of His madness. Nevertheless, I know God in his awesome wisdom has created an awesome universe and placed it in the hands of His best creation to enjoy it; us. I never apologized for being with Iris and I never will.

Sometimes I took Iris to Coney Island Amusement Park in my sister Janice's blue car, because I needed some money and sold mine for $300. My sister did not even know that the car was gone because I would just take it while she was in her house. It wasn't like stealing, but it was as if it were revenge for her telling me to steal my father's money, then saying she did not. Taking her car was also a pay back for her beating me up so often. I liked eating the French fries at Nathan's restaurant. On our way home, we would stop the car under the Verrazano Narrows Bridge in Brooklyn, to tell each other how much we cared about our relationship. We liked doing that and we did it often.

My most memorable time with Iris was when I went to a lake with her and her family in Pennsylvania. She wore a two-piece bathing suit that I didn't appreciate because it was too revealing. We played as little school kids that day splashing water on each other in the lake and laughing a lot.

I tried to expose Iris to my family as much as possible and I spent a great deal of time in her house relating to her family. I sported a Puerto Rican flag on my army jacket. It helped me feel a sense of oneness to Puerto Ricans and loyalty.

Iris showed me how special she was when I needed to study. Once we were sitting on the bench in front of her apartment, and I told her that I needed to study. She told me to go do it. I felt good about it because it showed me that she cared about my future. I called her on the telephone in order to find out if she were upset with me and if that is why she told me to go study. She told me that she was not upset with me and only wanted me to do what I needed to do.

I did win that community seat on the Red Hook Board and was asked to go to New Orleans, Louisiana to a conference. Iris, who helped me pack my clothes, was very special from the early days of our relationship. These are the invaluable things that people never knew about her. Her gentleness and her strength were often hidden from outsiders because the things, which she did for me were special to her and she did them privately.

Racism on a Grand Scale

New Orleans was a "trip" never to forget, because the American fiber of racial discrimination was there, and it affected me deeply. New Orleans was one of the main historical centers for jazz music, and Black people were at the forefront of it. Many Black people in New Orleans seemed to be shuffling around, while white people were having all the fun. I didn't realize it, but I was in the state of Louisiana, which was known for its hatred of Black people and which practiced racial discrimination openly. I went to a massage parlor in order to check it out. I found it in the Yellow Pages. When I arrived at the parlor, a middle-aged white woman told me, in a Southern drawl, "We don't have no Black girls here." An older-looking Black woman sat in a chair peering her eyes at me. At first, I thought that I didn't hear this white lady correctly. Then she said it to me again, "I said, we don't have no Black girls here." Then I understood. I never wanted to go to New Orleans again because I felt degraded. Maybe I disrespected myself, attempting to cross racial lines.

When I was in New Orleans, I met a person named Stoney, who was West Indian, and worked as a health center Administrator. He told me that he would help me get into medical school. Stoney lived in the Bronx, New York. The health center was in Valhalla, New York; a few miles from where he lived. He invited me to his house in order to take me to the health center where I meet some key people who were connected to New York Medical College. Iris did not agree. She believed that he had other motives, but I met him anyway. When I arrived at Stoney's house, he was happily waiting for me. He delayed our leaving his house in order to talk to me about going with him to California, where he claimed he had a beautiful house. He told me that he would take me to Europe and I would not have to spend a cent. He asked me to think about it. He tried to arouse me sexually by talking about dick sizes and having sex. I told him that I was not into it. He came close to me and did some funny motions with his tongue. He made me mad and I was sorry that I went to his house. He kept trying to get at me, and I aggressively retreated from him. I guess that he got tired and we left for Valhalla, New York. While we were in the car, he had calmed down outwardly. When we arrived at the health center, he introduced me to some people, but I had no idea if they had any influence in order to help me. I got tired of hanging out with him and wanted to go home. Stoney tried to keep me with him as long as he could. On the way back to his apartment he kept looking at me, rolling his eyes and sticking out his tongue. As for me, his being a homosexual was his business, but I wanted nothing to do with it.

When I arrived home, I was glad to see Iris. I missed her terribly. We saw each other as often as we could and she encouraged me to study and do well in college.

The Final Blow

Roslyn had become a bad habit. Nothing was going right between us; she brought the worst out in me, and it was dangerous for both of us. Iris wanted me to be hers and only hers. Nevertheless, I was lying to her big time and failing her.

One evening I was coming home from a youth meeting at the church and Barbara was with me. It was an unusual foggy evening. I held Barbara's hand while walking her home and Iris saw us. She knew that I was friendly with Barbara, but it upset her to see me holding another girl's hand. I did not understand it at the time, but Iris had a righteous jealousy for me because I expressed my love to her. Iris broke up with me after she could not convince me that my relationship with Barbara was not right. Roslyn called Iris and told her that I looked sad in church. She was hoping that she would create a disturbance and keep Iris and me apart for all time. Roslyn continued to harass Iris by calling her on the telephone, saying her name was Lorraine (which is Roslyn's middle name). She would say all kinds of things to Iris and sometimes she would just breathe into the phone.

Iris and I kept in touch and we resolved the issue concerning Barbara and got back together. One night I was supposed to meet Iris at 9:00 p.m. after youth meeting and Roslyn called Iris, harassing her. Iris told her that we were together again. Roslyn got upset and came to the church in a taxicab. She knew that I was to meet Iris. After the youth meeting was over, she asked me to take her home. The next day Iris was at my apartment and Roslyn called about seven times. I told Roslyn that I was busy and couldn't speak with her. On the last call, I didn't hang up the telephone. Iris asked me why Roslyn was calling me if we had nothing going. I told her that I didn't know. I told her that I didn't want Roslyn and she was annoying me. Roslyn heard the conversation. That evening she called Iris and told her that I was lying to her and I was seeing her and another woman. Iris didn't believe her until Roslyn told her intimate things about us. Roslyn told Iris no matter how much I messed around with her; I would eventually come back to Roslyn. Iris, who was shocked, took the straight approach with me. She asked me if I were still with Roslyn and did I convey information to Roslyn about us. I told her yes, and I was sorry. I told Iris that I felt trapped, held like a prisoner, by Roslyn and could not free myself. I was going finally to leave Roslyn. Iris was extremely distraught and hurt that I had deceived her. I didn't have a good answer for her. It wasn't really Roslyn who held me captive. My own weakness and inability held me captive to say I would not take any more guilt that Roslyn was ramming down my throat. Iris loved me and was willing to give me another chance.

One Monday evening during a youth meeting at the church, Roslyn had someone drop her off and leave her. After the meeting, she asked me to take her home. After taking her to her apartment, she said, "I know Iris was waiting for you tonight." I told her Iris was none of her business and it was over between us. I took the ring that she gave me, threw it on the floor, and crushed it with my shoe heel. I told her to give me back everything that I ever gave her, including the engagement ring, which I gave her years before. She told me no. I walked out of her apartment, got in the elevator, and she followed me in her wheelchair. We argued to the ground floor level. She followed me to the parking lot. I got in my sister's car, and she rolled her wheelchair in front of it, while she dared me to run her over. I got out of the car and pushed her to the side of it, and she rolled in front of it again. I got out a second time and rolled her away from it. She maneuvered it again in front of my car. I got out of the car a third time and smacked her face. A person was looking from his apartment window and yelled at me, "Hey, stop beating on that woman in that wheelchair." I jumped in the car, and sped away. That was the end to my relationship with Roslyn in any kind of way. I went to Iris's apartment and told her what happened. I felt terrible smacking Roslyn, but I was finally free from her.

Moving On

At the close of the college semester, I passed Microbiology and Organic Chemistry-II with B's and even got an A in Physics-II. I passed my English courses, getting two B's and a C, and was proud of myself. I had proved that I could get good grades, even if I had to work very hard in order to get them.

I still wanted to be a doctor. I was obsessed with it. I knew that if I became a doctor I would make a difference in medicine, and the world would benefit by it. I told Iris that I was continuing my journey to medical school, and reapplied. We spent time together, and some of it was writing postcards to medical schools for applications.

Reapplying to Medical School

I decided this time to apply to forty-one medical schools, including some foreign. I went to the Italian consulate in Manhattan, New York. When I walked into the consulate, I felt nervous not being Italian and being a Black, asking for an application to go to medical school in Italy. I still remembered that little Italian boy calling me a "nigger" on that Brooklyn Street. An Italian woman sat behind a wooden table looking very stern. I told her that I was there in order to get an application to medical school in Italy. She stared at me for a moment. I waited patiently for her to give me the documents, and then I left I was suspicious that she wondered if I spoke Italian, and who did I think I was trying to get into an Italian medical school. I went to the British, French, and Canadian consulates and requested their documents in order to apply to their medical schools.

Iris was very considerate of my desire to be a doctor and she never doubted for a moment that I would make it. She spent much energy convincing me that I would get in.

Graduation Again

I graduated on June 12, 1972 from Brooklyn College with a Bachelor of Arts Degree in English. I did not believe that I knew any more English than I did after leaving high school. My parents and Iris were very proud of me. I looked back over the six years that I had spent in college, knowing it should have only taken me four. I knew that I paid a price for sticking it out, and I paid the price in full with my sweat, tears, and prayers.

My relationship with Iris was going well and we were reading the Holy Bible together, and thinking about our future. I wanted medical school to be harnessed before we got into any serious thought about marriage. We had a few challenges. Many people were not happy about our being together, but we obviously felt different. Some people were still talking about the Black/white thing.

Iris had cerebral palsy from birth that left her with a limp and partial use of her left hand. Some people could not figure out why I wanted her. They had no idea how beautiful Iris was. They knew nothing about her gentleness, love, compassion, or strength. Some people did not understand that her physical condition did not make or break her. It had nothing to do with who she was. I loved Iris and I felt that she was a great person. Therefore, I knew Iris like no one else because her love for me became a part of my life. I did not care about her cerebral palsy. I noticed it the first week when I met her and she was not any less beautiful to me when I saw her limping.

After I applied to medical school a second time, I worried as I waited for the rejections. They started coming in within thirty days. I did not think that any medical school would accept me.

Tired of My Journey

I enrolled at Richmond College in Staten Island and took Black Study, Art and English courses. As I rode the Staten Island Ferry from lower Manhattan to Staten Island, I reflected on history and how it affected Black people. Often as I passed the Statue of Liberty in New York Harbor, I thought of the journey Black people have traveled. I wondered, was there any justice in America? Could Black people make it in a country that practiced such racial discrimination and bigotry? Does the symbol of the Statue of Liberty mean the same for me as for other Americans? These questions were before me daily.

I felt as though the fire and fumes covered me, as I imagined how the fire and fumes were in ancient Babylon before its destruction. I was very tired of my journey.

PART II

Kindling Flames

I put myself in the midst of this highly charged atmosphere

Chapter 9
Albany Medical College

If I ascend up into heaven, thou art there:
If I make my bed in hell, behold, thou art there.

Psalm 139:8

Affirmative Action was in full motion. Albany Medical College in upstate New York was looking for qualified Black applicants to interview for their freshman class. Previously they had not accepted any Black students in three years. The college was a private, predominately white male college with stiff requirements. A white student in my class asked me if I applied to Albany Medical School, and I told him that I wasn't sure. "You better look into it," he said, "because I hear they want Black students badly." They had rejected me the previous year, but I sent a second application for admission.

Two weeks after my conversation with him, I received a letter in the mail asking for an interview. I wasn't optimistic about the interview because I didn't think that it would go any better than the previous year's interviews at Downstate and Stony Brook Medical Schools.

I took a three-and-one-half-hour trip on a New York Trail ways bus to Albany, New York. I had plenty of time in order to think. I thought of how desperately I wanted to become a doctor. I would do almost anything in order to be accepted into medical school and was mentally exhausted. If I had any energy left, I would need it for the interviews.

When I arrived in Albany, I quickly caught a taxi to the medical center. I was dressed in a wool suit, and I carried my leather briefcase, which gave me a sense of security. I walked into the main lobby, and didn't see any Black people. I thought, "surely there must be some around."

A white woman approached me and asked if I needed any help. When I identified myself, she welcomed me to the medical college. She was very friendly and smiled all the time that I was with her. She told me that two doctors, a Psychiatrist and a Pharmacologist, would interview me. The Psychiatrist, Dr. Bell, to my surprise was Black. He told me that I had been granted an interview because the admission's committee was amazed that I had the nerve to apply to their medical school twice after being rejected. They wondered why with my marginal grades I believed that I would ever be admitted to medical school.

Dr. Bell said they felt that with my determination and their help, I might become a fine doctor. He said that the only problem in the interview would be with the Pharmacologist, Dr. Reynold. "Wilbert," he said, "he doesn't believe that you'll make it through this medical school and he's serious; you will have to win him to your side." Dr. Bell told me that I didn't have to worry about his interview. I thanked him for his frankness and anxiously awaited my interview with Dr. Reynold.

When Dr. Reynold came into the room, I was ready to speak to him with confidence. After asking me a few questions, he politely said, "I don't think you can make it through this medical school."

I said, "Yes I can."

He replied, "I don't think so."

I became aggressive with him. I said, "Hey, man, I can make it through this medical school." He told me that I would have a very difficult time there and he would recommend that I not be admitted to the college. I guess my grades were enough to convince him that he could judge me on paper.

I traveled back to Brooklyn with mixed emotions about being accepted to Albany Medical College. I didn't think that I had a chance of getting in.

My family was very supportive. My father kept telling me that something would come through. Iris continued to encourage and support me. She waited patiently, while I waited impatiently, for an answer from Albany Medical College. My studies at Richmond College became a burden. I didn't want to be there, and I didn't want to hang out on the street either, because I wasn't working.

Admittance to Medical School

After an anxious two weeks, I received a letter from the medical college, accepting me. I couldn't believe it. I called the Admissions Office and asked the receptionist if they had made a mistake.

"Are you Wilbert Williams, Jr.?"

I said, "Yes."

"Then we have the right person. It's no mistake."

When I told my parents that I was admitted to medical school, they were very excited because they knew how much it meant to me. I went to Iris's house and told them the good news. Everyone was happy, and I still couldn't believe it. I quit college because I was tired of undergraduate school, and my brain was saturated. I applied for a job at Long Island College Hospital to work in the outpatient clinic department where I would pull and deliver medical records. Paul Garguilo, who was my boss when I worked there before, was still there, and would still be a friend to me.

Getting Married

Iris and I decided to get married. We told our parents about our decision and they were not happy. They wanted time to prepare a wedding for us, but we felt that there was too much confusion surrounding us. We had a few days in order to prepare for the wedding and it created its own confusion. Mr.

Santiago was grieving over losing his first daughter, and my father informed me that there would be plenty of pretty girls in medical school. I didn't hear anything negative from our mothers. We had a small wedding at Calvary Baptist Church in Red Hook. There weren't many people there, but our families were represented, along with a few friends. We had our honeymoon at Howard Johnson in Manhattan and it was Iris's first time in a hotel. Within a few days, our honeymoon was over and I was back at work, and Iris was being a new homemaker.

We found a small apartment in an Italian neighborhood in Brooklyn's Carol Garden section, a few blocks from my job. It was a dreary place with black ceilings and dark painted walls. The only window in the living room looked at an adjacent red brick wall of the next building, where there was an alleyway. We repainted the apartment and settled into our new home.

While I worked, Iris stayed home. She had a little dog-named "Mudley", which didn't seem to like me. I constantly complained about her dog. My dog Amani was with us. In addition, the more I complained, the more the dog didn't like me. One day while I was at work, the dog ran into the street and got hit by a car. When I got home, Iris was crying and I cried with her. It was our first tragedy in our brand-new family.

My job was challenging because I didn't like pulling medical records and going up and down in the elevator and occasionally running up the stairs when charts were needed. It was, however, bringing in needed income and I needed to be responsible; especially as a married man.

I often walked to and from work, which was about seven city blocks. When I was working, I was able to sit in a little room and read a Gross Anatomy text. I went to the store across the street from the hospital and bought a $6 stethoscope and a $10 blood pressure cuff. By studying medicine, ahead of time, my own style, helped my impatience to enter medical school that August. The admission's committee at the medical college believed that I, and the other incoming Black students, would benefit from a special orientation program for minority students. They planned for us to take Physiology and Biochemistry for three weeks before the entering freshman class.

I didn't work very hard at the hospital. Many of the people who knew me when I was in college were happy that I decided to work at the hospital before going to medical school.

One time I was walking home from the hospital, which was only a few blocks away, and I walked through my boss's, Paul's, neighborhood. A little white boy stood in front of me and called me a "nigger." I looked straight in his eyes, and he looked at me and walked away. My heart broke. I felt that he was too young to understand what it meant to call anyone a "nigger." Either he heard that word in his neighborhood or someone encouraged him to say it. I went home and told Iris that a little Italian boy called me a "nigger." We didn't discuss it, but for a long time I never stopped hurting over it.

My family lived only a few blocks from where Iris and I lived. I missed them and wanted to see them. Iris was upset about it. I wasn't prepared for this side of marriage and I became angry. I told her that I no longer wanted a sexual relationship in the marriage. I wanted a platonic relationship. She thought that I was crazy. She missed me terribly when I left the house and this took an emotional toll on her. I didn't understand how important my relationship with her was. She was a good wife, constantly trying to please me. I was too immature to accept all of her.

We had the opportunity to save some money. My friend Raymond's mother, Angelina Scott, was dying from cancer and was in the hospital. She offered her apartment rent-free to Iris and me. We took it. Iris didn't want to go back to Red Hook, but she knew that it would save us money. We stayed there until I was to start medical school.

I Love My Wife

Eleanor came into my life again. She called my mother's house and asked for me. She was visiting her sister in the Bronx. I hadn't completely gotten over her from my days at Harvard, but my marriage to Iris meant a great deal to me now, for I loved Iris. I called Eleanor and arranged to meet her at Flushing Meadow Park in Queens, New York. When I saw her, I was surprised with myself because I was excited having not seen her in more than two years. I took a blanket from the trunk of my car to sit on. I spread it over a small patch of green grass and we sat. I kept enough distance from her in order to relay the message that things were no longer the same between us. We talked about Harvard and the good time that we had. She looked at me in a way, which I understood that I could have her, but Iris kept flashing in my mind. There was nothing left for Eleanor that was romantic or intimate to me and there was no way that I would give into her. I talked to her about her boyfriend, Poncho. She told me that they decided to break off their relationship for all time. I asked her what happened between us, and she told me that she thought that she felt more for Poncho. I reminded her that I was married and couldn't get involved with her. She moved closer to me, and I believe that she wanted me to kiss her, but I didn't. I was proud of myself that day because I did the right thing for once and remained true to myself and faithful to Iris. When we parted, I told her to take care of herself.

I never saw Eleanor again.

Going to Medical School

A few days before August, I quit my job at the hospital to go to Albany. On the day we were leaving Brooklyn for Albany, I had a mixed bag of feelings. On one hand I wanted to start medical school as soon as possible, but emotionally I was tied to my family. Leaving them would be difficult regardless, but medical school was the road that I had to take.

Iris was ready to hit the road in our old Ford Torino with its bald tires, and which was painted with aqua blue enamel paint. We brought it a few months prior. After loading our car with the few things, we had and after saying goodbye to our families, we headed for upstate New York for a three-and-one-half-hour ride. I kept thinking about medical school and how long and tedious my journey had been, and still couldn't believe that I was really going to become a medical student. I envisioned myself with all-white clothes and with a stethoscope around my neck, and with books stuffed in my coat pockets. I mentally saw my parents smiling at me, full of pride.

Driving up the New York State Thruway, I thought about my journey from Red Hook projects to medical school. I had worked very hard to walk into the ivory hall of that institution, and I had no idea what was awaiting me. When we were two miles from the exit to downtown Albany the radiator was steaming and the car slowed. I prayed that the car wouldn't shut off until we reached 566 Madison Avenue, where the one-bedroom apartment we were to rent was. I didn't know it, but we would spend the next five years in Albany, New York, instead of four and it would be the most trying five years academically and otherwise for me that I would ever experience. When we reached the block where the apartment was, our Ford "buggy" just stopped running. I rolled the car down the inclined street in neutral and parked it in an open area in front of our window.

There was a beautiful park called Washington Park across the street from the apartment, and it would become one of my places to steal away to. I loved it. Iris was excited about being in Albany, and I was excited about becoming a medical student, but I quickly put medical school on the backburner for the moment and was worrying about my car. After we settled in our new apartment, I went outside to start the car and the engine wouldn't turn over. We went to bed early that evening because I was due in medical school the following day.

Black Peas in a Pot of White Rice

I got up early the next morning and anxiously went to the medical center. I met three other students who were Black. We were scheduled to take a special orientation in medical school. The admission's committee believed that our educational backgrounds were weak and we would benefit by studying Biochemistry and Physiology before the incoming freshman class.

Jimmy Stevenson was the first Black student whom I met. He graduated from Brooklyn College, but I had never seen him on campus. He told me that there were two other Black students coming. Sure enough, within a few minutes I saw two Black guys come into the main lobby looking lost. When we realized that we were searching for each other, we started laughing. We joked about being four peas in a pot of white rice. One student, Oswald Hayes, who was from Brooklyn via the island of Jamaica, said, "Well, they got four 'niggers' in this school. Here come the 'niggers.'" None of us said a word; we chuckled. Harrison Lenoir was the quiet one. He was a graduate from Howard University who was the only one of us who had a master's degree; his was an advanced degree in science. His father was a dentist in Los Angeles, California.

There were three professors scheduled to meet us on our first day. Dr. Procitor, a professor of Pharmacology, greeted us and ushered us up to the third floor for a talk. He greeted us warmly and I liked him from the start. He appeared to have an honest streak in him. He told us that he was going to be our mentor. He spoke with us about the Affirmative Action program and stated that we were able to get into the school because of it. He made it clear that we were also picked on our personal qualities and ambition, but compared to most of the students in our incoming class we were probably in for a rough ride. He then took us to various department heads and introduced us to them. Dr. Procitor told us that Physiology and Biochemistry were the two courses, which most students found the hardest, and that's where the first point of separation began as far as who would probably make it through medical school.

Dr. Beeler, the Biochemistry professor, whom we met, told us that his course, along with Physiology, would separate the men from the boys. "My course is a difficult course and I teach it fast so you better be ready to keep up with me. Steroid Chemistry is a lot to know and I'm going to move fast." He wasn't joking.

Professor Gumbos taught physiology to us. He taught the electro physiology portion of the regular course during the year. I wouldn't understand a thing that he would speak about in electrophysiology, during and after the orientation to medical school. The final professor whom we met that day was Professor Edmunds. He taught the Anatomies and started us out in cell anatomy and the electron microscope.

All of these professors treated us well and were very polite, but Professor Gumbos seemed to have a devious streak in him. When he spoke to us, he had a half-smile, as if he knew something about our future, which we didn't know.

Beginning the Nightmare

The first couple of days with these professors were very challenging to me. The other Black students appeared confident in their abilities to do well.

When we had our first Physiology lecture, I sat in my seat as I listened and watched Professor Gumbos draw the electrochemical potential wave and did not understand any of it. After class, he lit a cigarette, walked slowly in front of the room, smiled, and asked us if we understood the material. I didn't understand a thing and was very confused. I didn't know why because I had read the textbook. After Dr. Gumbos asked us a few questions, he realized that I was confused about the material and said, "What is it you don't understand, Williams?"

"None of it," I answered.

"I can't go over all of it again; tell me what specifically is bothering you?"

"All of it," I said.

While he dragged and puffed on his cigarette, he looked frustrated and drew that circle, which represents a human cell and the sodium and potassium ions and started making all kinds of lines with the chalk again, and I was confused even more. "Do you understand it now?" he said.

"No," I responded.

He went over it two more times and I still didn't get it. He told me to go home and read it again. Oswald, Jimmy and Harrison didn't say a word to me about what happened in class. I kept saying, "I don't understand that stuff." I had my usual mental block and was again behind my classmates.

Biochemistry was more interesting than Physiology, but Dr. Beeler talked as fast as a person in an air traffic control tower did. He moved through Steroid Chemistry as if he were reading his Social Security number. He wouldn't stop scribbling with that chalk while he bounced up and down like a basketball. I thought that he was acting like a neurotic. Steroid Chemistry was coming out my nose. I literally felt sick after that lecture, but it was just another day for Dr. Beeler. After the lecture, he asked us a bunch of questions. "What do you guys like to do after hours? You know you guys are not going to be able to dress the way you did before coming here, because you are in medical school now with other priorities. The social life up here is going to be a bit difficult for you guys." We didn't understand where he was coming from and left the classroom baffled.

We set our minds on our next lecture, with Dr. Edmunds. I liked Dr. Edmunds because he was straight with us. He told us that he was going to talk about Cell Biology, and if we had any questions, he would be glad to answer them. He started asking us about the human cell and seeing if we understood high school-level biology and abruptly stopped. "Hey, what am

I going over this stuff with you guys for, you know this stuff. How would you guys like to do some things with the electron microscope?"

We jumped to the chance. I saw some things under that scope which I had never seen in my life and I was fascinated. After the session, we all walked out of his lab feeling charged up.

Oswald said, "Now I could dig that shit. What do these guys think?; we're some damn high school students or something?"

Iris had a new job in the medical college library and was doing fine. She made some friends quickly and was enjoying it. I was missing my family in Red Hook and wanted the security of being there. I needed to grow up and understand that what I had embarked on was a serious decision to get a piece of America's apple pie; namely medicine, and that it was going to be a tough part of my journey.

Medicine had been offered to influential white Americans for more than one hundred years, and America wasn't fully ready to give any of it to Black people. I didn't know it, but I was in a war with the white establishment. I needed to muster up strength and endurance because it was going to get hot, while the kindling flames of racism and bigotry began to burn.

Physiology continued to be challenging and I still didn't understand anything Professor Gumbos taught. When I thought that I understood something in the textbook, he proved me wrong. It was very frustrating being taught by him. I felt stupid.

Biochemistry was also challenging, but at least I was able to understand the material. I labored more over Dr. Beeler's ignorance concerning Black people than I did about Steroid Chemistry. Dr. Beeler kept pounding us with questions about our social life. One day after a difficult Biochemistry session, he said his children had not been around any Black kids and he didn't know if it were good or bad. "I raised them this way, and I'm not sure."

I lit into him. "Dr. Beeler," I said, "you talk all this stuff about not having any problem with Black people, but if I wasn't married and asked to take out your daughter, I don't think you would like it."

He looked at me and didn't say a word. The Black students looked straight ahead at him and were speechless. They told me I was crazy for saying something like that to him. I told them I didn't care and was tired of his nonsense. They shook their heads and wondered what was wrong with me. I knew that I had stepped out of bounds, but I believed the real reason was that I was frustrated with not understanding the material. I was on my way out of medical school before the regular year began.

When the orientation was over, I was convinced that I was in for a rough journey. Iris was encouraging me through my period of low self-esteem and fear of failure. I would have had a very difficult time coping in medical school, even though I was religious, if Iris had not been with me. It was confirmation to me that Iris and I belonged together.

The First Official Day

The first official day of med school was like standing in a soup line. Everyone was running around like chickens with their heads cut off. Confusion was everywhere. We were standing in threes in the hallway, waiting to have our mug shots taken (as if we were criminals). I felt like I was in undergraduate school again. Some things don't change.

A few days after the "official" orientation to medical school had cooled down, people began thinking seriously about studying. The scheduled courses for that semester were Physiology, Biochemistry and Psychiatry. Three courses seemed like very little, yet I had no idea until the first week was over, just how much material would be covered that semester.

I studied hard from the first day. I didn't put down my books for almost anything except to sleep. Occasionally, I tried to study and watch TV, but that game ended after the first few tries. Most nights, Iris would go to bed without me. It was difficult for her to stay up while I was studying, even though she tried many times. I felt abandoned when she would go to bed, but I never said anything. Most times, she watched the TV with an earphone to keep from disturbing me.

When the weekend arrived, I was so geared up that I couldn't stop studying. The weekend just seemed like extra study days. I studied every weekend and didn't tire easily. My energy came from two endless sources, fear and God.

The First Test

Our first examination was scheduled to be at the end of the first four weeks. I was trying to study in advance, but it was nearly impossible to do that. I had a lot to read, and the material was becoming more difficult to understand. Every time when I thought that I was ahead, there was always some new material that took extra time to study. The night before my Physiology exam, I stayed up until early the following morning and tried to put the last pieces together. The exam was "an open book," and we were allowed to bring with us any material that we wanted. I walked into the lecture hall with five physiology books, which Iris helped me carry to school.

When I arrived, some of my classmates were already there, talking about Physiology as if it were the most important thing in the world. I disliked jam sessions like that; they always made me more nervous. I couldn't help, but listen to all those "monkeys cracking peanuts and running their chops." Sure enough, they only served to exhaust me mentally and made me more anxious. As I sat waiting for the professor to bring in the examination, my body felt as though it were falling apart. I felt as if something heavy was weighing on my chest and my heart would beat right through it. When the professor arrived at my row and handed me the test, it felt like a book. When I started writing my name, my hand wouldn't stop shaking.

At first sight of the questions, I realized that no books were going to help me. The questions did not require direct answers. I had to think them out. All reasoning escaped me. The fear of failure filled every part in my body because I felt that I didn't understand the material. I could not hold my pen steady. At certain moments, I felt like crying. I started speaking to myself aloud, while grabbing at my head and pants. When the exam was over, I picked up my books and left the hall.

That afternoon, the Biochemistry exam was scheduled. I ate lunch and sat around, praying that the following exam would not be anything like Physiology.

I went to the lecture hall just about the same time the exam was starting. The professor was handing out the papers. I made up my mind that I wasn't going to let what happened on the Physiology exam happen on Biochemistry. I tried to remain calm while turning the exam pages. I saw matching questions on the last page and began to complete them. I answered seven out of ten. I did the entire exam from the back working my way to the front, which was the wrong way to take the exam. The exam was designed to aid the student in answering the following questions by working from the front page, though I actually felt confident that I had a good chance of passing.

The next few days I walked around extremely worried. I sat in class impatiently, and wondered if today were the day, that they would return the grades. I had diarrhea after each lecture. Finally, the day arrived. The announcement was made that the exam papers were in the Physiology and Biochemistry lab rooms. Everyone started running like a bunch of apes headed for a mountain of grapefruits. I wasn't acting like a human either. When I reached the lab, people were pushing and grabbing for their exam papers. They were in alphabetical order on two large tables, and like a dummy, I looked on the wrong table for mine. My hands shook like someone having convulsions and I felt like I was going to have one.

I ran around to the other side of the table, but still didn't see my paper. I saw handwriting that looked like mine. It was! It was my exam paper. I went for it like a lunatic. With my paper in hand, I headed for a nearby corner. I began to pray. There was a big "U" written on my exam paper, "U" for unsatisfactory. I glanced at the crowd of students still at the tables; a few of them were jumping with joy because they passed. I overheard other students talking about how they almost got "excellent" on their exams. I felt embarrassed.

I went to the library where Iris was working and told her about it. She tried to console me, but I felt too low to be picked up. She knew what it meant to me to fail. That evening I was depressed. Nothing else mattered more to me than knowing that I had failed the exam.

A few days later, there was an announcement that the Physiology examinations were in the lab room waiting to be picked up. I spotted my paper and picked it up. I was stunned by another failing grade and almost passed out. My body felt as though something was draining it. I couldn't believe that this was happening to me. I was convinced that nothing could help me. I imagined my dream to become a doctor vanishing away.

Iris tried desperately to encourage me. She said that God would not allow failure to win out over His plan for me to become a doctor. She realized that my faith was the key. Every chance she had to reinforce my faith in God, she did.

I studied like there were no tomorrow and concentrated on those areas, which were the most difficult to understand. I tried to relax, but it was difficult. Two failures in the most important subjects in the first year of medical school were enough to cause anyone to have a nervous breakdown.

"Buddy, You Should Have Known Better."

I went to Professor Gumbos and asked him what he thought about my being in medical school. "Do you want my honest opinion?" he asked.

I said, "Yes."

He looked at me with a smile on his face and said, "I think you're not cut out for medical school, you need to go into the paramedical field." My heart felt like it would stop. I just looked at him, and then I tilted my head to the floor. I left him standing in the classroom puffing on a cigarette. I went straight down to the emergency room and asked to see a Psychiatrist. I broke down and cried in the emergency room. My dream to become a doctor seemed so far away and impossible.

I called Steve Goodman, who befriended me. Steve was in the sophomore class. I trusted him. He and his wife were friendly and they accepted us like family.

The first time that I ever went water-skiing was with his father's boat in Lake George Resort near the Adirondack Mountains. I used to go hunting there for deer and bear. Steve wasn't home, but his wife said that she would let him know that I called. I was still crying and she sensed it. She asked me where was I and was it an emergency. I told her that it was an emergency and I was in the Albany Medical Hospital emergency room.

When I got home, I told Iris what occurred. She consoled me and said, "Buddy, what did you expect him to tell you, asking him a question like that, you should have known better. You know how he feels about you being in medical school."

I was so depressed that I eventually went to sleep in order to try to forget what Dr. Gumbos told me.

I thought about my cousin Leray's words to me that "doctors are born and not made," and I wasn't going to become any doctor, when I was living in my Aunt Doris's house. The words were still haunting me. I was wondering again if she was right.

The following morning Iris told me that Steve came to the house after I fell asleep. He told her that he would catch up with me and he did. I told him what happened and he got upset. He asked me if I believed Gumbos had anything against me. I told him I wasn't sure. That week some of the upper-class students held a meeting in the student lounge and asked me to attend. In the meeting I was asked why did I think Professor Gumbos was always calling on me to answer questions. I told them I did not know. Steve said, "Well, you won't have to deal with him much longer, because his portion of the course is almost over." The meeting was positive, at least to the point that the students understood that one Black student was discouraged and hurt and needed some help coping with the courses.

Steve decided to help me with electro physiology and I was glad to accept his help. I did get frustrated at times trying to understand the stuff. I found the energy and courage to continue to face Professor Gumbos. I didn't stop studying hard and I read the material repeatedly in order to absorb it.

When I took the second Physiology exam, I tried being positive. I was convinced that I could pass the test and I did. I remember the feeling, which I had when I found out that I had passed. I was now convinced that I could do the work. The Biochemistry exam did not yield the same return; I had failed and was extremely disappointed. I knew at this point that I would probably fail the course. It was a setback to think that I would fail the course after having worked so hard. I went through countless measures in order to study for the final exams. I visited every faculty member I knew who would sincerely encourage me. It was plain that some of them had given up on me. In fact, some didn't have any hope to begin with. I studied for long hours, burning the light into the morning, hardly speaking much to Iris. This was it; the last chance to pass Physiology and Biochemistry during the regular school year. I took the Biochemistry exam with confidence. Though it was difficult, I believed that I had passed. The Physiology exam was no joke. The exam was 230 multiple choice questions, to be completed in three hours. This was cutting it a bit close, and by the time I finished it, I knew that I had failed. When the exam was over, I was so upset that I took my exam and stuffed it in my pants. I wasn't going to turn in that item of shame. My plan was to let them wonder what happened to the exam and get a retest. I walked the halls for about ten minutes with the exam in my pants. I couldn't decide what to do with it. I finally decided to turn it in. I walked into the Physiology room. While the professors were sorting through the exam papers, I slipped mine on the table. Professor Gumbos was there. I looked at him, and said to my self, "You must be right; I'm not cut out for medical school." I stood there to notice their reaction when they saw this wrinkled paper. No one questioned my being there. Someone noticed it and summoned me. Of course, I was there instantly. A professor asked me to sit and transfer my answers to another sheet, one that was not wrinkled.

Later that day, I went to see the chairperson. I told him what I was going to do with the answer sheet. I think he must have felt I was foolish to tell him that. As I talked, I explained to him what medical school meant to me. Tears rolled down my face; I couldn't hold them back. I broke into an uncontrollable cry. He asked me to calm down. I'll never forget that moment. I was very disturbed. He suggested that I go on my Christmas vacation and not worry about the exam. He said that there was nothing I could do about what had happened. Of course, he was right.

When we arrived in Brooklyn, I tried to hide my worry from the families. I wanted to go back to Albany for my grades; at the same time,

I wanted to remain in Brooklyn to rest and spend time with my family. When Iris and I finally did return to Albany, the report still had not been returned. It was agony waiting for it. One day I went to the mailroom, and there it was visible through the little peep window; folded nicely. I was shaking while I opened the mailbox door. A feeling of despair came over me when I saw a "failure" in both Biochemistry and Physiology. As I walked through the halls, I wondered what I would do with my life. How could I ever live, knowing that I would never achieve my goal or fulfill the dream to be a doctor? I didn't dare go back to Red Hook and let people see that I had become a failure.

Worst of all, Iris was going through all of this with me, sharing every ounce of my pain, while having her own. My frustration in school and failing during those past months didn't make my life easy at all, and I fell along the way.

I tried forgetting about my problems in school and the problems at home and being frustrated with Iris when I felt that she didn't understand what I was going through. It wasn't that Iris didn't understand what I was going through. She knew that in order to help me that she had to be truthful with me and tell me what she felt concerning my attitude. I was going through the fire of my journey. My problems at home were, not wanting to face the fact that Iris was right in everything that she told me. Iris loved me and treated me like a royal king and if it were not for her love for me, I would have not made it through my first few months in medical school.

I enjoyed the open woods and sometimes I went to the railroad track a few blocks from my house and hunted squirrel and rabbits. Most of the time I came home with a squirrel, skinned it, and hung the skin on my wall. I guess in some ways I was working some of my frustration out by being in the woods and killing animals.

The first half of the year finally ended. Our grades were sent to the registrar's office. Two failures were sent for me in Physiology and Biochemistry, while I did receive a passing grade in Psychiatry. For the time being, these troublesome two courses were over.

The second semester included Gross Anatomy, Histology, Neuroanatomy, and the remainder of Psychiatry. I couldn't wait for the courses to begin. This was my second chance to prove myself. The Black students wanted me to work with them in Gross Anatomy. There were four students to a cadaver, and they wanted me to be the fourth student. I didn't want to study with them, and I expressed it. I didn't want them to feel as if they helped me in any way during the first semester. They never offered me any help in Biochemistry or Physiology. Harrison was the only one to encourage me. He told me many times not to worry about what some of the professors thought about me because they had no idea who I was. He knew what he knew and no one was going to tell him otherwise. I believed that Oswald and Jimmy only cared about themselves, and all of Oswald's talk about being Black brothers and sticking together was a bunch of lies. They kept pestering me about being the fourth student working on the cadaver and I gave in. I spoke with Iris about it. Before I did, I already had an idea what she would say. She told me not to do it, and against her advice, I said yes to them. Iris warned me that I would find myself in the same situation as before.

Finding Friends

I liked Histology. It was an interesting course and I discovered I was good at recognizing differences between tissue specimens. One day a thin white woman named Judy was walking around the lab helping students. She was taking a special interest in helping the students understand the material. When she approached my table and talked to the other students around me, I listened to her. I didn't feel she would show the same interest in me. As she passed by me, I spoke to her. I told her my life story and don't know what got into me. Everything was pouring out as if I were just waiting for her to come along. She was attentive and didn't interrupt me at all. I asked if she would be willing to help me with the Histology lab portion of the course during her spare time. She told me that it was no problem and she would like to. She arranged some off school-hour studying with me. The next day, the Chairman of the Anatomy department, Dr. Cowden, who was a white Southerner, came over to me in the lab and introduced himself. He said that while he was talking to one of his staff members (Judy), it was made known to him that I asked for special help in Histology. I told him that I was in scholastic trouble; on probation, and needed the help. He wanted to know more about my situation. I told him that I didn't think the people in the Physiology and Biochemistry departments cared much about my success in medical school, and as far as I was concerned, few other people cared. He replied that he was concerned and realized the school accepted me in order to obtain federal monies, and they didn't really care if I made it or not. He told me that many schools in the United States were involved in the same practice because they had been pressured into accepting minority students against their will. He felt it was an explanation for their attitude. He stated that the college didn't know how to handle minority students, and no medical school had the right to accept minority students without the willingness to help them through the program. In his opinion, the school had made a commitment and had refused to live up to it. He said the school would not purposely try to fail me but, on the other hand, would not fight too hard to keep me either. He assured me even though many people did not care if I sank or swam, he wasn't one of them. He was happy that I had asked for help, and offered his services to me. After having that conversation with him, I became concerned because I wasn't sure if Dr. Cowden was being honest with me or was just collecting information. I didn't know if I could trust him.

Another exam was on its way. Whenever I thought I needed help, I went to Judy, who was Dr. Cowden's assistant in the Histology lab. She went over the material with me. Although she was busy sometimes, she would stop whatever she was doing in order to help me. These sessions were very rewarding, and I learned a lot from her. She showed me some memory tricks to identify certain information on the Histology slides. On the day of the exam, I was definitely confident. When I walked into the exam room, Dr. Cowden and Judy looked at me and smiled. I knew at that moment, I had found friends. The exam was set up in a musical-chair fashion with 68 slides. When the start bell rang, I quickly looked in the microscope. I knew the answer at first glance. The exam went smoothly. The written exam took more time, but I was satisfied with it. The following week the exam was returned. I passed both exams with good grades.

As usual, my grades went to every faculty member who asked for it. Faculty members outside of the Anatomy department knew my grades without my telling.

The Gross Anatomy exam was coming up soon. Iris helped me with learning the bones, muscles and nerves. She would ask me to tell her what nerves worked certain muscles and the attachment of muscles to bones. I would go to school early in the morning before the nine o'clock lecture, and study the cadaver. Sometimes, one of the Black students would see me there, and it raised their suspicion about my trying to get ahead of them.

During the lab sessions, we hacked away at the cadaver. We had a male who was 76 years old, who died of cardiovascular disease. It was a bit difficult at first to deal with a dead body that smelled to me like cooked barbecue spare ribs. I had dreams at night that I was eating it and it tasted very sweet, like sugar. I asked our Anatomy Professor if he knew what human meat taste like. He told me he personally didn't, but a friend of his had to eat some in Africa among some cannibals, and he told him that it tastes like any other kind of meat except a little tough. Sometimes I would clown around, like when I was in Junior High School 142. One day I pulled the intestine from the abdomen of our cadaver, hooked it up to the water faucet, and turned it on. I waited until the water came to the end, and laughed about it. After a couple of weeks, I developed respect for the cadaver. I understood it was a privilege to learn from it, and it once was a real person like me. I came to thank God for it and even talked to it when no one was around but me.

Iris came to the lab often and watched me as I cut on the corpse and ate my lunch. It made her stomach turn. On the day of the exam, I went to the cafeteria to get some food in order to calm my stomach (I was now getting diarrhea every time I took an exam). The test was easy; except for some relationship questions, which would even have confused a surgeon. The following week, we were informed that the exams were in the Histology lab. I ran as fast as I could to the lab. When I got there, the papers were spread over the table in alphabetical order. Two grades were on the exams; one for the lab practical and the other for the written exam. I did very well on the practical, but not so well on the written. My overall grade was a solid "Pass." I was not, however, satisfied.

Black Conflict

I was sorry that I decided to work with the Black students because we argued a lot and never trusted each other. I often went to the Anatomy room when I knew they would not be there to study the cadaver. They thought that I was trying to get information without them, and Oswald especially wasn't going to let that happen. I was beginning to see Oswald for what he really was; a separatist who acted as if he hated white people, and one who said he was a brother to all Blacks. Iris didn't like him, and I liked him even less.

Passing

I eventually passed Gross Anatomy with a good grade. The struggle of working hard had paid off, and I realized the true value of the friendship of Dr. Cowden and Judy. It didn't matter to me that they were both white.

I knew for sure at that point I could make it through medical school, and the system could be beaten.

Iris was very happy concerning my performance. It made me feel good to know that my wife was with me "100 percent."

Pharmacology was also a course that gave me trouble. It required an integration of Biochemistry and Physiology. I failed the first Pharmacology exam. I don't think it was the material; I couldn't get my conceptual thinking together. When it came time for the second exam, I was more prepared and passed it. I also passed the final exam, with a marginal grade.

It was during the Pharmacology course that I worked out my differences with the Black students. I told them I didn't think they cared about me. I told Jimmy I didn't like him because he was always bragging about how he was going to "ace" some exam. Oswald voiced his concern and said, "If you don't want to study with us anymore, it's OK." I told him that wasn't the whole situation with me. I believed that they only cared about themselves and to hell with me and anyone else.

Neuroanatomy was the course that was supposed to separate the men from the boys. Only one exam was scheduled and if a student failed it, he would fail the course. I didn't appreciate having only one exam because it took me some time to get used to the style of each course. I remembered what happened to me at Brooklyn College with that History of the English Language course, and how I failed the one and only exam they gave, and spent six additional months in school because of it.

I approached a South American medical doctor who did not have a license to practice medicine in the U.S., who was helping in the Neuroanatomy lab. I asked him if he would tutor me and he agreed. He met me twice a week through the course and he didn't charge me anything. If I didn't understand the material to his satisfaction, he would stop the session and tell me to go home and study. Oswald found out that I was getting help from him and I believe he got jealous. He approached me and asked if I was getting help in the course, and I told him yes. This was the last time Oswald spoke with me about studying with the Black students. I was glad to be rid of him. My tutorial sessions helped me tremendously, and I passed the course.

I passed Pharmacology and received no failures that half of the year in any subjects. The pace was now beginning to slow. The time was approaching for me to concentrate on taking the Biochemistry and Physiology reviews; these results would determine if I would graduate to the second-year class.

The medical college had a policy that gave students the opportunity to retake a subject or two when they failed, in order to be retested. The promotion's committee felt that one subject should not cause a student to be left back, if he or she could achieve. What bothered me about the review policy was that 100% on the final exam would not have given me enough margins to pass the course; my grade was too low. The maximum percentage that could be received from the Biochemistry review was 25% on the makeup test. As far as I was concerned, they were sending me through the motions.

Conspiracy in the Working

I spoke with the Chairman of the Anatomy department, about the possibility of repeating the school year. He told me that he didn't feel I needed to repeat the year because two white girls in the class didn't do much better than me and they were graduating to the second-year class. In my opinion, it appeared to me that he said, "It definitely appears to be a conspiracy against you." He promised that he would do everything in his power to help me get to the second year. He asked for time to investigate the matter. When I saw him the next day, he told me the Physiology people simply felt that I didn't know enough Physiology in order to go to the second year. The Chairman of Biochemistry was sticking to his guns as long as I had a failure in Physiology. He told the Chairman of the Anatomy department if I had passed Physiology, I would have been given the passing grade. I was furious. The two departments wanted a guarantee that I would be repeating the entire school year so they both failed me.

The Chairman of the promotion's committee confessed it all to me. "Wilbert," he said, "If the promotion's committee had received one failure for you, they would have requested the faculty to give you a reexamination." He told me that his hands were tied, however. When I reminded him of the conversation, which I had with him about the matter of passing earlier during the year, and how difficult I believed it would be because my grade was so low. Also, he was the one who told me my passing or failing the course would be based on how I did on the review course test, he became angry. He told me that the school reflected society and that society unfortunately was racist.

I went to the Dean of the medical college about my case. He said that he couldn't figure out what was wrong with the Biochemistry Chairman. The Dean then told me that he would tell me some thing in confidence.

He said that three faculty heads from the Physiology and Biochemistry departments came to him after two months into the academic year. They requested that two other students and I be thrown out of the medical school because we obviously were not medical school material. He told them not to ask for that because we had paid tuition for a full year. He was not about to throw anyone out. "I told them that we took you for a year and we were going to keep you for a year. After that they would decide", he said, looking straight at me.

I told Dr. Cowden what the Dean told me, and he assured me that he would talk to a few people. Dr. Cowden asked the Dean to help me graduate to the second-year class. He told the Dean that he believed a conspiracy was in the works and the Dean told him not to use words like that in his office. According to Dr. Cowden, he and the Dean cursed each other. The Dean then told him he would talk to some of the faculty members and was sure they would swing the decision in my favor. It was becoming a matter of who would persuade whom to let me go on or leave me back. The Biochemistry department took a vote to decide if I would pass or fail. The vote was taken, and one person voted in my favor to pass the course. The promotion's committee voted and decided that I would be better off repeating the entire academic school year. Dr. Cowden and Judy, his assistant, were the only ones in the entire school who had tried to help me at this point.

He recounted a meeting, which he had with the Chairman of Physiology. They sat around a table during a conference with the executive faculty committee and literally cursed each other out concerning my situation. Dr. Cowden made it clear to me that though he was a Southerner and didn't particularly love Blacks, there was something about me that encouraged him to fight for me. He regretted there was nothing more that he could do to help me pass Biochemistry and Physiology. Very little was left to be done on his part or my part, I was out of energy to deal with these powerful people.

I thanked Dr. Cowden for his courage in helping me through the racist system. Even though he was from the South, from where my father was born and from which my father ran, Dr. Cowden proved to be a friend to me in the midst of kindling flames. Whether he realized it or not, I was probably the first Black person in his life whom he loved. He summed up his relationship with me by saying, "I never did what I'm doing for you with any person, but there is something about you, and it makes me want to fight like hell. What they're doing to you is wrong."

I was probably paying for my statements about some of the professors, for I had referred to them as racists when I was taking Biochemistry and Physiology. What I said got around the school, but I didn't care, because some of them were racists.

You Can Leave Medical School Now

I was sent a letter from the promotion's committee. It simply stated that I could leave school for good, go on a decelerated academic program (take fewer courses than the rest of the students), or repeat the entire school year. No way was I going to quit medical school, to go back to Red Hook or move to another place. I wanted to be a doctor, not a failure. I decided to repeat the entire school year.

Harrison, the Black medical student, whose car I washed, and who gave me Mary Jane candies during lecture class, was terminated from medical school because he failed every subject (he did even worst than me). The day he left, he was still saying nobody was going to tell him what he knew. Oswald and Jimmy did well so they were promoted, to the second year, and I was to repeat.

Iris was mentally tired, and I felt bad for her. She was by my side during the entire ordeal; never for a moment visibly shaken. Her wisdom and strength had been unbelievable.

Trying to Relax

The summer of 1974 was trying. I was upset about repeating the entire year, but resigned myself to it. Iris and I decided to go camping. We bought camping equipment and went to a lake called Thompson Lake, near the Helderberg Mountains. When we got there, I was the only Black person. At first, it didn't bother me but as we walked around the camp, I felt intimidated. Perhaps because I was a Black and was with Iris, who was white. No one said anything to us. It was just the stare. This was a beautiful lake on the side of the camp where I went fishing in the morning early before Iris got up. I didn't catch anything worth talking about. I just relaxed, throwing the line in and watching the little red and white float move up and down in the green water; then, dip under, as I was pulled by a small fish. I wondered where all the Black people were; didn't they know about Thompson Lake?

It was the same atmosphere as when I went to Lake George with Steve and his wife. I was the only Black person I saw. I began to feel that somebody wasn't letting Black people onto some of the good things in life. We enjoyed our camping trip and vowed to do it often. It helped me to forget some things I wanted to forget.

I tried not going to the medical school, because I felt rejected and humiliated. Iris was trying hard to keep me balanced; the more she consoled me, the more I sulked. I knew that there were trying days ahead. I was on a long journey that would challenge every fiber in my being.

Iris told me God hadn't left me alone to fend for myself, but at that time, I felt He did. I had never thought I would charge God for my troubles, but I felt He left me alone in the kindling flames of this life. It really wasn't my intention to put Him in the background when I failed my wife and my vocation, but I was afraid His promises were not enough to keep me going. I made the excuse that Iris didn't understand me. Iris knew this and that is why she constantly talked to me about God. "Buddy," she would say, "God is not going to leave you alone, He is going to fulfill His promise to you."

God and Religion

We went to a Baptist church on Albany's "other side of the tracks." There really weren't any train tracks separating where we lived from the church. The imaginary track identified where the Black neighborhood was beyond. It reminded me of Harlem, New York where Black people hung out on the front steps of brownstone apartment buildings; all the aspects of how colorful I feel by Black people being present. They were cooling out, hanging near the local liquor store and going in and out of the little grocery store (with its high prices). Children were running up and down the street in the midst of garbage and broken glass. Adults were looking out windows at all the commotion in the street. It was familiar and typical to me. I had seen it all before, even to some extent in Red Hook. The made-up slang words, the remote handshakes, the hugging and the kissing that give Black people much of their inner support in the midst of racism. I understood it and why we felt compelled to those things, some of the few things that bind Black people together, besides our color.

One Sunday morning we put on our best clothes and went to the other side of the tracks on Clinton Avenue. We went to Reverend Roland's church, which I don't remember the name. I do remember it was a Baptist church. It was a huge concrete structure. My first impression was where these Black people got this historic sanctuary. It was probably given, or sold to them after so many Black people moved into the neighborhood. That is how it's done. If too many of us move into a neighborhood, the whites run like hell. A good strategy would be to stay where you are; then, Blacks can't move in.

When we walked into the main sanctuary, Sunday school was in progress. Rev. Roland was teaching and he was on the topic of tobacco companies' sales, profits, and employees. He stated that if the tobacco business were halted, there would be many people out of work and that was justification to support it. He wasn't condoning smoking. He was just concerned about its effect on the economy. I differed with him and verbally stated so publicly. Eyes and ears were attentive while I spoke. Rev. Roland and I started arguing. Immediately Iris and I vowed not to return to the church.

We tried other churches in Albany and none satisfied us. We were invited to a church function by someone who knew we were Christians, and met a woman who was called Mother Smith. We met Mother Smith at a church we visited. Mother Smith attended a church called Refreshing Springs Church of God and Christ. She was full of energy. She grabbed our hands and asked Iris and me to attend her church in Schenectady, New York. It was only fifteen miles from Albany. She had a gleam in her eyes and a smile on her face. As she talked to us, I saw her face tense when she spoke about God. I believed she had the kind of heart that cared for people. We told her we would visit.

The following Sunday we went to Refreshing Springs Church of God and Christ. They were meeting in a small building. The service was charged with fast music, speaking in tongues, and seasoned throughout with bursts of Hallelujah. A woman, well dressed, sat on the left side in front of the church looking elegant. She held her head high, praising God and occasionally saying, "Let Him have His way, Doll baby." (She was coaxing someone in allowing God to fellowship with him or her.) I came to know her as Sister Georgetta Dix. Sister Dix was beautiful and had a heart for people hurting and needing God. And if a person believed they didn't need God, she knew differently. She was strong spiritually and a lighthouse in the community. People knew and loved Sister Georgetta Dix. Her husband, Rev. Eugene Dix, who had passed away, founded refreshing Springs Church. Sister Dix was still in love with him and didn't hesitate to tell it. She took an immediate liking to us, and the feeling was mutual. The service was high-spirited, as most Pentecostal services are. I don't remember who was speaking that day but the message was dynamic.

They Loved Gospel Music

We met a couple named Michael and Margie Owens and they had two children. Michael was outspoken, being very positive about his ability to keep my attention with his gift of speaking. His wife Margie was a bit reserved, but nice and introduced herself to Iris; then, to me. They invited us to their home and we accepted the invitation. That Sunday afternoon we went to their house in Albany. Margie fed us her famous fried chicken with vegetables and plenty to drink. I found out later that there was always plenty of Kool-Aid to drink because Michael had a large glass all the time. Margie satisfied him. I enjoyed Michael's company and adored Margie.

Our going to Refreshing Springs was to become an integral part of our lives. We met a Puerto Rican couple named Ephraim and Yoli Donez, who were from New York City. Ephraim was college-educated, working with a community health center called Carver Health Center. Ephraim was bright and reserved. Yoli was the typical homemaker, taking care of their daughter and being a wife to Ephraim. They were a happy couple. We saw them for the first time when they came to Refreshing Springs Church. They sat in the back of the church in the middle section. I noticed Ephraim moving his head from side to side, back and forth while the music was playing and the song, "I'm Going All the Way with the Lord" was being sang. He had that Puerto Rican rhythm for which Blacks are supposed to be known. When the music stopped, he stopped with it, but I noticed a smile on his face. Yoli sat next to him trying to control the children, not appearing to enjoy the service very much. Sister Dix stood in the front, as near to the middle as possible with a microphone saying, "This is the little church in the heart of the city, with the people of the city in its heart." She said this every Sunday morning after the choir marched down the aisle (Michael and Margie were in the choir).

Running Like Hell

Refreshing Springs Church moved from the little building to a massive church edifice with stained-glass windows. I remember our first time in the building. A white minister, who was the pastor, said his congregation would turn the keys over to Refreshing Springs Church. It was the last time his congregation (which was white) would be worshiping in the sanctuary. Apparently the neighborhood had turned Black and Hispanic so the whites, as usual, ran like hell out of Clifton Hill (the ghetto section of

Schenectady), and surrendered the neighborhood to the incoming peoples from other places. The same thing, which occurred in Albany on Clinton Avenue (in the Arbor Hill section), was occurring in Schenectady. The pastor gave a strong message to the white and Black congregations. As if he were speaking from a megaphone he said, "I hope and pray that at some time we can find ourselves worshiping in the same house of God." He and the few whites who were with him bid the building and the Blacks in it farewell and the service was terminated. It's a shame that some people don't feel they can live with Blacks, much less worship God with them. They must think Black people are crashing down doors to hang out with them. It's not true, and I don't believe it ever will be. Therefore, the neighborhoods had changed for all time, and even the so-called houses of God took up other residence, and ran like hell.

God's Shadow Over Me

After church, Michael, Margie, Ephraim, Yoli, Iris, and I huddled together and we all became friends. This friendship was a part of God's protective shadow over me. We spent a lot of time together and many of my great moments were with them.

Medical school was still a major issue ahead of me. Even though I had to repeat the school year, and had resigned myself to it, it was a burden upon Iris's and my shoulders. I didn't tell my new friends about my plight. I didn't want them to think I was not good enough to be in the prestigious private medical college that was highly praised in the tri-city area of Troy, Schenectady, and Albany. The hospital with which the school was connected took care of people as far away as 75 miles. I had put myself in the midst of this highly charged atmosphere, and was frightened to death of being a failure.

Washington, D.C.

Before the summer of 1974 ended, I took Iris to Washington, D.C. We got in our old Ford Torino (with the bald tires) and traveled more than 350 miles one-way. We stopped in New York City to visit our families. For the same reason I didn't tell my friends, I didn't tell them I had to repeat the year. I didn't want them to think I couldn't become a doctor.

When we got to Washington, we checked into the Howard Johnson's Hotel and had a ball. The only damper on our vacation was Iris's almost drowning in the swimming pool. I forgot she couldn't swim and I threw her in on the deep side. She was going down for the third time before I rescued her. The remainder of our vacation was great.

I was upset about repeating the school year and I deliberately arrived at school two days late to let the school officials believe that I was taking the repeating of the year without stress. I was notified by the registrar's office that they had called my mother to find out if I were going to return to school. No one told my parents that I had to repeat the year.

Repeating the School Year

When the summer ended, I returned to studying Physiology and Biochemistry. The Chairman of the promotion's committee told me that it would be my choice to repeat the subjects I passed, but the school would not force me to take them. I didn't want to take Psychiatry, Gross Anatomy, Histology, Neuroanatomy, Biostatistics and Epidemiology all over again. The committee allowed me to sit in with the second-year class, if I had the time. I opted to sit in the Hematology course. I found it interesting and not as difficult to understand as Physiology. Some of the faculty members were upset that I was given these options, but apparently there was nothing they could do. I studied my behind off and prayed to God to help me the second time around, and He did.

I passed my first set of Physiology and Biochemistry exams. One of the Physiology professors told me don't have a false sense of security because some students who do well on the first test may do terribly on the second, if they don't study as hard. He didn't have to tell me anything about studying, because I knew I had to read those textbooks for longer hours than my classmates did.

Four new Black students were in my class. Richard and Loretta were both from New York; Richard via the island of Jamaica in the West Indies, and Loretta from Brooklyn. Both of them were having a stormy time with Biochemistry and Physiology. Loretta kept to herself, but Richard and I became friends. His wife, Barbara, was studying to be a nurse and they had two children in Jamaica living with Richard's mother. Barbara was a Christian and Richard had not committed himself to any religion as far as I knew. I tutored Richard in Biochemistry and Physiology toward the end of the course. Loretta did some crying over her struggles. I was able to relate to them well. Both of them knew I was repeating the year.

Frustration

I went down to the railroad tracks to hunt when I had the time. Although I saw many rabbits run past me, I wasn't quick enough. Sometimes I sat on a rock thinking about my future. I thought about Red Hook many times. My heart and soul were in Red Hook projects. I often thought about the people with whom I grew up and who were still living there. Some of them got involved in drugs, and they were literally losing their lives. I wanted to help them and there was nothing that I could do. I had my own problems. My marriage to Iris wasn't going well. We constantly fought about my wanting to go to Brooklyn each time holidays came and even on some weekends. Iris wanted to spend time with me because she hardly had any quality time with me. I was either studying or we were in church or she was working.

My temper flared out of control and many times, I got violent. I smashed up things in the house and fought with Iris. I knew that I was wrong, and each time I did it, I felt terrible and apologized later, but the damages were done. I did not know that I would pay for the rest of my life for what I was doing.

Fried Chicken and Friends

When we got the chance, we had dinner at Michael and Margie's house (the couple we became friends with at Refreshing Springs Church). Margie would feed us her famous fried chicken and we enjoyed it. After eating, we lounged around their house "teasing" Michael. He was a bit heavy, and would sit at the table and eat his heart out; then, fill a big beverage glass, then fill it again. Margie would sit at the table and shake her head. It was all fun for us, and Michael never got offended; he just enjoyed the food.

On occasion, Iris and I went to Ephraim and Yoli's apartment (our Puerto Rican friends whom we met at Refreshing Springs Church) and had lunch or dinner with them on a Sunday afternoon. Ephraim was particular about many things and he encouraged me to be more disciplined. He would even go so far as to polish the soles of his shoes. The first time I saw him do it, I didn't believe he was serious.

I thought that he was joking. When I saw the serious look on his face, I was shocked. Another time we went to the Price Chopper Supermarket (local supermarket), where he opened a carton of eggs and touched and rolled over each one to make sure that they were not cracked. I openly laughed at my friend and he laughed with me. I loved Ephraim because he truly cared about my family and me. He had a beautiful heart. Michael, in contrast, loved my family and me also, but I had to work on our friendship. Ephraim and Michael's wives were super and I adored them both.

Golden Friends

We met some new friends who attended Refreshing Springs Church who were a bit older than we were; John and Doris Belton. The Beltons loved us from the beginning without effort. He was the Principal at an inner-city school in Schenectady and she worked for the state government. They lived comfortably in a modest house in a beautiful neighborhood. He was cool, calm, and assertive. He and his wife always projected a positive image and they were my cherished older friends. I respected and loved them dearly and they were to take a very important role in the health of my mind and my marriage.

I continued to pass all my tests in Physiology and Biochemistry. School was going great and my relationship with Iris was good. One time a professor approached me and said, "Wilbert, it's nice to see you here, I'm glad you're not bitter having to repeat the year."

I looked at him and said, "Thank you." I didn't have the time to be bitter, for I was pleased with myself.

Beating the System

I enjoyed our Christmas holidays and New Year also. I passed Biochemistry and Physiology. I did it! I beat the system again: the system that was never geared to help me succeed or encourage me to be a better person or a doctor or any professional for that matter. The same system that hurt my father for just being Black. The same system that geared my mother to work in factories and clean house for people. The same system that reminds all Black people that we are not accepted fully as Americans because we are not white enough. The same system that reminds all Black people that we are not accepted fully as Americans because we are not white enough.

Chapter 10
Roads

Thou has beset me behind and before,
And laid thine hand on me.

Psalm 139:5

During the summer of 1975 I worked with Dr. Marjorie Smith in East Berne, New York on a summer preceptorship (medical student working in a private doctor's office) on a farm in the Helderberg Mountains in the country. I enjoyed going into the country and especially liked the Helderberg Mountains because the area was so beautiful. I always looked for deer crossing the road or peeking from the edge of the woods. Dr. Smith's office was about twenty-five miles from Albany. She was a white doctor who took care of white people who lived in the surrounding area. I was a little apprehensive about going there because I had not been around country folks from any rural area and my experience with whites in general had been painful. When I called Dr. Smith about the position, I told her I was a Black medical student and wanted to know if I could work with her that summer in her office. "I don't care what color you are," she said and told me that she would have an answer for me in a few weeks.

When I called her back a few weeks later, she agreed to the preceptorship. I felt foolish thinking that my color was the most important credential I had. The preceptorship offered $600 for two months, and we certainly needed it to supplement our weekly income of $115 from Iris's job.

Dr. Smith was friendly, to the point, and open with me. She would not guarantee me that there would not be any racial problems, but she assured me she was on my side. She told me she just wanted things to work well. I visited her office before the preceptorship to see how the patients would react to me. When I got to the farm, I saw a bunch of cows and a big barn where they milked them. Dr. Smith was practicing in her home; there on the farm. She started out in a trailer and built around it. It had a beautiful fireplace and wood logs were stacked around it. It was my kind of setting. I loved animals and one of my boyhood dreams was to one day live on a farm.

She introduced me to her husband, Harry Garry. He was a big guy with a gentle disposition, and I found out later that he didn't like seeing interracial couples. He never said anything to me about it but Dr. Smith, in her openness, told me. Harry was always nice to me and if he had a "hang-up" about seeing white and Black couples, it never appeared to affect our relationship. He treated me as if I were his son.

From the first day, I was seeing patients. I was well received. When I told Dr. Smith how well her patients treated me, she said, "That's because my patients know I wouldn't put them in bad hands, they trust me."

I enjoyed watching Dr. Smith take care of her patients. She was very attentive to their needs and I learned a lot. She told me that she was sure things would work well and looked forward to seeing me in a few weeks. I was to commute to her office daily from Albany, which was about twenty-five miles away. Iris would stay home.

When the time arrived for me to work in her office, I was excited. My first official day went well and Dr. Smith was supportive. I was shy with her patients and kept thinking someone was going to refuse my care because of my color. Harry was encouraging and he kept talking to me all day, wanting to know if things were going OK. Harry ran the dairy farm, which they lived on. Their three children, a girl and two boys, helped him with the farm chores. I liked seeing them interact. We ate dinner at noon each day and while at the dinner table, there was a friendly bickering between the Smith family. It was strange for me to think of eating in the afternoon and calling it dinner. Dr. Smith told me that we need our biggest and best meal at noon because that's when most people expend the greatest energy. It made a lot of sense to me. I never saw so much meat and milk on one table at one time. With all the cows around, we had plenty of meat and milk daily. I got along well with her children and I believe they enjoyed having me with them.

As the preceptorship continued, Dr. Smith gave me more responsibility in the office. There were a few people who wanted to see her and I understood why, because she was both loving and considerate and they trusted her.

Some people drove many miles to see her and it was disappointing to them to be taken care of by another health provider. I made many home visits with her to elderly people. We also visited a nursing home weekly. She hugged her patients, held their hands, and let them know that she cared.

We had an emergency call one day. A man was pinned under his tractor. He was riding it on an incline and it turned over. When we arrived, he was trapped under the tractor, in pain, but he wouldn't accept any pain medication. She stayed until he was freed and taken by ambulance to Albany Medical Center Hospital.

I only had one experience in Dr. Smith's office that shook me. She asked me to see a little boy who was with his mother, whom I had treated before. On this particular visit, his mother stood attentively watching me. When his father came into the exam room, he looked at me with piercing eyes. As I talked to him and his wife, his facial expression stayed fixed on me. I started playing with his son and he became upset, and I left the room. I'm not sure if this incident was racially directed at me, but I never had any other encounters, which I thought was because of my color.

Most of the patients expressed to Dr. Smith that they liked me very much. She enjoyed telling me things like that because she knew I needed to hear them. She told me that she knew I had come a long way from Red Hook projects in Brooklyn to Albany Medical College and that I had the opportunity to be an asset to many people in the ghetto.

Dr. Smith was a good doctor and my friend. She never failed to try to encourage me. We talked a lot about racism, and the system. She listened to me and consoled me when she felt it was appropriate. I learned a great deal about preconceived reactions and stereotyping people. For the most part, the people whom I thought would react adversely to me did just the opposite. It was my first experience in building my confidence as a future doctor. I will always remember and love Dr. Marjorie Smith and Harry Garry, her husband. The last I heard, she is still practicing medicine and he is still running the dairy farm in the Helderberg Mountains.

Where Have We Gone?

I began seeing racism as a permanent fixture in America. Like even in conservative upstate New York, there were clear signs that the people who have made racism a part of their lives did not intend to remove it. I was seeing first-hand how it affected Black people. There were two

Black doctors on the staff at Albany Medical College Hospital; Dr. Alls, a radiologist and nephrologists, Dr. Hinds. Neither of them were involved in any committed way to alleviating the ills that we Blacks suffered emotionally in the medical college, as far as I knew. I went to Dr. Alls and she just told me to work harder. The fact that the school had not dealt with Black students in the past three years, she was Black and that didn't seem to make any difference to her. She could have involved herself at least by trying to help me in getting help from professors. Dr. Hinds had a comfortable position at the veteran's hospital and he never sat with the Black students to see how we were doing. Maybe Dr. Hind's being married to a white woman had something to do with how quiet he was through my first year in medical school.

None of the professors who taught us were Black or Puerto Ricans. The Chairman of Physiology was a white from Mississippi, who acted very distant to us Blacks. I wasn't surprised when the Biochemistry professor said he wasn't sure if raising his children in a white environment was good or not. I could tell he had a feeling of relief that he kept his children away from Blacks. He didn't fool me for a moment. I believed he was a bigot just like the Pharmacology professor, Dr. Reynold. Apparently, that's why it was so easy for him to be cold and apathetic with me. He didn't take into consideration that I was from the projects in Brooklyn and what it might have taken me just to reach the corridors of that great college. I may have been just another Black guy to him who thought I was good enough to have what white people have and he was going to tell me differently. I'll never forget how he told me boldly that he didn't think I could make it through medical school. He said it entirely without effort.

A Southern Gentleman

Dr. Cowden was a Southern gentleman. I remembered his words to me, telling me he was from the Deep South, and Blacks were the least of all people he thought he would stand up for at that time. I believe he was hurting inside for me. He understood the injustice and hypocrisy in which the school was involved, taking federal money for each Black head; then not caring if they sank or swam. I remember how upset he was, blaming the system for giving Blacks a hard time. He sounded off in front of me and said, "It's a shame, Wilbert, this goddamn country hasn't moved beyond this. I don't have any special liking for Blacks but you've been handed a dirty deal and it upsets me."

He told me there were some people who were out to force me to repeat the year, and there was nothing that he could do about it. I saw the hurt in his eyes. He was a man of integrity who followed his convictions, white or not, and I respected him. It was the first time any white person ever told me personally, that he wasn't fond of Blacks.

I was very critical concerning racism and bigotry. I didn't hold my tongue, and besides my inexperience dealing with white people, it cost me a lot. Iris kept telling me to shut my mouth and concentrate on learning. She called me a rebel. She was suffering my pain. When I was hurt, she was the only one I could go to for true comfort. I knew she wouldn't play a game with me because she loved me.

Sticking With Me

Iris was doing well at her job in the medical college library. Everyone at the library loved Iris. Even the professors who didn't care about me were polite and kind with her. Iris, in spite of her disapproval of some of my ways and actions, stuck by me. I was her man and she never let me down not once.

I was the one who let her down many times and blamed it on what I was going through. Not that I don't believe my reasons for letting her down, but it was never ever justified. I needed to grow up and learn how to deal better in the face of adversity.

I loved people, trusted them, and wanted them to love me. This is the way I was raised; to care. It was what my mother taught me and it was in grained in my soul. My father's stubbornness was inside of me, and in many ways, I was like him. I wasn't ashamed of anything about myself and I believed I was raised well.

The Precious Hand of God

Church and religion had become a greater part of our life. I went to church a lot. On Sunday mornings, I was able to release some of the hurt, anger and frustration I had pinned up inside. It was at Refreshing Springs Church of God and Christ in Schenectady that I was able to release myself to God. The people at the church who cared about me and loved me had no idea what I was struggling with. I held these things even from my friends. All of my friends were important to me. They were like a shield from the blistering heat of racism over me, that's why I saw them as the shadow of God in my life. They had no idea what role they played in their relationship to me.

Elder Mac Daniel

Our pastor, Lovell Mc Daniel, whom we referred to as "Elder Mac," was precious to me. He was raised in Brooklyn, New York. He had the gift of oratory and held me spellbound every time he spoke. He had a way of unfolding the Scriptures from the pulpit to the pews in such a way that people drew near to God and sought to know more about Him. Elder Mac wasn't your typical Pentecostal minister and I once heard a member in the congregation refer to him as such. He didn't throw a bunch of Bible passages at you sprinkled with flowery words from the pulpit. He spoke to the souls of the people and they received him well. Sometimes he would sit with me and talk about non-spiritual matters. I believe he understood as a man first, then as a minister that I needed his attention. I spoke with him about many things, but never about my pain at school. He gave me the impression that he thought the world of me. I listened to him sermonize many times and he never failed to have a positive message. When Elder Mac wasn't at church, the congregation shrank. Elder Mac lived in Waterbury, Connecticut with his beautiful wife and three children (who were adorable). They weren't angel children, but respectful of their parents and the members of the congregation. His wife carried herself with dignity.

He drove for more than two hours from Waterbury, Connecticut to Schenectady twice per week to minister. We didn't have a permanent pastor and the people wanted Elder Mac to fill the position. He was torn between being established in Connecticut and uprooting to Schenectady, New York. It was a big decision for him and his family and he never made the move. He did look at homes, but still stayed in Waterbury. I don't know what his reasons were for not moving, but he did tell me it wasn't as easy as some people believed for him to move. I feel he compensated for it because he spent a considerable amount of time in Schenectady. He didn't do a half job ministering to us or the people in Waterbury, Connecticut from what I heard. He spent many counseling hours speaking to the souls of people.

Mrs. Mc Daniel was always polite with me and smiled often when I spoke with her. I could tell she was being tried by fire. Some people looked down at Sister Mc Daniel and spoke ill of her, and she knew it. Her husband was feeding the flock and giving his life for it in many ways. She watched it and endured it.

False Security

I made a new friend at Refreshing Springs Church, Richard. Richard was a fascinating guy who was an ex-pimp and ex-drug dealer. I loved to hear him give his testimony. When it was time in church for people to get up and tell the congregation what God has done for them, up popped Richard. He'd say, "I wanna thank my Lord and Savior Jesus Christ for what He took me from. He truly has saved my soul." I used to be 'everything,' you name it, that's what I used to be, yawl don't know what I used to be but I know. I ran me some women. I was a devil and the Lord rescued me from the streets. "I'm gonna try to serve the Lord for the rest of my life. Yawl pray for me." If one kept his eyes on him, one might catch him doing a Holy Shuffle (dance in the Spirit). Richard would get "amens" and "hallelujahs" resounding off the chandeliers. Richard had a limp, so his legs and hands were not well coordinated. As he put it, he was so full of hell when he was pimping and drugging it up, God had to stop him by allowing him to be in a car accident. He was laid up in the hospital for months and nearly died. He credits his survival to his Lord and Savior Jesus Christ.

I liked Richard. He represented the salvage of some of the worst street people who believed they were safe from tragedy, padded with the false security of money and things. He represented hope to me. I was proud of Richard because he had a heart for people and was very active with ex-drug addicts and alcoholics.

Richard once told me if he had known me when he was pimping, he would have had me take care of his women and I would have made lots of money. I will always thank Richard for his testimony and his honesty (and for offering me a job, even if it were too late).

God's Love

John and Doris Belton were two very special people to us, and many other people. We affectionately called John "Brother Belton" and Doris, "Sister Belton." We never referred to them without these distinctions. They loved us like family and we loved them the same way. When we had marital problems, they were always willing to help us. They never got involved in our business unless we invited them to. They lived in a beautiful house in a predominantly white section called Niskayuna, not far from the city line of Schenectady.

I was encouraged by the way; they took care of their belongings. They had a nice motor home in their driveway and a little portable swimming pool for their daughter Jane. One time we were at church and after the service, I saw Brother Belton with a motorcycle helmet in his hand. He told me to look across the street from the church. He had bought a motorcycle. At first, I didn't believe it was his until he put the key in the ignition. He gave me a ride and it was great. Brother Belton was unpredictable and I'm sure that's one of the reasons I liked him. Sister Belton was as sweet as anyone could be. I never saw her angry and she treated me like a golden child.

When Iris and I were having financial problems, Brother and Sister Belton came to our house and prayed with us. We didn't have any food to offer them. Brother Belton pulled me to the side and asked me if I needed any money. He had no idea we didn't have any food or drink for them. I told him we were OK. He gave me two ten-dollar bills and told me to pay him back whenever I could and if I couldn't, it was OK.

I know by experience that Brother and Sister Belton were some beacons of light for many people and if it were not for their openness, a few people would have had more problems than they already had.

Sex and Medicine

My second year in medical school took off like a rocket. The first course was Hematology. I understood the material because it made sense and the professor made a world of difference. Professor Tartaglia, who was a medical doctor, taught the course and he made it interesting. Other required courses were Community Medicine, Microbiology, Human Reproduction, and Introduction to Medicine. Albany Medical College was a bit aggressive in teaching us sexual human reproduction.

A guy in my class had a Ph.D. in sexology from Johns Hopkins University. He helped in the course construction. He told me he had a basement full of pornographic material from his study. Some of the material was included in the course. The college wanted to desensitize the students sexually before we took Obstetrics and Gynecology. They put a notice in the classified section of the newspaper asking women who had a number of deliveries to apply for pelvic examinations by the medical students. Three women were picked.

Our first desensitization session was in the auditorium where we had our lectures. We sat with popcorn waiting for the cinema "The Devil and Mrs. Jones" to start. We were wild during the movie. For a so-called pornographic movie, I wasn't impressed. We didn't know it, but the heavy porno material was to follow in the next couple of weeks. They showed us hard porno where women were having sex with animals and posing with their sex organs, men and women having hard-core sex, and homosexuals playing with each other. It was all sexually stimulating. One session they showed us a Masters and Johnson film where a woman was hooked up to wires and diagnostic devices, which included measuring her vaginal, clitoral and vital signs to self-masturbation. I had a hard time watching that one. I don't think that there was a person in the auditorium who wasn't sexually excited by the stuff. We also had a lecture where they had a transvestite in the audience and he was sitting next to me, looking and smelling very much like a woman. When they introduced him and he got up and spoke, I was shocked. I didn't recognize "he" was a man with a sex change operation. The whole course was freaky and I know it didn't desensitize me. For the culmination of the course we had to do pelvic examinations on the women who responded to the article in the newspaper. When it was my turn, the nurse said to me, "Don't worry, we only watch your hands." They were expecting some of the guys, if not all, to get erections. Who could get an erection in that setting? I discredited the course for failure to desensitize me like a rat or a monkey in a Physiology lab.

I didn't enjoy Microbiology. It took me back to undergraduate school. At one point, I was having difficulty with it. The professor pulled me to the side and asked me if I wanted to repeat the year again. I looked at him as if he were a crazy fool, because I wasn't doing that badly in his course. At the end of the semester, I passed my courses, including Microbiology.

There weren't any overt incidences of racism in my second year. For the most part, I was comfortably learning the subjects. I began to feel a part of the school. I was still disturbed that we had so few Blacks in the school. The one or two Hispanics we had hid themselves between the white and Jewish students, which I did not expect to happen.

I remember one Hispanic female, Pam. I never heard her speak of Hispanics nor push for greater numbers in the school. I did see her hang out with a few white and Jewish students. When I saw her, I felt bad toward her. I spoke with her a few times about the horrible minority record at the college and she never had anything significant to say.

The Rat Race

It was definitely a rat race in medical school. If one couldn't keep up with the pack, he or she was lost in a separate world. One girl in my class was having emotional problems and she went crazy. The promotion's committee allowed her, as crazy as she was, to take a year leave of absence from school and to return the following year. In contrast, the only Asian student in our class was a male who also went crazy. They promised him if he saw a Psychiatrist and took a leave of absence for six months he could come back to school. He went to Manhattan, New York's Chinatown and stayed with his family. I found out later that they did not intend to let him back into his class. We never saw him again. We heard he tried to return, but failed to be re-enrolled. Double standards like this, made me angry. Racism wasn't easy to hide, and some of the professors were denying that it existed. They were either blind, ignorant or a bunch of liars. During the next semester, I continued to study hard, and I passed all my courses. I was due to graduate to the third-year class.

My grants and loans had run out. I didn't have enough money to complete school or even buy enough food. We went to the food stamp office, applied for food stamps, and got them. For $12, we were able to purchase $114 worth of food. Every two weeks I religiously went to the bank around the corner from our brownstone apartment and exchanged the coupon for stamps. One time I believed the teller mistreated me because she spoke rough verbally with me, so I told her off. I called the bank manager. He told me since I told her off; there was no need to chastise her. I stormed out of the bank, upset.

Not Enough to Eat

Sometimes we didn't have meat to eat or milk to drink so I went down to the train tracks to shoot squirrels, but this time for food. I would put the smelly thing in a pot of boiling water and Iris and I forced ourselves to eat it. One time Iris's parents came up from Brooklyn and caught us boiling one in a pot. Her mother Doris said, "What is that smell?" I tried to hide it, but it was too late. When we told them what it was, they commanded we get rid of it. They broke out with a cardboard box that had steak, plantains, and vegetables in it. They were great and were always willing to help us. We just never let them know what we were going through. My family also had no idea we were at welfare status either.

Black Students

From the beginning, the Black students were unsure about each other. Like most Blacks, they had not learned that we needed to help each other. They didn't understand, or were not willing to stand for what was right, even though the odds were not in their favor. At least as Black people, we are free to choose our own destiny with dignity. However, most Black people had to worry about their survival and it put some in a frame of mind that shackled them. Though the chains of slavery had been released a long time ago, minds were now shackled with fear of reprisal from white people. Every Black person lives daily with the reality that in most situations we are vulnerable to the whims of most whites, even where the law is concerned. It's a part of America at her worst behavior.

From the first time I met Jimmy in the school lobby, it was like being with a white boy in black face. He used phrases, which I wasn't accustomed to hearing in Brooklyn or any other place I had been. He kept showing his teeth and laughing aloud and never uttered a word about Black people. Maybe because he didn't know much about them. His father was in the military and Jimmy was stationed with him all around the world. I knew Jimmy's exposure to the outside world was greater than any of ours and maybe that made him more open to white people and narrowed-minded to his own; even though both his parents were Black. He just wasn't raised to relate to Blacks. As a result, I had mixed feelings about Jimmy. I liked him at first because he wasn't a threat to me. Later, however, I disliked him because he never saw me. He never saw my near-end in Albany Medical School.

Oswald was a character. He was the "uppity Black man" from New York City via the island of Jamaica, West Indies. He liked to use the "nigger word" like it was conventional and acceptable anywhere. He did, however, have enough sense not to use it in the presence of whites. He was what I call a conventional Negro. He was a hypocrite around whites. I guess many of us Blacks are like that. It's like kissing up to "Massa boss" when he comes into camp; then, talking about how you'd like to beat him down when he leaves. Its slave mentality and it belongs to phony conventional Negroes who are frightened like hell around white people.

Oswald was smart academically. He wasn't as sharp with the academics as Jimmy was, but he held his own. Oswald was cold and calculating. He was a separatist. He said if all the "niggers" had to go back to Africa one day, he was going to Jamaica because he was a Jamaican, a true "Island Man." He let the rest of us know from the beginning that he wasn't one of us, but we were too caught up in the white stuff to deal with the Black stuff. Much to my surprise, I tolerated Oswald. Although I didn't think Oswald was a great human being, he was what he was because he was a victim of the Jamaican and American systems and didn't know it. He was as far removed from Black people as Jimmy was, but Jimmy had innocence about his position. I felt sorry for Jimmy.

Harrison was my man. He was an honorable human being full of energy. He didn't care if you were Black or white when it came down to dealing with you. He spoke his heart. He was a lot of fun and if anything, taught me how to eat Mary Jane candies in lecture class and kept me asking him for more. Harrison saw me. He understood my pain, tried to console, and heal me. "Buddy," he would say, "don't let these people shake you up. All they want to do is get you upset so you can flunk out; that's all they want. I know what I know and can't anybody tell me differently."

Harrison knew what the good comfortable life was like. His father was a dentist in California. Harrison had a Master's Degree from Howard University. He was driving a new Buick Le Mans. Sometimes he would pay me to wash it. I would wash that car and wish that I had one as nice. Harrison never talked down to me about any of the Black students. He did at times talk about how we as Black people need to stick together and that was our problem. The bottom line was Harrison didn't care what the professors thought about him. He was a lover boy. Sometimes he would sit in lecture class with a beautiful girl from Washington, D.C., and some of the professors would be checking him out. When he was kicked out of school, Professor Cowden told me personally, "We're gonna throw this guy Harrison the hell out of this school. He thinks everything is roses around here, bringing all these women to class. That guy failed every course he took, he didn't pass one. He's on his way out of here."

I should have had something to say to Professor Cowden about what I thought about my friend, but I didn't. Maybe I didn't because I was also shackled in my mind and didn't have the strength or courage to tell Professor Cowden not to talk about him the way he did. Maybe to some degree, bigotry and racism had me bound.

Harrison really told them all to go to hell the way he wanted to and that was good enough for me. He was intelligent and could have done well. I don't think his heart was in becoming a doctor anyhow.

When I think about brothers of mine, I see Black America clothed in someone else's garments. I see us still very much in slavery. I know it is a game, which has been played on us to believe we have to do some kind of shuffle for white people to survive. We don't have to shuffle for anyone, and if we do, it's been our choice, and we'll pay for it. Life is full of choices and some of them are very tough. Nonetheless, we can survive as people in America, and if we have to dance in fire, we will.

Dr. J.T. Henderson, a Black Doctor

That summer I worked with Dr. J.T. Henderson in Schenectady, N.Y., on a summer preceptorship. He was a Black family doctor. It was a wonderful experience. He was by far one of the most compassionate doctors whom I had ever met. His practice included both Black and white patients. All of the white patients who spoke to me were thoroughly happy with him and respected him very much. To my surprise, Black people who were not his patients spoke of him negatively. They had various reasons for not going to him, which were as far as I knew and it made no sense to me. Sometimes Black people are critical of their own kind because of their ignorance and preconceived ideas that if a person is Black and professional compared to a white, he can't be as good. This is a bunch of garbage and has no credible foundation. Black people have been successful in every field of life and have proven their ability to excel. Society has done a hell of a mind game on us. I feel most Blacks who knew Dr. Henderson took pride in him, because he was a Black professional. Some, however, were jealous because he had achieved an academic level, which they, as Blacks, had not. My experience working with him was contrary to anything, which I heard.

He constantly tried to build up my low self-esteem. He was a graduate of Fisk University and later Howard Medical School. He knew medicine well and enjoyed the interaction with his patients. I was in awe of him. He was the first Black doctor with whom I had the opportunity to rub shoulders; just being with him boosted my self-worth.

Dr. Henderson spoke with me often about my outlook on racial issues. He believed that one's respect for himself was the ultimate in success. He didn't let what people believed about him surface in his interaction and relationship with them. He told me that one time a white woman was referred to him. When she walked in his office asking to see Dr. Henderson, he told her he was Dr. Henderson. She told him that she was looking for another Doctor Henderson. He assured her that he was the only Dr. Henderson in Schenectady, New York. She told him she made a mistake and walked out. He told me the story with such coolness and ease. He even had a smile on his face. He said he wasn't concerned about people's reactions to him as a Black doctor because he saw himself as a doctor first. I watched his ability to heal the sick and he did that very well.

My direct involvement with patients in his office was least. I did a lot of listening and watching. Many times, I sat in his office and read. It was different from the preceptorship I had with Dr. Marjorie Smith. I don't know why he didn't give me more hands-on with his patients, and I thought about it a lot.

Each day at 12:00 noon, we had lunch, which for him was usually peanut butter and jelly sandwiches, Coca-Cola, and ice cream. This was really the most enjoyable part of my day, watching him put away what I called the "bomb." After lunch, he would insist that I go upstairs and lay down in the bed. He didn't care if I fell asleep. He just wanted me resting in the bed. Most of the time I read a book or waited for the time to pass.

When Dr. Henderson relaxed, it was usually talking with his beautiful wife. They had a good relationship. She called him "Hon" and he would call her "Babe." He told me a couple of times that he loved his wife very much and she was one of the best things that ever happened to him.

She would often speak gently with me about my career and assured me that things would turnout well, no matter how they appeared, if I remained strong and confident. Often she saved me from school. I adored the way she balanced her time at home doing what needed to be done and enjoying it. I felt very close to her.

Most of the time we saw routine day-to-day medical problems like sore throats, bronchitis, urinary tract infections, hypertension, and diabetes. A couple of times a week a drug detail sales clerk came into the office.

One day a woman came into the office complaining of a headache. Before Dr. Henderson could check her blood pressure, she made a high-pitched scream, grabbed her head, and fell on the floor. I wasn't sure what happened, but Dr. Henderson knew right away that she suffered a ruptured blood vessel in her brain. He called the ambulance and they took her to the hospital. When I saw her in the hospital the following day, her face was swollen and she was connected to a respirator. Tubes were going into her and coming out everywhere. The machines were making their customary sounds. I believed that she didn't have a chance to live. Dr. Henderson told me that her condition was poor and the likelihood that she would live was slim. I felt sorry for her. One day she was standing in Dr. Henderson's exam room and the next day she was fighting for her life. Dr. Henderson visited his patients each day in the hospital and we visited her each day until she stopped breathing on her own.

One day while sitting in Dr. Henderson's office reading a book, Iris called me. I knew right away that something was wrong. She spoke to me with shallowness, as if she couldn't tell me what was on her mind. Then she told me the bad news. "Buddy, you didn't pass your national board exam." It hit me like a ton of bricks. She started to cry and apologized for opening my letter. She felt terrible about the disappointment I was feeling. We both knew that I needed to pass the exam to start the process of getting a license to practice medicine after medical school. Once again, Iris was sharing my pain.

I asked Dr. Henderson if I could go home. I explained to him that I had failed the national board exam and just couldn't work the rest of the day. He told me that I shouldn't take it too hard because I had another chance to pass it. I spent the evening with Iris and remained depressed. She tried to console me, but I was too stuck in self-pity.

What I took away with me from the preceptorship with Dr. Henderson was priceless. He gave me a gift; himself. I understood much better that I needed balance in my life. However, more than that, I needed self-confidence. I realized that Blacks were solid competitors in the field of medicine. It established a basis of Black pride for me. When the preceptorship was over, Dr. Henderson and his wife invited us to dinner. It was a happy parting. I gained an enormous amount of respect for him and loved his wife. In her own way, and probably not even realizing it, she comforted me many times by just listening and speaking gently with me concerning my life. Her relationship with Dr. Henderson gave me a first-hand look at why Dr. Henderson was content. He and his wife loved each another deeply. I will never forget their warmth and the love they shared with me.

Chapter 11
Moving On

If I take the wings of the morning and dwell in the uttermost
Parts of the sea; even there shall thy hand lead me,
And thy right hand shall hold me.

Psalm 139:9,10

The snow and cold of the winter months in Albany took a heavy toll on Iris, because she was pregnant with our first child. I remember many times walking to school with her early in the morning. She had to be at work about the same time I had to start class. We had to stop on the way, so she could catch her breath. Our hands would be freezing, and I would switch my books from arm to arm while trying to keep Iris from falling on the ice. She braved the winter months and hardly complained of the weather. Sometimes it was so cold a few feet from the house we couldn't go any further; we'd turn our back to the wind and just stand there.

Shoshanna

Iris was in excellent health and her prenatal course was going well. I thought it would be easy to be pregnant and easy to deliver a baby. The evening she went into labor we waited until she couldn't bear the pain, and then I rushed her to the labor and delivery room. After the doctor examined her, she was sent home. They said she wasn't ready. I took her back a few hours later and they sent her home again. The third time I caught some of the amniotic fluid (birth water) in a bottle and proudly walked into the hospital with it. They registered her, put her in the bed and

171

she was in labor, huffing and puffing about how she wanted more water from the nurse. I felt she was being rude when she started demanding things be done for her. At that time in my career, I didn't know that's how women behave during labor. I got angry with her, walked out of the labor room, went to the student lounge, and started watching TV. About an hour later, I was called to the delivery room over the page. Iris was on the delivery table, but I didn't hear the page. I thought to myself, "It must be about time for Iris to have the baby."

I was casually going up the stairs. When I reached the delivery room, a nurse told me that I'd better hurry because my wife was having our first baby.

I rushed into the change room and put on the operating room clothes. I dashed into the delivery room, and there she was with her legs aimed at the ceiling, trying to deliver our child. The doctor was making everyone laugh.

"Pu-ha, pu-ha," he said in Spanish, and he was telling Iris to "push." He knew my wife spoke English, so he must have been trying to learn Spanish. He told her that the baby was not coming, and if she didn't push, he was going to get the forceps, clamp the baby's head and pull the baby out. Still nothing was coming, so he proved he wasn't joking.

"Nurse," he said, "get my forceps." The nurse brought in something wrapped like a baby. "Pu-ha, pu-ha," he screamed. His tone was one of jest, but he meant business. He then pulled huge spoons out of the towel wrap. "Pu-ha, pu-ha, I'm going to use these forceps."

I looked at Iris and said, "You better push, or he'll use the forceps."

"Pu-ha, pu-ha," he commanded once more.

Like magic, out came a bloody baby girl with a long head and big cheeks. I was shocked. "Am I going to take that home?" I wondered.

Iris was on the table, but half in another world. I told her the baby had ten toes and ten fingers and didn't tell her at the time that it scared me. I gave her a kiss, patted her on the head and left, carrying the baby to the transfer nursery. The nurses were asking me about a name for the baby. Iris and I had not really agreed on a name, so this was my opportunity to plug my choice for a name without any interference. "Shoshanna," I said.

"What?" the nurse asked.

"Shoshanna," I repeated. Shoshanna is a Hebrew word which means "lily" or "rose." Then there was the question of "How do you spell it?"

When Iris recovered, naturally she had some complaints. I did two things, which she didn't like. First, I left her twice, once before going into the delivery room and again just after the delivery. The second and perhaps the most important thing was that I named our baby without any further input from her. Nevertheless, "Shoshanna" was her name.

Iris soon got over the naming problem, and we simply enjoyed the presence of our new daughter. I called just about everyone of our family members in New York City and they were overjoyed.

When Iris left the hospital and came home, we were faced with a couple of problems; some old and some new. At the top of the list was my medical education. Then there still was the question of money and whether Iris was going to be able to return to work.

The $4,000, which I had needed and used to repeat the first year of medical school had left me, broke. My financial aid was exhausted. Banks and lending agencies really were waiting for needy medical students to snatch up their money and make a long-term commitment. As a result, I applied for a Public Health Scholarship. Within a few weeks, I was notified that the money was granted. I was very happy because I didn't want Iris to return to work. I knew that she and I both wanted her to stay home with Shoshanna. The scholarship paid for my tuition in full, which was $6,400, and we were given $750 tax-free to live on every month. She quit her job and became a full-time mother.

Chapter 12
The Hospital

Thine eyes did see my substance, yet being imperfect; and in
Thy book all my members were written, which in continuance
Were fashioned, when as yet there was none of them.

Psalm 139:16

I believed Psychiatry was a wasted discipline in medicine. I saw people with mental problems being spaced out on medications, which didn't seem to help them. I didn't like Psychiatry because I rarely saw people get well.

"Ron" was my first psychiatric patient. He came into our unit via the emergency room, handcuffed by the police. Ron lived on a farm and spent much of his time reading. He got a hold of The Late Great Planet Earth and proclaimed to be John the Baptist and Jesus Christ. His mother told me after he read the book; he locked himself in his room, refusing to talk to anyone.

Then one day he started praying for her, trying to cast demons out of her. He prayed with such zeal that he leaped at her and grabbed at her head; then ,ran away. When the police found him, he was lying in chicken manure beside the barn, saying he was John the Baptist. I was asked to care for him after the Chief Psychiatrist, Dr. Conner, injected him with a high dose of thorazine (a mind-controlling drug). He was diagnosed as having had a psychotic episode. After spending some time with Ron, I believed there was more to his experience than just a crazy episode. As the week passed, he continued to confirm his experience, though he had trouble speaking because of being drugged. He told me it was not fair to drug him, but when they found him, he was in a crazy state and needed to be calmed.

When the medication began to wear off, he went through the ward preaching to and counseling other patients concerning their problems. After a few days, he started writing poetry about all the staff members. It was very sensible and precise writing. His poetry became so popular that Dr. Conner wanted to read it. When Ron was better, he helped get a couple of other patients' heads together, because he was able to relate to them.

He was given the diagnosis of manic-depressive illness (a person who has this illness is depressed for months; then, crazy for a number of months). I wasn't sure that's what he had. Instead of contradicting the diagnosis, I suggested to Dr. Conner that he might consider decreasing or stopping Ron's medication of Thorazine, which is given to manic-depressive patients. Dr. Conner yelled at me and asked me if I wanted to throw Ron out of the hospital. I was stunned. I told him that my intent was to make things better; not worse. I realized that I had challenged Dr. Conner's authority and it had offended him. Dr. Conner said nothing to me for the next few days. He simply ignored me. I was left with almost total responsibility for Ron.

I went to Dr. Clement, the only Black Psychiatrist on staff. I told him what had happened, and that I felt there was no-good reason for the Chief to tell me off in public. I felt the issue over medication was a learning experience, and it was the Psychiatrist's responsibility to teach me the correct way. He assured me that he was very surprised and would speak with Dr. Conner.

After giving the matter further thought, I went back to Dr. Clement and suggested that he did not say anything to Dr. Conner. I informed him that things were better and the Chief invited me to do rounds with him. Unfortunately, it was too late; Dr. Clement had already spoken to the Chief.

Ron proved that he wasn't a threat to himself or anyone else and was sent home on psychotropic medication. I wondered if we helped Ron and if what we did would last long enough for him to do something positive with his life. I hoped that he would remember my concern for him.

Dolores, another patient, was too much to believe. She came through the emergency room with a delusion that was out of this world. Dr. Conner asked me to accompany him immediately to the emergency room. A middle-aged woman lay on a stretcher; she was very emotionally disturbed.

She was shaking and talking to herself. Dolores's hair was wild and she had a dry mouth. I asked the Chief what was wrong with her.

He said, "She's crazy."

I said, "What?"

He said, "She's crazy."

She told us, in a fast pace, that she was standing on the corner at night and some white men captured and raped her; then, put razor blades in her vagina. I questioned her repeatedly about her story, and she never changed it. Dr. Conner assigned her to me. That evening, I had a captive audience with Iris telling her about Dolores's doctor/client relationship.

A couple of days later, Debra, another patient, was brought in by the police. She was violent and talking like Donald Duck. She was quite muscular for a woman. Dr. Rosenberg asked me to see her. He was a Psychiatrist to whom I was assigned. When I walked into the room, Debra told me not to come any closer or she would break my face. She warned me about three times and stated that she wasn't kidding. She was so violent I couldn't stay with her. I walked out while telling her I would see her the next day. She said, "No, you won't."

The following day I walked boldly into her room and said, "Hello." She told me to keep my distance and don't touch her. I moved slowly in her direction, challenging her until she told me to stop where I was standing.

I told her I was from New York City, and she said, "so what?" She asked me how could I relate to her. I told her I grew up around people who used drugs, and she went to curse me out. I told her that I cared about her. After three days, she was calm and let me near her. She told me that she was part Native American Indian. She also said her father abused her and because of that, she didn't want anything to do with men. She told me that she would speak with me if she could trust me. I assured her that she could.

When Dr. Conner went to see her, she wouldn't cooperate. She told him that she would only speak with me. He approached me and asked that I get information from her and then give it to him. I gave Debra my word, and I silently refused his request. Debra told me that she was a homosexual and asked me to swear not to tell anyone. When Dr. Conner realized he was getting nowhere with her, he turned her case completely over to me to manage. He suggested that I make the decision as to her care. I had full power to do with her what I believed would benefit her greatest.

In the meantime, Dolores was still complaining of razor blades in her vagina. She was given Thorazine, but it didn't help her depression. Dr. Conner decided to give her shock treatment.

This was the first time I had ever seen electricity applied to a human being. I watched in horror as she stiffened up while the electricity rushed through her body. The little stick with gauze wrapped around it that was placed in her mouth had her teeth prints on it. It served to protect her from a sliced tongue and broken teeth, which would have occurred without it. They then rolled her out on a stretcher and she appeared dead.

The following day she was up walking around, smiling and cooperative. That was a bit of Psychiatry I had seen which appeared to have a clear benefit.

Debra told me that she needed eyeglasses because her vision was blurred. She said that she would not cooperate with me any further unless she got eyeglasses. I asked Dr. Rosenberg if I could take her downtown to get a pair of eyeglasses. He told me that I could, if I had a note from the Optometrist stating that she had glasses to pick up. I told him that she would get it. She wasn't able to get the note, but I took her anyway, without telling Dr. Rosenberg. After she got her glasses, she was more confident that I was her friend. The Psychiatrist continued to probe her for information, but she still would not cooperate with him. Dr. Rosenberg told Dr. Conner what I did in taking her downtown. Dr. Rosenberg told me that I did not have permission to do what I did. From that point on my relationship with him, Dr. Conner, as well as with Dr. Rosenberg, was destroyed.

Though I was busy taking care of two patients, I was assigned to a third one, Sarah. She was a heroin addict. She was young and pretty. When I went to see her, she was very friendly. She motioned for me to sit on her bed. She told me that she was on drugs and needed to kick the habit. She didn't feel that she belonged in the hospital; although she was suicidal. I went to see her every day and sometimes-on weekends.

Dr. Rosenberg had a meeting with me and questioned my motives for visiting her so often. Then he went to tell me that I didn't know how to speak very well. He said, "When you say 'asked,' it sounds like "axed," and people will think you don't know how to speak."

I was very confused and did not understand what his motives were. I didn't understand why the way I spoke made any difference to him. He may have thought I wanted to get in Sarah's panty. One thing I knew for sure, I was very embarrassed and felt he was upset with me for having visited Sarah so often; after all, she was white, pretty and female. When I left his office, I was very angry, but I knew there was nothing I could do, which would secure my grade if I sounded off to him.

I had my hands full and was burdened on Psychiatry. At first, treating patients there was exciting and rewarding, but now I was dealing with my own emotions toward these professors. Dr. Clement, the only Black psychiatrist on staff, also had his own problems. I was told he had a nervous breakdown, and used to take patients, whom he was treating to his house. It was too much for him to bear, dealing with their horror stories, and as a result, he had a nervous breakdown.

I was assigned a fourth patient, Mary, who was also white and female. There I was a Black medical student from Brooklyn, New York, thrust into a very white environment with white patients and being challenged by white standards and attitudes. In spite of their attitudes toward me, all of my patients were doing very well. They all spoke highly of me and the Psychiatrists still weren't able to get through to these patients. Dr. Conner and Dr. Rosenberg didn't make themselves available enough to help people who were confused, angry, and hurt. None of these doctors' psychiatric education had taught them how to help people to be restored and healed mentally. I have no doubt that at some time in their careers, they may have been different, but now they too were caught up in the system.

Mary was depressed because her children were taken from her. She wasn't able to cope because of family problems that extended a generation back to her father, who had molested her. Ironically, she needed to forgive herself for being molested, and then forgive him. I spent a lot of time trying to show her that she would recover from depression and be well enough to care for her children, and it worked. She left the Psychiatric Ward and did get her children back.

Debra could see better and was enjoying her new glasses and found a friend in me in whom she could trust. She cried the day she left the hospital and she couldn't stop hugging me. I also felt like crying that day, but I was too worn out to shed a tear.

All of my patients gave me a great sense of satisfaction in knowing that they appreciated me as a person and thought well of my care. The person I felt the saddest about was Dolores, because she was still convinced that she had razor blades in her vagina. I suggested to Dr. Conner to perform a mock operation in order to pretend to take the razor blades from her vagina, but was put down about the suggestion. He felt it was stupid, and I felt he was closed-minded. Dr. Rosenberg and Dr. Conner acted as if I belonged in the Psychiatric Ward myself. Maybe I did belong there, but if I did, they all needed to be here with me also so I could take care of them.

During the last week of the Psychiatric rotation, we were asked to attend a meeting with a couple of Psychiatrists in order to discuss our rotation in Psychiatry. The professors sat with us in a small room where we were huddled in a circle. The Psychiatrists asked us questions of a psychiatric nature. They had misled us. They didn't want any feedback on the rotation and wanted to test our knowledge of psychiatry. Three other students and I were upset. There were only four of us doing the rotation. I personally believed that Dr. Conner and Dr. Rosenberg wanted to take me down a peg or two because of my independent attitude. I sat with them and practically ignored their questions and didn't play their game. After the session was over, we were even more upset because we suddenly realized that it was an oral exam. The other students soon cooled off, but it wasn't as easy for me, I remained upset.

The following day we were given a multiple-choice exam. I passed the exam with a good grade. I didn't attend the last day because I had a scheduled appointment with the Associate Dean. I left a note with Dr. Conner before leaving the previous day. A few weeks later, the grades were returned. I wasn't allowed to have my grade from the Psychiatry Office; it was in the Dean's office. After speaking with the Dean, I learned that a special letter had been prepared, which stated that I had no respect for authority, no relationship with my patients, and didn't get along with my peers, and staff. I was given a grade of passing, but that wasn't all. They also wrote that they had reservations about my being in postgraduate training in their department. I took it up with one Associate Dean; then, also with one person after the other. I even took it up with the very doctor who had written the letter. It didn't take very long to realize that I was not going to get justice. I remembered being angry that the Psychiatrists downplayed even the positive things that happened while, I was doing the rotation.

The patients, who were the very people who had been helped by me, seemed not to matter to the Psychiatrists. Nevertheless, because these people had been helped, I was able to see more of my own self-worth. I was glad the Psychiatry rotation was over, and I knew for sure I didn't want to be one.

Medicine

I looked forward to being in the Coronary Care Unit for one month at the Albany Medical Center Hospital. I was on general rounds one morning when I heard on the public address system that a patient was having a cardiac arrest. We stopped what we were doing and ran to the patient's bedside. When we arrived, as usual half of the hospital staff was there. My medical preceptor grabbed the paddles to the cardio-verting machine and put them on the patient's chest to get the heart beating properly with an electric shock. I was standing near the EKG monitor with the paper readout in my hand. It was a policy of mine to get involved as much as possible because sometimes nurses would ask people who were standing around idle to leave. I looked at the EKG strip while the doctors were trying to revive the patient. His heart was beating forty beats per minute. This was too low to sustain his life. My preceptor asked the Neurologist what he wanted to do. The Neurologist replied, "Nothing." I was astonished, for I couldn't believe what I was hearing. There we were, appearing to revive a man in cardiac arrest with a brain tumor and only going through the motions. They were actually saying, "Let him die."

The family was waiting outside the patient's room, believing that we were doing everything in our power to save their loved one who was dying. The doctors stood there and looked at each other for about forty-five seconds, doing nothing. They were waiting for the patient's heart to stop beating, but it didn't. Staff started moving out of the room while the patient's heart continued to show forty beats per minute on the EKG machine. It was crazy. They were just letting him die. The thing that disturbed me was their dishonesty, convincing the relatives they were doing their best to revive their family member. Someone was preparing a great lie to tell them, and I wasn't going to be part of it. I asked the intern if he thought what we did was right. "If it were my father with brain cancer dying in the hospital, I wouldn't want him to live," he responded reflexively. I then understood exactly why he said what he did, but I felt bad for the family.

We were supposed to save lives, not give them up. I knew we weren't gods, but the attitudes were so cold. I kept wondering, "What if that were my father, would I have wanted him alive with brain cancer?" Maybe not, but I wouldn't have wanted him and his family to be treated that way either. It almost seemed a blessing to many in that room when he died. Physicians are trained to not waste energy and time to revive terminally ill patients. The rationale is that it is neither beneficial nor cost-effective to the patient or the family. I didn't like what I believed were some of the cold and inhumane aspects of my chosen profession.

Pediatrics

I didn't like Pediatrics. The children made too much fuss. No medical values, which I had learned in adult medicine seemed to apply with children. There were many new things to learn. I continually felt like a learning machine. I decided to do the Pediatric rotation in a small hospital in Albany. It was a very friendly place, and it made taking care of children a bit more pleasant. I was with two doctors in training on Pediatrics. Dr. Degnan was the attending doctor in charge of us. He asked me to follow children with medical problems of interest, which appealed to me.

My first patient was a boy named Kevin, who was about twelve years and who had muscle weakness and partial paralysis due to an unknown cause. He had a history of streptococcal sore throat for one-and-a-half weeks. He had been prescribed penicillin by his local family physician; however, his symptoms did not subside. He was left with severe muscle pain and weakness. He had a staggering type of walk, slowed speech and a fine tremor in his hands.

I was asked to follow his case. After doing the history and physical examination, I came to the initial conclusion that his streptococcal sore throat must have been somehow related to his present state. I presented my findings to the attending physician, Dr. Degnan. He quickly dismissed them. He said that there was no relationship between the two and to forget any such theory, and don't try to "write another textbook." He suggested that I stick to documented medicine and not try to invent any.

The following day, a group of physicians discussed the case and they were confused. They had no idea what had happened to Kevin. Some believed that his inability to walk without staggering was due to his extreme weakness and fatigue. Others believed that there was possibly something taking place in his brain and spinal column. They really didn't know whose guess was the right one. No one wanted to take into account his streptococcal sore throat. They wouldn't even mention it, but it still seemed to me to be the most obvious possible cause. I wanted his strep throat to be high on our list of possible causes. Dr. Degnan again asked me to drop the whole idea.

The guessing continued for days. We did manage to agree on one thing; he had a muscle illness of unknown cause. Everyone imaginable was in on the case. The various opinions concerning Kevin prevented a proper early evaluation of his case. Some wanted to perform a muscle biopsy. One doctor was bitterly against it. All the time Kevin was getting sicker. The attending physician felt that the interns were too aggressive. I was checking Kevin at least twice a day and sometimes at night. He was so weak and sore in his muscles that he had to be fed. A Physical Therapist had been working with him everyday. I became a friend to him. Many times, I was asked by the staff to encourage Kevin to cooperate with them. He was, after all, a bit stubborn. On one occasion, the Physiotherapist wanted me to be there during the sessions to help in encouraging Kevin to work harder.

Kevin responded to me. Though he was responding, he was not really getting any better. I was asked to present Kevin's case at a Friday morning conference. That week Dr. Degnan agreed to have a muscle biopsy done. It took days before the procedure was performed. I carried the biopsy to another hospital to have it read by one of the best Neurologists in the northeast, Dr. Hansen, a female Neurologist, and gave the biopsy to her secretary. After two weeks the report was finally returned, the biopsy was not suggestive of any known muscle disease. The muscle specimen was a normal piece of thigh muscle.

I was asked to present the case that Friday to the staff. Dr. Degnan who was the pediatric attending physician supervising me was there and other important faculty members. I presented the case just as it was worked up with our findings and the opposing opinions.

I researched the subject of a muscle weakness and streptococcal sore throat and found no connection. I gathered the pertinent clinical and laboratory findings and presented the information. Halfway through the talk, Dr. Degnan stopped me and said, "You're running out of time, wind up your presentation."

I needed more time, and I told them that I had more to say, but could not do so because of time.

After the presentation, Dr. Degnan told me that I messed up the talk. He said it was not educational and that no one learned anything from it. When I returned to the ward, the interns wanted to know how the presentation went. I told them that the attending doctor didn't like it. They were surprised and didn't understand what had gone wrong. They told me that my outline was great. When I told them how I presented the case, they said, "That's how we worked it up." I ended the conversation because I didn't want anyone to overreact or relay it back to Dr. Degnan.

After rounds that afternoon, Dr. Degnan approached me and told me he had heard I was disappointed. He wanted me to know that he didn't feel that I should have presented the controversy concerning the case. I didn't say anything to him.

I continued to take care of Kevin and he still wasn't getting any better, so the house staff made the decision to send him to New York City to be seen by the best Neurologist in the area. Many months later, I learned the doctors at that New York hospital also concluded that Kevin's muscle problems were due to his streptococcal sore throat.

After the Pediatric rotation ended, we had an oral exam. I didn't do very well, but I wasn't worried because I had done my work and was given good recommendations from the staff. The following week I received a note in my mailbox asking to see Dr. Degnan.

He told me after my presentation he wanted to fail me in the course. I looked at him as if he were crazy, and I wanted to choke him. I knew he had no grounds to fail me. He gave me two reasons why I received only a "Pass" grade instead of a better grade; namely that the oral exam was not up to standard, and there was my "poor performance" in the outpatient clinic. Otherwise, he said I would have received a good grade. I asked him if my presentation influenced his decision to give me a mere passing grade instead of a grade of "good." "To be perfectly honest, it probably did," he replied. I was upset with him because the presentation was not supposed to decide a part of the final grade. He was upset because I had discovered the truth concerning the case, while he and his colleagues looked bad. They didn't know what was wrong with the patient, and I didn't find any need to hide it. The case was interesting and that was the way I presented it. My intent was not to injure anyone.

I made an appointment to see the Associate Dean, who was the Chairman of Pediatrics and who taught me in the clinic. When I saw him, he acted as if he had no idea why I was there. He told me he gave me the grade I deserved. In his opinion, my performance in the pediatric outpatient clinic was inferior to that of the other students. I asked him to show to me by name which of the patients I cared for in an inferior manner. He got defensive and said, "I don't carry around the names of patients in my pocket." He did remember one patient whom I had seen and he believed I didn't know what was going on with the case. When I asked him to help me, remember which patient, he was speaking of, he got upset. He told me that there was no way he could recall the incident any more than that. We argued for about ten minutes. His final words were that I had not performed as well as the other students, and that was his opinion.

I then went to the Associate Dean and explained to him what happened in Pediatrics. He promised to summon the people involved to explain to help settle the matter. I knew I was on a merry-go-round again with my professors and that bothered me. There were a few other things to deal with besides the grade. The Chairman of Pediatrics told me that the interns had informed him that they had to look over my shoulder to make sure I didn't do anything wrong. I didn't believe it, because the interns had given me good evaluations. When I called up one of the interns, he said it was a lie, and that "looking over my shoulder" was something suggested by Dr. Degnan. The intern felt that Dr. Degnan twisted the truth. The intern did not appreciate what had been said about him and volunteered to call the Chairman who taught me in the clinic. The intern maintained that he couldn't have said anything like that; especially after giving me a good evaluation. He informed me that the other doctor with him also gave me a good evaluation. I had also received another evaluation of excellence from the Neonatology (the newborn specialist from the first day of birth to thirty days old) who was also a Pediatrician. I thanked the intern for his frankness and decided to let the case rest. At least now, I knew what the deal was.

These unfair situations depressed me. I began to question my own style: was I rubbing people the wrong way, and I questioned whether I was the problem?

I couldn't help but think that the whites in this profession believed that as a Black man, I must always stay in "my place." These confrontations also made me critical of the profession itself. I was finally beginning to realize just how unimportant the patient appeared to be. The priority seemed to be not so much the patient's survival, but that of the doctor's ego. I couldn't see myself conforming.

Obstetrics and Gynecology

When I started Obstetrics and Gynecology, I found myself lacking the energy needed. Iris was determined in her mind that I was a rebel trying to fight every cause I believed was unfair. She was tired of my rebelling. Iris asked, "When are you going to learn that you cannot do well in school if you are on a crusade?"

She reminded me that I wasn't in school to fight, but to learn. She was sick and tired of seeing me suffer for it, for not heeding her warnings. I knew that she was right, but I just couldn't see sacrificing all of my values to please people who knew little about me. I wondered if I could benefit, in the end, if I continued my apparent rebellious behavior. I was tired of some people trying to bring me down, such as the professors who gave me bad grades just because they didn't like my attitude. I decided to keep my mouth shut to see if my academic and social life would change any.

I took Obstetrics and Gynecology at a hospital in Schenectady, about fifteen miles from Albany. All of the residents there were foreign trained and were very friendly. They made me feel very comfortable and relaxed. They took an interest in me as soon as they met me, and I appreciated that. I was encouraged by the fact that I got along with nearly everyone there. I hope that I thought, nothing would come up to rock the boat.

There was a lot of work to be done on the ward. The Operating Room was constantly booked with cases and it was all very exhausting at times. We were on call every third night, and when we were on call naturally, we didn't get much sleep.

Abortions

Each day we had from three to five abortions to perform. I had previously vowed that I would never do one, for it was against my religious beliefs. I spoke with my minister and family about it, and their general attitude was that I should participate for now because, unfortunately, it was a part of my training. No one was advocating it, and the hospital staff stated that it would be okay if I refused. I did some heavy thinking about the abortions on the ward, and decided that it would be in my best interest to help the other physicians. A couple of doctors told me that I didn't have to help them. I, however, decided not to trust that advice. I didn't want any attending physicians questioning my willingness to help. I felt it was going to make a difference if I didn't get involved.

The following day, I started doing abortions. Many of the women having the abortions were white. I'm sure this was because Schenectady is predominantly a white city. Only occasionally did we have a Black patient. In abortions, we used a device that operated like a vacuum cleaner. The patients were premeditated before the procedure. Then, the instrument was placed into the uterine cavity, and the fetus was destroyed by the suction. We had one case with miscalculated gestation (age of the fetus). While suctioning the cavity, the fetus' spine broke away from the body and wouldn't pass through the suction catheter. The doctor had to manually pick it off and push it through. He looked at me with a sick face. It was a horrible sight. Everyone in the room was visibly shaken. I realized something. I was involved in murder with consent; unfortunately, not the consent of the murdered.

Within two weeks, I was actually doing abortions myself. I knew it was wrong, and it disturbed me to know that I'd gotten accustomed to murdering so easily. Perhaps it was most disturbing because the murdered never spoke. I had paid a terrible price to join the fan club of my colleagues. I believed I had lost my self-respect and dignity, so my value system had crumbled.

After the rotation was over, I received my grade of "good." Not only had it been a successful rotation academically, but socially also, because the staff liked me. At the end of the third year, I felt reasonably pleased with my performance in medical school. At least I completed the year without any failures. This helped to compensate for the indifferent attitudes of many physicians. Many times, it seemed like a chore for them to share their wealth of knowledge with me.

I eventually told my family what had happened in the first year, the one I repeated, and kept secret from them. The secret couldn't be kept any longer because four years had passed, and according to their calendar, I was due to graduate. I was ready to tell them anyway. They seemed to understand and weren't upset with me for it. It was just another bridge crossed.

Chapter 13
Hanging Out

The earth is the Lord's, and the fullness of it,
the world and they who dwell in it.

Psalm 24:1

When I wasn't studying or in church, I spent time with my friends. Being with them was my chance to be free of stress and have fun. It made me feel good. Sometimes I got in touch with Eddie. Eddie worked in the medical college Physiology lab. I liked Eddie because he helped me forget about medical school. Ironically, his working in the college encouraged him to try to forget about anything connected to it. He liked hunting and we often talked about hunting together. We did go hunting one time and it was freezing but I enjoyed being in the woods. Sometimes I stopped at Eddie's house to talk with him and his wife. His wife liked talking about all kinds of stuff and I liked her. She was a beautician. She and Eddie spent quality time with their children at ball games and other activities. I respected both of them and enjoyed their company. Eddie had completed a number of years of college and once wanted to enter medical school (I don't know why he didn't). On occasion, we talked about racism and how it affects Black people and I felt he was bruised by it, like most Black people in America. Whenever I visit Albany, I always make contact with Eddie because he was true to me when I was in school.

Ephraim was another hangout; a partner of mine. I tried to make contact with him as much as I could because in many ways he was my idol of a cool minority, being Puerto Rican and coming from New York. He understood well the racism game played on us, but acted as if it didn't exist when he had to take care of serious business. One time I told him I started writing an autobiography and he said, "Hey, bro, I don't advise you to do that. It's going to make trouble for you."

Ephraim was a man who fought for what he believed, but he had a particular cool style in doing it, not letting his opponent know his moves. In many ways, I have wanted to be like him.

Paul Larber was another guy I enjoyed being with. I don't know where he is today. He wanted to be a doctor, but didn't get into a U.S. medical school. He was accepted at a school in Tampico, Mexico. In some ways I feel I let him down because he had money problems when he was there, and asked me for help and I couldn't. It wasn't because I didn't want to, for I was having money problems myself. Paul trusted and believed in me like all of my friends whom I hung out with (spent time with). Paul was a student at the State University of New York, at Albany. He had a Bachelor of Science degree and all the premedical requirements. He was working full time at a job at which he was determined to stay. I encouraged him to apply to Albany Medical College, which he did and was turned down. Paul and I spent many hours talking about racism and how it was messing up Blacks and Hispanics. I loved Paul very much and I still hurt that I didn't come through for him. As it is said, "hindsight is a bitch," and it is.

I probably spent more time with Michael than I did with any of my other hangout friends. I liked Michael because he kept me on my toes with everything. He was always asking me questions about some situation either of us was in. He seemed to be the most inquisitive about my future career as a doctor. I felt at times that he was fascinated to have a friend who was going to become a medical doctor. He made me feel extra special. "Hey, man," he would say, "I'm really proud of you making it, and I want you to believe that. If I had done what I was supposed to do in school, my situation would be better instead of having to deal with these white folks," he said.

Michael worked for General Electric and he never felt they did right by him and I agree. Michael was proud of his job because he understood that in spite of his feelings about not applying himself in school, he had come a long way. His job paid fairly well and he was able to buy a house at a young age and raise a family. I think Mike's problem was that he hated depending on anyone for the next day's subsistence. Mike was really the independent type who had just not found the right break to make it on his own in his own business. I saw the possibility of work independence in Mike and I saw him in his own business.

Michael was very close with his parents, they were nearing retirement and he was always concerned that he wasn't doing enough for them. I often told him always to remember, honor, and cherish his parents because it was right and they were all he would ever have.

I spent hangout time with Brother Belton also. The fact that he was older than I never made any difference to either of us. I looked at him as I did the other guys because he was energetic, full of surprises and enjoyed having fun. Most of my hangout time with him was in his house, and Iris was usually with me at these times. Sister Belton was always there and willing to share with Iris and me. I had many memorable times with him and most of them were quiet times talking about life and God.

If I had to say which one of my hangout, friends I enjoyed being with the most, I just wouldn't try. They all were very special to me and still are.

Chapter 14
Medical College Admissions
Committee

How precious are your thoughts unto me,
O God! How great is the sum of them!

Psalm 139:17

During my fourth year in medical school, because of a Minority Affairs Committee having been formed, I was able to assist in a decision-making role in who would be admitted. We had a number of white students on the committee, and most of them recognized the lack of minority enrollment and they too were concerned about improving the terrible discriminatory record at the medical center. We had about six Black medical students in the college out of 500-plus students. The medical college still accepted a small number of Black students. They claimed that there were few minorities who applied and those who did apply were not promising. One sure way of getting Blacks into the mainstream of the system was to get on the Admissions Committee. A number of students were running for the available positions. No seat, however, had been designated as a minority seat. I imagine they felt due to so few minorities in the school that there was no need for it, but that's the very reason they needed a minority seat filled.

The student Minority Affairs Committee asked me to run for the position. I never imagined ever doing anything like that in medical school.

I had been a controversial figure and didn't imagine anyone would want me on the Admissions Committee, because it meant working closely with the faculty without prejudice. I agreed to run anyway.

On Election Day, we gathered in the auditorium lecture hall. The students were all excited, waiting for the chance to elect their friends. Apparently, I wasn't in such good favor, because all the candidates had been required to write a letter explaining why we wanted a seat on the committee. I wrote about the minorities and their situation and mentioned the class as a whole, but that didn't overemphasize my minority pitch. A few believed my letter was too strong and prejudicial. I had the letter rewritten by a couple of classmates but I remained strong on the minority issues. I felt if I couldn't win by speaking my heart, then I wasn't going to win at all.

On the day of the voting, students were tense, because naturally they had their favorites to win. The result ended in a tie. When they voted again, some of the students who had voted for me the first time changed their minds and didn't vote for me. Even the few Black students didn't vote for me, apparently because, one told me, they believed I had no chance of winning. It was just another time that the Black students failed to stick together, as usual, and showed their asses to everybody. I lost the election.

The Minority Affairs Committee (which was, ironically, white) had a meeting and decided to ask that a minority seat on the Admissions Committee be filled. We made a lot of noise and were finally allocated the seat. It was planned for me to have it automatically, but they voted on the candidates anyway, thus making it democratic. This was an important move for me. I saw it as an excellent opportunity to pull some people over the wall who might not otherwise have been admitted to medical school. My role on the committee was equal to all other students. I was to screen and interview minority as well as non-minority candidates. I took home applicants' folders and sat with Iris to screen them. Iris would be my second opinion and my "checks & balances." If I didn't like a candidate without looking through the folder, she would say something to me that usually caught my attention.

I remember one applicant whose father was a judge in California. He tried to use his influence to get his son an interview. The judge had spoken with a friend of his, who knew the Chairman of a large department in a New York City hospital. The Chairman, in response, had written a letter to someone in the medical college asking for a return favor. It angered me.

It was obvious that his son was a good student and had excellent grades. I didn't understand why he felt the need to get a favor returned for his son. I immediately handed the letter to Iris. I told her that I would not consider the applicant for an interview. I thought about the less fortunate who had no one to speak for him or her. I wanted so much to be fair, but it was difficult to do so while at the same time dealing with the way the system worked by feeding itself.

There were times when committee members didn't know where I was coming from. They couldn't predict what kind of attitude I would have at any given meeting.

The students whom we interviewed on Friday were voted for on the following Tuesday. Each person who interviewed students was required to present or plead his case to the entire Admissions Committee. Sometimes, during these meetings, I wanted to respond to certain issues but did not do so for fear that, the subject of racial prejudice would arise, and I might be accused of giving a racially motivated interview and possibly be discredited. Many times, I held my peace and sat quietly.

A situation arose once with a Black student whom I had interviewed, who had decent grades and average medical college admissions test scores. One of the committee members from the Microbiology department questioned the student's ability to get through medical school. This student was better than most minority applicants we had interviewed up to that point. It was evident to me that the student had the qualities needed and did have a good chance of getting through medical school. This wasn't the first time this had happened. "Why is it that we evaluate Black candidates with such negative feelings?" I asked. It was a while before anyone answered me. When someone finally spoke up, he said that Black students, regardless of their educational background, didn't seem to achieve as well as the average white student. Before I could say anything, another committee member added, "Minority students just have a difficult time dealing socially."

I told them I believed it was unfair that Black candidates with good solid grades were evaluated poorly. The moderator of the meeting put a halt to the conversation, and we continued our presentation of cases.

Whenever I spoke what was on my mind, I always left the meeting feeling as if I had said something wrong, and usually I did.

I enjoyed the interviewing on Friday afternoons. I tried to tailor every interview according to students' first comments to me. After they had their say, I knew what position to come back to. I tried not to give a pressured interview, since the interview was a very crucial part of the selection process. In addition, I remembered my own interview and didn't want to subject anyone to what I had gone through. We had been given guidelines concerning which questions to ask, but were given liberty to ask our own questions also.

My first goal was to sort out the possible bigots. I would ask the white students if they thought it was wrong that so many Black people voted for President Carter in spite of his Southern background. I would question them about their feelings on minorities in medical school.

The Blacks didn't escape my piercing questions either. I asked them if they were anti-Semitic and what they thought about the attitudes of whites toward minorities in the medical profession. I remember one Black student, whom I questioned about the movie "Roots." He told me that he didn't have the time to see the television version, but that he had the book at home, although he hadn't read it. I was upset with him and asked why he hadn't read the book. He informed me that he just hadn't. At that point, the interview was over. I knew I couldn't give this candidate, Black or not, a positive evaluation. My attitude may not have been fair but that's how I felt and I acted on my feelings. As I look back on my actions today concerning what I did with some students and reading "Roots," I don't think I would do differently. Something about him appeared to me to be phony. I believed he was apathetic about his own people. I was personally offended over his passive decision not to share the Black experience through one of the most historic epic stories of our times, "Roots." This attitude did not match his blown-up outward rhetoric about Blacks. Another interviewer asked him the same question about "Roots," and got the same response.

If a candidate was honest during the interview and didn't try to pull the wool over my eyes, I considered him. Black or white, I didn't care. I was looking for people who were willing to admit their weak points as well as their strong points. I met a few people like this; when I did, I was quite impressed. Sometimes, I felt as though I had unfairly judged an applicant, and it bothered me for days. As I looked at credentials on Tuesday morning, before the meeting began, my doubts always surfaced. I was not always sure if my approach in evaluating candidates for medical school was correct. Suppose I was preaching the same kind of discrimination that, I objected to so much. In spite of my doubts, I ultimately generally felt comfortable with my judgments.

I advised a few college students whom I knew to apply to the medical school. Their credentials were not usually as good as the average candidate's, but they had shown the ability to do satisfactory work. I was very optimistic about getting them at least an interview.

The Assistant Dean had offered to let me help him screen all the minority applicants. He wanted me to question his decision on anyone. I took full advantage of that opportunity. I was able to convince him to reconsider about five applicants, two of whom I knew, Paul and Cheryl. I wanted to interview one of them, but I knew that it might not have been fair. I desperately especially wanted them in medical college. I asked one of the committee members, named Barry, to interview one. I asked him to interview Cheryl. He agreed and assured me that he would seek out another interviewer to give her the second interview. I made it clear to him that I wasn't trying to put him on the spot, but I believed he was the best person I could have approached about the matter. The student's interview was Friday, and I had no worries about it. I knew she would do well. We had gotten together and I had coached her on some ways to sharpen up her interview. I saw the Assistant Dean in the medical college. He told me that he wasn't sure she could get through medical school at that point in her life. He suggested that she would be wise to attend graduate school, take a few courses, and reapply the following year. My heart started pounding. I was mad enough to kill that guy.

That night I called Cheryl and explained what had taken place so far. She said that she didn't know what had happened at the interview that made him feel so negative about her, because she felt he was positive during the entire interview.

The following Tuesday morning at the medical center, we discussed the students. The Associate Dean said that he had interviewed her and liked her. He was willing to give her a chance until he found out how the other interviewer had evaluated her. My head was about to take off. I turned to an interviewer on my left and told him that I knew the applicant personally and deliberately did not interview her for that reason. He wanted me to mention this to everyone at the meeting in case they might reconsider her. I couldn't, for I had selected her application in the Assistant Dean's office and I was being impartial in my selection, which I wasn't, and it would have been a clear conflict of interest because I was not supposed to be selecting people whom I knew personally. Barry and the Dean would have felt I set the whole situation up for my own reasons. I was sitting on the edge of my seat, halfway between speaking up and walking out. I thought that any public admission that I knew Cheryl might bring on unfavorable reactions. The interviewer next to me kept speaking to me in a low tone, asking me to speak up. I couldn't. I wouldn't even look at him.

One person raised an issue about the split decision between the Associate Dean and Barry. He asked why another applicant was considered more favorably than Cheryl, the previous applicant having been white with no better grades. This opened up a new assortment of problems and people became defensive concerning their decisions. One group felt that the racial angle wasn't the point. The point was that there were two different groups, which were evaluating similar credentials in different ways.

One group felt the credentials presented were terrible and not acceptable, and the other group didn't. The entire situation had me boiling. As far as I could tell, it appeared to be racial and very few people were ready to deal with that.

After the long meeting, I picked up my coat and departed without saying a word to anyone. I dreaded the thought of telling Cheryl what had happened. This little difference in opinion was to shape her future goals.

When I spoke with her that evening, she broke down and cried. I felt terrible. Being zealous to get a fair interview may have hurt her. She cried so much I couldn't even speak with her over the telephone, so I told her that I would be over to pick her up. I explained the situation to Iris and immediately left the house. When I returned to the apartment with Cheryl, we sat in our living room that evening and talked until we both felt better. After that experience, I understood so much better how the system worked and how I could be an integral part of it.

I lost contact with Cheryl. Paul was also turned down. I became friends with a young Black man named Simon, who was a janitor mopping floors at the medical center. He had a college degree from The State University at New York. He wanted to be a doctor, but according to the system, didn't meet the mark to be accepted into medical school. Simon and I had many discussions concerning Black people. He converted to Islam and became a Muslim. That brother believed in himself, applied to Albany Medical College, and was accepted. He's a doctor today and I'm very proud of him.

Pregnancy and Finances

Financially, Iris and I were in trouble again. Iris was pregnant with our second child (who would be called Taina. We had overspent our Public Health Scholarship money. I had received a check every month for $750, tax-free, not realizing that some of it had to be saved for the summer months. The checks were only to come for the school year of nine months. We had no summer income in sight. We took the remaining few dollars we had and paid our current bills. After doing that, we were looking at $375 for the entire three months ahead. I knew something would work out, but I just didn't know how or what. I kept telling Iris that everything would be fine. As the weeks passed, the money dwindled rapidly. Often I was worried, but I didn't tell Iris.

I went into the preceptorship to find out if they had any openings to work with a private doctor in his or her office. There was an opening in a small town in the county, outside of Albany. The position was offered by Dr. Gifford (not his real name), a white family physician, who had no Black patients in his practice. It paid $252 for three weeks. In one-and-a-half weeks, Iris and I spent the $252.

The preceptorship didn't have much educational value. The doctor refused to let me help in doing anything of importance. In fact, whenever a white female patient was to be seen, he would make sure she was all covered up, as if I wanted to peek at her private parts. Whenever a woman had to have a pelvic exam or be checked for any female problem, he would make some excuse for me to take a tea or coffee break (and I drank neither). A few times, he just told me straight out that, he wanted to see the patient alone. I believed his actions were racial, but they may have been sexually motivated toward some of his female patients. It never seemed to bother him about his actions and I felt terrible. I was in another racially compromised position.

Dr. Gifford exhibited a lack of patience with most of his clients. He also appeared not to be very professionally honest. I watched him examine ears with an otoscope from two feet away (most people in medicine know you have to stick the thing in the ear). Well, I never saw him do it the correct way. He would tell them that their ears were fine. He looked in the eyes in the same manner.

Dr. Gifford complained about having to do histories and physicals on children and college students. He used the excuse that most of them were well and cut short the exam. He never complained, though, when he took their money after doing a sloppy job. Every time a patient complained of a headache, he would give them Valium and blame the headache on their nerves. If a patient complained of an upset stomach, he would blame it on their nerves and give them Lomotil medicine. Dr. Gifford never completely examined any patients while I was there. New patients were no exception. I guess I did learn one thing from him, and that is, I didn't want to be like him, ever. The last day of the summer preceptorship, I barely said goodbye to him. I didn't tell him I had a good experience because it was terrible.

I spent some of that summer fishing with my friends Ephraim and Paul in Schenectady on the Mohawk River. I bought a yellow inflatable raft that I purchased with some of our income tax money. We had a great time with it. We fished on a little island until we got tired. Ephraim took me back to land and returned for Paul. On the way, back the water got rough and Paul fell out of the raft. I laughed so hard my side was hurting. Ephraim almost fell out of the boat himself. Sometimes it was hard to get Ephraim to laugh, but this time it was no problem. Paul didn't get hurt; just a little wet. We all laughed about it.

I went fishing on the Mohawk River many times and it helped me drown out some of my stress.

Doing My Job

After my summer preceptorship with Dr. Gifford, I applied for a job at a local hospital, St. Clare's Hospital. I did histories and physical exams. I called up the Medical Director, and he gave me the job. It paid $15 per hour plus meals and a place to sleep. I rarely slept there because I didn't want to leave Iris alone at home with Shoshanna. I worked twice a week for six hours each day. The income kept my family afloat. I liked that little hospital, and in addition working there would help us pay bills.

The Last Miles

During my last miles in medical school, I began to feel like a doctor. I wore a clean white jacket every day. I was on call (had to stay in the hospital and care for patients). I was awakened at 3:00 a.m. I had to see a patient with excessive weight loss, fever and generalized pain. When I arrived at the patient's bedside, I took one look at her and knew she was very sick. I tried to draw blood from her, but her veins were hidden and small. When I stuck her with the needle, she cried like a child. I stopped and told the nurses that I couldn't draw it. After taking her history, I learned that she had lymphoma (cancer of the circulatory system), diabetes and a peri-rectal abscess. I ordered the necessary medications, lab tests and went back to bed. When I got up, I felt like I hadn't slept for a whole day. Morning rounds started at 8:00 a.m. I presented the patient to the staff. They listened as my voice shook from anxiety. I stumbled through the presentation, but I managed to finish with the staff smiling. I spent the rest of the morning and afternoon speaking with the patients.

Each day, I tried to see all of my patients before 8:00 a.m. and write a brief note before rounds. I tried to catch those with problems before the big shots arrived. I used the remainder of the day to do procedures and work on current problems. It gave me a chance to test my ability to take care of patients with minimal extra professional help.

My patient with lymphoma wasn't doing well. She was going to die and she knew it. She showed a lot of courage and never stopped hoping. Sometimes, I would enter her room while she was asleep. I would stand at her bedside and just look at her. Knowing that this life, which existed, would soon be no more, I had to come to grips with life's mortal finality. She finally left the hospital only to return later and die. It affected me deeply.

The Matching Program

The time arrived for me to decide where I would do my postgraduate training after medical school. I needed to first decide what field of medicine I would enter. I picked Family Medicine. Iris didn't want to leave Albany because she came to love it. It was a safe place for her away from Brooklyn. She told me she would go to another place to live but not Brooklyn and definitely not Red Hook. I understood how she felt, but I had made a promise to some people in Red Hook that I would practice medicine there one day.

The decision-making process involved the matching program where one tried to match up with internship and residency (doctor in training). Upcoming new doctors applied to various hospitals by way of selection and interview. There was no guarantee that I would be placed where I wanted to be, even if I had been given a verbal confirmation. It was more a matter of God's grace and chance. Early in the school year, I had gone to Brooklyn for one month with my family in order to do a preceptorship in a Family Practice program. I liked the program, and the Director of the program informed me that he wanted me to practice there. I was told to put that Family Practice program first if I felt the same way. When the match came through, I had been given the Family Practice residency in Brooklyn, just as I wanted.

Acting Internship in Surgery

I took on an acting internship in surgery at St. Peter's Hospital in Albany. I regretted it later. I tried to get out of doing it, but the schedule was already made up. I hadn't enjoyed surgery in my third year and knew it was going to be a drag. They wanted me to be on call every other night, and I really didn't want to. Surgeons, as everyone in the medical profession (except other surgeons) believes, have rotten attitudes. They walk around like gods, treating interns and residents like trash. My second week in internship surgery convinced me that I might never survive in a surgical residency. The chief resident(who was Black) placed me with a surgeon who gave most of the students a hard time.

It was said that this surgeon was so smart that he got 100% on his surgical boards. Once during a lymphoma staging, he got very upset with me. I was holding a retractor in order to keep a patient's abdomen open so he could stage her cancer. My hands were holding the retractor so long that my fingers felt frozen . He shouted at me, "Wake up, you're not in any pet shop with puppies." That wasn't so bad, but then he smacked my hands away from the patient. He was behaving crazily. I told the chief resident that I wasn't working with that surgeon again. One day that same surgeon needed a student to work with him, but I refused when they asked me. I didn't care what he or anyone else thought. This guy wasn't going to have a second chance to smack my hands.

These surgeon guys didn't seem to care about anyone. Most of them weren't even kind to the patients. Many patients didn't even know what they were going to have done in the operating room. Rarely would the doctor who operated on the patients take care of them postoperatively. Quite a number of the patients had post-op infections, which were probably avoidable. There was one woman who was left for two weeks in her hospital bed with no lab work done, just running up a bill. Many of the surgeons were unsanitary, going from patient to patient without even the minimal washing of their hands.

The most challenging time in my fourth year rotations was when I was in the veterans' hospital and had to give a presentation on lung cancer. I prepared myself well and all the residents were rooting for me to do well. Halfway through my talk, a big-shot surgeon named Dr. Wald yelled out, "Why don't he sit the hell down, he doesn't know what the hell he's talking about." The resident doctors believed his remarks were not called for. I did sit, but not before, I finished my talk.

Taina

Iris gave birth to our second daughter, Taina. The experience was not as frightening as the birth of Shoshanna. Though she didn't look that great either at birth, as Shoshanna didn't, I was sure she would be beautiful. Taina was an excellent baby. Iris says, she was the best baby in terms of behavior and attitude. She was a very calm child.

I got an excellent grade in surgery and I am not sure why, because I will admit that I didn't take any harassement from them and I spoke my mind. I really think things went OK because I exhibited the same attitude that they had; say what you have to, do what you have to, and keep on going.

Finishing Up

The remainder of the fourth year was pretty much routine. I had taken a number of other rotations like Cardiology, Neurology, and Urology and I hated them all. I did well, though I had some problems academically. Some people on the faculty reassured me that they knew I would be a good physician. Not all of my stands for or against certain matters were appreciated, but I made my point known. I gained the respect of many people.

During my last few weeks in school, a professor of Epidemiology and Biostatistics approached me. He said, "Wilbert, the only problems some of us are concerned about with you is, will you ever get a license to practice medicine after graduation?" His statement stunned and hurt me and I thought seriously whether he was right. Nevertheless, I was leaving that institution to enter another situation just as challenging.

Chapter 15
Graduation

Search me O God, and know my heart:
Try me, and know my thoughts.

Psalm 139:23

It was May 25, 1978. My friends and relatives in New York were excited. My friend Raymond came up with a host of "Brooklynites." They were all really special to me, but Raymond was my best friend. They came to see me through the graduation ceremony. It was a great day in my life, and many in my family were there to share that moment of euphoria with me.

Brother and Sister Belton drove me in their motor home to Saratoga Springs, New York, where the graduation ceremony was being held. As usual, they treated Iris and I like royalty.

Elder Mc Daniel was there, as well as many people from Refreshing Springs Church, including Sister Dix, my friends Michael and Margie, and Ephraim and Yoli. Dr. J.T. Henderson and his wife were there. They gave me a brand new Littman stethoscope. I was happy that they all were there because they were a part of my life. I called them God's shadow over me.

The graduation ceremony was great and, as usual, too long for those graduating. When my name was called to receive my large old-fashioned medical degree certificate, I swiftly walked onto the stage. When the Chairman of Anatomy shook my right hand and handed me my degree he asked, "What are you doing here?" I looked in his eyes and laughed. I was told later that I was screaming on the stage. It was over. The grinding task to achieve my goal to be a doctor. I had finally made it, in spite of all the fire I had walked through.

Refreshing Springs Church had a celebration for me and Iris said I grinned the whole time. When it was all over, I knew for sure that I beat the system and I did it while holding my head up high with erect shoulders, and full of pride.

I understood the words, which my father spoke to me years earlier in reference to his native state in Chesson, Alabama when he said, "I wasn't gonna let them treat me like a low-down no-good nigger." When he spoke for himself, he was speaking for me also.

During this tim, Iris and I had many confrontations about where we were going to live while I did my internship and residency in Family Medicine. I wanted to go down to New York City. I felt that I had to fulfill my promise to the neighborhood: I would return when I made it. Various people told me that when I became a big-shot doctor I would forget about Red Hook and the people there. I told them that they were wrong. No way did Iris want me to go back to Brooklyn. She believed that it would destroy our marriage. We were having differences about what was best for the entire family. Iris even told me that if I decided to make Brooklyn, New York the location for our new home, she was not going. I didn't think that she really meant it, but she was quite serious. She was willing to go anywhere, but New York City. We had a great falling-out about it when I insisted on going back. Iris made it clear to me that whatever went wrong in New York City with us, would be my fault, and that I was not to forget it.

John and Doris Belton sat with us and counseled us with respect to our marriage and our future. They were great and tactful. Doris took me to the side and gently and quietly spoke with me and John spoke with Iris. She showed us that what mattered was our family and God's place in our plans. They were always willing to give of themselves unselfishly to us and it was one of the things that made them special (not only to us, but also to many people).

Flames

My father was the first one to ever call me a "nigger," and I understand why. He believed for a person to steal from his own father, that person had to be a low-down no-good person who was capable of doing anything. The second time I was called a "nigger" was by a white guy in junior high school for no apparent reason. The third time I was called a "nigger" was by a little white boy in an Italian neighborhood who probably didn't even know how to spell his name. Maybe a lot of people wanted to call me a "nigger," but for whatever reason didn't. I've been dealt some dirty deals by some white people in medical school who felt that I was too aggressive. None of them dared to call me a "nigger"as far as I know (at least not to my face).

But I never thought a bunch of bigoted, hateful white people who amounted to a mob of cowards would threaten to kill me and my family for trying to rent a nice apartment on a tree-lined street in Brooklyn, in a Norwegian and Irish-American neighborhood. It was the most bitter experience, which I ever had with white racism, and it inflicted a deep scar in me and left me feeling bitter toward white people for years to come.

It started when my future Family Practice Director at The Lutheran Medical Center Hospital in Brooklyn promised me a nice apartment on a tree-lined street a few months before I graduated from medical school. He asked me to get in touch with his own real estate agent, who was selling the Medical Director's house. When we arrived at the agency, we were told that most property owners really didn't want children and that we should visit other rental agencies.

They didn't know we had visited a number of agencies who only showed us roach infested apartments. Iris and I visited them again, and insisted on being shown something. The agent took us to two places. One was a nice apartment in a six-family complex that was still being built on 78th Street in Bay Ridge, Brooklyn. Another was on Staten Island, a cheap apartment in an otherwise nice building. He tried to convince us to take the latter, yet the Bay Ridge apartment was really, what we liked, and we told him so.

He called us the next day and fed us some line about the Bay Ridge apartment would not be ready in time for us to move in because of a building permit, which was needed.

After returning to Albany, I asked my friend Richard, who was due to graduate with me, to accompany me to the real estate office and pose as my lawyer, and he agreed. Richard, being Black, would present them with the challenge of dealing with two educated Black men. We were hoping that they would think Richard was my lawyer. The following week Richard put on a suit(which I never saw him wear while we were in school), and both of us headed back down to Brooklyn in order to confront those racist bigots. When the real estate sales agent saw us, he quickly summoned us to his desk. Richard and I sat before him as fake client and attorney. Richard never verbally stated that he was a lawyer, but his mannerism spoke otherwise. Richard sat silently with his hand on his chin. The agent looked frightened. The agent told me that he still didn't have anything available for my family, but he would continue to search. When we left the office, Richard and I looked at each other and started smiling. "Did you see how scared that guy looked?" I said.

"Yeah," Richard said, "he got the message." I thought that we were on top of the problem.

After my return to Albany, I prepared myself for the last few miles of medical school. A couple of months passed and the Swift Real Estate office was still playing games with me. I felt terrible that I had to walk the flames of racism and bigotry.

After graduation from Albany Medical College, I bid my friends farewell and returned to Brooklyn, New York. I felt like I was entering kindling fire.

I called the Human Rights Commission in Manhattan, New York. I was told by an agent to put a deposit on the apartment.

The whole situation spiraled afterwards. Mr. Swift, the agency owner (who attended the same church where my friend Raymond was a member), tried to steer me to other apartments in run down neighborhoods, and tried to give us our deposit back several times. Raymond told me that Mr. Swift was caught in a bind. He found out from Mr. Swift that some of the Norwegians and Irish-Americans in the neighborhood had threatened to mess up the building and kill my family if he rented to us. They even threatened the builder's daughter. They told him, "If those niggers get the apartment, we're gonna rape your daughter." Her bra and panty size were quoted on the telephone with the builder (who was her father). He became hysterical, and as a result sent her to Norway. Mr. Swift received calls of threats to blow up his real estate office. Someone from the neighborhood even went inside the establishment and spit on a sales agent. Mr. Swift claimed that he didn't feel the way the people did who lived in the neighborhood and he was more concerned for my family than for his business. I didn't believe him. He was a part of the racial discrimination being practiced against us. The people who were threatening us, he says, were threatening to burn down his business.

I was angry with the Swift Real Estate Company in the Bay Ridge section of Brooklyn and its owner, Mr. Swift, for allowing his company to be racist, while he claimed to be a Christian. He had deceived me. They had a real estate agent take me to two unfit dwellings. They tried to get me to rent one.

Along the line, Mr. Swift invited his friend and me on a fishing trip off the coast of Staten Island, New York, one evening. They took me out in their boat, and then stopped it. They scared me. I thought that they were going to throw me overboard. When they took me ashore, it was, by then, already dark. They drove me to an isolated street on Second Avenue in Brooklyn. Mr. Swift threatened me. He yelled in an uncontrollable rage, saying repeatedly, "You better not take that apartment." His saliva sprinkled my face. He wouldn't let me out of his car until I said, "OK, I won't take it." When I finally got out of that car, I thanked God for my life. I was mad as hell and still scared.

After I arrived home, I told Iris what had happened and she begged me to forget about the apartment. She said that we could find another apartment in a neighborhood where people didn't care about color and race. After she spoke with me, I understood her fear because I was again frightened for my family and myself. The thing that kept ripping at me was that not even at this point in my life was I protected from racism. I had proven myself educationally, and had struggled so hard to become a medical doctor. Not anyone in his right mind would ever make my color and my race a focal point concerning me and calling me a black "nigger." I had never felt so low and broken in all of my life.

My Family Practice Director urged me to drop it (but then, after all, he was trying to get his own house sold). The Human Rights agent told me that we should not bow down to the apartment residents' pressures. He believed that they were just bluffing with their threats to the builder, the agency and my family. Iris had been strong throughout the ordeal, up to that point. However, after the personal threats to our family, and after a brick was thrown through the balcony sliding glass door, we thought that we should back off and live some safer place. I just couldn't, however, bring myself to back down so soon. I believed that my manhood was somehow at stake. I was in the flaming fire again, but this time I had Iris and the two children with me.

The situation got worse. The builder refused to complete the apartment, so even though we had all the paperwork to move in we couldn't do so. The neighborhood residents were using the word "nigger" as if it were a new household product. All the other tenants in the building had moved in, even though they had applied after we did.

Both of our families started urging us to forget it all, but I was stubborn. I wanted to feel like a real man who could protect his family, no matter what the cost. The Human Rights Commission had given the builder and real estate agency until July 15 to have the apartment ready. July 15 arrived and it was show down time. I was still resolved to have that apartment. I met the Human Rights officer and together, along with police escorts, we went to the apartment on 78th Street.

There was a good-sized crowd of people outside the apartment building. There were two police officers with the Human Rights agent and me. One of the officers had a gun strapped to his lower leg. When I got out of the car, a man standing across the street grabbed his groin and shook his dick at me; an exercise in mental castration.

The Human Rights agent asked the builder if the apartment was ready, and the builder replied, "No, I'm not going to get killed." The Human Rights agent asked him to show us the apartment. He didn't want to, but the agent insisted. While we stood there talking, a white woman named Mrs. O'Keefe ran up to us, threatening the builder right before our eyes. We tried to ignore her, but by this time, more people had gathered around. As we walked up the stairs to the apartment, I felt someone was going to shoot me; I was scared. Inside, the apartment fixtures were not completely connected, wires were hanging from the ceiling, and the floor and walls were not finished. The brick, which was thrown through the dining room window, was still there, on the floor next to the broken glass. At that moment, I knew that I couldn't bring my children around these kinds of people. These people were like animals running wild and we didn't mean anything to them; they were ready to kill us.

After viewing the condition of the apartment, the Human Rights officer asked the builder when he could have it ready. "I won't," the builder answered. "If you want it ready, I'll give you the money to fix it up. They're going to kill me." When he said that, I became engulfed with fear. I finally told the Human Rights officer that Iris and I didn't want the apartment. He was disappointed.

We settled the matter down town at the Human Rights office. Iris and I were given an apology and $700. I requested the money in personal checks from Mr. Swift and Mr. Hansen to show my children one day, and they gave me the checks.

I felt less than a man that day; effectively castrated. The whole experience threw me into a deep psychological abyss where white people were concerned. I resigned myself to feel that not even my medical degree and all the respect that comes with it were enough to make some people treat me as a human being. Not even my nice car and my white intern clothes would change the racist attitudes of many. I was wounded deeply, and once again, I was angry with the white establishment.

Someone who heard about our plight found an apartment for us, ironically in an Italian neighborhood, in the Bensenhurst section of Brooklyn.

My Mother, Laverne Williams.

My Father, Wilbert Williams, Sr.

Left to right: My sister Janice, acting crazy, as usual. My usual calm self, and my sister Shelly.

I was handsome when I was 8 years old.

Graduation from Boy's High School, 1966.

Contemplating my life's journey at 25 years old.

Graduation from Medical School, Left to Right:
Iris' mother, Doris Shoshanna, Me, Iris Taina, and
Iris' father, Zacharias.

*I couldn't believe I finally had the Medical Degree
diploma in my hand!*

*My pastor - and friend, Elder McDaniel, as usual,
supporting and encouraging me at Graduation from
Albany Medical College.*

*Iris and I on our
wedding day. She was
19 years of age and I
was 24.*

*Iris and I, with our new family. Left to right:
Saladine, Shoshanna, and Taina.*

*My new Piper aircraft, my "Cocoon," tied with a red ribbon at the
former Alexander Hamilton Airport, St. Croix, U.S.V.I.*

*Awaiting a flight in our new Piper aircraft
are my wife Iris & daughter Cilicia.*

*Hurricane Hugo destroyed my "cocoon" and my
escape from the stress, and gave me even more stress*

*Cilicia, our daughter, enjoying
something sweet.*

*Daughter Ariana with her very
enticing smile.*

*aughters Shoshanna and Taina   enjoying
a vacation.*

Son Saladine studying diligently in the Good Hope School library.
Photo-Vaughn

Jamal, really getting with it on vacation

*Wilbert, smiling, as usual —
he is from St. Croix,
not Washington, D.C.*

Oh, happy days!
Iris and myself
on vacation.

My lovely and loving
wife, Iris with a
Valentine Day Rose.

Ready to go to the office
after visiting Pelican Cove
on St. Croix
Photo-Vaughn

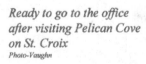

215

*My Grandmother Maggie, my
Father's mother, who lived
In Alabama.*

*My Aunt Queen as a young girl,
my Father's sister-in law*

*My Aunt Doris, my
Mother's sister from
Brooklyn, who taught me
many lessons, including
cleaning up after my dog
(see my book
Dancing in Fire).*

Left to Right: Back - Felisha, Oscar, Orlando, Louis Jr., Jackie, Myra; 3rd Row - Angie, Katie, Elmira; 2nd Row - Anginetta, Shayla, Patrick; 1st Row - Aunt Queen.

Uncle Louis, my Father's Brother, in graduation regalia.

My cousin Louis, Jr, son of Uncle Louis.

Hurricane Hugo devastation to our home on St. Croix, when we all suffered trauma — including our horse.

Our family smiling through it all, even though traumatized at our Hurricane Hugo destroyed home

PART III

Lost

Professional or not, I had to protect my family and myself and play the "hard up nigger."

Chapter 16
Lutheran Medical Center

Though, I walk through the valley of the shadow of death,
I will fear no evil, for You are with me.
Your rod and Your staff, they comfort me.

Psalm 23:4

When I first saw Lutheran Medical Center, I was shocked. I remembered it as an old rundown factory. I passed it many times while going to Coney Island and heading to Staten Island across the Verrazano Narrows Bridge. It connects Bay Ridge, Brooklyn with Staten Island, New York, where Iris and I used to park and tell each other how much we were in love.

The buildings surrounding the hospital were old and falling apart. Many Puerto Ricans lived in the neighborhood. The area was nicer-looking when I was growing up. However, as usual, the white people ran like hell when they realized some darker people than they wanted housing as decent as theirs. When they left the neighborhood, so did the quality of services; such as the sanitation and police departments, and the public school system. Those people left the neighborhood in the hands of minorities until the hospital moved in; then, they tried to get it back.

The Family Practice residency program was housed on the other side of a highway called the Belt Parkway, which separated the rundown area from the more kept up one. The Hispanics occupied the houses on the rundown sides. The other side had some Hispanics mixed with whites and their homes looked better than the ones surrounding Lutheran Medical Center.

The Family Practice clinic was in a three-story brownstone building. I had an office in the rear of the building; it faced an ally. It was comfortable in our center, but I didn't like it. I felt as if I were in prison. Steel bars were on the windows and a special buzzer system was used in order to get in. There were four Black doctors in the program; one white, and one Filipino. They never had that many Black doctors at one time. We had a number of females on staff making sure the clinic functioned well. Mickie was a Puerto Rican and she was the head receptionist. Wanda was Black, and she was one of three nurses. We had two white nurses and two Hispanic female aides who worked with us. As for ethnic diversity, I felt the Family Practice program was balanced for the population of people, which we took care of. Our boss, Dr. Fanta, was an older man who was very dedicated to the program, which was the first Family Practice program in New York City.

Early during my internship in the Family Practice program, I was assigned to the Cardiac Ward at Lutheran Medical Center. I didn't enjoy working with cardiac patients; one minute they were fine, the next minute they were dead.

Most of my patients there had emphysema or heart failure. Cardiology was not one of my favorite areas. Much of my time was spent reading electrocardiograms with the resident and deciding how much medicine to give, and I hated electrocardiograms because they teased my brain.

One night, I had first call. I checked each station, and made sure that no problems were missed before going to bed. A couple of nurses approached me and suggested that I stick around. They thought that a patient was about to have a cardiac arrest. My adrenaline shot up so fast; I immediately became anxious. The nurses started to laugh, but I didn't know what I was going to do if the patient died. I quickly recalled the protocol for instructions during a cardiac arrest, which I'd never fully researched. I paced the floor, hoping that the patient would take a turn for the better. A nurse in the patient's room calmly stated that the patient just coded (heart stop beating). In a hurried frenzy, I tried everything that I could think of in order to revive this dying man. By the time the other doctors arrived, the patient was dead. The nurses encouraged me not to be too concerned because the patient wasn't expected to live anyway.

From then on, cardiac arrest became an everyday occurrence for me. I actually waited daily; I expected to hear the code alarm. A Doctor experiences a weird high feeling as he runs to a code with everyone watching him. The feeling that he may save a person's life all by himself seems to take over. He runs through the hospital; as a crazy fool, he lives out his fantasy, and when he gets to the bedside, he sees the other fools in white coats too.

There comes a time in every conscientious doctor's life when the realization of just how crucial he or she is to the sick and dying really sinks in. This realization came to me during those first five months of my internship. Three patients died during those months when I was on call; not only had I watched them die, but through what I believed was my own foolish behavior or neglect, I apparently helped in one such death, and it affected me deeply.

I was on call on another night, and I had neglected to take the blood of a patient with pulmonary edema for blood gases (checking the amount of oxygen in the blood) before she went to sleep. She was dying the following morning when the nurses called me. I called in a code 66, which is for cardiac arrest, but the patient died before the other doctors could reach her. I remember that time quite vividly because I walked the third floor corridor crying. I promised myself that no other patients would ever die because of what I thought was my neglect. Another time, I was in the emergency room, and a patient came in with a similar pulmonary edema from which three of my other patients died. As soon as I saw her, I knew what the problem was. I immediately ordered the nurses to give her lasix and digoxin. I ordered a chest x-ray and summoned the senior resident. When the senior resident arrived, I informed him that the patient came into the emergency room looking as if she was dying with a pulmonary edema. She was fine; she sat up in the bed in a matter of thirty minutes. She was sitting there comfortably, smiling. The senior resident examined the chest x-ray and told me that he did not like the fact that I treated the patient for a pulmonary edema without consulting him first.

I wasn't going to take the chance of the patient dying in order to stroke his ego or wait for him to be a hero. I wasn't concerned about his feeling or his ego. All I knew was that this patient was dying and she was now alive and doing well. I made another promise to myself that no patient of mine would die due to procrastination.

Many people on the Cardiac Ward thought that I was organized and one of the best doctors they had. I never took the comments seriously because I felt more lost than found. I became very friendly with the staff, and we had a good working relationship, but sometimes we went too far. Working in a hospital with so many females doing what I asked them to do gave me a sense of power.

Ordinarily, I would start my day by saying something nice to everyone. Occasionally my behavior would be flirtatious, and so would be some of the nurses. Occasionally we hugged, and kissed on the cheek. Every now and then, someone would say, "You think you're cute, don't you?" This bothered me, but I tried not to let it show. I simply enjoyed relating to people.

On-call nights were more interesting than on-call days. That's when all the day's gossip was rehashed in detail. One evening while I was doing my rounds, a Black nurse named Jenner approached me and told me all the white nurses were "checking me out." I looked at her in surprise, but she continued, "Come on, you know what's happening," and she started giving me names and faces. "They want any Black doctor whom they can get their hands on," she informed me. I was flattered that some of the nurses were after me, and not long after that incident, I became known as the "lover boy" of the hospital. I tried to find out the source of the rumor, but the only answer I received was that everybody knew it.

Some people, however, seemed to be bothered that I was so friendly. They believed that I was out to get in the nurses' panties. At first, I thought that it was all a joke, but then it got serious. Soon people weren't smiling anymore when it was mentioned. I was touchy about the matter; especially when a Christian woman approached me, saying, "I heard all about you. So you're the lover boy of the hospital." Every time I saw her, I felt compelled to explain myself. It all seemed to be an exaggeration that I couldn't take too seriously. In fact, being on this ward turned out to be a real test of my marriage.

One evening while I was on night call in the hospital, one of the day-shift nurses named Cookie called me. She wanted me to give her some advice about some trouble that she was having with her boy friend. Since she was going through some stress, I sincerely wanted to help her, so we talked for a while.

The next day, Cookie spoke to me about the advice, which I had given her. After that, we talked frequently. I didn't think that it was unusual because I talked with many nurses. In no time, however, we seemed to be putting aside time to be together and talk about anything and everything. It didn't take long before we stepped over the boundary of friendship.

My image as the "lover boy of the hospital" now took on a new reality though I kept denying it.

I tried to not let what I was doing interfere with my marriage, but it didn't take Iris long to figure out that I was doing more at the medical center than trying to save lives. Iris called my friend Raymond and spoke with him concerning my behavior and our marriage. He suggested that she dress up nicely and surprise me at the hospital. One evening when I was on call, Iris came to the hospital; she looked very pretty. She caught me talking with Cookie. I couldn't suffer being caught, so I got upset with Iris. Iris didn't accuse me of anything; I just felt stupid.

As time went on, Iris realized that I was being unfaithful. The integrity of my relationship with Iris was being tested. I loved Iris. I decided to save my marriage; therefore, I stopped seeing Cookie.

I didn't know what was driving me to do some of the things that I was doing. As long as I was busy with medicine I kept out of trouble, but as soon as I became bored or stressed I messed up. We started attending Calvary Baptist Church after our return to New York. The church wasn't exciting to me anymore. I knew that there was something missing, but I didn't know what. Calvary Baptist Church had become a way of life with me. It was traditional to go there. It still had something to offer people, but my life was so much in conflict that I needed more. It wasn't the church's fault that I couldn't focus on God. I was distracted by what was available to me since becoming a doctor. No longer were people telling me what I wasn't or how dumb I was. They were offering almost the sky in return for my attention and sometimes affection. I had a difficult time handling it all. Iris knew I was distracted, but she felt helpless as usual to draw my attention to it. Therefore, it was my fault and no one else's that I had separated myself from God, and it wasn't Calvary Baptist Church's fault or Iris's.

I spent time with Shoshanna and Taina, but it wasn't a lot of time. I loved them dearly. When I wasn't with them, I was in the hospital on call or at the Family Practice program late into the evening. Iris suffered a lot without me.

Chapter 17
Emergency Room

Do not I hate them, O Lord, that hate thee?
And am not I grieved with those that rise up against thee?

Psalm 139:21

The emergency room was both an ordeal and a learning experience. I enjoyed working there because I had always enjoyed emergency medicine. The challenge of a new problem with a new patient every half-hour or so kept my interest high. That first day I must have treated two head wounds, a few fractures, vaginitis, cervicitis, multiple upper respiratory illnesses, pulmonary edema, myocardial infarction, and one patient with cardiac arrest. Each day was as busy as the one before. Before long, though, I ran into some problems, some of which were engineered by several nurses. I found that I lacked the tact and humility that were apparently needed in order to deal with these problems. Some of the nurses were treating patients before I gave the okay. They were trying to help, but sometimes it was at a risk to the patients. Intravenous lines (IVs) were being inserted on cardiac patients without doctors being informed. Aspirin suppositories were being inserted into children's rectums without regard to an allergy, which is a known complication if the child has nasal polyps and asthma. Consultations were being ordered without the doctors being notified, even though it was the doctor's responsibility to decide what was necessary. I knew these things were improper, but I let them go on for a few days.

Finally, I approached one of the nurses and told her what was happening wasn't proper and I didn't want her to use these procedures with my patients. We got into an argument, and she asked me if I threatened her. I didn't consider what I had said a threat, but I told her if that's the way she took it, then I guess it was.

The following day, the word was out that I had overstepped my bounds in dealing with the nurses. Many doctors feel that to get a nurse on your bad side is the ultimate in stupidity. Well, I wasn't concerned about that.

Some of the doctors informed me of some of the things that they were hearing. "I don't know what you did," one doctor said to me, "but the word is out to 'get' you." I wasn't surprised, and I knew that this was only the beginning of my struggle to practice good medicine regardless of the consequences.

Shortly after this, a young boy of about fourteen years of age was admitted to the emergency room for a head wound. I immediately ordered a skull series with appropriate laboratory data and evaluated the case as a possible concussion. His blood pressure was 150/90, which was clearly too high for him. I requested that he be observed for any changes in vital signs, such as blood pressure and pulse, and asked a few nurses to notify me if anything happened. I had written a note that if the child was okay within a few hours, then he was to be sent home and requested to return to the outpatient clinic in five days. It was very busy that day, but before I went home, I informed the oncoming physician of the child's status.

The following morning the Director of Family Practice, Dr. Fanta, asked to see me in his office. With the emergency room sheet on his desk, he accused me of being medically incompetent and told me that the hospital was not in need of any publicity, as it already had a number of cases pending against it. I tried to explain to him, to no avail, that some of the nurses were out to get me. Apparently, before I went home, the nurses neglected to inform me that the boy's blood pressure was still elevated. After I left the hospital, someone on the nursing staff decided to call a neurological consultant (a specialist for the brain and spinal cord), after which the child was admitted to the hospital.

The conflict between the nurses and me continued. Some of them accused me of doing too many pelvic exams. The nurses alleged that every time a young, pretty female came into the emergency room, I wanted to put a speculum into her. When I asked the nurses for medication and other things for patients, they sometimes tried to embarrass me by saying loudly, "Wait a minute! I'm busy; I only have two hands."

As a result, patients whom I saw in the emergency room were often neglected and forced to wait unnecessarily long. Most of the time, I, myself, would get the items that I needed for the patients. People sat in the emergency room suffering from seizures and asthma attacks, waiting until some nurse felt that they were sick enough to be brought in the treatment area. Sometimes workers would approach me about patients (usually Hispanic) whom they thought were being treated unfairly by the nurses and I was expected to do something. Many workers knew that I had a heart for the people. Upon such lay advice, often I was hesitant, I but would try to help anyway.

One time a young man came in with blood on his T-shirt, and was made to wait on a chair inside the reception area. A Puerto Rican aide approached me saying, "Hey, Doc, you've gotta see this guy." A nurse had looked at him and said, "He just has a little blood on his T-shirt." When I spoke to the aide, however, she told me that the patient had been stabbed in the back.

Often times, incidents occurred where a nurse's judgment was incorrect, and no doctor was notified. It seemed to be such an indifferent, apathetic way of dealing with all the sick and dying.

Ethnic Bias

Minority groups suffered the most in the emergency room. Biased comments were often made by a few of the nurses about Hispanics or Jews. Many of the Hispanic people were harassed publicly. I burned inside every time I witnessed this.

Once I heard, a nurse make the statement that all Hispanics say, "No speak English." Although I've heard Italians and a few Scandinavians say the same thing, I never saw them being treated as poorly. Some of the nurses there appeared to have it out for particular ethnic groups.

They rarely mentioned anything about Black people because there weren't many being seen in our emergency room.

A big Black security guard acted just like an "Uncle Tom" whenever something was said about Blacks. He would laugh and joke with these same nurses, who were white nurses. Many times, they even made racial slurs about him, and he would just laugh. I believed that he needed a good swift whipping. I despised him for doing the 'Slave camp shuffle' for those bigots.

Some police officers weren't much better than the bigoted nurses were. I was once sewing up a man's head, and a police officer punched him in the face. I left the treatment room to tell the head nurse about it, but she only said, "Williams, don't get involved." I don't remember if the man was white, Black, or Hispanic. I couldn't believe what she was saying.

I was tired of what was happening. Frustration was mounting because I felt that the patients were the only ones suffering, while the medical staff closed their eyes, made money and went home.

The racism and racial prejudice that existed in the emergency room were blatant at times, and I never heard anyone speak against it, not even a Puerto Rican nurse whom I felt was in touch with her roots.

Racist Liars

On New Year's Eve night, my tolerance was at its lowest. A patient came to the emergency room after having had a seizure. An aide came to me because she felt that the patient had been waiting a long time. She told me that no nurse had seen the patient, even though he had been processed. No vital signs had been taken, and the patient was sitting in the waiting room feeling very sickly. I asked the aide to bring the patient in.

After taking initial lab work on him, I requested a nurse to take him back to the intensive care area. When another nurse heard that I wanted the patient transferred to the back area, she cursed me aloud.

I asked the nurse who was transporting the patient to put an intravenous line with dextrose water in his arm.

The patient was left alone in the intensive care hold unit for about an hour, after which time the nurse checked on him and came running out, yelling that the man was having a seizure. I instructed her to get 10mg of Valium and give him 5mg of it. When I went into the intensive care area, there was no IV line to put the medication in. She had not followed my previous orders. The patient convulsed, making it impossible to establish an IV line. After the seizure, I asked the nurse to order an emergency chest x-ray.

I was so angry that evening I could not stop talking about how the roof was going to come off the emergency room. I told a few of the staff people whom I trusted what was on my mind, and that I wanted something done about the inhumanity to the patients. Their advice was for me not to disturb the waters, because I could get hurt. They were concerned about my losing the internship residency program and not being able to work in any other hospital due to being "blacklisted." Some people were also concerned about my family and my own mental health. Most of them tried to calm me down, but were not successful.

I told everyone that I would go to outside sources if I didn't get any positive results at the medical center. I was ready to expose the emergency room situation to the community; I was ready to call the Daily News of New York.

When I mentioned these things to a couple of emergency room administrators, one told me that if I did that, one would have to go, either the hospital or I, and it would be me, even if I were right. He told me that the hospital had to survive. They were not going to let me destroy it.

I then approached the Family Practice residents. When I told them what was happening, they were reluctant to get involved. Most of them believed and agreed with the allegations against the emergency room, but felt that there was nothing, which they could do about it. I told them that there had to be a time in their lives when they would have to deal with problems of this sort, which affected the patients and physicians alike. If we really believed in competent medical care, this was our time to defend it. I made it clear to them that I didn't think that they really cared, but with or without them, I was going to do what was necessary.

The Family Practice Psychologist, Dr. Sheldon, was present and asked the other residents if they were going to let me bear this burden alone. One resident made the suggestion to have a letter written by the residents in Family Practice, in order to state their support for me. They all agreed, though some of the residents appeared worried and hesitant about this position.

A meeting was arranged with the general house staff, who believed some of the issues were questionable and didn't want to get involved at the time. They wanted more time to think about the issues, but I thought we didn't have that kind of time.

Meanwhile, a meeting had been arranged with a couple of head nurses of the emergency room and the emergency room administrators. My original outline for the meeting was dismissed because it was thought to be too personal. Some of the residents got together and wrote up a new agenda. They also asked me to sit back and say very little, because I was too emotionally involved. They were to give me cues for when to expound on a particular point in the discussion. In their opinion, this would be more effective and would not readily turn people off. I didn't agree with the new set-up, but I went along with it.

People gathered for the meeting in a portion of the hospital designated by the emergency room administrators. Two nurses from the emergency room entered without making any eye contact with me. When the meeting began, I thought that the issues were going to be dealt with effectively.

The conference turned out to be a disaster. The Family Practice Director, who was also in charge of the emergency room, was very uncomfortable. He had not even wanted this meeting held. He sat in his chair, protecting his emergency room staff and throwing me to those racist liars.

When I realized what was happening, I refused to hold my peace any longer. I challenged a statement made by one of the emergency room nurses. She said no patient had ever waited in our emergency room for hours without anyone knowing that they were ill, and that patients were not doubted as to the seriousness of their complaints. I refuted her statement; I cited a couple of my own patients who had waited unnecessarily long, and a few patients, thought to be constant bothers, who were left to wait in the waiting room. I told the personnel present that the issues were not being dealt with, and the nurses who sat face to face with them were not telling the truth.

At that point, Dr. Fanta made a motion to end the meeting. I was furious and felt like turning over the tables. I rose and walked out.

The situation seemed to be a total loss. People were suffering in the community, and it seemed as if very few of our professionals cared. I knew that before there could be healing, the system would have to heal itself. This was part of the problem that seemed impossible to resolve.

After the meeting, I was ready to do anything in order to get results. I thought about calling up "Eyewitness News."

Some people approached me that day; they wanted to know why I walked out of the meeting, but they were already out of my mind. I didn't want to have anything to do with them. They were not involved in any cause, which I was fighting for, and I did not need them. I had it with Lutheran Medical Center that day. I didn't trust the opinions of anyone. I only trusted how I felt.

In a few days, I went to see the emergency room administrators in order to express my displeasure over the meeting. I told them that the people of the community had only us to fight for their rights in the hospital in order to assure them of decent medical care. The administrators said that they were concerned, but that my cause wasn't clearly stated. They also questioned whether I stood to make any secondary gain in this matter. I informed them that I personally was looking for no gain. I only wanted to do something positive for the patients. I explained that they were my people (Hispanics and Blacks), and I had to help them.

One of the administrators, a Puerto Rican, assured me that if I went to the community and exposed these problems, even he would be forced to side with the hospital, although these were his people also. They may have been his people, but from where I sat he didn't seem to care what happened to them as long as he kept his job. I was told by the other administrator not to threaten him because if I did, he would give me nothing. If I pushed them, they would push me back. I went back three times to see the administrators, and each time they told me that they would do their best to improve things.

For weeks, I continued seriously thinking about contacting the Daily News and informing the community. I was even considering letting the seven Puerto Rican gangs in the neighborhood know that I believed some of the hospital emergency room staffs were racist against Hispanics. I did speak with some community people, but it didn't go very far.

Burn Out

After all the energy I used to stand up against those racist, I was exhausted and disappointed. I was burning out, but didn't realize it. I knew that there was some way to handle the fight against this inhumanity, and I was determined to find the answer.

As the weeks passed, I began to feel isolated and alone. In my efforts, I didn't want to be bothered with anyone. I tried using my energy to think. I wanted to crack the system wide open and to use it for the benefit of the people.

The World on Fire

I wouldn't talk to anyone for weeks at a time. I felt that there was no use in it. Some people wanted to know if I had a problem. They questioned my sitting alone in the cafeteria, and why I didn't visit the nurses' station anymore.

I tried not to reveal anything to them, but sometimes it didn't work. Usually they would tell me to simply take care of my family and myself and leave the problems of the hospital to the hospital. Their attitudes just pushed me further away from them. I'm sure that they meant well, but there was work to be done. I Stayed to Myself More.

My home life was intense because I had many problems thinking about the hospital garbage and how some people were treated there. I didn't enjoy the raging fire I was in, but if I were in the fire, what were the people in, those who were less fortunate than me? As far as I could see, they were being consumed by fire. I couldn't stand seeing people hurt. I kept thinking about my roots and how I came out of Red Hook and I was supposed to make a positive difference in people's lives. It was a burden that at times was terribly difficult to bear, but I had to bear it. I made promises to myself and to God that I would stand for what I believed was right rather than sit on what I felt was wrong. The world to me was on fire, and it was consuming masses of people; especially Blacks and Puerto Ricans where I was living. I knew the same thing was occurring all around the world--and in me.

I Wanna Quit

There were days when I got up and told Iris that I didn't want to go to work. I was sure that I didn't want to be a doctor anymore. This was the first time that I considered leaving medicine. I don't think that she took me seriously.

The months following the emergency room experience showed me the reality of being burned out. I was mentally and physically exhausted. I was no good to my patients, my family, or myself. Not only did I have problems with the emergency room, but also I had a problem with myself. The conflict with the nurses in the emergency room grew worse. I tried to get my head together, but the thoughts of what I had gone through with people whom I had thought were fair kept hurting me. I wanted to resolve the bigoted problem in the emergency room, not fight with nurses. Even when, however, I held my peace, the trouble continued.

Deep Bigotry

"Cathy," the head nurse in the emergency room, who was white, made a statement about not wanting any more Black doctors to ever work in the emergency room. I was told that she made the statement because of me. She knew that I was onto her bigotry and racial prejudice, and she set herself on fire thinking about me. She was the main nurse involved in the racial prejudice remarks against Hispanics and Jews. When I sat with the hospital staff at the conference table meeting, Cathy was there. One evening she was in the emergency room supervising. I was on call in the hospital. Someone called me on the telephone and said, "Hey, Williams, come on down to the emergency room." I was upset that I was referred to that way (I was Dr. Williams, not hey, Williams). When I got to the emergency room, Cathy was attending to my patient. When she saw me, she stopped taking care of him and walked out of the treatment room. She wouldn't even tell the patient's status to me. This happened on a number of other occasions.

When someone mentioned my name, she would go into a rage, and display her disgust for me. No one could say anything to her about me without her making a scene. Sometimes, I was stopped in the hospital, only to be told how Cathy hated my guts.

Cathy converted a few other nurses with her hatred and bigotry for me. Those nurses, however, were more conservative. Occasionally they would make themselves scarce when I needed them, or they would speak to me in a nasty tone of voice, and a few times, I was just plainly ignored. Nurses with whom I had a good relationship previously changed their attitude and behavior toward me. I felt terrible about it.

The situation grew worse and worse. I began to loathe going to the emergency room. The atmosphere was such that I couldn't relax, and it interfered with patient care.

Cathy was the leader of the pack for one entire year; she succeeded in making my work hell. I have to give it to her. She was an expert at calculating and practicing hatred and bigotry in the midst of minorities and she had a good show going on in the emergency room with that big Black "Uncle Tom" washer cheering partner. He was a stupid fool.

Family Support

I didn't spend much time at my parents' apartment in Red Hook. When I had some free time, I called my mother and spoke with her. It was hard not unloading my problems on her. She often listened to me with patience and would tell me to calm down and take it easy. She understood my energy, being my mother. There were few things that changed about me over the years. She knew that I was a fighter and wouldn't quit until the battle was over. She vividly remembered my early days at Calvary Baptist Church. I fought religious wars with Rev. Yarber and anyone else who dared to challenge me. She always encouraged me to release my weapons of warfare and move on. She hated conflict and had enough wisdom to know when to quit, but I didn't have enough wisdom to listen to her.

I didn't regret fighting battles the way I did. I only wished that there were none to fight. I was never able to convince anyone who knew me that I was not looking for fights to pick. My father was his usual self, as he encouraged me to do my best. He told me to stand up for what I believed in, but he didn't like all the confusion, which I got into. I learned to respect my father's opinion because he held his ground on issues. He had a soft heart for people, and one of his strong points was standing up for them if he felt that they were wronged. I also respected my father for his constant badgering of me; particularly his concern for me not to be too hard on people. In spite of his pain from being paralyzed, he shared the pain of others. I know that his, being Black and a man living in this country, challenged his human fiber and he passed the test. He loved people in spite of it all. Even when he talked about some people, being full of racial hatred, I know in his heart that he didn't hate anyone. He was hurt as a result of being oppressed because of his color and race. He never stopped telling me how the people in Chesson, Alabama ran the Black doctor out of town for taking care of a white woman. My father was proud of me and all he really wanted for me was to be successful. Being an extension of him would help me stand tall and move on.

My sisters were going through their own problems on a marital and social level. I tried not to burden them with my problems. Sometimes it was too much to bear, and I used them as a sounding board. They listened to me. but were upset that I was going through problems.

My Aunt Doris and Cousin Leray were in my life. I was glad that I had the opportunity to show Leray, that I was born a little "Negro" boy according to my birth certificate, and now I was a young Blackman, trained to save lives. I was a doctor. God helped me to become a doctor.

My aunt was so happy to see me practicing medicine. She would call me up and ask me all kinds of questions. She helped me to weather the heat that I was in by just believing in me. She hated the fact that I was always fighting the establishment. She didn't see any need for those kinds of battles for me. As far as she was concerned, I had made it and I needed to enjoy it.

A Trip South

In the summer of 1979, our friends, Michael and Margie, who still lived in Albany, New York, decided to take a trip to Vero Beach, Florida; they invited Iris and me. Neither of us had ever been to Florida. We had not seen Michael and Margie for a long time. We were in need of a break. We made a small bed in the back of our little Datsun 610 and headed for the sunshine state of Florida. Iris and I took turns driving. We were to meet Michael and Margie in Vero Beach, Florida.

Iris was pregnant with our son (Saladine). She was more than halfway through the pregnancy. We drove for 23 hours, alternating drivers. Shoshanna and Taina were comfortable as they slept on the makeshift bed, which we made for them. The trying part of the trip was driving that distance with the broken air conditioner in our car. It was working well before we left New York; then, it broke down and we were baking in it once we crossed "South of the Border."

When we got to Vero Beach, we were both relieved and tired. The children slept most of the way. We stayed with Margie's mother. Margie's sisters were there. Michael and Margie went to someone else's house to stay because her mother's house was too small. It was so hot and humid in Florida that I couldn't breathe well. Iris was braving the heat. Even being pregnant, she did better than I did with the weather. We took the children to Disney World in Orlando, Florida. We tried to enjoy it, but it was too hot and we couldn't relax. We didn't enjoy Vero Beach very much. We did go to a family gathering where people were very nice to us. Iris wanted to do more in Florida than just sit around. We decided to drive to Miami, Florida. It took us about two hours and thirty minutes. I just wanted to see what Miami looked like. After we got there, we stopped at a gift store, purchased some items, and hit the road back to Vero Beach. Iris was miserable, hot, and not enjoying how we were spending our so-called vacation.

One day Michael asked me to go with him in order to get fresh squeezed orange juice and I did. We got big glasses of orange juice for twenty-five cents. After we downed a few, we talked for a while, and then went to the car. A carload of white people drove by us and called Michael "a big black nigger." I looked at Michael in shock and Michael said, "That's the way them crackers are." That was my first experience of racial prejudice in the state of Florida. I was deeply hurt that they said that to my friend. I could see the hurt in his eyes and he appeared helpless. That ruined my Florida trip and I would never heal of its stain. I developed a fear in Florida because I felt out of my northern element. I knew that there was racial prejudice in the North, but for some reason I felt more protected. In the South, I envisioned mobs of white people stringing me up to a tree as my father told me that they did in Chesson, Alabama. Alabama was not far from Florida, which made Florida more threatening to me.

Michael and Margie left with Iris and me in their car. Iris and I were both glad to leave Florida for different reasons. On our way home, Iris got sick and started to vomit and have abdominal pains. We had to stop on the roadside in the state of Virginia. Michael had a cold, apathetic attitude about our misfortune. He didn't want to wait and help us. Gas was rationed according to odd- and even-number license plates and we were driving on the day when Michael could get gas, but it was about 11:30 p.m.and he was afraid he would be stuck without being able to get fuel. He decided to leave us on the roadside with Iris sick and our two small children. As a friend, Michael made the wrong decision. It hurt us very much and it only sealed our Florida trip with more disappointment. I loved Michael and I wasn't going to let what happened ruin our friendship. I believed that he would understand in years to come how to really be a friend.

Chapter 18
Second-Year Residency

I hate them with perfect hatred:
I count them mine enemies.

Psalm 139:22

I was well into my second-year residency, and even though Iris was encouraging me, and my family stood by me, I felt low in terms of my self-worth. My life was falling apart at the seams, while I was fighting the establishment. I was so depressed that I didn't want to go to work, ever again. I couldn't bear being put down continually, but I couldn't stop fighting either.

French Fries and Prejudice

One day, I went to the cafeteria and heard an Italian food clerk harassing two Puerto Ricans. She told them not to speak Spanish because English was the language of this country. At this point, I had it with white people. I told her that she had no right to say that to them. They were Americans, and Spanish should be the second language of the country. That was the end of that situation, or so I thought.

For the next three months, this same food handler placed very small portions of food on my plate. On the other hand, she would load up the plate of the person in front of me. She maintained a condescending and cold attitude.

One evening when I was on call, she and I got into an argument over French fries, which she refused to serve me. The nurse in front of me asked for French fries. The clerk told her to come back later; she would keep the French fries on the side for her. She planned to let the nurse pick up the French fries on the way out of the back door. When I asked for the same, she said, "Why don't you ask the cashier?"

I called her a racist. She warned me not to use that word with her again.

The following week, I was told that the cafeteria clerk reported me to the hospital administrators. She had accused me of harassment. The administrators evidently took her word. They never called me in for clarification, but sent a notice to my Family Practice Director about my behavior.

They Used My Services

That same week, I was asked to see a well-to-do, prominent woman who had political ties with a hospital administrator. She suffered with a severe nosebleed. She wasn't even my patient, but a hospital official who requested my service personally called me at home. I don't know why I was selected. I had never seen her before and she wasn't a patient in the Family Practice program. She was in the emergency room for a time, and then admitted to the hospital. She had no personal physician, and for that moment, I was it. I treated her by burning the blood vessels in her nose with silver nitrate and the bleeding stopped. One night while I was home, a nurse called me and informed me that the patient was bleeding again from the nose. I asked her to get me some silver nitrate sticks to stop the nosebleed and told her that I was on my way in.

When I arrived, the patient was sitting in bed bleeding, all over her face and on the linen. She told me that she had been calling the nurses' station, but no one responded. She was very anxious. The nurse who called me on the phone was giving evening reports before preparing to go home.

When I approached the nurse, she told me that she couldn't find any silver nitrate sticks, and if I still wanted them, that I could go get them myself. She wasn't nasty about it; just indifferent. I lost my cool and yelled at her. A nurse standing nearby told her to get the silver nitrate sticks for me. She took her time; in fact, I never got those sticks from her.

Someone suggested that I send the aide to the emergency room in order to get the sticks. The aide came back with one stick to cauterize the patient's nose. I sent her back for two more.

When I questioned the aide as to why she brought only one stick, she said that the emergency room head nurse was very nasty. The emergency room nurse told her to go get her own silver nitrate sticks and not to return because they only had a couple left.

I knew that they had more than just a couple because I had been in there earlier that day and saw an entire tube full. I asked the aide (who was Black) why the nurse had been angry with her, and she told me that she didn't know. I went down to the emergency room with the aide, took the required silver nitrate sticks and left six in the tube.

The nurse grabbed me and asked, "Who are you?"

"I'm Doctor Williams. You said that there were only a couple of silver nitrate sticks. You lied and were nasty to this aide for no reason. I needed more silver nitrate sticks than you gave her and I have a patient bleeding upstairs." I left the emergency room yelling at the nurse, who was boldly yelling back.

The following day, I was reported to the emergency room head nurse for harassment. Things just continued to happen. It was a crazy time, and the incidents were building up.

Cathy was still on the rampage, and I was sick of her.

Fire and Brimstone

I looked for a way out of all the hellfire and brimstone, which I faced at Lutheran Medical Center and medicine in general. I was involved in church again; I tried to help the young people. They looked up to me even more now because I made something of myself. Many of them knew that I worked very hard in order to become a doctor and I believe it encouraged them.

I was spinning my wheels at Calvary Baptist Church. For all the years I had spent there, I didn't see much of a change concerning the young people there. Some of them were married and others had joined the church looking for someone to guide and lead them spiritually. My life wasn't where it should have been, but I had spent many years at the church. I knew that I loved them dearly and I offered what I had to give at the time; unselfish love. The reality of my life's situation was that I needed help myself. I was sinking emotionally, depressed and in no shape to help anyone, but I tried. I convinced Iris to go with me to the pastor's house. She told me it wouldn't do any good and the pastor would not receive my suggestions well. Against her advice I went. It was a terrible meeting. I told the pastor that the young people needed better guidance and he listened until he couldn't take it anymore. He wanted to know who I thought I was coming to him, telling him what the young people needed. He politely told me that I couldn't speak for the young people in his church. I left his house in frustration and realized again the wisdom of my wife's advice.

After that meeting with the pastor, I decided to start a street film ministry called the "Agape Film Ministry." I showed religious films in neighborhoods. I showed "The Cross and the Switchblade" by David Wilkenson, not knowing I would come to experience God in a deeper way through it.

A Continual Source of Pain

My life at Lutheran Medical Center Hospital and the Family Practice program was a continual source of pain. I had an emergency pediatric case one evening, and someone telephoned me, saying, "Williams, you better come down here to the emergency room." By this time, I was fed up with all this "one minute personal, the next minute impersonal" stuff.

"Why are they calling me by my last name?" I wondered to myself. "I'm Dr. Williams, not Hey Williams or Williams." They don't have that kind of right, not after treating me like a dog.

Well, I don't know whom it was calling because I hung up the phone quickly in order to make my way to the emergency room. When I arrived, there was a hydrocephalic baby having seizures. Instead of devoting my full attention to the baby, I tried to find out who called me that way.

The nurse taking care of the baby wanted me to help her suction the baby and give oxygen. My senior resident was on the telephone, trying to contact the patient's doctor, so I stood at the patient's stretcher and helped in giving the oxygen.

After checking with two nurses, who told me that they hadn't called me, I saw Cathy and asked her if she had called me. She said arrogantly, "No, I didn't call you." I had it with her insolence. This had been going on for a year. I told her that I knew it was she, and she started to walk away. I told her that she was a racist and that she made racist statements about Hispanics, Jews, and Blacks. I assured her that she wasn't fooling anyone by laughing with the Puerto Ricans and talking about them like dirt behind their backs.

I let her know that others and I knew she was a racist, against not only Hispanics, but Jews and Blacks also. She denied it and said that I was acting like a crazy man. (I am sure she was somewhat right because I was steamed up.) I also told her that she hadn't treated my patients or me

241

professionally. I reminded her of how she, for one entire year, never gave me information about my private patients, for whom she was the primary care nurse.

Cathy phoned the administrator and said, "There is a man down here who calls himself a doctor. I think he has gone crazy. You'd better call King's County Hospital Psychiatric Ward to take him to the G building" (crazy section of that hospital). Then, she walked into one of the treatment rooms. As I followed her, we continued to argue, and she repeatedly called me insane.

When the administrator and two nursing supervisors arrived, they tried to calm me down. They wanted to know what happened and didn't seem to be surprised about my complaint. They advised me to document my complaint if I could.

The following day, I put in a formal complaint to the nursing supervisor; it pertained to the year-long vendetta against me.

A few days later, my chief resident in Family Practice informed me that Cathy was suing me for assault on her person. He told me that she was accusing me of bodily handling of her in the treatment room, that I threw her up against the wall and threatened her life. The hospital and the nurses union, which would supply her with a lawyer in order to pursue the assault charge against me, backed her. Not only that, but she had a witness to verify that I had attacked her.

The chief resident thought it looked very bad for me, and he, along with others, suggested that I forget about the whole thing. I told him that I wouldn't. "You'd better," he said, "because you're going to lose. She has a witness against you. Do you understand what that means? What about your family and your career?"

I told him that I didn't care about the career. He told me that the hospital was ready to back Cathy, and if they had to, they'd destroy me. "You don't even have a license to practice medicine," he continued. "How will you live? Let it go." I told him that I would not.

I couldn't believe that Cathy was telling an outright lie. I had never threatened her or put my hands on her person. I never even made a gesture to harm her.

White Power

The hospital emergency room administrator immediately terminated my being in the emergency room. Up to this time, the hospital administrators had not summoned me or anyone else for verification and proof of the charges. They took Cathy's word for what had happened and then took action against me. They had come to her aid immediately. There I was, their salaried doctor, with an assault charge against me, and they "iced" me without any hearing or any spoken word to me.

All this news came by way of the chief resident in the Family Practice program. My Family Practice Director, Dr. Fanta, didn't even have the guts to tell me himself. He sent all words of "condolence" by way of a carrier doctor.

After a couple of days, the chief resident came back to me and asked me to think about letting the matter go. The hospital now wanted to suspend me from the staff, and the administrators had asked the Family Practice Director to get rid of me. He told me that my boss let them know that he wouldn't do that. Things were mounting against me.

The chief resident informed me that Cathy was now threatening to sue the aide whom I sent to the emergency room in order to get the silver nitrate sticks. The nurse who grabbed me when I took the silver nitrate sticks was now saying that I assaulted her also.

The chief resident warned me that if they fired me, I would be in a fix, and probably no one would hire me in the whole United States.

Within a day or two, I was called into my director's office. He and his staff were there, along with the chief resident. The director politely invited me to sit. They started discussing the serious implications of the matter. My director said that it was the consensus that I see someone who could help me with my problem; a Psychiatrist. He went on to say that, it was his responsibility to me in order to make certain that I received the kind of help that I needed.

I stopped him immediately and asked, "Whose opinion is this?"

"This is the conclusion that we all came to," he replied.

"Who?" I asked again.

"We," he answered.

"How can you come to that conclusion about me when you know nothing about me or what's going on?" I pressed. I told him that if they wanted me to see a Psychiatrist, I would after they all had seen one first.

"How can we help you?" he asked.

I said he could not help me, but maybe they could help some of the residents who had similar problems. I told him that it wasn't my problem, but it was our problem. The Director told me that they couldn't help me if I didn't cooperate.

"Good," I responded, "Because I'm not going to see any Psychiatrist." I knew what that meant.

When the meeting was over, they must have thought that I was really one crazy doctor. The chief resident continued to speak with me. He told me that the hospital was ready and anxious to fire me.

Saladine

Iris had just had our third child, Saladine, and he was only five weeks old. He was my first son. He had distinguishing eye brows that raised when he was stressed. I decided to give him an Arab name. I named him after an Arab warrior who is highly respected in Arab history. A medical resident who worked with me had the same name. He was a Muslim. I admired him because he was cool and calm.

I thought about Iris, Shoshanna, Taina and Saladine and my responsibility to them. Again, I felt trapped, chained to the rap and frightened for my family and myself. He asked me to think about it because it would probably be one of the most important decisions in my life I'd ever have to make. The emergency room administrator wanted the matter resolved. He asked me if he arranged a meeting between Cathy and me, would I come. I kept thinking about my new son, only a few weeks old, Iris and my daughters at home, in light of the decision I had to make. At that moment, I knew I had to "take the rap." At that point, professional or not, I had to protect my family and myself and play the "hard up nigger." I told the administrator that Cathy was lying. "Yes," he said, "I know she is lying. What do you expect her to do? You forced her by putting her job in jeopardy, and this was her way out."

When the meeting was called, Cathy lied so much that she made no sense. I called her a liar to her face, in front of the administrator. She asked me if I had a tape recorder to prove it. I told her that I could prove her a liar by way of another nurse.

"Well, did she record any conversations?" she asked.

I wanted to jump across the table and beat her. When I asked how I assaulted her, she started stumbling in her speech and fabricating her story. The emergency room administrator asked her to consider my family. She told him that she would drop the action to take me into court. It was a cheap and dirty situation.

The "Hard up Nigger"

The hospital backed Cathy all the way, while never considering the truth of the entire ordeal. They never questioned me as to my complaints. They never followed up the assault charge with the witness. They wanted to settle the matter any way they could, and they did, at the expense of my respect and integrity. With little regard for me or my family, they put us aside like trash. I felt castrated by the whole system that was supposed to protect us.

My attitude changed. I convinced myself that I didn't care about anyone or anything except my family. This was my lowest point during the residency program. Patients were dying, and I wouldn't blink an eyelid. I lost something valuable.

When I took care of patients in the emergency room and the wards, I cared very little. Many times, I would be impatient and in a hurry. Occasionally, a nurse or two who were sharp enough to take notice would talk to me about it. One nurse told me that the good, caring Doctor Williams had died, and she wanted him back. I explained to her why he was never going to surface again and that he cared less about the patients' problems, and the hospital's as well.

This wasn't the only time that I sounded off. People were surprised and shocked. They couldn't understand how I had allowed myself to become so hard.

One of the Family Practice doctors (who happened to be white) came into my office and tried to talk some sense into me. He told me to stop crying like a baby and put my efforts back into being a good doctor. I argued with him, and soon we were throwing ammunition about each other's medical competency. It all ended in a cursing match with nothing being accomplished except many nasty things having been said.

Not all these medical incompetence accusations were helping matters, especially when I was told that the hospital was ready to defend itself against my charges of their medical incompetence. They wanted me shut up for good. The medical incompetence game was their backlash against me.

Patients were suffering under my care. I knew that I wasn't treating them well. All the continued frustration and depression had me fixed on destruction. Unless I changed my attitude, I was doomed and didn't know it. Cardiac arrest calls were being made in the hospital, and I took my time getting there. My patients at Family Practice were rushed out of the office at times. I was refusing to see people who had previously been a headache to me.

One day a patient of mine died, but I just didn't care. At that moment, I realized that I was dying from within. Whatever had sustained me in the past had been shut out. My relationship with God and man was at a low ebb. God was shelved away in a dark corner of my mind. I was literally lost in my anger and depression, and it was destroying me--not what Cathy had done or said, not the administrators, nor the hospital staff, but my own anger was killing me.

God and Me

Ever since I could remember, as far back as age five, my parents had kept us in the church. They knew that the church would be vitally important to our survival. I was accustomed to forgetting God one moment and crying out to Him the next. Through it all, I knew that God's mercy was abundant and great, that He really loved my family and me, but now all that church going, twenty-five years' worth, didn't seem to be enough to unshackle me. I was in desperate need of spiritual healing. It was my only hope. I knew that God's mercy and love were still there, even though I had not felt it. I prayed, but I couldn't be healed. My wounds were wide open for the world to see.

One day I was singing some spiritual songs in the operating room when I was doing Gynecology, and this guy Nefty, an operating room technician, heard me. He asked me if I was a Christian. With inward hesitancy, I said, "Yes." I wondered if he knew anything about my attitude and behavior. I didn't want this Christian Brother to think that I was a hypocrite. We started talking, and he asked me to attend his church, Brooklyn Tabernacle. I accepted his invitation, but didn't show up.

When I would see him, he would tell me how beautiful the services were. Each time I felt bad because I told him that I was going to come. I wasn't completely out of the church, but I might as well have been.

One evening I suggested to my wife and a friend that we go to Nefty's church. During the service, the feeling that came over me was a calm excitement. It was a while before I began to heal. There was a big job yet to be done in my life, however; there was this stubborn kind of depression inside of me. As I continued to attend that church, I opened up more until I could see myself in all my ugliness.

I saw that I was badly in need of healing, and most important, that God could do it. Soon my home life improved. Iris was happier and doing better because I was doing better. The children greeted me each day at the door with kisses. I was still concerned about the injustices I saw in the hospital, but somehow I knew God would fix it all.

Where Is St. Croix?

One day I got a call from the Public Health Service. They told me that a doctor had visited their office from the United States Virgin Islands. The Virgin Islands was in need of a doctor. The Public Health Services asked me if I would consider practicing medicine in St. Croix or St. Thomas. I asked, "Where is St. Croix? I never heard of it, but I do know where St. Thomas is." The woman laughed, and tried to mentally direct me to St. Croix in reference to St. Thomas and Puerto Rico. I told her that I wouldn't mind checking it out.

After speaking with her, I couldn't believe that I was being given the opportunity to practice in the Caribbean. Iris was shocked. We both agreed to accept at least the interview process. When we told our families about it, they weren't too excited because of the distance it would take us from them.

The Public Health Service sent Iris and me to both Caribbean islands, and we decided on St.Croix because it had more space and looked just as beautiful. We had a ball playing in the warm Caribbean Sea while there was snow in New York. We accepted the opportunity to work and live on the beautiful island; we believed that it was God's will.

MD Degree and Licensing

Though I had a medical degree, I didn't have a license to hang out a shingle and practice medicine (you have to prove yourself knowledgeable and worthy of a license by taking an examination). As far as I was concerned, this was my next great hurdle.

I had failed the National Boards Examination while in medical school, after taking parts one and two. The examination to obtain a license, called the Flex, was said to be tougher and it was given throughout the United States. If anyone had the opportunity to take the National Boards, they had to be crazy to take the Nationwide Flex Examination, because the

Flex was believed to be harder. For me it was my only way to getting that license, short of repeating the National Board Exams.

One of the doctors told me about some American students who had studied in Mexico. She said they had a lot of good information and suggested that I ask them. I did.

I had not forgotten about the Kaplan course while a student at Brooklyn College. What happened with the medical college admissions was my failure to take advantage of materials that other people were fortunate to have, but it wasn't going to happen again. My delay then cost me a failing grade. Whoever had the prep exams to the National Flex test would give them to me because I was going to be aggressive.

When I approached one of the students, he at first was very reluctant to give up the material. He said it had cost each one of them $60 to get it copied, and that's what it would cost me. I spoke to Iris about it. We got the money together and gave it to the student.

I was due to take the Flex exam that December, but because half of the material was delayed, I could not take it at that time. I knew that I had to take it soon, because within one-and-a-half years the residency program would be over.

I applied to the state of Massachusetts to take the exam there, but I was too late in applying. I was warned not to take the exam in New York City because it would be more difficult to pass. People were going to Georgia, Maine, and Vermont to escape the New York grading. I was tired of running for a place to hide. I was a New York State resident. I was educated in New York State, so why not take the exam in New York. It was as "simple" as that.

I started studying seven months before the New York exam date. I studied everywhere and anytime, in the bathroom, in the car, I would even take the stuff to church. Iris would ask, "Where are you going with that?" I told her if I had a chance to study, I would study anywhere. I took the exam at Pratt Institute in Brooklyn. It consisted of sixteen hundred questions covering almost every aspect of medicine, including basic science. After the first day of exams, people were excited as they talked about how difficult it was. I didn't think so, but that was no guarantee of my passing that day. People were trying to remember the answers they had put down while comparing their answers to others. It all seemed childish to me.

On each of the three exam days, I got a headache at the same time of day. Sixteen hundred questions, six-and-a-half hours per day for three days, made me ill. I was glad along with thousands of others, to be rid of that test.

I told Iris I didn't think the exam was difficult, and I thought I had passed. She told me she knew I had. I tried to dissuade her a little bit, but she had enough confidence for both of us.

Three months passed, and I hadn't received my grade. A few people had taken the test out of state and had passed the exam. I became more anxiety-ridden. I knew that God was still with me, but here again was my shaky attitude.

Two more weeks had passed with no grade. I was getting the news that a couple of people failed. Even a couple of people from New York had their grades. I called the New York State Licensing Bureau. They informed me that I had to wait along with everyone else in New York for the grade, and that it would be sent out the following week. All that week I was asking Iris about the mail. Sometimes, I would get prematurely excited because she didn't answer me fast enough.

Oh God, I Passed

One day that week, I was in my landlord's apartment taking care of his daughter's injured arm. On the way out, I asked if they had any mail for me. His wife said, "No, not today, Doctor." Something caught my eye on the china cabinet. It was a large white envelope. I asked her if that was my mail.

"Oh yes, that must be your mail," she replied.

I quickly grabbed it and went out the door. As I stood motionless after the door closed behind me, I said a little prayer and opened the envelope. I looked, slowly, for some numbers, not really wanting to pull the paper completely out of the envelope. I had passed the exam. It was the greatest moment of my life; greater than anything that had ever happened to me except graduating from medical school.

Moonlighting Madness

The residency program in Family Practice was nearing its end. This meant that I would be finished with my formal post medical training.

I had made a two-year commitment to work with the federal government in St. Croix, U.S. Virgin Islands.

We had no money, and there was no way that I could foresee any extra money coming in on which to live. Iris was beginning to worry about our lack of money. Her constant reminder made that reality haunt me. We were buried in bad investments and $20,000 worth of loans that needed to be repaid. I kept saying to Iris not to worry, God would provide all we needed financially and otherwise. That didn't prevent her from letting me know that we still had no money.

My New York medical license finally arrived in the mail. I knew that the license was my answer. Even though I was not supposed to moonlight while a medical resident, many third-year medical residents did so. That was no license for me to break the rules, but I did.

I applied for a job with a medical supplies company. I made house calls all over New York City. After working there for a couple of months, I applied for a job with a health center in Red Hook. In a short while, I had three jobs. I worked almost twenty-four hours a day, six days a week, and sometimes-on Sunday. The money began to roll in.

Now Iris was complaining that she wasn't seeing me enough. I told her that she couldn't have her cake and eat it too. We had our problems over my tough schedule. The more money I made, the harder I worked. My goal was to make $25,000 in a few months.

Making house calls in New York was a trying experience. Many of the people whom I treated were elderly, white or Jewish and alone. Some were living alone by choice, but most were abandoned by their families. Many things I encountered broke my heart. What I saw reinforced in me disapproval for abandoning the elderly. Often before leaving, I would say a word of prayer for them. Sometimes I felt like crying. I met some people who had been in Hitler's concentration camps. Sometimes they would freely speak about it. I wanted to find out in detail what some of them went through. I couldn't believe that I was speaking with people who had been hated so much, and some with all family members killed and still enduring life's hardships today. Sometimes people would point to some memorable picture or plaque on the wall. I enjoyed looking at old photos, and I often encouraged them to pull out more for me to see.

My driver, John, who was a minister, would look at me funny. Sometimes, he would even say, "Let's" go, Doc. We have more people to see." The driver had to actually walk out the door in order for me to realize that he was serious about leaving me there running my mouth.

Many times, we had three or five calls to make. On some of those occasions, I was called early in the morning to see someone who really didn't need medical attention. They just wanted someone to talk to. It was frustrating, and I got angry, only to be hurt by my own anger.

John spoke with me many times about my life. He told me that he was concerned about me. We talked about everything from illegal drugs to sex, church, God, and the whole universe. John would tell me, "Doc, there ain't no justice in this world." He told me that many times, and I did not know how right he was until I became a man. I believe John really cared about me, as a brother would have. I love John.

Some of the house calls were in tough areas of New York, such as Harlem, Bedford Stuyvesant, and East New York areas, which looked as though a nuclear weapon had discharged in their midst. Winos, drug addicts, and prostitutes roamed the streets and hallways. It was only the grace of God that kept us from being harmed. Often I prayed that God would get us in and out with our clothes still on our backs, not minus skin or money. If I had as much as $150 in my pocket, I knew for sure I would give it and the drugs in my bag to thieves who might hold us up. I would have even told them where they could get more drugs, if it came down to that. John and I would look at each other and shake our heads. It was a bad scene and dangerous.

Harlem on My Mind

One of my worst experiences was in Harlem about two o'clock in the morning. We were called to see a man who was ill with a chest infection. The morning was cold and icy, and we drove to Harlem in John's Ford Grenada. The windows were cracked so he could get some air while he smoked his mini slim cigars. The smoke made me sick. I was half with my nose pinned to the window and half wanting totell him off. However, it was his car, and he could do what he liked in it.

After about forty minutes, we arrived in Harlem at a tenement building ten stories high, with rough-looking teens in the hallway, and no operating elevator. The driver and I debated whether it was swise to ascend the stairs. There wasn't much to debate; the call had to be answered.

As we were going up those stairs, I kept saying to myself, "Do you realize, Doc, there is no safe way out of here if someone comes behind you?" Every window next to the stairwell was open. A person could trip and fall out the window or easily be thrown out. When we reached the top, we were out of breath. I thanked God nothing happened.

Promises to Keep

At times, the health center would call Iris so she could inform me to show up for work. Sometimes, I had to refuse because of conflicts in time with the residency program. Usually, I worked something out. Often I didn't go to a rotation or would leave the operating room and go to the health center.

Many people in the health center knew me from my pre-medical school days. They remembered my struggles and could see my success outwardly.

I wanted desperately to give some service to Red Hook projects. I had made a promise that I would return to the neighborhood in order to help out. I never realized it was going to be for money. I had envisioned some volunteer work. The people were delighted to have me. I wanted to do a good job, and I worked hard and confidently. Being in Family Medicine made me somewhat popular. I could work just about all of the clinics.

One day I even tried running the surgery clinic. When the surgeon arrived, he just smiled and told me to continue doing what I was doing. Almost every Saturday, when they had no Obstetrician/Gynecologist, I filled in.

I was making $180 per day. My other job, making house calls, earned me $1,500 per week. With the residency giving $620 every two weeks, I was in the money. Almost all the money went in the bank. Iris was a little happier, but she was still concerned about me. I was too involved in making money, and caught up in the cares of this life.

Pain and Confusion

I got involved with a woman named Esther at the health center. On the very first day, I ran into her while I saw old acquaintances. When she saw me, she gave a big smile. I had never known her by name, and we crossed paths a number of times my first week there. She asked me if I would make a house call to visit her if she were ill. I replied, "sure."

That week she asked me for a ride to the train station in Brooklyn Heights and I took her. When I was at the health center, she frequently visited my area and told me that she just wanted to say hello. I knew that she wanted me. I proposed in my mind that I was going to take her up on her offer. I told her that I was interested in her. She outright told me that she could not do that because she knew Iris. She felt that I wasn't going to be around always, and she didn't want to be hurt by my short stay in New York before going to the Virgin Islands. I didn't understand where she was coming from; she played interested in me; then, she backed off. I told her that I understood, but that week I kept thinking about her, and she kept coming to my work area. I knew that I was wrong for wanting her.

We finally made a date to meet. I took off from the hospital and met her in her Queen's apartment. We spent the day together, both having full knowledge that we were wrong, and we spoke about it. About this time, I decided to take scuba-diving lessons, in preparation for enjoying St. Croix, and I used the opportunity to visit her at her apartment before returning home.

The strangest thing happened. Iris knew that I was cheating on her. She saw me in a dream. She described to me the building, which I went into, where Esther lived; mailboxes on the right-hand side that were bronze, an elevator, and the stairs that led to an upstairs apartment. I was shocked when she told me these things. Many people would think that she had me followed or knew by some other means where I was, but I knew that she didn't. Iris didn't lie to me. God, to save my life, revealed it to her. Knowing she had that information frightened me.

I didn't understand why Iris let it go on so long. She later told me that she knew we didn't have much longer in New York and as far as she was concerned, our departure would end the relationship.

One morning I came in about 5:30 a.m. I even told Iris one of the guys had a birthday party, and I had gone to Sheephead Bay in Brooklyn in order to eat hamburgers. I was lying through my teeth, and she knew it.

Although I was attending Brooklyn Tabernacle, and Nefty was still encouraging me, there was an obvious wedge between God and me.

They Loved Me

In some ways, it was hard for me to leave the Family Practice program because I was fond of some people there. My last day while I was cleaning out my desk, I wondered how I ever survived the ordeal of being there. It didn't take me long to figure out how. Mickie, the receptionist, constantly spoke kindly to me and respected me as a person and a physician. I respected her for her honesty and sincerity. She told me that day that she loved me and she wanted me to remember it. When she said it, I paused and took serious notice of her and she had tears in her eyes. She hugged and kissed me and I felt as if I were going to fall apart. I love Mickie. Wanda, the nurse called me to her side, encouraged me many times, and related to me as a Black person. She told me that she always cared about me and was with me when I was going through hell in the Family Practice program and at Lutheran Medical Center. I thanked her for caring about me. She told me to continue to be strong. I love Wanda. The two aides who were Puerto Ricans whom I harassed terribly, hugged and squeezed me that day and I felt their affection for me. I love them also. I believe all of these precious friends knew some of my pain and in their own way hurt for me. When I walked out of the center, knowing that chapter in my life was closed; I knew it would be hard to find friends like them again.

I Needed a Change

Our departure for St. Croix was nearing. I signed a two-year contract with the United States Department of Public Health as a way of paying back my student loan. The residency program was at an end soon, and I had just about reached my goal of $25,000. I purchased a new 1981 Toyota Celica (cash) for Iris and a motorcycle for myself and we still had cash in the bank.

Even though I was making a lot of money, I wanted desperately to leave New York. I realized my life wasn't what it should have been. I thought to leave New York was one way out of a bad situation that put my marriage on the line a second time. Iris was definitely ready to leave.

The morning we were to leave for St. Croix was warm and quiet. My family was up early, as we hurried the last belongings to the car.

I took a few moments to reflect upon Red Hook projects. I still wanted to help with the many problems that plagued the people who still hung out in droves with idle minds. I spent so much time dealing with Lutheran Medical Center's bullshit and white bigots that I lost touch with my dreams. Those racist on 78th Street who threatened my life, called me a "black nigger," and Iris, a "nigger lover," and viewed my children as half-breeds, didn't help my focus either. I spent a lot of time hurting for three years over their treatment of me and my family. The wrong turns I made on my own hurt my wife in ways I didn't fully understand. I loved Iris as I loved no other woman, but I was too immature in order to deal with it. I was responsible for the choices, which I had made and I was about to make another one, to leave New York and go to a place I considered Paradise on earth, St. Croix, United States Virgin Islands. I tried to leave without regrets.

Red Hook was plagued with murders, drug addiction, and crimes of all sorts. I loved Red Hook and I considered it my true home. God knows I hurt for Red Hook. While riding to Kennedy Airport, it hit me that I was leaving my birthplace. What disturbed me most was I knew that I wanted out mentally, but my heart was still there. I thought about my wife, Iris, and my three children, and how they deserved more than what I had given them. Iris certainly didn't deserve what I gave her. I believed that St.Croix would be what my family and I needed.

So many thoughts and memories flowed through me.

When we finally reached the airport, I realized how real my leaving was. I didn't want to see anyone cry, but I knew it was inevitable. My niece, Nina, was going to St. Croix with us. She had some disciplinary problems, and we wanted to help her. I didn't know it at the time, but she was soon to give our family heartaches in St. Croix.

As we waited to board the jumbo American Airlines jet, Iris's mother and father began to cry. Shoshanna was crying, and then Iris started. I could feel something inside of me breaking, and I wanted to board the plane quickly.

My life and my family were at crossroads. I didn't know what awaited us in St. Croix, but I believed it would give me a fresh start at being a good husband to Iris. While we walked the ramp to board the aircraft, I noticed Iris crying and my heart broke. I felt like crying, but it wouldn't happen.

A Pillow of Cloud and Warmth by Fire

I remember many times while in the different churches, which I attended reading and studying about the Israelites, when Moses bought them out of Pharaoh's house in Egypt. As they crossed the wilderness, God protected them at night by fire in order to keep them warm, and protected them during the day with a pillow of cloud from the blistering heat of the dessert. He loved them, and loves us all even now.

When I was a little boy, I dreamed about God's protection over me. I had no idea, how He would protect me when the time came, as I knew it eventually would. When I became a teenager, I had the same dreams, but with visions. I saw myself adoring tropical islands in the sea. There was peace in my heart and excitement filled me. There were no struggles, no tears, and no anger. I was content. I believed it was God speaking to me, telling me no matter what happened in my life that I would be OK because He was with me and that He was protecting me. When I was a medical student, the dreams and visions became more real and vivid. I would awaken with my heart pounding after a dream, gleaming, because I had just finished a pleasant journey in some warm tropical island. I always envisioned it as Hawaii, but there was nothing ever confirming Hawaii. After I finished the medical school, the dreams disappeared as fumes from kindling fire. Just like the children of Israel were protected from the raging flames on the surface of the sun, creating ignited heat, so I stood in the midst of the fire and was dancing in it, while God was protecting me.

I believed that God's gift to Iris and me for enduring the pain, which we suffered was sending us to the beautiful island of St. Croix. We were hurting so much that the thought of ever going to a place in the sun, with palm trees, blue turquoise water and new faces was unbelievable. However, it was all real and it was soon to become a reality. In a few hours, we would be where my dreams took me many late nights and early mornings; one of God's islands in the sea.

We anticipated a brand new beginning for us and our three children whom we adored.

PART IV

Shouting at the Rain

And the princes, governors, and captains, and the king's counselors, being gathered together, saw these men, upon whose bodies the fire had no power, nor was a hair of their head singed, neither were their coats changed, nor the smell of fire had passed on them.

Daniel 3:27

Chapter 19
Shouting at the Rain

Surely goodness, mercy, and unfailing love
shall follow me all the days of my life,
and through the length of my days
the house of the Lord shall be my dwelling place.

Psalm 23:6

As the jumbo jet soared through the air at 35,000 feet, I wondered what wonders awaited us on the beautiful island of St. Croix. St. Croix was resting in the blue turquoise water of the Caribbean Ocean. When we reached the huge beautiful island of Puerto Rico, I thought of the many Puerto Ricans whom I had met through the years. I thought also of Rosa, Ana, Hector, and the Puerto Ricans I grew up with. I wondered how could a Puerto Rican leave a beautiful island like this to live in New York's rat-infested tenement houses and projects nestled in concrete. How could a person give up the clear colorful water of this part of God's creation for the murky brown polluted water of Coney Island, Reese Beach, or Far Rockaway Beach? As I was thinking, the pilot announced for passengers to fasten their seat belts for landing in St. Croix. I looked at Iris and she was happy. The tears dried up a few hours before and she was smiling. I was happy for her.

Later when we reached the coast of St. Croix, I looked down and saw the beautiful multicolored water, and the bright beige sand on a section of the island called Sandy Point. I was excited. When we landed, Iris and I looked at each other, knowing that we were on our own. I had no family within driving distance to go to if I wanted as in the past, and she had God and me to depend on. As I walked down the steps of the aircraft, the air felt so very clean and refreshing to my lungs. I believed my life would be changed forever in St. Croix and I would begin to heal from the wounds I received in New York.

The St. Croix Hamilton airport was small and busy.

We were met by the landlady, who seemed very glad to see us. We got our luggage together, packed them into her car, and headed for our new home in a section of the island called Estate Whim. Iris and I were very curious to see the house because we never had a house all to ourselves with a yard. As we drove a couple of miles, I saw horses running wild on the roadside, chickens, goats, and sheep all over the place. I saw palm trees, just like the ones I saw in my dreams. I said to myself, I want to get a horse, and some coconuts like those on that tree. We entered a dirt road that ran alongside a gas station. The road was bad, and we weren't terribly encouraged. We looked at each other. We saw abandoned cars along the road, and a couple of the homes, which looked shabby. We expected to see something similar for ourselves. Suddenly, a pretty green house with flowers and two huge fruit trees came into view.

The house was fenced in with a beautiful yard and various fruit trees. This was our new home. We were excited; we went through the fire and survived. We were Beyond the Fire and the Rain, and now we would dance in our own happy home with our beautiful children.

I was alone. The Health Center Administrator, the Medical Director, the two doctors who were in charge of seeing to my starting work as scheduled on August 4, 1981, expected a good year from me caring for patients. I was a brand new doctor fresh out of my internship and residency (medical training after medical school). I was expected to start right in seeing patients and wasn't familiar with the health center procedures. I only knew that I was expected to put in a full day's work and see about 100 patients per week for the government of St. Croix, and it would be reported to the federal government in Washington, DC.

St. Croix is one of three United States Virgin Islands nestled in the tropical waters of the Caribbean. The Atlantic Ocean is on the north side of the island, and the Caribbean Ocean on the south side. If there existed a roadway, one could drive from the south side of St. Croix to South America, which is about five hundred fifty miles away. One could take a mental flight and reach the continent of Africa from the eastern tip of the island. Africa is about fourteen hundred miles away. From the northern portion of the island, one could go a little west, say ten or fifteen degrees, and reach New York City, which is about eighteen hundred miles away. The little twenty-seven miles by seven miles wide island is unique in that it's strategically located, and from its shores, one could easily by modern-day commercial jet within hours be in the bustling city of New York or Miami, or be in the thick forest of Brazil, South America or on the plains of Kenya, Africa. The only place I was concerned about reaching if I needed to was Brooklyn, New York. My mother, two sisters, and a host of relatives who loved me were in New York. My mother and sisters lived in a housing project called Red Hook, in South Brooklyn. It wasn't that I didn't like being on the island of St. Croix. I just missed my family. I loved my wife and my three children, but I felt there was no place like home (where I grew up).

Nevertheless, I had to make the best of being away from the only place on the face of this earth I was in love with.

I signed on with the Public Health Service, in Washington, DC. I promised them for the two years, which they supported me financially, while I was in Albany Medical College, I would pay it back by working anywhere in the United States of America where there was a physician shortage. The United States Government wanted me to work as a doctor in Mississippi, Louisiana, Arkansas, or Tennessee. My father, Wilbert Williams, was from Chesson, Alabama. Chesson, Alabama, which is in the South, like Mississippi, Louisiana, Arkansas, and Tennessee. Though Chesson was over seventy miles from Montgomery, Alabama, Montgomery was the most racially divided city in America. My father told me, when he was a little boy, some white people got together late one night at the house of the only Black doctor in town, and gave him twenty-four hours to get out because he attended to a white woman. That was enough for me to hear. I never wanted to go to that place, even if my father was born and raised in Chesson, Alabama, which is in the same state. Well, I had a two-year hitch with Uncle Sam on the beautiful island of St. Croix. I missed going to some of the United States war zones, so I thought, and rested in the sun and tried to enjoy myself in Paradise.

The first week, I waited for the other physician to show up for work. I was then informed that she wasn't coming in for a couple of weeks and that I would have to run the clinic. I worked that first four weeks alone, seeing over five hundred patients. It was exciting, but I became exhausted.

When the other doctor finally arrived, she came with her father, who said his daughter wouldn't be coming to work for a few days. I remember being furious. Dr. Smart and her father had some nerve! When she started working, it was a great relief. I still had the large patient load, but the feeling of working alone was gone.

The months to follow were much like the first. I worked very hard. Many people began to greet me as soon as I was in sight. They wouldn't even let me go through the clinic doors without a host of questions and requests, which didn't happen in New York.

It wasn't too bad at first, but after a while, it got annoying. I wanted very much to take care of the needs that people had. It just seemed that the more I did, the more the needs kept coming. Some people even began to use me, which wasn't very hard, since I listened and responded to every sad story that came along.

Conflicts and New York

I was lonely for New York and wanted to go back and see Esther. An opportunity with the Public Health Service came up for me to attend a medical conference in Boston. Iris wasn't too keen on my going to New York. She was still hurting over the difficult times she spent there and she didn't trust me going there alone. When I left, Iris cried. I felt bad, but I still wanted to go. While I was in Boston, I met Esther and she wanted to know if she could come to St. Croix. I told her that it wasn't a good idea. She was insistent, but I wouldn't lead her on.

When I returned to St. Croix, Iris met me with open arms and a big smile. The children seemed to have grown so much in just a few days; I was happy to be at home. I thought to myself as I looked at my wife, that I really loved her.

It was so refreshing being back in St. Croix. The following months had their difficulties. There were times, however, when I felt like leaving the island again. I convinced myself that maybe St. Croix wasn't for me. Iris adjusted to being in St. Croix better than I. I didn't want to stay in St. Croix because I felt cut off from the rest of the world with which I was familiar in New York. The size and quietness of St. Croix did not help my homesickness. I couldn't believe that I had ever decided to come to a place like St. Croix. Not even the beauty of this island "paradise" was encouraging. I was working hard at the health center and enjoying it, but I felt locked away.

Esther wanted to still come to St. Croix. I had not written her in over a month. I'm not sure why I didn't write her, but it was probably my wanting to straighten my life out. Our relationship was dissolving, and in my heart, I believe that's what I wanted, because it was ruining my marriage.

To add to all my confusion and despair, I went and got involved with a woman about ten years older than me. Her name was Selma, and she had two children who were teenagers. She just approached me one day and started talking to me. I didn't think much about her forwardness, and felt she was friendly, but each time I saw her she wanted to talk. I never imagined that she was interested in me. We started spending time together during lunch breaks from work. People with whom I worked saw me with her, but never said anything. I assumed that they felt it was none of their business. Sometimes we would see each other after lunch for a few moments. This went on for a while. Iris knew about the relationship because someone who worked at the health center had told her, but she never said anything to me.

I eventually had an affair with her and the relationship became demanding, because she pressured me to see her at times when I knew I should have been at home. After a while, I wanted to see her. It was partly due to my loneliness for Esther.

I was sneaking off in order to play husband with a divorced woman who had teenage children. One night I told Iris that I was going fishing, but I ended up on the other side of the island, parked in the car with her. Iris checked the car the next day; she smelled perfume radiating throughout the interior. She knew immediately that I was in it with a woman. She didn't waste any time getting to me. Of course, I denied everything repeatedly. I knew that my rope was getting short. I wanted to stop, but something was driving me.

I loved Iris and the children, I thought. All of my behavior seemed so natural to be a man, but I was a married man, with children. I convinced myself that it wasn't as bad as it seemed.

Nina

Things at home weren't going so well. There were so many things to set up and organize. My niece Nina had even brought some of her troublesome ways from New York to St. Croix with her. She started keeping company with a few of the guys who lived nearby. One night she went somewhere with one of the guys and returned home late without my permission. Another time, the same guy came to our house and asked to take her on a date. I was hesitant, but he promised to have her home by ten o'clock. When Nina finally came home at eleven o'clock, she had alcohol on her breath. That same evening I beat her with a belt. I felt stupid chastising her that aggressively, but I was upset.

Her same behavior continued, and soon she became a burden to us. After a few weeks, we sent her back to New York. Even though she often did not behave well, we missed her. Iris cried at the airport, and even my heart felt heavy.

I stayed away from Selma for one month, only to allow her to sweet-talk me, and I started seeing her again. For the next few months, I was sneaking around with her. Some people at the Family Practice Clinic knew what was going on. I was leaving for work early in the morning and arriving home late at night. It was so obvious to Iris what I was doing, but she held her peace and prayed for me.

The Nazarene Church

I started attending the Church of the Nazarene and I was trying to be content and settle down. One evening while in my pastor's house, watching "The Cross and the Switchblade," I became a born-again Christian. I decided not to tell Iris that my life had changed. I wanted her to see it for herself. She had to confirm it for me.

Two months after I became a born-again Christian, my second son, Wilbert, was born and just two days before my birthday. He was a cute, strong, massive-looking baby. He came at the right time for me. I was living my new life as a born-again Christian and he was to receive the blessings of that. Iris had Wilbert without any complications. We were very happy.

As the months passed, Iris didn't say anything to me about my change. Even though she said nothing, I didn't doubt the change. One day we were talking about spiritual matters, and she mentioned that she had noticed a change in me. I was encouraged. Of all the people in my life, Iris had to see something, for she had suffered the most.

The days following my experience of new life were challenging. Some people doubted my conversion. I told Selma that my life changed and when I finished telling her, she just looked at me and said, "I know it's good," and then she left. As the weeks went by, the flame that was extinguished tried to re light, but I knew I needed to go forward.

Selma came into my office with all kinds of vaginal problems, and picked me as the doctor to examine her. I never once thought about her romantically again. The relationship was dead. Iris spoke with Selma on the telephone and told her to leave me alone. Selma told Iris that I wasn't completely innocent in the affair.

It is so easy for many men to cheat on their wives, and have all kinds of excuses to justify their actions. There are no justifiable reasons. Marriage is sacred, and it should be an intimate and trusting bond, between two people who claim to love each other. I failed to hold up the banner of marriage early on, and it would take until I became a real man to deal with my emotions.

I had no idea at the time how much I hurt Iris, and it would take many years to repair some of the damage. However, not even a lifetime of her living with me would ever wipe the pain from her mind and heart, and I would forever pay for my mistakes.

My New Life

Iris, though convinced of my new life, had her doubts about all my plans. She wasn't convinced that I could hold on to my new life. She felt that the influence of the world had too strong an effect on me. I didn't blame her. She had all the data to feel the way she did. It was challenging and frustrating to me. I wanted desperately to be seen as healthy, both mentally and spiritually, before Iris. I was scheduled to return to New York City for a medical conference, and I was to go alone. Iris was worried that I would meet up with Esther in New York again. Iris and I had a big argument the evening before I left. I called the pastor and his wife and asked them to come over. Until early in the morning, he and his wife counseled us, and prayed for God to give us more love and trust for each other. During that session, I became hostile and angry. I didn't want anyone doubting my life changed. My new life was on the firing line, and it hurt to have my past life before me.

The greatest challenge facing me was me. I had to trust God to see me through. When I arrived in New York, it was gray and cold (what a contrast, I thought, from 86-degree weather). My father-in-law picked me up at the airport. He was always willing to do something nice. On many occasions, I have thanked God for him. My family was glad to see me, and the feeling was mutual.

The following day I got up early, and my mother fixed me breakfast. I was a little nervous because I knew what had to be done. I was destined to tell my friend about my new life. When I left my mother's house, I by fate saw Esther. She lived more than twenty miles from Red Hook projects. Just my fortune, we were approaching each other quickly. I said, "Oh Lord, this can't be her." As I got closer, my heart felt as though it hit my feet. I knew it had to be plain and quick. I asked God to give me the strength I needed.

We stopped and stared into each other's eyes without saying a word. I asked her how she was, and she responded, "Okay." We shared some words and began to walk in the direction of her job. I showed her a few pictures of St. Croix, and she quickly looked through them.

When the air between us was gentle, I explained to her that my life had changed. She looked at me and said, "I told you that the relationship wasn't any good. I hope you practice what you preach." I was embarrassed.

Here I was telling the woman with whom I'd had an affair that I was a born-again Christian and wanted out. She must have thought that I was trying to play holier-than-thou. Well, it was done. I was relieved. The guilt was released.

Ellenville, New York

I left Brooklyn and went up to Ellenville, New York, to the conference. It was icy cold. My little frail, underweight body had lost its fat pads in St. Croix, and I was freezing. The medical conference went well, and I visited Michael, Margie, Ephraim, and Yoli in upstate New York (which was like being in Alaska in mid-winter). It was a joy seeing my friends, but I was glad to leave the cold. I became anxious and wanted to return to St. Croix. The 86 to 90 degrees daily had spoiled me. I wanted to see Iris and the children.

When I returned to St. Croix, Iris met me at the airport. It was a good feeling seeing her and the children fresh in the island sun.

Those months following my conversion were trying. I wanted so desperately to live for God. I felt closer to Iris and the children; it was no longer a struggle to be happy. Every day seemed to be brighter and better than the day before. I carried my Bible daily. Frequent meditations in my medical office were common. From moment to moment, I sought God's direction in my life. Constantly, I talked to patients about being born again.

A Christian brother asked me to go with him to a Full Gospel Businessmen's Fellowship meeting. After a couple of sessions, I decided to become a member. It was an exciting experience. I thought that I would never come down from my spiritual high, but I also saw that life's problems were still there.

I wanted to witness to people about God's love for them. I had asked God to show me the needs of the people of St. Croix, their spiritual and physical needs. I had asked Him from my own comfortable little world.

I had a horse called "Hope" and he was stolen. When I found him miles away from where I lived, I knew who had him.

I went to his house. He was a 17-year-old high school student. He denied stealing the horse. After speaking to him about stealing, I took a New Testament Bible and a Christian tract out of my backpack. I told him that God loved him very much. He gave me his attention. I told him that God had something special for him. As we talked, my heart felt heavy, and we both began to cry. I embraced him and told him that God had forgiven him.

When I left that young man's house, I knew that God's power had shown itself. I knew that it was no strength of mine that caused things to happen the way they did. The loss of my horse, its return, and the embrace of a stranger . . . It was clear to me that I had witnessed a small miracle.

The experience helped me to go deeper into the area of forgiveness. I prayed that evening that God would always intervene in crises in my life. I was confident and full of faith that He would. The months following that incident, I had many opportunities, I grew more.

My life was very busy as far as medicine was concerned, but every chance I had to share my new life with someone I did.

I was seeing about twenty-five patients per day at the health center, plus walk-in patients. Iris and I had begun a film ministry called "Agape Outreach." God had put a street film ministry in my heart for young people, again. I concentrated especially in project areas. We were involved monthly in showing films and sharing testimonies, and God was blessing that ministry. We carried the financial responsibility of the ministry. I was sure that was the way God wanted it at the time and the hustle and fast paces involved were quite evident.

Exams Again

My first year with the government was nearing an end and everything worked out well. I helped many people and was liked by most. One more year remained for me to complete my two-year stretch with the Public Health Service. The government of the Virgin Islands would not accept my New York State license, so I had to sit for the exam a second time. It was stupid because it was the same type of test given by the same testing agency on the United States mainland. The first time I took it in New York, I studied for seven months. I was now on the second time around and into my fourth month of studying. It was a drag, and I definitely didn't want to do it. I knew, however, if I didn't, and wanted to practice in St. Croix privately, I couldn't. I asked God to see me through my exam-taking days again.

As usual, when I sat for an exam, I took my Bible and had fellowship with God in song and prayer. I sat for three days in St. Thomas and attempted to answer sixteen hundred questions. I was given one-and-a-half hours for lunch and two fifteen-minute breaks. On the third and final day, my head started pounding. I knew that I had studied and answered enough questions.

I waited two months for my grade to return and when it arrived, I achieved an 78%. I thanked God for His faithfulness to me.

I wondered after I passed the New York State and the Virgin Islands Boards what Dr. Carroll at Albany Medical College would say to me having questioned if I would ever get a license to practice medicine.

I took the family on a trip to New York. We needed the change. Iris wasn't sure that she wanted to visit New York. We had talked about taking my father out of the nursing home where he had been for almost one year. I just couldn't stand the thought of leaving him there any longer.

When we arrived in New York, the first thing we realized was that not many things had changed. I thought of the great opportunity, which God had given me to escape the concrete jungle.

Imagine how many people there are who may never get the opportunity to see anything other than projects, slums, and concrete. My heart was bleeding for the people of my home. I wanted to give them all a ticket to leave if they wished, even if it were just for a moment.

We spent our month in New York visiting family, friends and going to church. A friend of ours was going through a spiritual problem. Iris and I counseled her. She had a tremendous fear of death and dying. She felt that if she surrendered her mind, soul and body to God, He would take her life. It was sad and unfortunate. We prayed and read Scripture and counseled with her until early morning hours.

We kept going around in circles with her, but we finally convinced her to attend church with us one Sunday.

That Sunday, Nicky Cruz, the former gang leader in "The Cross and the Switchblade," was at Brooklyn Tabernacle. I became born again under his ministry. My friend Nefty spoke with the pastor, who summoned

Nicky and called our friend to the front of the church, where Nicky Cruz prayed for her. She said that she was better, but her words spoke otherwise; she refused to give up her fear of death and dying.

It was the first time in my life where my wife and I together gave spiritual counseling to another.

We had a nice time in New York. When we neared our last week, I reflected on the previous three weeks and made an assessment on my attitude and behavior. I believed God was pleased. Opportunities given to me by God were clearly visible, and I had acted upon them. I was happy, and more than being happy, I felt God's victory in my life.

Loving My Father

My father was in a nursing home, and I wanted him out. I had prayed to God to give me the answer. I didn't want the decision to be mine. I discussed it with Iris, and she believed God might have been speaking to us. I wanted a positive verification from her, but she was careful in her opinion. I believed God wanted me to take my father out of the nursing home, and I continued to seek His approval.

Everything pointed to my compassion and love for my one and only earthly father. I loved my father dearly and needed to take him out of that situation. He had become mentally unstable and aggressive. My mother couldn't take care of him, and her dreaded alternative was to place him in a nursing home.

Our last day in New York, I was happy and excited to leave. It was like being released from bondage. With all of my love for New York, it became an intolerable place after a few weeks. I guess being away in a very different and perhaps favorable, more relaxed environment like St. Croix had spoiled me.

We headed for the nursing home and got my father. Iris's family followed behind us in her father's car. We arrived at Kennedy Airport a little late, loaded down with many boxes, bags and packages. The baggage attendant suggested that in order to save expenses I unload one box and transfer some items to a plastic bag, which he would give me. This took time, but after that was taken care of, off we went to the loading gate.

I pushed my father in a wheelchair. Iris and our four children came next, followed by a host of carry-on packages. There were many people at the gate ready to board the jet.

The ticket attendant, after telling me that we were late, gave us our boarding passes, and we all boarded the plane.

Suddenly, a Black flight attendant walked over to me and asked if I would kindly follow her to discuss a seating problem. As I got off the plane and went through the gate door, the jet door closed. The check-in desk clerk told me that I couldn't fly to St. Croix on that flight. I was shocked. They sent me to Pan American Airline to catch a connecting flight to Miami; then to St. Croix. The flight wasn't scheduled to leave for three hours. I had breakfast, read the newspaper for a half-hour and boarded the jet. I sat on that plane for three hours and the plane never left because they couldn't close the cargo door. I was told to speak with the Pan American attendant; however, he told me to wait my turn because he was busy. By this time, there was no way I was going to St. Croix that day. I went back to American Airlines, and the check-in attendant told me that I couldn't fly to St. Croix unless I gave them $100 for a reissued ticket and then I could fly the following day. I was shocked. I had been ushered off their aircraft from a seat that was mine and sent to another airline that couldn't fly, and now I was being told that because I originally arrived late they wanted more money from me. The computer didn't realize I had originally been given a seat and then it had been taken away.

It was now 4:30 p.m., and I was frustrated and exhausted. I told the ticket agent that I didn't have the money. He sent me to the information desk.

The information desk employee told me that she couldn't do anything about it. She advised me to speak with the manager above her.

The manager was so busy that when I told him I had a serious problem, he said, "So do I, I have others before you. I'll be right back."

When he finally returned, I explained the situation to him from the beginning. He typed something into the computer. A few seconds later, he told me that I was late and had to pay the additional $100 fare. I explained to him that I was already on the original plane. "You were late," he repeated.

I put my ticket before him, and he pushed it back to me. I told him that I wanted to return home to St. Croix where my wife and children had already arrived. He informed me that he couldn't help me.

I wanted to punch him in his face. Instead, I grabbed the telephone and pulled it off the wall. Then, I took some documents off the counter and threw them across the terminal floor. I told him to call the police, and that's exactly what he did.

My father-in-law had just arrived at the airport a few moments before my episode because I called him and told him that I was stuck at Kennedy Airport. Just in time, he arrived because he said a man was about to hit me from behind, but he stopped him. The police arrived, handcuffed me, and took me to the police station at the airport. A police sergeant there asked me what happened.

When I started explaining to him what happened, I broke down with tears. I felt humiliated, lost and afraid.

There my father-in-law was, standing outside trying to speak sense to the police. I had prayed at his table many times. He was fully aware of my church-going, and he knew I was trying to live for God. After all the praying, witnessing and speaking with Nicky Cruz about my new life as a born-again Christian, here I was in handcuffs; arrested! I was no better than any criminal was. I had reacted violently and had broken the law.

I finally told the sergeant that I was a doctor in Uncle Sam's military. He was shocked. "You're a doctor," he exclaimed.

"Yes," I replied, "a Lieutenant in the Public Health Service."

He asked for ID. After looking at my service card, he demanded that they remove the handcuffs. "You're a doctor in Uncle Sam's Army, and you don't know how to control yourself?" he admonished me.

My father-in-law was by then outside the room; he threatened to sue the airlines. The sergeant excused himself from the room. When he came back in, he asked, "If we send you back to St. Croix, will you promise not to give us any more trouble?"

"Yes, sir," I answered.

My father-in-law then took me back to the terminal. Laughing, he said, "I don't believe what you did." He told me that he understood, but he couldn't believe I went crazy like I did.

The manager who originally said that he couldn't help me went inside the airline terminal and came back with a first-class ticket for the next day. He apologized and asked me to fly in style back to St.Croix. I thanked him and apologized. My father-in-law told me later, that he laughed all the way back to Red Hook projects.

From that experience, God showed me more of me. That night I prayed and asked God to forgive me.

My father was a burden on Iris and myself. He was not mentally alert, and when we took him from the nursing home, he was taking medication for his intermittent psychosis. The medication worked in keeping him calm, but it also slowed him mentally. To make matters worse, my father could not control his bowels. I was constantly cleaning after him. Often he didn't want to take a bath. Iris frequently complained about his odor. She had her hands full with the children, my needs as well as her own. It was difficult for her. I continually asked God for strength. Sometimes, I would get upset with my father and threaten to put him back in the nursing home. I knew I could never do that. I believed at least I owed this to my father. I wanted to take care of him in his old age. He had always cared for me, and never really denied me anything. After five months on St. Croix, when he felt better, we all agreed to send him back to New York where he would live with my mother.

Though I passed my test to practice medicine in St. Croix, it took ten months before I received my license. I was even given an oral exam a couple of months after passing It. I threatened to sue the Virgin Islands government. When it did come, I was grateful. I believe it was an administrative problem.

Wilbert

On February 9, 1981, my son Wilbert III was born. He was the first child whose diapers I changed on a regular basis and bathed him. One day Iris was tired and I asked her to go out and relax. When she came home her breast were full of milk. She wanted to breast feed Wilbert. Wilbert had slept for hours because I fed him concentrated formula from a can without diluting it with water. I did not realize what I did was the wrong thing to do at six weeks old or any age. He made it through the ordeal but he slept longer than usual. He had a hardy appetite. He would eat a whole bowel of cream of wheat. After eating the bowel of cream of wheat, he would fall asleep for a few hours. When he woke up, Iris would give him juice and lunch. He was a thick child.

Jamal

On March 21, 1983, Iris had our fifth child and I named him Jamal. He was a beautiful baby boy. I called him "Blondie" because he had blond curly hair. At times, I would ask him where he came from. He would get up in the morning and say to his mother, "Good morning mommy I love you." Jamal loved stuff animals. Every time we went to Woolworths Department store, he wanted a stuffed animal. He was a happy baby. Iris says, "He was a good baby."

Chapter 20
Red Monday

I cried unto the lord with my voice:
With my voice unto the Lord did I make my supplication.

Psalm 142:1

It was a Monday morning, and the Frederiksted Health Center was busy. The waiting room was filled with people, and the medical staff was already immersed in work.

While sitting in my office, the head nurse summoned me, because I was the chief medical officer. I was often asked to handle administrative problems, which affected the health center. As I entered her office, I noticed that she looked upset. She was concerned about one of the doctors who was working that morning and asked me to investigate his behavior. In her opinion, he had been acting strangely for a few days, and today she noticed that he was wearing dark sunglasses indoors. Her main concern, however, was that Dr. Martin had prescribed birth control pills to a patient without examining her.

I reviewed the patient's chart, and realized that the head nurse had a right to be alarmed. I decided to look in on Dr. Martin and found him speaking with a patient. I politely interrupted him. He did not respond to me. I continued to speak to him, and he still ignored me. I put my hand on his large shoulder, and he finally replied that he was "okay." I asked how his weekend was. He responded, "It was okay." I never did get around to asking him about the patient.

After I returned to my office, two aides came in to speak with me. Suddenly, Dr. Martin barged in and started cursing at me. Yelling at the top of his voice, he said, "If you ever put your mother-fucking hands on me again, I'm going to kill your mother-fucking ass!"

I was totally taken by surprise and so were the aides, who instinctively ran from my office. When he finished cursing me, Dr. Martin turned and left the room.

Surprised and taken aback by his threats, I remained seated on a stool as I gathered my thoughts. Then, Dr. Martin came back into my office a second time; he repeated his threats to kill me. This time, however, he came at me; he grabbed my neck, and pulled a scalpel from his left coat pocket. When I saw that the plastic sheath was removed from the new scalpel, I knew that he was serious. I caught his hand that held the knife and began to wrestle with him.

During the struggle, thoughts of my family flashed before my mind. I called out to God.

Somehow, I got loose from his hold and ran from the room. I held the door handle to keep him from getting out. I knew that would only work for a short while. He was a strong, big-framed guy, much bigger than I was.

I yelled to the head nurse to leave the building. When I saw her run out, I let the door handle loose and started to run. I could feel him just behind me. After escaping from the building, I found myself surrounded by a crowd of people.

Realizing that Dr. Martin could leave the building from the rear exit, I quickly asked a large man to hold the front door. While Dr. Martin was pacing the floor, shouting and gesturing with his hands that he would get me, I ran to the back of the building in order to hold the door. With all the strength that I could muster, I held the back door closed.

Dr. Martin pushed on the door three times and knocked it open. When our eyes made contact, I gestured to him that I was willing to give up. He continued to chase me. I ran through the Ingeborg Nesbitt Clinic and shouted that Dr. Martin was crazy and was trying to kill me. Many people looked at me with amazement and didn't know what to do.

When I saw that he was gaining ground on me, I ran faster, out through the main entrance and into the street. I saw two police officers approaching, so I ran up to them and shouted that the doctor was trying to kill me. Instead of helping me, one police officer put his nightstick on my back and said, "You get over there." I told him that I was "Dr. Williams," but my street attire was not convincing to him.

Dr. Martin was dressed in a white lab coat. He continued to pursue me, and the police officers did not keep him from approaching me. At face distance, he was still shouting his threats.

When I fully realized that the police officers were not protecting me, I called them crazy. At this point, one police officer lost control and called me a "mother-fucker." He placed a nightstick forcibly on my neck, while the other held my hands behind my back with the pressure of his body on mine. I was thrown on the trunk of the police car.

When I was pulled off and taken to the rear door of the police car, a nurse approached the officers and told them that they had the wrong man. One of the police officers pushed her with his arm. She approached him again, warning, "I want you to remember that I told you, you have the wrong man." People were shouting and trying to get the police officers to realize their mistake. During this time, Dr. Martin had not been apprehended. I was pushed roughly into the back of the patrol car, and I hit my head on the door molding. In the process, my glasses fell from my face.

I saw Dr. Martin open the door of a four-wheel drive police Bronco and he sat unhindered. As I was being driven to the police station, the officer wanted to know why I didn't tell him that I was a doctor. "I did," I responded. When we arrived at the station house, the officers took our statements. Dr.Martin was still threatening to harm me. By that time, the Medical Director of the hospital and the Hospital Administrator arrived. My immediate supervisor was there also. After we gave our statements, they released Dr. Martin after assault and battery on me, and, as far as I'm concerned, attempted murder. When I was advised that I could leave, one of the police officers told me that no arrest had taken place.

Iris arrived, crying. When she saw that I was okay, she calmed down. Some of the health care workers were telling me to sue the government. All I wanted to do was go back to the health center to take care of my patients. Iris was advised to take me home.

For the next few days, Iris and I tried to understand and deal with what had happened. I couldn't understand why the Virgin Islands government had put the patients' lives in danger by hiring a doctor who apparently was mentally ill.

The circumstances of my own life being in danger troubled me. The thought of what my family would have gone through if I were killed, plagued me. I wanted some answers pertaining to the commitment of the Virgin Islands Department of Health.

Various stories began to funnel in my direction.

Some people felt that I harassed Dr. Martin by pursuing the course of conversation, which pertained to his weekend. My immediate supervisor was saying that I was Dr. Martin's boss. The Medical Director in the hospital assumed that Dr. Martin's mental health had been fully disclosed to me. I didn't know that Dr. Martin was using psychotropic medication and he was a diagnosed paranoid schizophrenic.

These statements were not true. I believed that my superiors cared little for the well-being of the people of the Virgin Islands, much less its health-givers. It was this, which made me turn on them. As far as I was concerned, they were not representing the people whom I cared for. I began to get angry. Not only was I angry, but my body began to physically go through changes. My neck was hurting from Dr.Martin's hold on me. Iris noticed my mood and attitude changing; I was very nervous and short-tempered with people. She told me that I changed, and she didn't like it. I noticed none of these psychological changes, although I knew I was preoccupied with what happened.

When I went back to work, many people were concerned and sympathetic. A number of them were offended and angry about what happened to me.

I wondered what I would do if Dr. Martin returned to the health center. He never retracted his threat and had not been charged with attempted assault. He was loose on the streets within two hours of the incident. Even though no charges were filed against him, he did lose his job because of his violent behavior.

One day he returned to the health center, at which time the head nurse came into my office to advise me. I was stunned by the fact that he had threatened my life and was still coming to the clinic.

I decided to meet with the government in court. I called a lawyer who had previously helped to win a settlement for a patient of mine. After asking me to think seriously about challenging the Virgin Islands government, he agreed to take the case.

I received both praise and criticism from some people for what I was about to do. I was a Christian suing the government of the Virgin Islands and a few of my medical colleagues. It was not considered professional among physicians to sue each other. I knew, however, that my obligation went beyond any loyalty to the profession. I was also told that if I sued the VI government, I could not work for them.

Seeing A Psychiatrist

My attorney requested that I see a Psychiatrist; he felt that it was probably needed in order to help the case. He suggested that perhaps some things needed addressing by a counselor. I agreed.

After my first visit to the psychiatrist, he recommended that I return. He felt that I needed to talk out a few things. After the second visit, he asked for a third visit with Iris present.

By this time, I had second thoughts about ever visiting him. I didn't think that I needed a Psychiatrist, but he was convinced that I was under extreme pressure and needed to rest. He told Iris that he was very concerned about me and suggested a trip to New York. It wasn't what I felt I needed, but Iris agreed with the Psychiatrist's recommendation that I rest.

I was depressed in New York, but I didn't realize it. Iris did, however, and she told me after the trip.

My next visit to the Psychiatrist was trying. I told him that he would be asked to testify concerning my mental trauma, which pertained to the assault by Dr. Martin. He became furious and acted as if he needed a Psychiatrist. He shouted that he was not going to get involved in court proceedings. He wanted things dealt with out of court through conversations with the other physicians who were involved. I told Iris it was obvious that he was protecting the system, and since he couldn't control his own emotions, I didn't want to see him anymore. Iris and I agreed to stop the sessions with him.

It was fine with me; I wanted and needed to be free from the tentacles of the Virgin Islands Department of Health.

Chapter 21
Private Practice

I cried unto thee, O Lord: I said,
Thou art my refuge
And my portion in the land of the living.

Psalm 142:5

I was one month away from signing my termination papers with the US Public Health Service. I was scheduled to open my private office on the next street, next to the health center.

A few days before going into private practice, however, a couple of head doctors called me into a rectangular table meeting. In short, I was told of my need to work for the VI government Department of Health. Dr. King informed me that if I did not work for the government, he did not think I could make it financially with a family. Another doctor accused me of not practicing medicine "up to standard." He said that I didn't know how to read an EKG or take care of certain acute care patients. He stated that he had to stop another physician from encouraging a family to sue me for the death of a cancer victim. A third doctor in the same meeting told me if I sued the government, I could forget about employment with them. When I left that meeting, my confidence was shaken.

I was going through a lot of stress and my life was preoccupied with my personal problems. My life being put into danger with Dr. Martin was only a part of it. The people who were supposed to respect and protect me had lied to me and were now accusing me of medical incompetence. Now they had the nerve to try to control my life.

My Christian life was more of a burden to me than an asset because I wanted revenge for what my colleagues did to me. I wanted the whole island to know that they were a bunch of liars. That born-again excitement and total surrender attitude was gone. My job became more of a hassle for me, and my family became secondary in my life.

My First Medical Office

After I officially received my license to practice medicine in the Virgin Islands, Iris and I opened the office, which we had been preparing for about three months. We rented the bottom level of a house on the waterfront on Strand Street in Frederiksted. It was a beautiful spot, and ideal for the practice of medicine.

We rented the office space for $500.00 per month, and called the new practice "Agape Medical Clinic," "Agape" meaning "God's perfect and unconditional love." The least I could have done was to dedicate my practice to God.

Iris was my receptionist and she handled typing and financial matters. She performed her job well, even though she never got direct payment. Everything seemed to go very well. Patients were booking appointments every day, and we were full. People were walking into the clinic for on-the-spot care. There were occasions when we even handled emergencies.

During my first month in private practice, I made $12,000. We worked days and weeks and sometimes spent twelve hours in the office.

The medical problems were wide-ranging, and it was challenging to me. I tried to administer to the physical, mental, and spiritual needs of the people. The religions were varied; mostly Christians and some Muslims and Jehovah's Witnesses.

There were times when I was hesitant to talk about Jesus Christ to some people. Nevertheless, I freely talked about God, gave out Bibles, and prayed for patients. Most people, as far as I know, appreciated my attitude. We played Christian background music, and that set an atmosphere, which raised healthy conversations. Iris and I knew that people were being helped on a holistic level, because they were testifying for me. We were blessed financially; the Agape Medical Clinic was on its way.

Our lives were stable and we were satisfied with our business. We knew that we had done the right thing by staying in St. Croix and opening a medical office. I could have gone back to the states, but it wouldn't have been what was wise for us. St. Croix offered what we needed in terms of peace and an environment to raise our children.

One day while we were in our office, Yoli from Schenectady called us, and told us that Elder Mac died. We were devastated, and for a few moments didn't believe it. He was traveling on the highway coming from a church function and he crashed. The first thing I thought about was his wife and children. How was sister Mac Daniel going to make it without her beloved husband? Then, I thought about his wonderful sermons and how they made me feel great and there was never one that I didn't enjoy.

Refreshing Springs Church lost a good man. He was not only a Christian, but also someone who understood better than most Christians, that there was a lot more to life than calling Jesus' name as if He is a household detergent that cleans all of our dirty laundry.

I was going to miss Elder Mac Daniel very much. I looked at Iris and she had tears flowing down her checks. I knew that she felt devastated, but neither one of us could bring him back. All I had left of him were his great sermons, his love for me, and a role model as a pastor, and I would never have one like him again.

Williams vs. the Government of the Virgin Islands

My lawsuit against the government of the Virgin Islands and the two police officers had been set in motion. My attorney was not afraid to deal with the Department of Health and Public Safety of the Virgin Islands. After much soul-searching and some criticism, I decided that I had no other alternative but to sue the system that had promised to protect me and the people of the Virgin Islands, but failed.

After a few months, our case was called to the District Court of the Virgin Islands. Seven women and one man were selected for the jury. The doctors involved included the Medical Director of the hospital, the Assistant Commissioner of Health, and the Medical Director of the Frederiksted Health Center. I claimed negligence on behalf of the VI Government Health Department for hiring a physician with a history of mental illness and endangering my life, and police brutality on behalf of the VI Department of Public Safety. The stage was set, and we went to court.

The trial lasted for three days. The attorney for the VI government tried to discredit me and show that my character was questionable. He tried many arguments, pointing to my psychiatric visits, and making of

$12,000 in my first month of private practice, practicing medicine without a license, and stating that I was one of the most aggressive doctors ever to work at the Frederiksted Health Center.

When the trial reached its third day, I was confident that our case had been well stated. There was no doubt in my mind that the jury was aware of the tactics of the government's lawyer.

As the Judge made a statement on the final day of the trial, he mentioned how the defendants tried to make me look bad for three days, but he wasn't going to let them do that.

After the jury gave their verdict, we were awarded $137,000.00 in damages. I was not surprised concerning the VI government's verdict and the verdicts against the police officers. I was satisfied with the results.

Chapter 22
Suffering

You prepare a table before me in the presence of my enemies.
You anoint my head with oil; my cup runs over.

Psalm 23:5

Iris suffered a lot after our ordeal with the VI government. I knew that the stress of the trial was not good for her. Though she was stronger than I was, she disliked public confrontation. She was pregnant again. She was soon to lose the baby and very sad for a number of weeks.

Iris and I tried to get back to our daily duties of practicing medicine and raising a family. We were evicted from our home; the landlady wanted us to move so she could fix up the house. She raised our rent in order to encourage us to vacate the premises.

We looked for a new house to live in, but we quickly realized that we needed to finally start circulating our money into our own purse. We didn't have enough money to purchase a house, so we decided to start building one on a seven-and-one-half-acre piece of property, which we had bought a few years before. We had about $6,000 on hand, so we asked one of the men at the church, which we were attending to build the house for us.

It was time for us to make our first attempt at owning a home. We worked very diligently; we put in long hours in the office. As we made money, we paid the builder.

In a few months, we were encouraged by our landlady to move out quickly. Therefore, we decided to move into our new home even before it was completed.

For two weeks, we lived without any water or electricity. There were multiple inconveniences, such as no indoor plumbing and no refrigerator.

I was accused of not thinking about my family in my decision to move in prior to the completion of the house. It didn't make much sense to me to see so many people doing the very same thing on St. Croix; doing well in the end, while I played the big professional, and refusing to sacrifice. Our goal was to be in our own home and we accomplished that.

After a few weeks, we had a well dug and electricity was hooked up and the house was more comfortable. God was providing the house we began to live in.

The medical practice continued to flourish. God was bringing in people who needed our services. We tried hard to provide the competent care that people needed so badly in St. Croix.

In so many ways, the quality of medical care in the islands left much to be desired. There were constant complaints concerning the lack of proper diagnosis by some physicians, the prescribing of medications that do not help, and lack of compassion and competence. Many of these allegations from patients were damaging and did not help the general fear that locals and especially newcomers to the island had concerning malpractice.

Iris and I made a conscious effort to alleviate many of these feelings. Some of the allegations were true.

No matter what our effort was, some people were still not convinced.

Many were traveling to Puerto Rico for what they thought was quality care. I have to admit that the doctors in Puerto Rico are better equipped with modern facilities, which help them deal with the misgivings of the people. My personal opinion, however, is that some of those doctors in Puerto Rico were taking advantage of the fear that many patients from St. Croix exhibited.

I had to deal with the notion of some people that because I was practicing medicine in St.Croix, I could not really be that good a doctor. Sometimes people would come to me for medical care and then ask for a letter to go to Puerto Rico. It was hard to work within that framework.

To add to our troubles, my victorious lawsuit against the government gave me a terrible reputation among the doctors who still worked for the government.

In spite of the fact that many people preferred and wanted private medical services, the government had created a monopoly on medical services. I was making far more money taking care of people in my office during the morning hours than the doctors who worked for the government all day. When those doctors arrived at their private practices in the afternoon, I had just about put in a full day's work.

I worked long hard hours in my office, made house calls and delivered babies. Each time I delivered a baby, it gave me a medical shot in the arm, and I loved it.

Many evenings, Iris and I went home exhausted. After arriving home, the telephone was constantly busy with patients calling. Sometimes, they would come to my house while I was resting. Sunday was hardly a rest day. I thank God, though, that Iris and I had enough strength in order to endure it.

Helping Others

I was in my office taking care of a full load of patients and an attorney phoned my office and said, "Hey Doc, we got this guy who was hurt by a doctor at the St. Croix Hospital. We can't find any doctor with a private license on St. Croix and a stateside license to testify for him, would you be willing to help this guy? We know you challenged the government, and you're still here. So what do you say?"

He explained to me that the man was married with three children and with a borderline IQ. The man had lost the use of his right hand, which he stated was because he was brought into the St. Croix Hospital Emergency Room, psychotic and handcuffed. The handcuffs were on for a number of hours before they were removed. He was then placed in a straight jacket and laid on his stomach for about five hours. His hands became swollen, and no doctor examined him for five days. Because of that, he had to have two operations on his hand, both of which were not successful. He was a mason and could no longer do masonry work.

Three doctors from the St. Croix Hospital were apparently involved and they were being sued. The attorney wanted me to testify on behalf of the patient and against those three doctors for neglect. I agreed. Although I sat in court all day, I never did testify.

The patient won his case and was awarded $85,000. This did not improve my image with doctors at the hospital. I knew, however, I had done the right thing. My business was helping people; not the system.

Chapter 23
Daddy Died

The earth is the Lord's
And the fullness thereof;
The world, and they that dwell therein.

Psalm 24:1

My father was sick for quite a while and all the family understood that his condition was guarded, but what we did not know was how near to death he was. His kidneys had failed, high blood pressure destroyed his heart and blood vessels, sugar diabetes followed, and to top it all he suffered a number of heart attacks and a couple of strokes.

I visited him for the last time in the Veterans Hospital at Fort Hamilton in Brooklyn. When I walked into his room, he was in a stupor and I don't even know if he remembers me being there. My mother and my sisters were there. One of them asked me what I thought about his state and I responded that it didn't look good. That was the best answer I could muster up, as I stood in the room with all of them and my dying father. After all, I was supposed to have an answer that would be satisfying since I was a doctor. I knew my mother was hurting deep inside her soul; I could see it in her face. She looked at me and shrugged her shoulders and I felt helpless. I touched my father's hand and in my heart, I was telling him that I loved him dearly. He meant the world to me and I never told him. I did tell him when I felt that he was receptive that I loved him and he never rejected me when I did. So many things had occurred between us when I became a young man. We argued about God, man, heaven, earth, hell, good, and evil. He never changed his position on these issues as far as I knew and he believed 100 percent that he was on the side of right. The conflict rose when I thought that I was on the side of right. We butted horns like old rams until one of us got tired, or my mother told me to shut up. I think that we did it for the exercise of manhood between father and son. Sometimes the debates were so heated, the veins in my father's neck were bulging while his forehead wrinkled and his eyes fixed on me. My mother worried that he would have a stroke or a heart attack and she hated the arguments between us. I stood before my father; I believed that he loved me and forgave me for every stupid play on words, which I had with him because I was a college graduate. I never tried to make him look small. I'm sure he thought that I did at times, but he had no good reason to feel small in my presence. He was more intelligent than I was, had a better memory, was much wiser, and was more man. I was no real match for him even with my few pieces of paper from school.

I forgave him for calling me a "nigger" when I stole his money, but I believe that he had the right to speak his mind. I looked at him with intensity, as I tried to convince myself that he would make it through his ill health journey one more time, and I convinced myself that he would. I kissed my father on his cheek and told him that I would see him later. I told my mother his condition was more serious than I thought before we left his room.

When I went back to St. Croix, I was glad to see Iris. I told her about my father and all she could do was listen because there was nothing either of us could do but pray, and we did.

One early morning while I was in a deep sleep, my sister Janice called me. "Buddy," she said, "Daddy died." I do remember saying "Okay," hanging up the telephone and going back to sleep.

After waking up later that morning, the reality of my father's death hit me. I did not cry or speak much to Iris about it. I knew that there was a purpose in his death as in his life. I prepared myself to meet the family in New York City.

My father requested that I give his eulogy. Iris and the children stayed in St. Croix while I traveled to New York. While en route, I was constantly recalling the strength, which my father exhibited, even during his illness. As I watched the passing clouds from the jumbo jet window, I had a feeling of peace. God was ministering His peace to me.

I was so glad to see my family. Everyone was holding together well. When I went to the church that evening in order to view his body, my friend Philip was there along with some other people whom I had not seen in a long time. Their presence helped to comfort me.

When I approached the casket, my father looked at peace. After I touched his hand, I fell apart. This was the man who raised me. He had given so much to me, and I loved him dearly. I broke down and cried.

The day of the funeral was challenging to all of us. When it was time to give his eulogy, I sang the hymn, "At the Cross." The eulogy wasn't long. I tried to sprinkle it with humor and yet capture the reality of my father's life. I wanted the sensitivity of my father to shine through.

I told the crowd that my father didn't take nonsense, but he loved people. I told them of the time that I watched my father hold a dead puppy of mine with tears in his eyes. I told them of the times he beat me for misbehaving and how he always told me he was sorry. They laughed and cried when I finished. I saw people shaking their heads in approval of what I said. Later we buried my father on Long Island at the Veterans Cemetery. On that cold November day, my mother received his American flag with honor. It was over. My father's body had finally been put to rest.

Chapter 24
Hospital Admissions Privilege

A man that beareth false witness
against his neighbor
is a maul and a sword, and a sharp arrow.

Proverbs 25:18

My relationship with my colleagues and the hospital got worse. Though I did not work for the hospital, I did have admitting "privileges." I frequented the hospital if one of my patients needed to be admitted. The Chairman of Medicine, Dr. Evangelista wouldn't even speak to me. Each time I was in his presence, he ignored me. If I asked him a question or addressed him, he would never give me eye contact, he would walk away from me speaking some words into the air. He made me feel uncomfortable, but I continued to speak to him. He once complained to the Hospital Medical Director, Dr. King that I should not be able to dress the way I did with dungarees and sneakers. I knew that I was beyond being able to impress him and I wouldn't change the manner of my dress. Dr. King told me that I should try to dress better when visiting the hospital, because it was thought that I had no respect for rules.

Medical Discrimination

Adult medicine kept me very busy. A few of my patients were quite sick and needed frequent admissions to the hospital. I enjoyed the challenge of helping them get well, and 98 percent of them did get well. Another doctor admitted one of my extremely ill patients. He had a rare liver tumor and

I missed it. It was a tumor, which is often seen in Africa, but rarely in the USA. The doctor who diagnosed it held animosities against me. I never found out what her problem was with me. She suggested to Dr. Evangelista that the family sue me.

Within a few weeks my patient died. I had a difficult time holding my head up when I entered the hospital, because I felt that she spoke ill of me to other physicians.

After his funeral, I visited his wife in their home. They lived in a wooden shack that was kept very neat and clean. I watched her children playing in the living room (I thought of my own children and wondered how they would react if I had died). His wife was very hospitable with me. When I left her house, I felt empty.

The "Rectangular" Table

The Medical Director's secretary at the St. Croix Community Hospital called me and requested a rectangular table meeting along with a few physicians who stated that they were concerned about me. I didn't think that the meeting was to advance my stand in the medical community or the hospital, but to deal with me on their prejudicial issues. I wasn't sure, if seeking an attorney was in order or if I should go alone and try to handle the matter myself. Dr. Evangelista took it upon himself to show me just how much he disliked me. I never understood what his problem was. He would never speak to me when I spoke to him. He was never polite or friendly. His attitude didn't stop me from speaking to him and I think this annoyed him. I couldn't see myself being abrasive toward him and participating in his stupid game.

I had "privileges" in medicine, pediatrics, surgery, obstetrics, and gynecology. Taking care of my patients in the hospital gave me a chance to practice a more intensive form of medicine. Sometimes I had as many as five or six people in the hospital at a time. Occasionally a nurse would pull me to her side and tell me that some of the doctors were jealous because I had so many people in the hospital. I never took those comments seriously because it appeared so ridiculous and immature for any physician to be jealous or threatened because I was doing well at what I had been trained to do.

It wasn't only Dr. Evangelista who was acting out his own frustrations by taking it out on me, but Dr. Dizon, one of St. Croix's most well-known and respected Internists who was also acting out. He practiced some cardiology. St. Croix didn't have a heart doctor at the time, so most people sought his care if their ticker was acting up. I respected him for what he did, though I didn't know how well he practiced and understood cardiology. When I had a client who needed cardiovascular care, I encouraged most of them to see him. When I saw him, he avoided me. If I had the occasion to speak to him, he behaved, just like Dr. Evangelista. They were friendly with each other. It didn't take me long to figure out their abrasive attitudes with me had more to do with their shallow self-esteem and fear of losing something as physicians because someone new was around. The nurses were telling me that the Chief of Medicine was making negative comments about me.

As a result, when I was asked to attend the meeting I wasn't surprised when I walked in and saw Dr. Evangelista sitting at the beautiful rectangular wooden table with a pile of charts in front of him. The Medical Director, of the hospital, Dr. King and the Assistant Commissioner of Health, Dr. Christian were sitting with him.

At first, I wasn't sure what their plan was until I noticed my charts piled in front of Dr. Evangelista, the Chief of Medicine. He didn't have a smile on his face and the other two had half-smiles. I knew at this point that they were about to set me up for the slaughter. Dr. King asked me politely to have a seat and Dr. Christian, asked me to relax. The Medical Director, Dr. King told me that they had some concerns about the way I practiced medicine.

"In what way?"

Dr. Christian replied, "Tommy [Dr. Evangelista] has some feelings that you're not practicing medicine correctly."

"Yes," Dr. Evangelista said, "he doesn't even know how to read an EKG. He even treats his patients the same way. He gives all these men the diagnosis of prostatitis [prostate gland infection] and treats them all with ampicillin [antibiotics]."

I asked Dr. Evangelista what was wrong with the treatment and questioned him if they got well or not. He jumped to ulcer disease and said, "You even treat all your ulcer patients the same way."

I replied to him and said, "Don't they get well and leave the hospital better than when they came in?"

He then jumped back to the EKG business and said, "But you can't read an EKG." He was acting like a fool and the other two were taking it all as if it were all staged. I sat before them feeling insecure and full of rage because they were saying, in effect, I was incompetent as a medical doctor, and I had no medical doctors to speak for me.

Dr. Christian said, "We're only trying to help you Wilbert," and Dr. King remained silent. I wanted to get the hell out of there. Dr. Evangelista was still shouting in the air that I didn't know how to read an EKG.

I left the meeting furious and determined to continue to treat my patients the best way I knew how. There were many people in the hospital who could testify that my patients got well and left the hospital early. I knew I was not incompetent.

When I went home that evening, I felt torn up inside and started cursing the whole lot of those who tried to do me in. I didn't know what their problem was, but I was sure Tim felt threatened by me. I was too busy to worry about Tim and his low self-esteem and deflated ego. I did find out later that some were saying that he was upset with me. While he was working for the government, my office was open. It was said, that he apparently believed I was stealing his patients, because my office was open during those morning hours and our offices were near each other. I was treating many patients in the small town of Frederiksted where our offices were at the time, but I never stole any of his patients. In my opinion, if he did feel this way he was being paranoid.

Obstetrics Inferno

I was delivering babies in and out of the hospital. My first out-of-the-hospital delivery was done in my office. A white patient of mine who recently moved to the island from the States asked me to deliver her baby outside of the hospital because she had heard so many bad things about the delivery room. I assured her that she could have a safe delivery in the hospital, but she insisted on having it in my office. The delivery went OK except for unexpected bleeding. I had to drive to the hospital and get some medication in order to stop the bleeding. By the time I got back to her it had stopped. I later found out from her that she hemorrhaged with her first delivery; she had withheld that information from me. After that first out-of-hospital delivery, we started getting calls from people asking if I would deliver their babies at home. I wasn't too keen on it, but my wife and I decided to try it. This time it was in the patient's home and it went well. After my second delivery outside of our community hospital, I was sold on home deliveries. The clients kept coming and I kept delivering. I continued to deliver babies inside the hospital, and it was going well.

Midwives controlled the hospital labor and delivery rooms. This was the first time for me working in such a setting. My experiences had been working with doctors who controlled the labor and delivery rooms. The St. Croix Hospital didn't even have a doctor on call, so the midwives were making all the judgment calls, even concerning high-risk pregnancies and deliveries. It wasn't a good setup and it concerned me; especially when they tried to make some judgment calls on my patients. All of my patients were private and they didn't appreciate the attitudes of some midwives walking into their room and pulling back the sheets, telling them to open up their legs while seeing rubber gloves ready to assault them.

After it occurred a couple times, and I ignored some midwives' statements to me concerning what they thought was best for my patients, some of them got annoyed with me. I knew what I was doing and what was best for my patients and I wasn't going to let any midwife walk over me and do what she pleased with my patients without first consulting with me. My position with them was their lack of professionalism and disrespect for my patients and me. Dr. De Chabert, the Chief of Obstetrics and Gynecology allowed the midwives full authority in the labor and delivery rooms. It benefited him so there was little or no reason for him to correct them. While the midwives were working their butts off in the delivery rooms, sometimes two midwives to as many as five to eight patients, with no pediatricians around to receive babies that were born with medical problems, the doctors were home "cooling out." Sometimes the midwives would call one of them for advice and I witnessed Obstetrics being practiced over the telephone.

When I went into the labor and delivery rooms with my patients, I'd stay all day or night with them. I could see the midwives steaming because they wanted the control over my practice in their domain, but I wouldn't surrender it. Therefore, they put out the "word" on me, told Dr. De Chabert, the director of Ob/Gyn (who was also the Chief of the department) that I was difficult to get along with, and didn't want any one of them treating my patients. Those lying midwives only gave half-truths when they spoke to him and he believed them. He didn't help to improve the situation and he could have. His position was to protect the midwives no matter what. As a result, each time I went into the delivery room some midwife would chump up nasty charges on me. That wasn't all; they would also behave as if only half of me was there. When I asked for certain items to care for my patients, I was sometimes made to wait, only to never receive it. Many times, I had to get it for myself or do without it. When I asked for an intravenous set to start a glucose water drip, some of those nasty nurses would make some ugly faces. They would only screw up more what was already screwed up from the beginning. I tried hard to deal with their attitudes. I continued to greet them morning, afternoon, and evening. Some of them were more than determined to let me know that they were out to get me. One nurse named Duncan was very vicious, devious, cunning, and nasty. She was a bit quieter than the rest and almost sneaked around to talk about me, as various people on staff in the hospital told me. A few times, I caught her talking about me negatively.

Surrounded by Fire and a Impaired Doctor

All hell broke loose in the delivery room when a patient of mine had difficulty in the second stage of labor (when the head is coming down the birth canal) and she just stopped at that point. Midwife Duncan asked me if I wanted her to call in one of the Obstetricians whom she favored and I said OK. When he came about one half-hour later, he walked a bit unsteady with slurred speech. I looked at him in amazement; not wanting to believe what I was seeing. The three midwives in the room with me acted as if everything was normal. I couldn't believe their deliberate denial of the fact that this doctor was high on something. I had previously asked the nurse to start a pitocin drip (to enhance uterine contractions) which was running slow due to the seriousness of the medication. When he came in, he opened the valve and let the medicine freely run into the patient. I looked on in horror while the midwives acted like nothing wrong had been done. When she failed to deliver her baby, he requested that we take her into the delivery room. He made a midline episiotomy (cut from the vaginal opening toward the rectum) to ease her delivery, then put forceps on the baby's head and ripped her apart. The baby was born OK, but the patient was traumatized. Yellow fat tissue was protruding from the vagina and I looked at the midwife, who ignored my signals that all wasn't well.

Disbelief

I stood with that doctor and watched him in disbelief, knowing that he needed help as much as my patient needed a good obstetrician. He sutured her up like a Thanksgiving Day turkey and no one said a word, including me. I didn't appreciate Nurse Duncan's help because she didn't help my patient and I sure didn't appreciate the Ob/Gyn physician who didn't have the professionalism to be fully sober to practice medicine.

That evening a nurse asked me how the delivery went and I said, "Not good, the doctor who came in to help ripped my patient up." I told her that I believed he was drunk. The following day the word was out in the labor and delivery room that I accused the doctor of being drunk. Nurse Duncan stopped speaking to me. When I greeted her, she answered me with a grunt if she said anything at all.

I apparently had overstepped my bounds as far as loyalty and staying with the "medical pack" was concerned. I had once again breached the fact that doctors are supposed to stick together, but I didn't care. My patients came first, they trusted me, and I wasn't going to let any secret honor code guide my principles or channel the way I practiced medicine. I didn't spend the time becoming a doctor, sweating, and crying tears when I wasn't doing well in medical school, to now give it up for false loyalty and acceptance by them.

My office practice was as busy as ever and I had my hands full, spending sometimes ten to eleven hours taking care of the sick and dying while being a husband and father at the same time. Sometimes I wondered if I had made the right decision to become a doctor in the first place. I wondered if it were worth the tension, anxiety, and outright depression at times to help people.

Chapter 25
Stealing Away

He refreshes and restores my life;
He leads me in the paths of righteousness for
His name's sake.

Psalm 23:3

I tried burying myself in other projects. A guy whom I knew at the church, which I was attending (Church of the Nazarene) was gifted with his hands. We were sitting around one day when he and his brother (who was my pastor) decided to embark on making a Hovercraft (rides on a cushion of air and has a propeller blade on the rear to push it forward). It was agreed that I would finance the project and Steve, the pastor's brother, would build it. When the Hovercraft was finished months later, it functioned well on the ocean. Our plan was to start building them to sell, and it would be a way for me to quit medicine, but the plan never worked. Gary (my pastor), Steve's brother, along with Steve made the decision to leave our craft at someone's beachfront property, without consulting with me, and I objected. I told my pastor that it was none of his business and Steve took offense and decided that he didn't want to follow through with our plans.

Our relationship became strained and we fell out of friendship, with our emotions flying high. Gary, for reasons expressed to our congregation, felt a need to leave our church, which had nothing to do with our Hovercraft fiasco. Steve had left also and my heart was crushed. It hurt so much because I trusted both of them, only to find out that I had misjudged their characters.

I didn't stop my pursuit to leave medicine. I next tried the fishing business and purchased sixteen lobster cages with a guy whom I met in my practice. Again, I had promises of loyalty and dedication to a project that not only would benefit me, but the other person as well. The guy told me that he was starting a fishing business, and lured me with the promise of a boat, which he was buying. It took him so long to get a boat that the lobster cages, which I purchased through a friend of his rotted in the sun.

I tried a third time in the fishing business with a guy named Lennie, who made some fish cages with my money. He had a ragged car with bald tires and doors that barely closed and a piece of a wooden boat, which he made. For a homemade job it wasn't that bad, but he acted like he had a yacht and he was doing me a favor. Every Saturday morning at 5:15 a.m. I awakened and met him at his house to go on the ocean and pull our fish traps. Most of the time our catch was small. I stayed with him many Saturday mornings in his yard and sold fish to people. Sometimes I went home with no fish because I believed that he needed the money more than I needed the fish or the money.

After a few months of this, one Saturday he refused to speak to me. He wouldn't tell me what was wrong and the more I spoke with him the angrier he became. He kept saying, "I done with you." I was very confused and didn't understand what, if anything, I did to upset him.

I spoke with Iris about what was happening in my life. She seriously told me with force that I would never be successful at any project where I wanted to leave medicine. She reminded me that I had pleaded and begged God to help me to become a medical doctor and I agreed to give it back to Him in service to people and I was backing out. She said, "Medicine is the only thing you will do well because that's what God gave you." I listened to her more intently than she imagined. Her words continued to ring in my mind.

Pushing on

We continued to perform home deliveries and I began to hear the disapproval of some midwives. I once had a woman in labor at home and she ceased to progress in her second stage of labor, and after futile attempts to deliver the baby I took her to the hospital. I informed the midwife on duty that labor had ceased and I was sure she would need a C-section. The staff made her stay in labor with the baby's head pounding against her pelvic bone for hours. When they got ready, they called in an Obstetrician who, with another doctor, did a C-section.

I was not asked to help on these cases and was ignored by the Chief of Obstetrics Dr. Ralph De Chabert and his assistant. This wasn't the first time it happened. I always felt very lonely at these times and questioned my worth and importance in Obstetrics and this was their intent. Each time I had a hospital delivery most of the midwives, save a couple, would be apathetic to the needs of my patients, and had a bad attitude with me. Those midwives were mean as hell and made sure that they ganged together, right or wrong. I never once mistreated any of them and they had no justifiable reason to deal with me the way they did. As far as I was concerned they were wild, like a bunch of animals, doing whatever they pleased, and Dr. De Chabert encouraged it.

I was sorry not only for my patients, but other patients who were less fortunate than mine were because they didn't have a private doctor to stand up for them when some of the midwives leached out their terror on them. I experienced seeing women who were staff patients (having no private doctor) being talked down to as if they were some kind of low-life. Some of them were outright abused physically and verbally. A midwife would just slap on a surgical rubber glove and command the patient to do whatever she said. It disgusted me, but there was little or nothing I could do at the time to make their situation better. Those midwives did whatever they wanted, because they had virtually no check and balance system.

I began to hate each time that I had to go there; my stomach would fill with gas, and I often had diarrhea. Sometimes a midwife or two would act as if I weren't even there.

Early one morning a midwife named Fredricks told the Nurse Supervisor that she couldn't work with me, I was difficult to get along with, and I didn't want anyone helping in taking care of my patients. I was shocked because I thought that she was neutral and was not a part of the gang of those other devious, nasty midwives. I spent over five hours with my patient and I was tired as hell, and Nurse Fredricks was there with her lying mouth talking badly about me. I looked at Nurse Fredricks in disbelief and my heart was pounding in my chest so hard that my head was rocking and I asked her why she said such a thing and she didn't answer me.

I was so upset that while my patient was in labor I took a legal pad and wrote her a four-page letter, telling her that professing Christians are not supposed to lie and certainly not on each other and that, she had no foundation to say what she did. I reminded her that I was also a Christian and her brother in Christ Jesus. I ended the letter by telling her I would pray for her and that I loved her.

Almost all the conflicts with midwives caused some serious emotional and spiritual conflicts for me and I was in a state of personal turmoil and agony. From that point on, Nurse Fredricks had changed her outward behavior toward me. I, however, knew that I could never let down my guard with her. She was just another bearer of the flames that were trying to destroy me.

Home Deliveries

The home deliveries were increasing and the word was spreading through the Caribbean islands that I was doing them. As a result, my practice in obstetrics was more congested because women from other Caribbean islands were coming. I didn't mind it at all, because I loved delivering babies. I enjoyed taking Iris along with me because she helped tremendously during the deliveries. She had a way of relaxing the patients and she knew enough to deliver one if it were necessary.

Sometimes we packed our children in our custom van and headed for a delivery with excitement. We were all over the island. Many times, we traveled on bad roads into hilly areas and a few times, we had to travel through the rain forest. The children slept in the van while we delivered the baby. Most of my home deliveries went smoothly. I adopted a policy of trying not to deliver women who were pregnant for the first time. A few patients literally begged me to deliver their babies and I complied with their requests. These deliveries were usually long and exhausting. Sometimes we were worried that a patient was going to need a C-section, but thanks be to God they didn't.

One time I went to a home delivery and Iris decided to stay home in order to remain with our children. It was late at night, and I got in my car and rushed to the patient's house only to find her anxious and uncooperative. For two hours, I begged and pleaded with her to follow my instructions, and for the same two hours, she did what she pleased. I knew she was uncomfortable and in pain, but so were many other women whom I took care of. Because the deliveries were all natural, I wouldn't give anyone medication for pain and things usually worked out well. This time all seemed to go wrong. I was so tired of dealing with her that I did anything to relax, and as a result, I took off my shoes. She had to go to the bathroom and I followed her to make sure that she wouldn't have the baby in the toilet bowl. She defecated on the floor and I stepped in it. I felt like throwing up and was angered.

I told her to get dressed and I took her to the hospital. After arriving in the labor and delivery room, within one half-hour she delivered. When the midwife heard from the patient that she attempted to deliver at home, the midwife started complaining to the other midwife. I walked out, got in my car and went home.

After that delivery, I told Iris I was quitting obstetrics and didn't want to deliver any more babies. She assured me that by the time the next delivery came, I would change my mind and of course, I did. Sometimes when I went to the delivery room, I had patients on the medical ward, the surgical ward, and in the pediatric nursery. The staff frequently saw me going from one discipline in medicine to another. I took care of the babies whom I delivered and on occasion had to do a circumcision. A couple of the Pediatricians didn't exactly throw down the "welcome mat" for me in the nursery, in the pediatric ward or elsewhere. Sometime I went into the nursery and took pictures of my newborns with my Polaroid camera.

There were moments when I was complimented, and it made a world of difference to me. A pediatric nurse commented to me that she had never seen such a well-done circumcision before. A few people in the hospital were friendly and kind to me. I kept getting warnings from some of them to watch my back, because it was being said by a few important people that I was trying to do everything in medicine and I wanted to do my own thing. I didn't want to do my own thing; I wanted to practice medicine without them telling me how.

My relationship with Iris and my children was reassuring because they showed me that they loved me dearly. I tried to please Iris because she had sacrificed so much for me and for the children. She had not finished college, had married me, and gave me five healthy beautiful children. Much of her time was spent trying to help me stay in balance and deal with adverse circumstances concerning my profession and my personal life. She watched me helplessly sometimes make mistakes because I wouldn't listen to her and follow her advice. I knew that she was right many times in her opinion, but I had to do what made me feel useful and alive.

Iris constantly talked to me about what she believed I needed to do in order to escape some of the pressure that I was under. Most of the time, however, I wouldn't listen to her. As a result, my response usually drained her of the energy. Iris understood when she married me that I was full of energy and strongly committed to loving and helping people. I tried not to display or have a selfish attitude about anything, which I did for people or my family. I just wanted to do what I did best, care and love people. I found things to do in order to take up the lonely and depressed areas of my life. It was strange because in the midst of a loving family, and a couple of friends like Raymond and Michael, I felt lost and lonely. It was like being without something necessary to sustain happiness and peace. There were times when I had no peace and no joy. I thought there had to be more to life than looking down people's throats and listening to their hearts and lungs, delivering babies and caring for the sick and dying.

Ostracism from the Medical Society

The process had begun for my ostracism from the medical establishment and it wasn't my desire, but it was inevitable. I wouldn't conform to their rules because I didn't think that they were fair. Iris was again pregnant with our sixth child, only a few weeks from delivering. I was happy about the pregnancy, even though we had our hands full with the five children we already had. Iris as usual was doing fine and tolerating her pregnancy.

My troubles in the hospital became more intense. Dr. Evangelista continued to ignore me, and some of the nursing staff let me know that I was still disliked by a powerful few. I was ostracized from the medical community and it hurt. I wasn't asking them to overlook what I had done because I didn't feel I had done anything wrong. I was not going to apologize for what I believed was right and true. I had testified against my colleagues and as far as I was concerned, it was over, but they had other goals in mind concerning how to deal with me.

Chapter 26
Ostracism and Ob/Gyn
Insanity, Again

The Lord is my Shepherd
[to feed, guide, and shield me], I shall not lack.

Psalm 23:1

My troubles in the hospital became more intense and Dr. Evangelista continued to ignore me. Some of the nursing staff let me know that I was still disliked by a powerful few. Dr. De Chabert was outwardly displaying his mean streak toward me.

It was clear that I was ostracized from the medical community and it hurt. I wasn't asking them to overlook what I had done because I didn't feel that I had done anything wrong. I was not going to apologize for what I believed was right and true. I had testified against my colleagues and as far as I was concerned it was over, but they had other goals in mind concerning how to deal with me.

One of my patients who was thirty-six weeks pregnant was involved in a car accident. When she told the Ob/Gyn staff that she was my patient and wanted me to be notified so I could care for her, they were offended. Dr. De Chabert was on call and was told that the baby was dead and he refused to take care of her and told them to call me to deliver her baby. At this point of the baby's death, I was called in to deliver her in the hospital room. I delivered a dead baby and I believe this gave the two midwives

301

who were there satisfaction. Dr. De Chabert never came to see the patient before I got there and to my knowledge not after that. No fetal monitoring had been used prior to my arrival and no obstetric ultrasound had been done. The patient's husband, who was a police officer, was pacing up and down the hall talking about how he wanted to hurt someone for not caring properly for his wife. All I could do was try and console him and his wife. They sued the Department of Health and the St. Croix Community Hospital and won. I was happy that they got some compensation for the negligence, which they had to experience.

One medical crisis followed another and I was expending energy as I tried to maintain my sanity. I delivered a patient of mine who was pregnant for the first time and delivered a baby boy. The neonate (a baby less than thirty days old) vomited in the nursery and was diagnosed as having an outlet obstruction in the stomach. The surgeons found that the food could not leave the stomach to enter the intestine so they had to operate. After the success of the operation, the anesthetist placed an adult breathing bag over the baby's nose and mouth in order to help it in breathing during recovery. A few hours later the baby was bleeding from his mouth and nose. The surgeons were called back in and they rushed the baby to the operating room and diagnosed five holes in the baby's stomach. They operated in order to close five holes that were found in the baby's stomach. A few hours later the baby died. The conclusion concerning the holes in the baby's stomach was related to the bagging technique, which was done after the first operation. It was concluded that the surgeons did their job well. The parents wouldn't have an autopsy done unless I was present. It was mandatory in order to decide why the infant died. I reluctantly went and was glad that I did because I saw first-hand some of the trauma that our people were going through because the Virgin Islands Department of Health was not doing its job. The father, in his distress over his first and only baby's death, went to the morgue and took his baby out of the hospital. He went to a friend's house and buried it in the back yard. He called me up on Thanksgiving Day, cried, and told me that he wanted to kill somebody and he didn't feel like living. I spoke to him and reassured him that he could still try to have another child. I told him to dig his baby's body up. He did what I asked and had a proper burial for his baby. He and his wife decided to sue the St. Croix Hospital and the Department of Health and they won their case. I felt very sorry for them because they not only lost their first baby due to malpractice, but the father lost his desire to live. If it were not for his wife holding together, I don't think that he would have made it.

Iris knew about these tragedies and told me that there was nothing, which I could do that would be greater than the impact of the parents pushing for the system to change by being vocal and complaining to government officials. I, on the other hand, believed that I needed to do something constructive in order to help improve the conditions concerning medical care, but I didn't know what to do. The hospital officials didn't want to hear what I had to say, because as far as many of them were concerned I was a troublemaker and needed to be silenced. Iris saw my frustration, anger, and depression each time that I had to deal with medical issues in regards to the system. It made her angry that I wouldn't follow her advice. She was tired of seeing me hurt.

Church Business

Our pastor at the Church of the Nazarene was having tons of trouble with some of the members and he had confided in me. Some of the church members decided that he wasn't spiritual enough to be the pastor and decided to make their feelings known in the church. It overwhelmed him and he got distressed and didn't know what to do. I promised him that I would stand by his side. I even fired a member of the church who worked in my office and had a few words with her about her attitude toward him and his wife. I was caring for the pastor's wife, who was pregnant and having a difficult time with the pregnancy. The baby died in her womb and the uterus did not expel it. I sent her for a second opinion in order to decide if the baby needed to be aborted, but the physician decided to allow her to go into labor on her own. Usually within a few days, the baby will be expelled from the uterus. She got angry with me because she believed that I had kept the knowledge of her dead baby from her. I couldn't convince her that she was wrong. My relationship with the pastor and his wife was strained and it became pounds of trouble for me. Because the pastor needed my support, he continued to have a good relationship with me, but his wife was very upset with me and decided to stop speaking to me. I found myself in a painful position with people whom I loved and wanted to be a part of.

While I was attending my own church, I had engagements to speak in other churches on the island. Sometimes two pastors would ask me to speak on the same day and hour. I was busy studying the Bible and practicing medicine while my mind and heart were under pressure at the hospital. I felt that my relationship with God was good and He was pleased with me. It never dawned on me that it was my responsibility to say no when someone asked me to speak when I had something in medicine to do. I believed that I was being a dedicated Christian by putting my patients on the back burner and meeting the church program commitments I had taken on because I trusted and respected the pastors who sought me. I was immature as a Christian and I believe some of the pastors knew it and used me not only for what they said was my gift to the world, but also my money in their bank account. I gave money to the church because I felt it belonged to God. I was entangled in the church pastor circle and preached around St. Croix and my family followed me wherever I went. I gave my testimony and told everyone what God had done for me, how He saved my life from destruction and I became a new person in Christ Jesus. I believed every word of it then, as I believe them now. The greatest miracle God ever performed as far as I was concerned was changing me.

I was loyal to my pastor because God had changed my life through His Son Jesus Christ, but when the pastor revealed to me that he was going to resign from the church, but before doing so would go on a pastor's conference and use the church's shallow bank account first, the loyalty abruptly halted. He had not told anyone else as far as I knew, but me. I was on the church board and when the topic came up concerning the pastor's plans to resign from the church and some members said that they didn't understand why, I offered what I believed was his reason. When the pastor heard what I said, he believed I betrayed him and he aggressively attacked me, and his wife called me a dog. When I asked him to control his wife and not allow her to continue her behavior, he wouldn't. The board meeting deteriorated and I resigned from the Church of the Nazarene effective immediately. It hurt me to leave the church, but I had it with Christians saying one thing to the world and doing their own thing in church. Some of the members asked me to return, and the acting pastor asked me to return, but I refused.

Religion and Race

In a couple of weeks, we joined another church called Community Christian Fellowship. I previously heard about the church for years, but never had any desire to go there. The pastor met me at a Full Gospel Men's Fellowship meeting (a Christian organization composed of businessmen who believe strongly in speaking in tongues and that it is the evidence of one having the Holy Spirit in one's life). The Church of the Nazarene strongly opposed this belief and made it known. I personally never believed it, but was constantly reminded that I didn't have the gift by some Christians and to say the least, it bothered me. Second, the pastor was white and from Montgomery, Alabama. I weren't keen on being in a congregation a second time with a white minister after the fiasco with Gary (the pastor of the Nazarene church); especially from Alabama. The pastor at Community Christian Fellowship seemed more interested in if I spoke in tongues than my walk with God. I never forgot our first meeting when he asked me if I were a Christian, then followed it with, "Do you speak in tongues?" Because of that first encounter and some aggressive members from his congregation, I never had any desire to go there. I finally went after being asked a few times.

Iris and I enjoyed the church service and decided to visit a second time. We became members in spite of their beliefs and we were again on our way down another path seeking God.

Deliveries and Conspiracy

My life in the hospital was draining and at times, I had to literally force myself to go there. Some of the midwives were still raising hell with me. Midwife Duncan decided that she would finish me off finally.

I had a delivery early one morning and midwife Duncan refused to speak to me when I went in. After not addressing me professionally, she tried to take over my patient. I said good morning to her and she wouldn't speak. When I repeated it, she verbally charged at me, yelling without giving eye contact in the presence of my patient. I was stunned, not knowing what to do and I pretended as if nothing occurred. I was embarrassed and hurt. I tried to compose myself and I only felt worse so I asked God for strength. The delivery went well and as usual, I took care of the baby in the nursery. Each time I went to the nursery, the reception by some Pediatricians got colder and some of the nurses were hesitant to be friendly with me. I didn't know what was happening.

Emotionally I started falling apart after I delivered a baby of someone I personally knew and the baby died hours later in the nursery. The neonate developed respiratory difficulty. It had amniotic fluid in its lungs. It needed a respirator, but the hospital had no one trained to use the one they say that they had. I requested that the baby be transported to Puerto Rico or Miami, Florida, but the Pediatrician in charge decided to wait until dawn the next day. During the morning hours the baby died. I was furious and the family of the baby was devastated and in shock. They tried for eleven years to have a baby and finally had a baby boy, only to have it die. The word was passed that the baby's death was my fault because she was a high-risk patient and I allowed her to be in labor too long. I felt partially responsible because I knew that she was high-risk and thought that I should have asked her to see another physician. I didn't because she begged me to deliver her baby.

All the other Ob/Gyn physicians had abandoned me and some of the midwives were slowly cutting my throat, and I was in a very vulnerable position. After they bonded together against me, I was finally intimidated by the midwives and the Ob/Gyn physicians, and I dared not seek any help from them. It was the way they wanted it and they made it hard for me to fight them fairly. I was wounded emotionally. Dr. De Chabert finally mustered up enough nerve to tell the midwives to tell me if I wanted any consultations done in his department, it wouldn't be given. I was to give my patients to his staff if they needed help. He sought my total humiliation and end in his department. This left my patients vulnerable where I could not help them. I wasn't sure how to deal with it all. I didn't know it at the time, but it was against the Virgin Islands' bylaws for the Ob/Gyn doctors on call to deny my patients consultations that they were entitled to under my care. I let the fat cat have his way and didn't make waves. Dr. De Chabert was out right rude to me and refused to inform me of what was being done to my patients when a medical team needed to perform a procedure. Each time I saw him in the hospital, I spoke to him politely and he would grunt like a pig, if he did that. I felt like a fool trying to engage myself with him. My being a Christian required that I treat him with respect and love him, but I didn't want to love him anymore. I hid my emotion. I wanted him out of my life and flushed into oblivion. I submerged it deep into my subconscious mind and it was eating me up inside. My commitment to face injustice and prejudice was what kept me fighting them. It was ironic that we were all so-called "people of color," and they were just as evil, if not worse than some racist bigots whom I encountered in my life. They were just a bunch of Black racist bigots who lived in the West Indies. They would have slaughtered me without mercy if I stopped long enough to smell the thorny roses in their presence.

I believed that I was to remain in St. Croix and follow my heart and care for and love people through medicine. An evil force didn't motivate me. I never had in my heart or mind to hurt anyone. I unloaded a lot of my despair on Iris and she tolerated it well. I told her that I didn't want to go to work anymore and was finally going to leave medicine. I didn't feel that she understood why I felt the way I did. I don't think that anyone understood or felt to any degree my agony and pain. It wasn't anyone's fault. I realized that I was a complicated guy under the surface. I am the first to admit that I was fully committed to what I believed was right even when the odds were against me, and maybe this is what drove people mad. I wanted to hear someone tell me to fight those ugly racist and some people did, but not in the way, I wanted to hear it. One prominent physician, who Iris and I met in a shopping plaza, advised me to kiss Dr. De Chabert's behind, he said, it would do to make the amends. I wasn't going to bow down to Dr. De Chabert or anyone because he had a little bit of power. That doctor told me that, in front of my wife. That physician also asked me to make contact with the medical administration, but they were all in the same basket feeding each other. The few times that I confided with those in authority were futile. I believed that it was a waste of time trying to confide in the system because it was feeding itself with its own greed.

Nurse Nethersaul, the Nurse Supervisor of the midwives, one afternoon listened to me patiently while I told her that Dr. De Chabert wouldn't speak with me or be professional as a physician. She asked me why I thought he behaved the way he did. I told her that I had no idea. She asked me if I wanted her to speak to him because she had a good relationship with him. I encouraged her to speak to him because I believed that she was neutral. After a few days, she told me that she found out from him that he believed we had a personality problem. I told her that I didn't have a personality problem with him and I didn't understand what he was referring to. Much to my ignorance, Nurse Nethersaul was on his side. I was foolish in not realizing that these two people fed each other's egos. While the Ob/Gyn physicians were allowed to stay home, Nurse Nethersaul and her crew of midwives were in the delivery room working hard. There was never a doctor on call in the labor and delivery room while I was there, and patients were suffering medical trauma because of it. The midwives many times made critical decisions that physicians were trained to make. I and some other people understood that the labor and delivery room was left vulnerable to the whims of the midwives. When a baby in distress was born, there wasn't even a Pediatrician to receive it until hours later. A few times, I experienced a midwife calling all over the island trying to find a doctor and the operating room team when a patient needed an emergency C-section. Sometimes it was over an hour before anyone arrived to scrub for the operation. It was irresponsible and unprofessional and they all got away with it because they covered each other.

One time I had two patients in labor at the same time and both of them needed C-sections. When the doctors arrived, the emergency for one patient had escalated too critically and a serious need prevailed to deliver the other because the baby was pushing against the pelvic bone with each contraction. After the operations, both patients needed intravenous antibiotic therapy and had lengthy stays in the hospital. I couldn't figure out what went wrong. Why were two patients who were operated on by the same doctors seriously ill? One of the patients considered suing the hospital. When these kinds of things occurred, very little was said about it and business went on as usual.

Nurse Duncan was on the warpath with me, full time. Besides her hating my guts, she wanted to see me professionally destroyed. She was determined to see the chapter closed on me and she didn't care who had the honor of doing it. I continued to speak to her and it made her more vicious. Not all the midwives approved of the treatment that I was receiving, but they were scared to speak out because their lives in the department might end like mine. There was a white midwife who spoke her mind pertaining to other matters in the labor and delivery room and a Black West Indian midwife smacked her. The midwife who smacked her got away with it and the white midwife transferred to the island of St. John. One of the midwives, who knew I was a Christian, never spoke any words of encouragement to me while I was going through all the fire and brimstone in the labor and delivery room. I had fellowship with her in a Pentecostal church, occasionally. She had a chance to speak with me, and she never did. She would go about the labor and delivery rooms telling women to say, "Thank you, Jesus" for everything she could think of asking them to thank Him for. I don't think she once cared that not everyone practiced Christianity. I don't feel what she was doing showed a great love for God; it showed a disregard for others. She played herself off as a strong Christian and from what I heard and saw for myself, it appeared that way even if she were a bit insensitive to the religions of others. She knew that I was a Christian and was aware of what I was going through and many times witnessed ill-treatment of me and never said a word to me. I received no words of encouragement or warning from her. She was old enough to be my grandmother and her attitude later hurt me the most. I believed that she was a hypocrite because when I saw her at a church or in the street she would greet me with "praise the Lord" and "thank you, Jesus." Some people no doubt were just too committed to their own survival so they chose not to deal with my unfortunate situation and I tried to understand.

Cilicia

Iris was due any day to deliver our third child into the world. My mother and our friends, Brother and Sister Sing were with us. Iris was groaning because of the uterine contractions. Sister Sing and my mother were in the bedroom at our home with Iris. Brother Sing was with me in the living room while I was negotiating with a man on Long Island, New York to purchase his airplane. My mother came out of the bed room and scolded me. She said, "You better get in there while your wife is having your baby and stop talking on that telephone." My mother had the right to tell me to stop my nonsense because I was to deliver our baby at our home. It was a beautiful delivery. My mother and Sister Sing attended to her. When I delivered Cilicia, Jamal told Iris to put her back in her belly. When we took her to our office to weigh her she was nine pounds and six ounces. She was our biggest baby.

I Want Out

I wanted more than ever to leave medicine, and I continued to call around the country in order to look for an airplane. I finally found one in Florida and arranged with a guy whom I knew, named John, to go with me in order to fly it back to St. Croix.

John lived in St. Croix. He spent many years in the South and had a strong Southern accent. John said that he took a liking to me the first time he met me, and I thought that John was prejudiced. There was something about him that most Black people can detect when they come up against it. I didn't know it at the time, but I was right.

We went to West Palm Beach, Florida to a small airport called Lantana Airport. I had not forgotten Florida and that my friend Michael was called a big black "nigger" in Vero Beach. I was still frightened of the South. The first night in Florida, we stayed in a small motel and the following morning got up at five o'clock in order to catch a taxi to the airport.

The weather was chilly and we were blowing smoke as we waited outside a small wooden shack where we would meet the person who was flying the aircraft, which I was to buy. As the early morning sky got lighter from the rising sun, I saw a strobe light in the distance and it was the aircraft that I was to purchase. I had an $18,500 banker's check in my briefcase to purchase the plane. After checking the aircraft for any possible damage, I flew it with John and I didn't hesitate to buy it. I was the only Black person at the airport until a Black guy came in, grabbed a broom and started sweeping the floor. I got some serious stares from the pilots, who were all white. John noticed them, looking at me, but he didn't address it. Every fiber in my body was on edge and I felt intimidated by them.

We went to a restaurant where pilots often ate and had an old-fashioned breakfast with home fries. There were no Black people there. I was uncomfortable being around all those Southern white people. While we were eating, I spoke with John about the stares and he admitted that he witnessed it all, but I was not to worry about it. John, being white, did the best he could in order to change the course of my conversation. I appreciated his honesty by not covering over it, but I felt once again alone in the midst of company. John was himself prejudiced against Black people, but it was his best-kept secret from me for a while.

When we went back to the airport, I made sure that anyone who was looking at me saw the banker's check, which I handed the seller. We filed a flight plan with Miami radio and prepared to leave West Palm Beach, Florida for Freeport, The Bahamas.

I called Iris in order to let her know that we were on our way home. She told me that I had a patient in labor and she asked Dr. Camoes, one of the Obstetricians who worked with Dr. De Chabert, to deliver the patient, and he refused. I felt terrible not being able to get assistance from colleagues to help my patients in Obstetrics. I should not have been surprised by his refusal, but I was because this doctor at least spoke to me. I had no known problems with him and he never gave me any indication that I was on his black list. It was obvious to me that he felt threatened by me. When I hung the telephone up, I knew for sure that I would quit medicine and leave that stress behind me.

Flying Home In My Airplane

As we were flying over the Atlantic Ocean to Freeport, The Bahamas I hated having to make the decision as to whether or not I was to continue practicing medicine. My new airplane gave me a sense of accomplishment and I tried not to care about anything, but my family. When I saw the island of Freeport, it looked so beautiful from the air. I pulled back the throttle, put the aircraft in full rich position, and prepared for landing.

When we landed in Freeport, the black Bahamian custom agent walked to John and me and asked, "Can I help you?" and John arrogantly said, "No." The man just looked at us and didn't say a word. John felt threatened by that Black man in his uniform because it represented authority and power and it was too much for him, being a bigot, to handle. John kept saying, "Who does he think he is, asking me if I need any help; if I needed help I would have asked him for it." It upset me to experience that. A missionary from the States who was also from the South picked us up and took us to his house. It was a trying ordeal. A black Bahamian who was a Christian stopped by. I was talking to the missionary's daughter, who was in her teens, about some of my experiences racially in the states and my journey to become a doctor. She was very friendly, but inquisitive about my background, being a Black doctor. I spoke with her about some of the racial things, which I went through. The black Bahamian, who didn't consider himself Black because of his light skin and British heritage, started talking about Black Americans. He said that they were lazy and didn't work hard enough in order to improve themselves. He spoke as if he hated Black people. I was "pissed off" with him. I called him a Bahamian "nigger" in my mind and loathed him.

I went to a church service where the Bahamians and Haitians worshiped with a wooden wall between them. These people really thought that they were serving God while they were practicing bigotry and racial prejudice. It was sad. After I spoke with the missionary I was convinced that he, along with his clan, besides his daughter and maybe his wife, who I spoke with in depth, were prejudiced. I couldn't wait to get out of that place. The following morning we went to a small restaurant with that bigot Bahamian and I could hardly eat in his presence. I flew the aircraft from Freeport, The Bahamas to Georgetown, The Bahamas, then to South Caicos Island. We fueled up and flew more than 350 miles of the Atlantic Ocean to Isla Grande in Puerto Rico. I sat in the pilot seat of command (left seat) and flew for over three hours. We hit a head wind of 20 knots and lost vital time and our fuel was running low. It got dark and hazy. John was nervous and started poking his face with the pen, which he had in his hand. I was flying for over three-and-a-half hours in a haze and it was raining and dark over the ocean. We had not been able to make contact with San Juan radio in Puerto Rico and were running out of fuel. The gas gauge needles were registering 10 gallons in each tank. We had 2.5 gallons of reserved fuel in each one and had no idea how far we were from the coastline of Puerto Rico. I watched those needles touch the 5-gallon marks, then the 0-gallon marks. I prayed. John was saying, "I sure will be glad when we see the coastline of Puerto Rico." It was pitch dark and all I could see was the strobe light flickering off the propeller blades. I watched the needles touch the empty marks for at least 15 minutes. I told God I wanted to see my family and I didn't want to die in that ocean. I had survived Dr. Martin and I didn't want to be consumed by the ocean. When we saw the coastline of Puerto Rico, I put the throttle to the wall. When I landed at Isla Grande Airport and got out of that piece of metal, I touched the ground with my hands.

Flying Like Fools and God's Grace

We got a warning from customs because the guy in the tower at South Caicos Island, didn't notify Customs and to top it off we arrived late The gas pump was closed and they wouldn't accommodate us. John said that he didn't want to stay in Puerto Rico overnight. He asked me if I were willing to fly over a lake (lagoon) to the International Airport. I said, "You're the instrument pilot." He said, "Let's go." Like a fool, I started the aircraft with no fuel in the right tank and we had to shake the wing to see fuel in the left. I put the throttle to the wall, roared down the runway and headed over the lagoon. I had the nerve to ask God to guide us safely. It seemed like we would never get there. When we finally touched down on the runway with our main wheels, I knew that God had hung out with two fools. When I arrived in St. Croix, I hugged and kissed my wife and told her about my foolishness.

I cut my practice hours down to three days per week and enjoyed the rest of the week flying and being with my family. For a number of weeks I had less stress. The financial side of it was not as rewarding, but at least I obtained a greater peace of mind. I spent quality time with Iris and we enjoyed each other more. Even the children were more relaxed and that pleased us all.

Every chance I had to fly my airplane I did. Sometimes during lunch break from the office, I would fly to the small island of Vieques in Puerto Rico in order to get gas. It was my excuse to soar in the air and be free of all the stress, which I was dealing with at the hospital.

I wondered if I would survive mentally all the things, which I had allowed my mind to suffer. I really didn't know any other way to live, but to forge ahead in the face of resistance when it appeared. If I could have traded my medical license in for some professional airline pilot's license,

I would have. Reality was that what I knew to do best, I was doing; practicing medicine.

I had helped many people and the people were my greatest witnesses. People kept telling me that I was a good doctor. Nevertheless, I wanted a different kind of life and a different job.

Chapter 27
Testimonial Retribution

I will say of the Lord,
He is my refuge and my fortress:
My God: in him will I trust.

Psalm 91:2

I wasn't surprised to find out that as I went my separate way from the stress at the hospital, I was being trailed. My practice was busy, though I worked fewer hours. People made sure that they got their medical needs attended to.

I thought that some of those bitchy midwives had enough of my hide. They cooled down for a while, so I thought. A few of them were plotting like Satan to burn me and throw me away to die. I went into the delivery room late one evening. I had a patient in labor that was very obese and midwife Duncan was working. She was quiet this evening; it was strange behavior in my presence because she was often aggressive with me. I figured maybe she had come to enjoy life and finally joined the human race.

The patient had difficult labor and for hours was pushing and the baby was descending slowly. Early into the morning, she became fully dilated (10 centimeters, when the cervix is opened to a maximum diameter). The baby was now able to freely make it through the birth canal. I told Nurse Duncan that she was ready to deliver and she took her into the delivery room quickly. It was about 2:30 a.m. and I had stayed with her the entire time. I informed Iris at intervals what was happening. After standing in the delivery room for about 15 minutes, the baby descended through the canal and I delivered it. Nurse Duncan took the baby from me in order to suction the nose and mouth for amniotic fluid and vaginal secretions. I was busy trying to stop the bleeding from her uterus, which was heavy with blood clots. A large mass came from the vagina and I put it in the stainless steel basin on the table behind me. Midwife Duncan was supposed to check it and tell me if it were the placenta so I could give the patient Pitocin (medication to help the uterus to contract to stop the bleeding). She didn't say a word and I didn't question her. The bleeding stopped and I congratulated the mother, and checked on the baby. I thanked Nurse Duncan for her help and went home. I was very tired. I had not slept from the night before and it was almost 4:00 am... I couldn't wait to get home and get in my bed and sleep.

That morning I got up at 8:00 a.m. in order to go to work. My office was full and I saw a number of patients. Iris told me that a midwife from the hospital was on the telephone line and wanted to speak with me. The midwife told me that I needed to come to the hospital right away. I asked her if it could wait until I finished seeing my patients and she said I needed to come then. When I got to the delivery room, she pulled me into a little utility area and with a half-serious look on her face said, "Do you know that you left the placenta in the patient?"

"What patient?" I asked.

"The patient whom you delivered this morning." I stood before her in disbelief. I asked her how she knew that. "Because we got it out," she replied. "I just wanted to let you know you left the placenta in the patient, but we got it out." When I asked her where it was, she told me that they threw it away. I knew that they were doing it to me, but I had no proof that I got the placenta out. Nurse Duncan wasn't going to back me up. She was trying to cover her own behind because she was supposed to identify the tissue in the basin and she said nothing. I believed she did this on purpose. I left the hospital depressed. I spoke with my patient and she told me that she didn't know what they took out of her. They told her that it was the placenta. She was doing fine and I discharged her from the hospital in a couple of days. I thought that the matter was settled until I got a call from the Medical Director's secretary requesting that I meet with Dr. De Chabert I knew that if I did leave the placenta in the patient, it was not a benign matter, but there was no evidence. I had no proof that they were telling me the truth. They didn't show the placenta to me. Many OB/GYN physicians have at some time in their career left a portion of the placenta in a patient. Midwife Duncan had eased herself in the clear and she had goons protecting her.

When I walked into Dr. De Chabert's office, he was sitting behind his desk with a long white lab coat on. He hardly gave me a chance to sit before he said, "Why did you leave the placenta in the patient and deliberately leave the hospital?" I told him it was not consistent with my character to do that. He said, "But why did you deliberately leave the hospital, knowing you left the placenta in the patient?" I told him that I did not deliberately leave the placenta in the patient and leave the hospital, and please don't say that again. He repeated it a third time. I told him that if I did, Nurse Duncan was just as responsible because she was working with me and was supposed to check the tissue in the basin. He acted as if he never heard me. I told him that other doctors have done it. "Not the whole placenta," he said. He told me I would be hearing from him. They were doing it really well to me and I had no way of stopping it. No one would verbally stand up for me.

After a couple of weeks, I was called into a rectangular table meeting full of doctors with wet blood on their mouths. Like a pack of wolves, they cornered me. They had Dr. Hendricks, (a "Psychiatrist"), Dr. De Chabert (Chief of Ob/Gyn), Dr. Endriga, (a Pediatrician), Dr. Pedersen, (an Orthopedic Surgeon), a General Surgeon, and Ms. Safe, (the Medical Director's secretary). They were all sitting at the table looking blood thirsty. I was asked by Dr. Hendricks, the Psychiatrist, to sit, and then he pushed the button on a black tape recorder on the table. I said, "I thought I didn't need a lawyer." I spoke with the Medical Director's secretary a week before the meeting about getting one and she told me that I didn't need one. Dr. Hendricks asked me if I had anything to say. I didn't know what to say. I didn't even know why I was there. However, it didn't take me long to figure it out. They wanted to systematically destroy my credibility. Dr Hendricks told me that there was a serious concern about how I practiced medicine. The situation with the placenta came up. I told them that some midwives were out to get me and I believed that they set me up. I looked at the Dr. De Chabert and said, "For two years you refused to speak to me and I have done nothing to you. Tell me what I have done and I will publicly apologize." He didn't say a word. He tilted his balding head to the table edge. I told him that I loved him and he was wrong for treating me the way he did. Everyone was silent except the Psychiatrist, who told that me they weren't there for any purpose, but to help me. He was a liar and he knew it, and they did. They wanted to lynch me as high as they could from the rafters of the hospital.

Dr. Endriga, the Pediatrician presented a letter asking to have me removed from the nursery. I looked at her in shock because I used to go to a Bible study with her. I reminded her that she could have talked to me about any problem, which she believed that I had because we were both Christians. She looked at me stupidly. Dr. Pedersen, the Orthopedic Surgeon, who I didn't even know, told the committee that I gave a patient inappropriate medication. I told him that the patient whom he was referring to was my private patient in my practice. He said that she was not my patient and we argued. "You're wrong," I told him. "What is your problem with me, I don't even know you." Dr. Hendricks asked me if I had anything else to say. I told him yes and held them for almost thirty minutes until the tape in the recorder ran out. I assured them that I knew they were lynching me. Those evil people hung me up.

Conspiracy Completed

A few days later, I was sent a letter by Dr. De Chabert . The letter stated that I needed an Ob/Gyn physician to back me up if I wanted to deliver any more babies in the hospital. I asked him to back me and he said no. I asked all the Obstetricians and every one of them said no. I wrote Dr. De Chabert and told him that he asked me to find back up and everyone refused, and would he consider doing it because he was the most experienced. He responded with, "No." He knew that he asked me to do something, which I couldn't accomplish. One of the doctors was Dr. De Chabert's associate; both of the doctors worked in the same office. The third Ob/Gyn claimed to be recovering from chronic ulcer disease and he stated that he was already backing a physician and couldn't help me. The conspiracy was completed. The devil's work had been done and I was put out of the Labor and Delivery rooms. It was the price, which I paid for telling them all that I would not bow down to their images, their false gods, their hidden agendas, their secret codes of false honor, and their hypocracy nonsense. I can't say that I didn't care because I did. Matter of fact, it hurt terribly and it put me in a kind of grief and longing to be free from this earth. The only hope, which I saw was Iris and my sweet children and my love for all of them. I felt defeated.

It took me weeks to recover. I felt embarrassed though I had nothing to be embarrassed about and ashamed though I did nothing dishonest to be ashamed of. In addition, I felt like a bastard child who had been kicked out of his house. I, then got mad. I got mad as hell and told my wife, the next time I had a delivery I was going into the delivery room. For two years I defied them all and delivered babies in the hospital. Dr. De Chabert was his normal self, not speaking with me, and some midwives were angry concerning my insistence on being in the delivery room.

Chapter 28
Searching

Then I saw that human wisdom is better than folly,
as far as light is better than darkness.

Ecclesiastes 2:13

I started to cry in my car a second time. I didn't know what was wrong or what hit me. A patient was waiting for me in front of my office and I couldn't stop crying. I tried to stop, but the tears continued to fall from my eyes. I wiped them away and more came. I said, "God, whatever You want from me, I'll give it. Oh God, why me? Why do I have to feel this way?" With the tears still wet on my face, I got out of my car and greeted my patient. She didn't give me any indication that she thought there was something disturbing me.

I told Iris that I needed to go to New York again. When she asked me why, I told her that I needed to" share the word of God," and practice medicine free. She didn't understand any more this time why I needed to leave her and the children and go to New York than she did when I went to speak at the schools. I guess I appeared unstable to her, having come so far in our lives, sacrificing so much to become a doctor, and telling her that I wanted to preach God's word and give my learning away for free. We struggled over my decision and she gave in to me.

I went to some of the elders of the church: Orlando, Michael, Bob, Joseph, and John and told them that I felt God wanted me to go to Red Hook and rent a motor home and park it on the main street where drugs were sold, and preach the gospel. They had to think hard about what they advised me, and they prayed, and told me that they believed God was with me.

I got in touch with my friend Raymond in New York, and we planned the journey. The night before I left some dear friends of his wife, and ours, Bro. Singh prayed for the family and me. He told me that he believed it was God's will for me to go. I trusted Bro. Singh's opinion because he was a man who trusted God's Word.

Murder in the Street

When I arrived in New York, Raymond and I drove to New Jersey the following day in order to pick up the motor home I was to practice medicine in. I decided to finance the journey and brought $1,500 to handle expenses. It was great seeing my family and as always, they were happy to have me home again.

My first evening while sleeping in my mother's apartment, I heard gunshots all night into the morning. One particular shot was very loud. That morning a dead body was lying on the side walk behind the building where I was to practice in front of on that day and preach at that evening. I parked the motor home on Columbia Street where drug trafficking was taking place as usual. By 9:00 a.m. I was practicing medicine and people couldn't believe it was free until I took care of them. Some people asked me what was the catch, and I told them that there wasn't any. The people who knew me were proud to see me giving to Red Hook. It was a great feeling taking care of people who knew me while I was growing up as a bad kid. I enjoyed the entire day and the fact that we were parked on a street, which was known for a lot of crime. Things went well. People seemed to respect what we were doing. Some couldn't believe a young Black man not asking for anything would give free time to them.

That night as it was getting dark, Raymond and I set up the PA system and I was ready to speak. It was an emotional experience for me. My message was entitled, "The Word of God Will Set the Captive Free." I told the large crowd, who numbered a little over fifty people, that I traveled 1,850 miles from the beautiful Island of St. Croix in the Caribbean, to tell them that God wanted them to be free. "You don't have to be locked up in prison to be in slavery. You can be enslaved by drugs and crime. If you give God's Word a chance to change your hearts, it will set you free, and you'll never be enslaved again. I encourage you today to let the Word of God set you free." I told them of God's love for them and that He loved them. I became very emotional, and told them that I heard guns shooting all night into the morning, and I knew someone was killed. "One of you did it or knows who did it; you need to ask God to forgive you and He will. I don't care about my life and you can kill me if you want to, but God's Word will still stand. He'll still set you free. God loves you greater than anyone." I began to cry and I started praying for people, as I asked God to set them free.

When the meeting was over, my friend Raymond chastised me for becoming so emotional and I didn't receive his criticism well, but he meant no harm. I appreciated and loved Raymond and my heart was open to him.

That evening I didn't hear any gunshots. I asked my mother if she heard any and she said no. I practiced medicine the following day the way I did the day before and it went great. I saw some of my old friends. At night, Raymond preached. He was a bit quieter than I was and didn't cry. After he finished, I gave some parting words to the crowd. I told them that street crime, and drugs were killing us all, and it needed to stop. "God cares about you and He wants to set you free." I drove the motor home to Raymond's house to parked it. He lived in a better neighborhood and I didn't want anyone to break into it in Red Hook. Raymond and I shared some intimate words and bid each other farewell for a while. He took the motor home back to New Jersey.

I asked my mother on the day of my departure if she heard any gunshots the previous night, and she said, "No." I didn't either. For two nights, I didn't hear any gunshots and it was a confirmation that God was with me. I hugged my mother, kissed her, and told her that I would keep in touch. My sisters hugged and kissed me and gave me their support.

On my return trip to St. Croix I relaxed in my seat, I felt better than I had in years. It was as if my soul was revived and I was living again a productive life. I thanked God for His strength in me. For the first time in my life, I believed that I did exactly what God wanted me to do; believe, trust, and follow Him.

No More Tears

My life changed for the better after my journey to New York. The tears had dried up and I didn't feel like an emotional wreck and lost. I made copies of "The Word of God Will Set You Free "message, which I gave on Columbia Street. When I listened to the tape, I realized Raymond was right about me being too emotional. I could at times barely understand what I was saying. During the latter third of the message, I was crying. Nevertheless, I gave copies to those people whom I believed would be honestly interested. I talked about it to Iris and let her listen to the tape and I wasn't convinced that she believed I did my best. I didn't say anything to her because my going, in her opinion, was not the greatest idea.

I was tired of all the challenges, which I was facing. Tired of fighting, tired of my anger, and tired of the pain of rejection. I was exhausted and wiped out. There was no more fight in me. The same thing that happened to me emotionally at Lutheran Medical Center had occurred again. I still cared about my patients. I wasn't going to forget about them as I did when I was a second-year resident in Brooklyn, but for now I needed a rest.

There were major events taking place in my life and I was trying to cope with them: First, I had my six lovely children to love and be affectionate with. Second, my wife was trying all she could to help me through my challenges and she was loving me all the way. I appreciated her care of me and admired her strength once again. I was missing something in my life; I didn't know what it was, and I continued to feel exhausted.

I awakened one morning, looked at Iris and burst into tears. I didn't know why, but Red Hook was on my mind. She was not prepared for my outburst and wanted to know what was bothering me. Between the crying, I told her that the children in Red Hook were dying and I needed to go there. She didn't understand why I felt I had to go. She reminded me that I didn't owe anything to Red Hook and I paid my dues when I kept my promise to work there after medical school. I told her that somebody needed to care about those children. I knew that Red Hook was full of crack addicts, pimps, drug pushers, and there were illegal guns in the hands of children who knew nothing about the destruction, which they could cause. I knew that there were shootings almost every night because my mother told me about it when I called her. Sometimes while speaking with her, she paused because of gunfire in the street. "Did you hear that?" she would say. "They're out there shooting again."

Red Hook was a war zone and my mother and sisters and a host of relatives were caught in it. I wanted them to get out. They didn't see the urgency of leaving because it had become a part of their everyday life. It wasn't that they or anyone living there were comfortable with the gunfire, but they felt helpless. The police knew who had guns and who sold drugs, but what did some of them care; they didn't live in Red Hook projects. I heard at least two gunshots each time I called my mother. I couldn't comprehend it all. It was as if the whole city had fallen to the criminal element and the justice system failed to contain the convicted criminals.

People were in and out of jail before the next holiday rolled around. "Ma," I said, "how can you take what's happening in Red Hook, all the shootings, drugs, and crime?"

"What can I do, Buddy?" she replied.

I needed to visit Red Hook and try to make a difference. Iris believed that it was foolish and I understood how and why she felt the way, which she did. She was tired of seeing me trying to save the world and she told me so many times. She'd say, "Buddy, you can't save the world." I knew saving the world was beyond my reach, but I needed to try and be a part of the solution.

Taking Care of My Wife

I wanted to do something nice for my wife. It was her dream to one day have a Mercedes Benz and I saw one in the car showroom. When I first saw it, I thought, that's too much money, but I knew nothing was too much for my wife. I probably had the hardest-working, loving wife in the world.

I went into the showroom and inquired about the Benz. It was a beautiful 190 E Mercedes with a beige interior. Iris was partial to black cars; she felt that they looked elegant. When I told her I saw one at the dealer and was thinking about buying it, she didn't think that I was serious. We were driving a nice Subaru four-door sedan and we traded it in, added $3,000 as a down payment, and drove the Mercedes home. Iris was elated over her dream car. It was her third brand new car since my internship and residency. I felt great being able to please my wife. She was going through a lot with me and the least I could do was give her some things, which she wanted.

Tolerating My Situation

My medical practice was going well and I continued to work long hours into the evenings in order to pay our bills and try to accomplish day-to-day tasks and accomplish being financially independent. I didn't trust the system and the people in it and I realized that I needed to find my own financial "pot of gold."

I still wanted to leave medicine, but I didn't talk much about it because Iris got on my case each time that I mentioned it.

322

Red Hook was still on my mind. I told Iris that I was planning a trip there. I wrote letters to the public and junior high schools, which I attended, and asked if I could visit the school in order to speak to the students about medicine and career goals, and determination. I got a warm response and was welcomed with open arms. I bought two sport suits, two pairs of shoes, and packed my bags to leave. Iris was still trying to understand why I had to return to Red Hook, but she gave me her blessing. I knew that I was doing the right thing because the children of Red Hook were in my soul and I had to speak to them.

The three-and-one-half-hours flight to New York was different from other times. I had a butterfly sensation in my stomach all the way to New York and it wasn't going to go away until I fulfilled my purpose to tell those children my story. When I arrived at Kennedy International Airport in New York, my sisters and my mother met me. I was happy to see them. I missed them so much. My first night in Red Hook, gunshots were fired all night into the morning. I couldn't believe Red Hook had become a battle zone. No one was safe on the street during the day or night. While I lay in the bed my first night there, I heard a few gunshots and it startled me. I jumped off the bed and onto the floor. I slowly looked out the window and saw two young guys pointing a handgun in the air. I saw him discharge a round. There wasn't a police officer in sight. This wasn't rare in Red Hook; gunshots were the norms each night. I crawled into bed again and looked at the ceiling. "Oh God," I said, "I know you're in this place and You can help these people." I prayed for Red Hook while my heart was weeping.

Red Hook wasn't just any place. It was the place I once adored and defended. It was my first home, my running ground, and it was still in my soul. When I awakened that morning, the shooting was fresh in my mind and I told my mother about it. She said she heard it, and that's how it was almost every night. I put on my new white sport suit and pinned my name badge to it, which said Dr. Wilbert Williams Jr. I reflected on Red Hook and took an emotional journey looking at the places where I played, the cellar and bushes that I hid in while playing with my friends, the broken benches, the red fire alarm box, which I pulled, the street that the "Kovons" marched on, and some of the same people whom I grew up with. They greeted me and told me how good I looked, and I was amazed that they were so excited to see me. It made me feel very special and important.

I had some mixed emotions and felt somewhat guilty that I had made it educationally and socially, but some of them didn't. It was the guilt, which Iris spoke to me about many times, but I didn't want to recognize it.

I walked slowly to the school, as I wondered had I stayed in Red Hook and practiced medicine would I have made a difference. When I arrived at the schoolyard, I remembered how Ronald stomped on me and hurt me really badly. I didn't hate him anymore and I no longer called him a black gorilla. My mother told me that she heard that he was killed in California. She said that she wasn't sure, but she believed that he was dead. I felt sorry that Ronald and I never made it right between us. I would have gladly forgiven him if he had stopped messing with my mind. Even the beating he gave me would have meant little to me, if he had given me an honest hello. However, it was too late and many years were between us and now a possible death. In some ways, it was a tragic finale and it sealed a painful moment in my life. However, I was now able and strong enough to tell myself that I had nothing to be sad about, but it would have been great to know and love Ronald.

Precious Seeds

Public School 27 had just opened its doors to the incoming students. I was greeted at the door by the hall monitor, who knew me and took me to the principal's office. When the principal arrived, she had a smile on her face and said, "You must be Dr. Williams." I told her that I was. She excused herself after telling me how busy it was trying to help the staff get their assignments for the day, and helping some students who seemed to be confused about why they were in school. I knew that she was being challenged while trying to be polite and respectful to me. I didn't mind the delay because the butterflies in my stomach were getting worse. When she came back, she apologized, and told me that the children were going to the auditorium in order to wait for my presence. When I got to the auditorium, it was loaded with children. My mother and my sisters were sitting in one row from the front.

The Speech

When I stood up to speak, a quiet hush fell over the room. Some of the students had blank stares on their faces. One student in particular kept eye contact with me. He may have wondered what I was doing there invading his space and his life and trying to change the rules, which he was familiar with. I knew I had to say something to all of them that would affect their lives and change them forever. They needed to know the truth about me and hear as much of my story as I was able to give in the forty-five minutes, which they gave me to speak.

I began to tell them about my journey, and my mother taking me to a Psychiatrist when I was a little boy. The crowd broke in laughter. I looked at my mother and she was laughing as if we had a private joke between us. The laughter permeated the room like thunder in the sky. I knew at this point they would listen to me and wait for me to tell them more. They were captivated by my bluntness. I prepared a lot of information to tell them, but I didn't have the time. I told them that I was left back four times during my thirty years in school, and in the fifth grade, I was accused of tripping a substitute teacher. They could hardly sit still from laughing. They didn't have a chance to recover from laughing because I kept telling them my story. I told them that I spent most of my summers in summer school because I kept failing courses. I boldly told them that I was never cited for any outstanding academic achievements; except one time when I was in high school on the honor roll for six months. When I finished college, I said, "I had eleven F's and nine D's on my college transcript." I made eye contact with a little boy who was sitting in front of me distracting other students, and his eyes fixed on mine. I had at least one person who was absorbing what I was telling the students.

"I almost flunked out of medical school," I told them. "In the opinion of some of my professors in medical school, I didn't belong in medical school and one professor told me that he and some other people were concerned if I would ever get a license to practice medicine." I wanted them to know these things about me because they should believe that they could achieve anything, which they tried if they put their minds to it.

I paid a price to stand before them and tell them what I thought was best to secure their future. The price was paid by all the things that I went through as a Black man in order to be successful in America. I didn't have the right to tell them what to become, but I was sure going to tell them about their great potential. I had an idea what they were up against because I grew up in their neighborhood. There were years between us, but they were faced with similar problems, which I faced when I was growing up: drugs, guns, and crime. The difference in their generation from mine and most of the generations I ever read about was, children killing each other.

Living in Red Hook for twenty-four years was not a liability to me, but an asset because at least I understood after seeing what was going on around me that I needed to get out. Not everyone needed what I needed, but it saved my life and I did not become a victim to it.

I told them all these things and more, as much as they would allow me to and as much as my soul could reveal.

When they finally quieted down, they waited patiently to hear what else I had to tell them, and I paused. I paused long enough to see some of the teachers in a daze. Some of them looked tired, having listened to me for over an hour, but no one dared stop me. I had not finished what I wanted to say, but I had to end my journey with them. I didn't feel that I gave them any solutions to achieve success. Therefore, I told them to believe that God loved them and made them well. "Look at yourself, you're beautiful, God made you that way. You're strong and great like a seed with great potential, and your soil is the place you live in, and every place you go, and everyone you let speak to you. Every now and then, you will be watered by circumstances and the circumstances will be your life experience. There will be some dry spells in your life, but don't give up and die; be like a powerful seed and fight to live. Some of you might die before your appointed time, but you should never abandon your dreams and be committed until the end of your lives. You owe it to yourselves to reach your potential and be successful. You are not junk, but beautiful children who can become engineers, doctors, lawyers and educators." They stood to their feet, yelled, and applauded, and I felt like weeping because I was convinced that I reached their hearts and souls.

I was fully confident with God's help and grace that they all would make it if they stayed focused on their dreams and faint not. My soul was assured that I did my earnest best to give them myself without fear that they would think of me less than I ought to be.

Junior High School Days Again

When I went to Junior High School 142, I had an emotional rush. I remembered Rosa and how I sang songs from "West Side Story" to her. I remembered Betty and when I put that note in her violin case, which my homeroom teacher intercepted. I was remembering all of my mischief there and how I would sit waiting for the bell to ring in order to go to the next classroom. Mr. Manfreddy, one of my teachers whom I had when I was in the eighth grade, surfaced in my mind. One day I was clowning in class and he politely asked me to leave the room. Outside the classroom, he smacked me hard on my face and my whole body shook. I wanted to see him. I didn't want to say anything to him in particular. I just needed to see how he looked. He was a big strong-looking man and I was scared to hell of him then and still was. I saw him, not long after I entered the principal's office. When he walked in, he had that same walk with his shoulders riding high and that serious look on his face. He didn't recognize me and I spoke to him. "Hello, Mr. Manfreddy, how are you, I'm Wilbert. You were my teacher."

He had no problem recalling me and said, "Hi, how are you, it's good to see you."

"It's good to see you also, Mr. Manfreddy, I'll be speaking here today."

"Yes, I heard about it, I'll see you later."

When I arrived at the auditorium, there weren't as many students as I expected. The teacher in charge sat them together in the center section. The students looked at me with little or no excitement. There was something very different about them, something that frightened me; I couldn't figure what. Maybe the cares of life in 1987 made them appear dull and apathetic. I had a hard time getting prepared to speak. I wasn't sure what I was going to say and how I was going to say it. When I began to speak, I stumbled over my words and my trend of thought was not flowing. At one point, I didn't want to continue speaking because they wouldn't respond to me in a way that showed they were receiving my message. As I continued my talk, the students appeared as though they were tolerating me, so I ended it. When I finished, I was not satisfied that my being there was worth while.

Mr. Manfreddy stood up and told the students what a great student I was when I attended. He was lying through his teeth and he knew it or he never remembered how bad I was. I couldn't believe he forgot when he smacked me. I asked him to get me a T-shirt and he told one of the students to get it. I don't remember any of the students asking me any questions. I was glad it was over because I felt bad. Mr. Manfreddy thanked me for coming to the school and wished me well.

I did my part. I traveled 1,850 miles from the beautiful Caribbean island of St. Croix in order to give of myself to those students and it was all worth it, even if the reception was dull at Junior High School 142. I had to face the reality that times had changed since I was there and would continue to change with every passing day.

The night before my departure for St. Croix, gunshots were ringing out in the streets and it broke my heart to experience that kind of change in Red Hook. Life magazine did a story on Red Hook. It was called "Death of a Neighborhood." I read the article and looked at the familiar pictures of the project hallways and courtyard. It wasn't the same Red Hook, which I grew up in but it was still the place I loved dearly. On my return trip to St. Croix, I saw those children at Public School 27 as clear as I could see the seat in front of me. "Oh God," I said, "Keep those children and give them strength to fulfill their dreams and goals."

When I arrived in St. Croix, the experience of being in Brooklyn, New York had changed me and I was strong and renewed, knowing that I did something purposeful with my life. I gave all that I could and I felt confident it was exactly what I was supposed to give.

Iris, as always, looked beautiful as ever to me and I was happy to see her. I squeezed her gently but firmly and told her that I loved her. She looked at me sincerely and said, "I love you too, honey. "Iris was really my anchor and my confidante. She didn't agree with many of the things I did and some of my ways of thinking, but the fact that she loved me made a world of difference.

My children were at the airport and they were the other part of my life. They meant the world to me and I was glad that I had them. It was during the hard times in my life that I realized they were God's gifts to me and without them, my life would have been missing something vital for balance. There were times when having to care for them burdened me and created some anxiety; especially when I made a decision to challenge the system. That's when I saw their faces vivid before my mental eye. I loved my children with a passion and I would never regret their being with me. I went back to work and all the stress that accompanied it was waiting for me as if it had missed a partner for a few days, and my patients were waiting for me to see them also. Some of them had needs while I was away and when they saw me, they without pain let me know that they needed me. One person asked me what she was supposed to do when I left the island. I looked at her and said, "I'm sorry, but I needed some time off." It always bothered me when my patients let me know life would be difficult for them without me giving them medical care.

I didn't visit the hospital unless I had a patient admitted; otherwise, I tried to keep it far removed from my mind. It was a source of pain that I wanted to forget about, but it wouldn't go away because I decided when a patient of mine went into labor I would be there to deliver her. That time came and when it did, I boldly walked into the labor and delivery room with acid in my stomach, and the midwives who were there looked angry. Eyes opened wide and facial attitudes lit bright, and I acted as if it were business as usual. I wasn't going to let them take from me what I was entitled to have; the right to deliver babies in the hospital where I had privileges at. I had a permanent license to practice medicine in the Virgin Islands, and no one gave me a thing and therefore, I didn't owe them. I did owe the people of the Virgin Islands to practice good medical care and do the best I could according to my training. The midwife who was on call accompanied me during the delivery. All went well. I didn't detect any animosity from her. After the delivery, I walked out of there as boldly as I walked in.

I didn't hear anything coming from the Chairman of OB/Gyn's desk. He was probably tired of dealing with me. Each time I had a delivery; I entered the delivery room and delivered my patients' babies.

Every opportunity I had, I was at the airport cleaning, polishing, or flying my Piper 180-G single engine aircraft. That airplane was a major player in my life, and I was fascinated by its ability to help me soar like an eagle.

I started a flying club and called it the Agape Flying Club. I wanted to encourage the kids in St. Croix ,concerning aviation, to become pilots. I put a sectional aviation chart and a sign in my office window in order to advertise the flying club. It caught the attention of many people. When the kids saw it, they stopped and asked. Some parents even came in and inquired if I would teach them to fly an airplane. Before long, I had a number of children to teach; Dexter, Elroy, Elwin, Anthony, Richard, and Atom. We had one girl, but her stay was short because she moved to the States. Every other Saturday we met at my office for ground schooling and I taught them what I knew. The other Saturdays we gathered at the airport and the kids took turns; three at a time went up with me. I let the student in the co-pilot seat fly the airplane. Picking up the microphone, I'd say, "St. Croix ground, November 4496 Tango ready to taxi to active from east ramp parking, request permission to taxi to active runway."

The ground control would answer, "November 4496 Tango, permission granted to taxi to active."

It was great waiting at the take-off point, speaking to the tower, and waiting to become airborne. St. Croix tower, N-44976-T ready to take off at active, straight out to practice area."

"N-4496-T cleared for take-off."

I would tell the student to push the throttle to the wall and the airplane pushed us back in our seats and down the runway, we soared until the air speed reached 78 miles per hour. "Pull the yoke back," I'd instruct, and off the ground, we lifted into the air. Each time we went through this procedure was just as gratifying as the one before. We would fly to the end of the island, called the East End, and do all kinds of crazy stuff like: sharp turns, steep descents and ascents, stalls (turn the engine down to idle speed and point the nose of the plane up until it started to shake and fall), and weightlessness. They went wild when I did this. I'd push the throttle to the wall and soar upward, and then suddenly push the yoke forward and our butts would lift out of the seats. I usually tossed a pencil in the air and it would float until I couldn't take the empty-hole feeling in my stomach and leveled the airplane. It was great and we had a grand time with that airplane.

Sometimes, I took them away to another island like St. Martin, St. Thomas, or Puerto Rico. I liked those trips because it gave me quality time with the guys; especially the ones who wanted to follow aviation as a career. Dexter and Atom were two who put energy into moving in that direction. Dexter asked me for some information and I gave him three pages of addresses and telephone numbers. Atom was interested in joining the Army in order to enter aviation school.

Atom had a tragedy in his life. His mother, who was a friend of Iris and I, had a cerebral stroke and died. She was young and had severe high blood pressure. It was a tragedy for many because she was loved and well known. She was cremated, and her husband asked me to take her ashes up in the airplane and release it into the air. Atom and I took my little Piper 180-G and soared to four thousand feet. While he commanded the controls, I opened the side window and sprinkled her ashes into the air. I think some of Atom's pain was decreased when he saw his mother's ashes freely fading into the atmosphere.

Iris and I spent quality time together in that little airplane going to other Islands. We frequently went to Puerto Rico to shop and eat. We often visited my in-laws, who live in Corozal, near the mid-southern portion of the island. I loved being with them, they treated me like a golden child, and my mother-in-law fed me as if I were her own child. Being in the country of Puerto Rico was great and I marveled at the acres of banana and plantain trees. It was a very relaxing time for me and I never grew tired of going there.

One time I took Shoshanna and Taina with us to Puerto Rico. On our return back to St. Croix, I arrived at the airport while it was getting dark and hazy. I cleared with San Juan, Puerto Rico because the kids got shook up and started vomiting.

Sometimes I did stupid things like taking off in marginal weather, believing that we would be OK. I learned slowly from my hairy experiences while flying. One time I took off from Ponce, Puerto Rico and headed to St. Croix without an operating left brake. When I was twenty miles off the coast line of St. Croix, I radioed the tower and told them that I had no left brake. They cleared the runway and had a fire truck waiting to help put out the flames if I crashed. When I stepped from the aircraft a firefighter in a silver suit asked me if I were OK. I felt foolish.

My worst near-disaster came one Saturday after taking some guys to St. Martin. On the return trip, the weather deteriorated down to instrument conditions and I was not rated to fly in that type of weather. I couldn't fly an airplane well if I couldn't see the outside. Well, the outside disappeared because the first third of the trip was in haze and it was thick. The instrument panel showed the plane was not flying in straight and level flight. I lost full command of the aircraft because I panicked, knowing that I couldn't fly well in that kind of weather. I lost altitude and was less than one thousand feet above the water and the right wing kept dipping to a forty-five-degree angle. I called San Juan, Puerto Rico and told them that I didn't know where I was and should have reached St. Croix by then. They told me to hold on, and I lost contact with them. I called them back and they gave me false importation. Knowing the east end of the island had small mountains, I figured that I would hit one. I prayed to God as I did when John and I almost ran out of gas coming from South Caicos Island to Puerto Rico. "O God, I need your help, we can't die out here like this." Within thirty seconds, the haze broke and the mountain was in front of us; a few hundred feet away.

My Cocoon

The airplane had become a part of my stable mental diet. It even became my friend because when I should have died in it, along with others, it never once fell apart or didn't do what it was created to do. It didn't fail me like some people had, and when I had the chance I took the best care of it that I could.

In many ways, it was one of my escapes from all the fire and brimstone I was going through in St. Croix. Each time I climbed into it, it felt like a cocoon around me, and I'd sit in it and my soul would cry because I knew that the world was burning up. It helped me to survive and in some way dance in the fire.

I tried to spend more time with my children and it was a major effort because there was always something that needed my attention. My children meant the world to me and I know in ways I failed them, but I also failed myself, because they are an extension of me. I took them to the beach and played in the sand with them; we camped out in our yard and ran through the brush. We even stayed in our custom van overnight and called it a sleep-out while the mosquitoes ate us alive. I even built a playhouse for my daughters so they could put their dolls in. I enjoyed the time that I spent with them and I believe it was the highlight of their lives.

Iris was delighted each time she saw me giving to the children. She encouraged me to spend time with them. She realized it was best for the balance in all our lives because we were family. I spent good quality time with Iris. I took her away many times in our airplane just to let her know that I had not forgotten her in the midst of all the confusion surrounding us because of me.

I decided to upgrade the instruments in the airplane and I asked her to fly with me to Miami, Florida from St. Croix. I was a bit anxious about taking a long trip across the water even though we would be island hopping. I got the information, which I needed in order to successfully make the trip, and plotted the course to three islands. We left our children with a baby-sitter and headed to Miami/Opa- locka, Florida. Our first stop was Isla Grande in Puerto Rico. We cleared customs and headed for Borinquen, which was at the northwestern tip of Puerto Rico. We stayed in a motel and the following morning got up just as the sun was rising and flew along the northern coast of the Dominican Republic to a place called Puerto Plata. I took a heading north that I thought would take me to the island of South Caicos. I went to North Caicos island and had to be guided to the correct island. The Bahamas' islands were dotted throughout the beautiful water of the Atlantic and once again, it fascinated me. We cleared customs, went to the rest rooms and headed for Georgetown, Bahamas Island. It was a small airstrip with a dingy wooden reception building. We filled the Piper with gas and headed for Miami/Opa-locka in Florida. It seemed like a long haul from Georgetown to Miami. We flew over Andros Island, which is the largest island in the Bahamas. After flying over it, I called Miami radio and told them that I was coming in. They followed me all the way into Miami, as they spoke to me about air traffic and my position to them. When I reached the coast of Florida and saw all the tall buildings, I had no idea where to go. I didn't know where Opa-locka, Florida was. I told Miami radio I didn't know where to fly in order to reach

"Hanger-1" at Opa-locka airport. They coordinated my exact position and guided me exactly to the tip of the runway at Opa-locka. After landing, an attendant came out and parked my airplane in a designated spot. They literally had a red carpet for us to walk on from the airplane to the hanger building, which had chandeliers hanging from the ceiling. I checked my airplane in as if it were going into a hospital and left for a hotel. I didn't know it at the time, but my airplane's hospital bill would be $10,000.

When we returned to St. Croix via commercial airlines, our home was as we left it and our children were very excited to see us. The time that Iris and I spent together was very special to us and we will never forget it.

When I wasn't practicing medicine, flying my airplane, riding my horse, scuba diving in the ocean, growing vegetables, or doing something childish with my children, I was thinking about my entire life and what I really wanted to do with it.

Every five years I took an assessment of the road, which I traveled and where I ended. It gave me an idea about the progress of my life and if it was worth it to God to have made me. I wondered if it was worth my mother and father having labored over me, and if it was worth it to my wife to have married me. I usually came to some startling conclusions. The bottom line was I needed to continue to plot my journey and find my place at that time in my life. I needed to know who and what I had become, if I were a better person or a different individual, and if my life was worth anything to a world that was on fire. It was this world that I envisioned on fire that kept me focusing on my life. I didn't want to be burned and consumed by it.

The more I tried to understand my purpose, the more I was confused about it. I knew I was important, at least to myself, my wife, my mother, sisters, and a host of relatives, but something was missing in my life and I didn't know what. I was beginning to show signs of stress and depression again and Iris noticed it.

One day I went to the Mercedes dealership in order to speak with the owners, Clearance and Carol George. Carol suggested that I look at a white Benz, which was due in the showroom in one week. It was a white 300 SEL four-door sedan. It was one of the largest made, other than the limousine. Carol had one just like it, but hers was eight cylinders and the one coming in was a six. I told her that I wasn't interested, but she insisted that I look at it. "Buddy, you'll like it and you deserve to have something nice to drive around in. You work really hard delivering babies all hours of the night and morning. You need to treat yourself." I told her a Mercedes

Benz wasn't me and she asked me why and I couldn't answer her. When the Mercedes came in, I took Iris with me to see it and Iris agreed with Carol that I should buy the car. I told Carol and Iris that I didn't want it. They tried to convince me to buy it. They said I would look good in it. Carol said, "Buddy, your patients would like to see you in a Mercedes." I told her I didn't think so. Iris later asked me what was my problem with having a Mercedes, and I told her it just wasn't me. After a week or two, they both convinced me to buy it and I dug deep into my empty pocket and paid $54,000, which after bank interest, cost $74,000. I drove the car home, anxious that someone who knew me might judge me negatively for indulging in an expensive item.

The reason why I didn't want the expensive Mercedes Benz was I didn't believe that I deserved it. It wasn't because it cost too much money, because I was making a lot. I felt guilty that I left the projects and made it, and so many of my friends didn't. I didn't think that a Black man like me was supposed to sport luxury while so many Black men were in jail or living wasted lives. The system put us all at a disadvantage; here I am thinking that I owed my entire life to try and solve the problems of Black people because at least I had a piece of America's apple pie. Black people, overall, had to work harder than most in order to prove that they were entitled to all the rights that the United States spells out. Genocide was taking place on Black people and Black men in particular and we were all suffering because of it.

Even as a professional, I had not been able to escape the trauma. I had suffered on 78th Street in Brooklyn, at Lutheran Medical Center, and at Kennedy International Airport, and the suffering wasn't over.

I had a hard time fully enjoying my new car, as if it were borrowed. I gave people rides in it who were hitchhiking along the road. I didn't care what they looked like or how they were dressed and wanted to share that car with as many people as possible. I believed it would make me deserving of having it, because at least people who may have never had a chance to ride in a Mercedes Benz would ride in mine. I even offered some people whom I knew the opportunity to drive it. In spite of my personal problem, I did try to enjoy the 100-watt stereo cassette player. I blasted gospel music through the ten speakers while cruising with the windows rolled up and bathing in the cold air coming from the high-powered air conditioner. That car was able to reach 100 miles per hour with ease and feel like it was 35.

I had some emotional encounters in my Benz. I broke down and cried in it about four or five times. I went to a church service one evening at the New Testament Church of God. The service was nice and I felt lifted spiritually when I left. I got in my Benz and turned on the air conditioner and blasted a gospel song by Helen Baylor entitled "The Anointed." When I was almost home, I switched the cassette player to the radio. The news reporter stated James Baldwin died in Port De Vince, France. I didn't have any great affection for James Baldwin, so I thought. I had read some of his books: Giovanni's Room, another Country, Nobody Knows My Name, the Fire Next Time, and saw and heard him on a television program with the famous Anthropologist, Margaret Mead, rapping on race. I enjoyed listening to him speak because he spoke precisely, surely, and intelligently, spiced with big words. I sat in my car thinking of him choosing to live in Paris, France because of his need to feel like a real man because America had shown him her racist side. It was too much for him to stomach. He just couldn't deal with it and left his roots, his family, and his dream to be a full American with all the rights that the United States Constitution said he and other Black Americans had. I thought of my father in Chesson, Alabama, my mother having worked hard doing domestic work, the unfortunate Blacks in America. I even thought of the starving children of the Sudan in Ethiopia. My father flashed in my mind again and I could see his pain and agony being a Black man in America, and I broke down and cried. I cried so hard that I wept, my chest felt like it had a hole in it, and my heart would tumble out onto the carpeted floor. I said, "Oh God, what do You want from me? I hurt so much and I don't know what to do, what do You want?" I didn't get an answer from Him at that moment. I was confident that my journey was going to take me to a different level of emotional life. I was so tired of emotional pain I didn't know how to handle a simple rejection from anyone, not even an enemy. I didn't want any more emotional trauma, but it seemed to follow me.

Doing What I Did Best

My practice presented me with enough work to take my attention off all my problems. I was delivering a few babies and the midwives had come to painfully tolerate me. The Chairman of Ob/Gyn as usual didn't have anything professional or social to say to me. I finally wrote him off as a mistake in my judgment. I believed he and all people who behaved as he did failed to join the human race. Thank God, I didn't have any problems with my patients and they were pleased with my care. I admitted a few people to medicine and most of them got well.

One patient in particular slipped through my better judgment. She was about 47 years old. She came into my office for a routine exam with a chief complaint of a "rash" on her breast caused by mosquitoes. When I looked at them, they were clearly eaten away with deep pockets of infection. I asked her how long was her breast that way, and she replied a couple of weeks. I diagnosed it as an infection and gave her an antibiotic. A few days later, she was admitted to the hospital with the diagnosis of infectious cancer. I spoke with the surgeon who diagnosed it and he told me he had seen that type of cancer many times before. That Sunday I visited her and she couldn't breathe because of fluid accumulating in her lungs. I asked the nurse to give me a large-bore needle and I drained over one quart of cancerous liquid from her breast. She thanked me for helping her. Within five days, she died, and the family blamed me for her death. I was devastated. I didn't feel her death was my fault. She had cancer for a while, but I was blamed because I missed the problem. I admitted to my incorrect judgment and took blame for it, but the family wanted me to take all the blame. One of her daughters was determined to get revenge, and in a way, she succeeded.

Fellowship

Community Christian Fellowship had become a part of our lives and we were going to church every Sunday on a regular basis. Our pastor was a pleasant man who loved people, but his wife was a bit to the left of being sociable. In fact, I felt she was prejudiced, but my feeling was not confirmed until later.

There were a number of white people in the congregation and they were all nice and friendly: the St. Johns, the Realies, and the Hadros. I came to love them all and it was a break from the usual grind with whits. The fact that they were serious Christians who I believe honestly loved people I'm sure made a difference in their attitudes. I didn't believe any of them were prejudiced and would have trusted them with my life. Michael and Paula were gems. Sometimes Michael glared at me when he spoke to me. He heard me talking about how white people don't really want to be friends with or love Black people. Michael approached me one Sunday after church and told me that he was a white man who loved me and he kissed me on my cheek. I will never forget it, not because a white person did kiss me but because I believe it was from his heart. Paula was just as precious and she didn't hesitate to be friendly with me. Though she didn't tell me that she loved me and kissed me as her husband did, I believe she felt the same about me.

The services at the church were nice and it felt like family being there. It helped me to feel that my life was worth something and there were people who loved me regardless of color and race. In many ways, the white families at the church represented hope as far as racism and racial prejudice is concerned.

Iris and I didn't spend much time with the families in the church other than at church gatherings. Michael and Paula invited us to their house for dinner and we had a good time. We met Orlando and Annie, and Joseph and Bernadette, and they were friendly and open with us and our relationships would be tested.

For the most part our fellowship with these new people in our lives would be positive. A man whose wife was racially prejudiced was pastoring what became negative in my view. Others in the church questioned her position as far as race also. I came to both love and despise the pastor's wife and that wasn't my style. I tried to maintain a healthy attitude toward her but she continued to leave a question as to her sincerity of racial equality and acceptance, and the fact that she was from Montgomery, Alabama didn't help.

When I had the energy and the time, I called Michael and Margie in Albany, New York. It was so refreshing to speak with my friends. In many ways, I missed them because they were a part of my life. Michael and I talked about his job situation, the church, and his life at home. He was having some challenges in his life and he shared them with me. He trusted that I would speak my heart to him as a friend and I did. He was still thanking me for encouraging him to do all he could to have a fine relationship with his parents. It wasn't that it was poor; Michael was just concerned because they were getting older and he wanted to be a good son to them.

Ephraim and Yoli were having some challenges in their lives, we loved them dearly, and it hurt us to know that they were not happy. Iris and I knew what type of challenges presented married couples because we had our own battles to win in our marriage. I encouraged all my friends to continue to seek the best in each other and keep the love alive between them.

Since Elder Mac Daniel died, the church seemed to have a greater struggle being a family. Yoli mentioned to me that she believed not having Elder Mac around caused a weakening in the church. Elder Mac was really missed by many people. Sis. Dix was still holding the banner up with the rest of the congregation and she was doing a good job. Many others and I respected her and felt she would always do her best.

My life on St. Croix continued to be debatable. In one circle, I was considered one of the greatest physicians to ever come to St. Croix, in another a menace that needed to go back to New York. I wasn't going anywhere. My long-gone boss at the Frederiksted Health Center told me a number of times if I didn't like it in St. Croix; I needed to get some tickets at the travel agent to leave. It would have been so much better for some of my colleagues if I left, but there was no way I would. I had the right to live in peace in the Virgin Islands, just as much right as they had to be educated in U.S. medical schools. If it were not for the United States, many people would have found themselves on the backburner socially and economically.

I tried to maintain being happy, but considering happiness is a state of the mind and is subject to fluctuations depending on the cares of this life, I once again fell into depression. One morning while driving to work I, felt enslaved by my emotions, and just as I was entering the parking lot, I was thinking about Red Hook and my growing up there and now being a successful doctor, and I fell apart emotionally and wept.

Chapter 29
The Eye of the Hurricane

And there arose a great storm of wind,
And the waves beat into the ship,
So that it was now full.

Mark 4:37

After I came back from Brooklyn, New York, I thought that the greatest storms in my life were over. I found peace with myself having given back to Red Hook what I thought I owed them. It were as if I had purged myself of all the guilt and pain, which I suffered through the years. I didn't know that I was the only one who felt that I owed anything to Red Hook, and if there were, a debt owed, Red Hook owed me as much as I owed her. In fact, we are all in debt to each other according to the Bible, because it says, "We are to bear one another's burdens." Whether we believe this to be true or not, I don't think that it ruins us or makes us, less than what we ought to be, but rather purges us of our own selfishness and greed. So in some way my journey set me free and pointed me in a direction away from myself, and I became a greater part of life.

If it were not for Iris, I would have been consumed by my challenges, because many times, I was confused and wounded, and she patched me up and tried to point me in the best direction. Without a doubt, we were meant for each other and she was my greatest earthly asset.

Medicine had become something, which I had to do to be balanced and it was still grinding away at me because the problems in the hospital, although less, were still before me. When I had a patient in labor, some of the midwives would wait until she was almost ready to deliver before calling me. I would drive like a lunatic to the hospital, which was about three miles from my house on a winding road. It was impossible for me to arrive there in less than seven minutes and each time that they delayed calling me, I missed the delivery. I knew that they had delayed notifying me because my patients would tell me that they were in the labor room for quite a while before my being called. Sometimes they told me that they asked, pleaded, and begged the midwife on duty to call me, to no avail. These acts of deliberate unprofessional behavior hurt my patient and me, and it made me mad as hell each time it occurred. In spite of their behavior, I continued to deliver babies and I guess some of them were mad as hell. Each time I entered the labor and delivery area, mountains of acid poured into my stomach and I felt sick. My heart would pound fast and my legs were weak. There wasn't a time that I didn't pray to God asking Him to give me more strength, and He did. I continued to do what was best for my patients and they appreciated my care for them.

I was very active in the church ministry, telling people of God's great love and concern for all of His creation. I preached at a number of churches on St. Croix and was even invited to go to other islands in order to minister, which I never did. I felt that I had my hands full ministering on St. Croix. It got to a point where I was so drained with engagements so I typed a letter telling the pastors that I wouldn't be ministering for a while because I had other things to do. A couple of them approached me and told me when God called, I needed to answer and I should never turn down an opportunity to preach the Word of God. Iris believed different because she saw some of what it took and cost me to stay up late at night and early into the morning in order to prepare a message. This was one of the times that I didn't have a hard time agreeing with her. As usual, I did what I felt was best and allowed some of these pastors to put a guilt trip on me, and I continued to brave the preaching though my life was already busy and I was tired. I did turn down a number of pastors and I felt guilty when I did. One pastor approached me and said, "Come on, it's been long enough; come to my church and preach to my people,.They would love it, Dr. Williams."

I really respected a few pastors highly because I believed that they truly loved helping and wanted to help people by the Word. I also respected some of their diligence and ability to deliver the Word a few times a week, take care of their family, and remain sane. I knew what it took to work through a preaching message and it was no fun. It was tiring and anxiety provoking. Therefore, if not for anything else, I respected them for choosing to stick with their calling, for those that were called.

When I had the chance, I went scuba diving and spear fishing. I enjoyed being in the ocean. It is a very different world down there and it fascinated me. When I was beneath the water swimming around, I didn't think much about what was taking place in the world. I understood that while the world was burning up, the sea world that God created was doing just fine, except for the vicious hands of men who tried to destroy it by killing the life in it. I believe that man is the most destructive creation made by God, and it was never intended to be that way, because He made us in His image and in His likeness, but, we are bent on destruction, and that's why we kill each other without regard for life.

I called my friends John and Doris Belton in upstate New York. It was great hearing their voices. I was feeling down and I needed them to give me an energized shot in the arm. I told them how good I knew God had been to me, and I was grateful, but I believed that all of the things, which I had accumulated over the years were not important. I told them that I felt separated from my airplane, my house, and my property. I told them that I just wanted to be in God's will. Both of them spoke with me. They didn't rebuke what I said, but I detected that they believed that there were some things, which I needed to understand. They were my friends, I respected their opinion, and I waited for them to respond to what I said. As usual, they were supportive of my being in God's will and obeying Him. I did not know that I was soon to see them, and they would tell me face to face how they felt.

St. Croix was to go through a traumatic experience, and the integrity and fiber of my life would be tested, and my family would look to me for answers and I wouldn't have any. Life has many surprises, and if we live long enough we'll encounter some of them, and it will break us or make us stronger. Some of the encounters will even point our lives in directions that we never intended to go. Disasters are just as much a part of this world as we are made from the dust of the earth.

It was August 1989, and my life was set on the course that I desired. I earned $210,000 in the past twelve months. My Mercedes Benz car payments were one payment ahead, my mortgage was up-to-date, a two-acre piece of property was almost paid for, my airplane was paid for, and my practice was going well as usual. Iris was seven months pregnant with our seventh child, and my children were healthy and happy.

Living in the Caribbean was different in many ways from living in New York. For one thing, I never had to worry about storms and hurricanes, but in the Caribbean it was a yearly affair and highly unpredictable. My

Wilbert Williams Jr., M.D.

entire family and many families on the island of St. Croix and other parts of the Caribbean would experience the ravaging effects of a devastating hurricane. It would be one of the worst anyone in the Caribbean had experienced, called Hurricane Hugo.

Everyone in the Caribbean knew Hurricane Hugo was on its way; it was targeted for the eastern Caribbean, U.S. and British Virgin Islands, and Puerto Rico. The hurricane-tracking center in Coral Gables, Florida had notified nationwide news companies and they, in turn, broadcast it throughout the world.

Cape Verde, on the southwestern coast of Africa, is the breeding ground for hurricanes, it birthed a monster of a hurricane that would tear St. Croix to pieces and drive its residents to its knees, and the island would never be the same again.

The day of the hurricane, my family and I went to church at St. Croix Community Fellowship. The wind was blowing hard enough to force us to close the two wooden doors in the back of the church while we had service. Each time the doors knocked against the doorstop, members looked to the back of the church. When the wind became more intense, the service was quickly terminated and we went home. I don't think that anyone had the slightest idea that within a few hours we would be engulfed by a monstrous hurricane that would seem to have a mind of its own. The hurricane was one hundred miles in circumference, with an eye thirty miles wide, and packing 180-mile-per-hour winds. When it was about fifty miles southeast of St. Croix, it traveled at twenty-five miles per hour. When it reached the coast of the island, it dropped its speed to seven miles per hour and traversed the island, spending over ten hours chewing us to pieces and spitting us out like a dead carcass. My family and I were listening to the radio when our electricity shut off and the house became dark. Iris and I looked at each other. We lit candles and the children took out their Monopoly game as if nothing great had occurred, but Iris and I knew differently. The wind became more intense and it howled like a lone wolf in the night. I believed that we would have an intense journey as the hurricane and the sand, which it picked up from the ocean ,abraded the island like rough sandpaper. It was gripping, ripping, stripping, gouging the plant life to death, and blowing the earth. The coral in the sea was being destroyed and some of the life in it was tossed onto the earth. We put the children to bed, and Iris and I lay in our bed as water poured down our walls and the roof lifted from the sides and corners of our house. We were being drenched with water and moved to our daughter's room until it too started to come apart. The roof

342

was lifting, and we heard a loud bang in the boys' room. I jumped up from the bed and ran in there to find a large piece of concrete block near my son Jamal's head. I told everyone to get up and get out of the main part of the house and to go downstairs. They braved going outside in their pajamas and underclothes, while they tried desperately not to be blown off the steps, which led to our shelter. After we re-secured, someone remembered that our Rottweiler named Jemma was still outside, and I let her in. My horses were loose and they had the freedom to seek shelter, but Hugo stripped any possible shelter that there was.

Our shelter leaked from its concrete ceiling, while water accumulated in the main house. Iris cried all morning, and though I tried to console her, it did little to stop her tears. I slept in small spurts and each time I awakened the wind seemed to increase its howl.

When I awakened in the morning, Iris was huddled next to me, and I looked at her. Her face was puffy from the crying. I looked outside and saw my horses with their legs stretched in the direction of the four corners of the earth like statues. The howl of Hugo was gone, and Iris didn't want me to go. I touched her and told her I would be right back. When I went outside, I didn't recognize my property. It was as if something or someone had lifted our house like in the "Wizard of Oz," and sent it to another location. When I reached the top level of the house, the first thing, which I saw was our two Mercedes Benz and they were not damaged. I turned around and looked at the house, and most of the roof was off. I said, "Oh God, I praise Your name." When I went inside the house, it was full of water and our piano and other contents were soaked. My heart began to race, but I maintained my emotion. It wasn't until Iris and the children came out that I fell apart inside. I didn't cry outwardly, but my heart was slowly breaking. My children stood with Iris on a slab of concrete; they looked lost and weary. Their clothes didn't seem to fit them; it hung from their bodies, and I saw them without adequate shelter. I was supposed to provide for them and it hurt me to see them destitute.

I took a picture of them standing next to our ravaged house minus most of the roof, and that picture has stayed in my mind; haunting me.

Bankruptcy

It was days before I was able to get to my office. The roads were blocked with debris, and everybody seemed to be going to the same place, even though there were few places to go that weren't damaged. I tried going to the airport in order to check my airplane, but the National Guard and the police would not let me through. I told them that I was a pilot and needed to get to my Piper 180-G cocoon. I needed to know if my friend that protected me from the world that was on fire made it, I needed to know if Hugo had mercy on it.

When I finally arrived at my office, it was being robbed. Two people got out of a car, walked into my office as if it were theirs, and emerged with the cushions from the sofa, which my patients sat on. Iris asked one why they were stealing our things, and he responded, "You have insurance, what are you worried about?" She told him that we didn't have insurance and started to cry. I went to my car and pulled out of the glove compartment a brand new stainless steel Smith and Wesson 5-shot revolver in its black Swede holster. I tucked it into my pants near my back pocket. A friend of mine was standing by named Daryl, who worked in the pharmacy next to my office, which had also been looted and destroyed. He told the guy standing by Iris that I had a gun and was going to shoot him. He looked at me, spread his legs, and said, "You gonna shoot me, go ahead and shoot me." I looked up at the sky and said, "Oh God, these people are crazy." The things that were stolen from me weren't worth killing anyone for.

Though I had no insurance and almost all of my office equipment was stolen along with the furniture, and the office was trashed, I valued his life greater than anything, which I lost. It hurt me to know that people would take from me as those two people did, knowing that we were all Black people and it didn't matter to them what I shared in common with them. It just hurt to keep on hurting, but I had no more tears to shed. I looked at Iris and said, "Let's get out of here."

God, What Is On Your Mind?

After a few days of begging and pleading with the police and the National Guard to let me through their blockade to the airport, I gave up. When things were more in order, they let me through. I prayed to God to allow my airplane to be spared damage. After parking my car at the entrance to the air craft parking area, I slowly looked in the direction where I had tied down my cocoon to the ground. I made sure that it was not near any other aircraft. It was upside down on its back. The propeller was bent on each end like a pretzel and the wings were bent along with the rudder and fuselage. I walked to it and said, "Lord, I don't know what you're doing in my life, but it hurts. God, I praise Your name." I had a Bible between the two back seats, and I looked for it. It was lying in the wet grass. I picked it up and it was turned to the Book of Job. I told God that I loved Him. I went home and told Iris that the airplane was destroyed, and she told me not to worry; one day I would have another one. I returned to the airport and took my expensive instruments out.

I couldn't believe that we had lost so much to a natural disaster. I had no insurance on my house, no insurance on my office, an under insured aircraft, and $4,300 in Chase Bank.

Iris was due to have a baby in two months, and to top it off she was emotionally distraught. She was still intermittently crying, but I couldn't shed a tear. In many ways, I felt numb and unreal as if I were in a dream.

The U.S. Marshals, stateside National Guard, and the Federal Bureau of Investigation were on St. Croix trying to maintain order. The government let the prisoners out of jail because it was damaged, and crime was everywhere. We called my in-laws in Puerto Rico. They told us that we could go to Puerto Rico and live with them until we got our lives back together again. We went to Chase Bank and they would only give us $500. We had a few hundred dollars in cash. We went to the travel agent and bought one-way compassion fare tickets in order to leave St. Croix.

Iris said that I lost it mentally. I burned most of her clothes; I left her with a bra and some panties. I burned furniture and gave most of our children's toys away. I gave our new small gas stove away, and our towels and sheets. Iris tried to stop me, but I wouldn't listen to her. I told people that I would never return to St. Croix to live again. I was finished emotionally, wiped out, and ready to retire from island life. One of my patients came to the house and told me, in front of Iris, how much she appreciated me and I was a good doctor who had helped her a lot. I broke down and cried. The tears flowed from my eyes like two rivers. I thought that I had no more tears to shed, but I was wrong.

As long as I was able to love my wife and my children, still care about my patients, and love God and His creation, I still had tears to shed. In my heart, I still loved St. Croix and its people, but I was too hurt to stay, so I left.

The Exodus

The day that we left St. Croix, the sun was shining bright and we dressed in our best clothes and went to the airport early. Many people were there, as if most people wanted to leave. An exodus had begun weeks before; mainly white people who were afraid for their lives. John pulled out his gun on a crowd of Black folks whom he said were harassing a lone white woman in the street. From the way he expressed it to me I could tell that he was shaken and angry. I detected in his words that he felt they were a bunch of black "niggers" doing their thing again. He got out of St. Croix on a government airlift.

A murder took place on St. Croix. It involved Pharmacist. I had a loose business relationship with him when I first started my practice. Iris and I visited him a few nights before the killing took place. He told us there were people driving by his business harassing him, and telling him that they were going to rob it. It was all he had to make a living, and Hugo didn't destroy it. One evening he caught two guys trying to blow torch his safe, which had $14,000 in it. He approached them with his .38 revolver and didn't shoot or harm them; he just told them to get the hell out. He gave me some bullets for my .38 Revolver and water for us to drink at home. We thanked him and left. The following night he shot a Hispanic guy with a shotgun and killed him. He told me that the police tried to surrender him to a bunch of Black and Hispanic people as a sacrifice for the killing. He and a business associate managed to get to St. Thomas. After telling the National Guard soldier that his life was in danger, they airlifted him to the United States mainland.

I felt for Randy after Corcino was shot, but I also felt for Corcino. It was an unfortunate tragedy and both families would suffer for it.

It was now our turn to be airlifted to the States, not by the government of the United States, but American Airlines. While we sat in our seats with the massive jet engines running, I wondered where I would go to practice medicine. We were heading to New York, but I wasn't sure that we would stay there. I was glad to be leaving for New York to be with family, and see familiar faces, but anxiety was high because I didn't know if I were ready for the fast pace. My other alternative was going to Florida. When the jumbo luxury liner lifted from the runway, I looked at Iris and she was crying. I asked her what was wrong and she told me, "I'm leaving my home." I didn't know what to say, so I said nothing. When we arrived in New York, it was chilly and we were shivering from the cold. It was great seeing my family.

After a day or two, we visited Raymond and his wife Shauna. It was a moment of fresh air when I saw them because, as usual, they greeted us with smiles and hugs. Their children were happy, safe, and comfortable in their apartment. We all sat and Iris and I told them of our experiences and they listened until we were finished. We were sitting on the couch. A video of Larnell Harris, the gospel artist, was on singing "Amazing Grace." Iris started to cry and I followed. I sat with her; we felt vulnerable and helpless. I didn't know what to say to her, and the tears continued to flow. It was a very difficult time for us.

Raymond and Shauna took us to Sears department store and purchased winter coats and hats for our children. Raymond was my best friend, and he and Shauna continued to share their love with us.

We visited Calvary Baptist Church. They were in a new church building that they built from the ground with hard-earned money. They got out of that bigoted neighborhood where the people called us "niggers" and left anything that was dead on the front steps of the church. They didn't have to worry about being harmed or insulated by a bunch of people who were racially prejudiced. In some ways they did as many people have done in most neighborhoods when Blacks moved in; ran like hell. I understand how the people in the church must have felt when the authoritative clan said, "Let's get out of this place." I am sure that there were a number of reasons why they left.

Calvary had not changed much except for a few key members dying, and Rev. Crayton was a bit older. They took up a collection for us and we gladly received it.

I called the Florida and New York medical license boards in order to get information about working in either state. After thinking about Albany and Schenectady, I discussed our options with Iris, and we decided that Albany would be the best place for us to go. I told my family of our decision and we left.

Raymond let us use his Dodge van. We packed the family comfortably in it and hit the New York State Thruway to Albany. Iris and I were content and sure that we were doing the right thing. We stayed at Iris's brother's house with him and his wife Nancy and their two children. Tibbs, as he is affectionately called, was always nice to me and respectful. He never said anything to me out of the way, and things, which he knew that I didn't appreciate. He tried to not offend me. I always liked him because he carried himself well and confidently. He was my idea of a good family man who showed himself responsibly. We stayed in his house until we were able to find a place to live.

We got in touch with Michael and Margie and they were happy to know that we were in town to stay. That Sunday we went to Refreshing Springs Church of God and Christ. Refreshing Springs had not changed at all, and

Sister Dix was still her beautiful self, calling people doll-babies. The people were delighted to see us. I sat in the service and cried. I remembered all the good times that I spent at Refreshing Springs and how it refreshed my soul. I felt as if a million pounds were released from my body; I was revived again.

When the choir's turn came to give their selection, I couldn't believe what my eyes were seeing. My old girlfriend Gwen Newell was standing with the choir singing. I would have never missed her anywhere, with her full lips and crooked smile. My heart beat fast and I said to my self, "It can't be, she lives in Queens, at least that's the last place where I saw her." After church I went to her, kissed, and hugged her. She told me that her father died and her mother and sister were fine. Her last name wasn't Newell any more. She had been married twice and she wasn't with her last husband. She had two sons, and decided to move to upstate New York in order to work. It was nice seeing her again, remembering old times at New York City Community College and while we were dating. Gwen turned out later to be quite a surprise, considering that she called herself a Christian.

My next order of business was finding a job, and there were many available, being a physician. I went to the Whitney M. Young Jr. Health Center in Albany, by Arbor Hill. I wanted to practice as close to the inner city as possible and the predominantly Black neighborhood of Arbor Hill was it. The Medical Director of the health center was a Black male Internist named Dr. Bishop. He greeted me warmly and told me that they had an opening paying $75,000. Considering I had very little money it wasn't bad, but compared to the $210,000, which I made the last year, being offered low pay was discouraging. I told him that I would think about it.

Lies

I went to a well-known and highly respected health maintenance organization and they told me that they had a few positions, and I would be paid the highest salary, which they offered because of my years practicing and experience in Family Medicine; $110,000 was their quoted figure. They told me that they had a position available in Albany, and I told them that I would take it. They then told me that I needed to get letters of recommendation, my New York State license certificate, and my Drug Enforcement Agency certificate. Because they wanted tangible letters of recommendation and the telephones were not operating for the private sector on St. Croix, I had to return to the island in order to speak with a few doctors who would write the letters for me. Though I had no colleagues on St. Croix, these three physicians were willing to help me: Dr. Gardene, Dr. Sue, and Dr. Garcia. While I was on St. Croix, I went to our house and cleaned it the best that I could. I called the agency in Albany and told them that I was getting the letters and the woman told me that we had a problem. I asked her what problem we had. She said that they needed three recommendations and needed to talk to the people who wrote them. I told her that wouldn't be difficult and I would ask the ones involved to call her. She said, "We have another problem."

"What problem do we have now?" I questioned her.

"We need your Drug Enforcement Agency certificate, and a license certificate."

"That's not a problem," I told her.

"Well," she said, "we have another problem."

"What is that?" I asked.

"We don't have the spot available anymore."

After I hung up with her, I couldn't wait to get on the plane and head back to New York.

I went back to the agency with my letters, only to hear them tell me that they had nothing available for me. I may have been wrong, but I believed racism was staring me in the face again and I was angry. They didn't have an acceptable reason to turn me down. I pushed them on the issue of them telling me that they had a job for me; then saying that they had none. They offered me a position in Glens Falls, New York, about 45 minutes north of Albany. I told them that I didn't want to go that far. They offered me a second position in Westchester County, New York. I didn't want to be that close to New York City. I told her that I didn't want it. "What about jobs in the area?" I asked.

"Dr. Williams, we don't have any available."

I thanked her for her lying tongue and walked out of the agency.

White Fear and Black Pain

My second encounter with what I call racial harassment met me in a medical supply store on the main street in Schenectady. I was due to deliver my seventh child in November. I went into the store and Iris waited for me in the van. There were about five white customers inside. The owner of the business was a white woman. I walked over to the area where they had the diagnostic units and reached for a glucometer (device to check blood sugar) and the owner blurted aloud, "Can I help you, sir?" The white people turned around and looked at me. I told her I was looking for suture material. She said, "We don't have any."

"Well, do you have a suture holder?" I asked.

"No, we don't have any suture holders."

I responded, "This is a medical supply store and you don't have any suture material or a suture holder?"

"That's right," she said. The eyes of all the white people in that store stayed fixed on me as if I were there to steal something or harm them. The owner wouldn't address their needs until I made a move to leave. I turned around and walked out. When I got to the van, I was shaking and angry. I told Iris what happened and she didn't say a word. She knew that I was hurt and I guess she felt as helpless as I did. I thought of going back to that store dressed in a three-piece suit; except that I didn't have one. I didn't feel that I needed to walk into the establishment with a stethoscope around my neck, or telling the woman that I was a medical doctor, who graduated from "their" prestigious white private medical college up the road. Too many times Black professionals have to parade themselves around in order to get the same respect as their white counterpart. I was sick and tired of having to answer to the white establishment for things, which they think are important.

I thought about the Whitney Young Health Center. Maybe I belonged in Arbor Hill, taking care of my people and loving them. Maybe that was my place for now, but I didn't follow my heart.

I went to Ellis Hospital in Schenectady, where I did rounds with Dr. J.T. Henderson when I was a medical student. They were interested in placing a doctor in a white neighborhood outside of Rotterdam, New York. They told me that the town had no doctor for about three years. The previous doctor died. They took me there and made me an offer. They would pay to set me up in private practice and support some of my salary for a while. The only problem, as they put it, was whether the white people in the town would accept a Black physician. The hospital administrator took me to a doctor's office further out in the country in a small town. The doctor used to be a police officer; he quit the force and went to medical school. He had a nice comfortable white practice in the country. The hospital administrator asked him what he thought about my practicing in a small town with white patients. He said that he didn't think it would be a problem after they got to know me. He probably was right but by this time, I was sick emotionally and tired.

I also visited a white doctor in his private office in Schenectady. I was told that he needed someone to join his practice. He spoke with me about my credentials; then, he told me that I needed more Continuing Medical Education hours and flatly turned me down, but not before making me feel unqualified. I had it with their running me around. I felt that the only people who were honest with me was Dr. Bishop, who later turned out to have big problems of his own, and the Administrator at Ellis Hospital. I believed that the Administrator respected me being a physician, and white or not I respected him for his kindness.

I went to the Whitney Young Health Center, marched into Dr. Bishop's office, and asked if the job was still available. "Yes, it is," he said.

The Whitney M. Young Jr., Health Center

Whitney M. Young Jr., Health Center reminded me of the Family Practice program at Lutheran Medical Center. From my first day, it never felt right being there. When I was a fourth-year medical student at Albany Medical College, I did a clinical rotation at Whitney Young. A woman named Barbara remembered me from those days. When I spoke with Dr. Bishop the first time, I saw her and she greeted me as if she didn't remember me, and I reminded her who I am. She smiled at me and said, "I remember you, you were a student here a few years ago."

"Yes," I replied, "I remember you also, how are you?"

Dr. Bishop had a secretary named Margaret. She was the one he referred me to before I was hired in order to sign documents and give copies of my certificates and diploma. Margaret looked benign, but she was sneaky and cunning. Sylvia was a Head Nurse who gave immunization shots to people who were going abroad. She was also white. Her demeanor was very pleasant, but she was a coward when she used her power. If she had to deal with people below her position in her jurisdiction, she always had other people working to inject her venom. She tried to never show her true colors. There were a couple of middle-aged women, Helen and Bernice who were up-front and straightforward. They worked in the blood lab. In many ways, they were like water in a desert to me. Janet was my secretary. She made life bearable for me and she was the life of my office. I looked forward to going to work in order to speak with her. We had some deep conversations. I met a young man named El-Wise who turned out to be a super guy, who told me almost every day that he loved me, and I believe him to this day. He was a man who was bold, confident and wise. I never met a young Black man like him. I learned that I could trust him with anything and not worry that he would harm me or cost me. He helped me build confidence in myself every day.

The doctors at the center were each unique in their own way. I was closest to Dr. Brown, who was a Black Internist. He was younger than I was and intelligent, very fashionable and clean. I believe that I gravitated to him because he was precise, clear, and committed to not take, as he put it, "any of their crap, and stuff like that." He was talented and used to play the piano in church. Frank wasn't a religious person, but he respected me and never spoke ill about what I believed in. He was my strength outside of me; he helped me to focus better on major issues in my life.

On my first day of work, the health center was busy and stayed busy almost every day. My patients had various problems; most of them being high blood pressure, diabetes, stress or bronchial conditions. The racial spread was whites, Blacks, and Hispanics. We took care of many immigrants from Russia. They were given sponsorship by various organizations, and given jobs.

AIDS was a big problem and a number of my patients had tested positive. I didn't want to risk my health taking care of them and said (before the hurricane) that I would not, but I had to eat my negative words and be a real doctor to them as well as everyone else. I tried to understand what it means to a person to have tested positive for HIV, but no matter how hard I tried, I felt far removed from them.

I talked a great deal to all of my patients and realized that I needed them as much as they needed me because I felt like I was in a wilderness. I had little sense of my abilities, in what I called the real world, which was away from island life. I had a kind of shyness and I felt inhibited.

My secretary, Janet, was friendly, but professional. I asked her to "loosen up" a bit and smile. It took her a while to trust me because there were many "job politics" going on, and people were afraid to lose their job status. Without notice, people were switched to other job descriptions. Janet was smart enough to watch her back at all times, but sometimes she was paranoid, and it affected our relationship because she clammed up. When I walked into my office, as soon as I saw her face with a blank stare I knew that she was distraught. She was having a few personal problems and they too were taking a toll on her. We talked a lot about them. She was really a stronger person than she thought, if she weren't she would not have been able to help me with my problems. One day she came into the center with a pair of shoes and some ties that she got from her boyfriend, and told me that she wanted me to have them. She really touched my core with her concern. I proudly wore the shoes and the ties.

I was using the van to get around. Though Raymond and Shauna frequently used it, they agreed to let us have it until our cars arrived from St. Croix. We left our cars with Orlando and Annie, who were friends of ours, until we had enough money to ship them. With the salary I was making we weren't going to have enough money for a long time.

The Set-Up

Richard from Refreshing Springs Church found an apartment for us. His adopted daughter Jane agreed to let us stay at her house for $850.00 per month. He convinced us that it was the deal of a lifetime, and we bought it. It was a nice three-bedroom red brick house. The bedrooms were small, but the house provided a clean safe environment for us.

The insurance money for my airplane arrived for $14,500 and I was already $22,000 in debt. My aircraft was worth $30,000 when it was destroyed so I lost $15,500 from the start. We didn't have any money saved and all the money, which I was making had to be spent. We were shopping at the Price Chopper supermarket with coupons; we denied our family the things, which we could not afford to buy. We never had to select certain foods to not buy because of a lack of money since I became a doctor. I didn't feel degraded because I had to do it, but it made me feel inadequate as a provider. In some ways, it was therapeutic because it took me closer to the grass roots of how some people had to live.

Iris and I were tolerating our circumstances and having each other was a tremendous source of strength. We denied ourselves, purchasing clothes, in order to put food on our table. When Thanksgiving arrived, Refreshing Springs Church gave us a big turkey and some canned items. I was shocked when it was done, but I wasn't surprised because that was the way things were done there. We enjoyed our Thanksgiving dinner and it was an intimate moment for us all, as we reflected on people's love for us.

Ariana

Iris had our seventh child, and I delivered her in our rented home. She was beautiful, and Iris named her Ariana. I went to church and announced her birth, and Iris was a brand new mother for the seventh time.

The first snowfall, I took the kids to the park and we ran on the frozen lake and slid down the white hills. I had a lot of fun with them that day, and I forgot about my troubles. It was rare when I was able to do that.

I was elected to work with the young people in the church. As in most churches, the young people were to be reckoned with and the young people at Refreshing Springs were a handful. I really didn't want to get involved that way, but I agreed.

Gwen must have taken offense to my being elected because for no good reason known to me, she all of a sudden would not support the functions that we had. One time we had a church camp-out, and she refused to let her boys get involved. She rounded them up to take them home. She walked by me and said, "What do you think you're doing?" She stopped, turned and looked at me with her crooked smile and lazy eye. She smirked at me and made a grunt sound like a pig. I always catch the "pig grunt," because that's how one of my lost colleagues reluctantly spoke to me at the St. Croix Community Hospital. It hurt me to think so highly of Gwen and all she could think of to share with me was her arrogance.

Hidden Rage

Our cars arrived from St. Croix. They were in Ft. Lauderdale at Port Everglades. I asked Michael to accompany me to pick them up. I encouraged him to bring and wear it so we would not look suspicious, being Black and picking up two Mercedes Benz. We flew to Ft. Lauderdale, Florida, and met a Black preacher from the Church of God and Christ. Being a minister and having to do a funeral that day, he dressed in a suit. The three of us went to the port, and by mistake walked into the wrong door. We met a white custom agent fooling around with a couple of white women. The agent was highly upset and said, "Do you know you came through the wrong door?"

We looked at each other and I said, "We're sorry."

He didn't say another word. We went to the front entrance and composed ourselves. When we were inside, he didn't see us, and one of the women looked at him and jerked her head in our direction. He walked over to us and said, "Can I help you?"

"Yes," I said, "I'm here to pick up two Mercedes Benz."

He took his time looking at my documents and said, "Both of these cars are yours?"

"Yes, sir," I responded.

"What kind of gas do they use?"

"Regular," I said.

"We have a big problem here."

"What is the problem, sir?"

"You said these cars use regular gas and they're not United States inspected."

"Sir," I replied, "they are U.S. inspected."

"But you already said they use regular gas."

"Sir," I responded, "I made a mistake."

"No," he said. "You already said they use regular gas."

At that point, I realized that he was jerking me around as if I were beneath him. My heart was pounding fast and I said, "Sir am I going to get my cars? I came all the way here from New York, and I've been waiting months for my cars to arrive from St. Croix. They are U.S. inspected and use unleaded gas."

He looked at me and said, "I think there is a duty to be paid on these cars." The duty had already been paid on the cars when they were shipped to Montvale, New Jersey. He wanted to slap me with a $6,000 duty. I took out my documents, which verified that the duty was paid. Fortunately, I had called Montvale, New Jersey and asked them to fax the duty-paid documents to me on the same day that I left for Ft. Lauderdale. After he finished whipping me, and satisfied his sick craving to try and make me look small by harassing me, he said, "Come back at one o' clock."

I looked at him seriously and said, "Sir am I going to get my cars?"

"Come back at one o'clock," he repeated. I collected my documents and walked out.

I hated the South, like my father hated it, and I understood why. If I had to put up with bigotry in order to get what belonged to me, I couldn't even imagine what those people did to my father in his day. At least I had the passage of some key Civil Rights Bills in my favor, even if the whole place was a threat to every Black man who has to depend on the system. I couldn't wait to get out of Ft. Lauderdale and hit I-95 North.

What I experienced in the medical supply store in Schenectady, New York was worse than what I got in Florida. Like a naive fool, I never expected white Northerners to treat me as if I were less than they were. I was aware of certain attitudes and understood anything could happen, given the wrong variables. The sorry truth of the situation was, I trusted white people more than I did Blacks. That's why they were able to hurt me the greatest. The hurt, which I suffered in St. Croix by the hands of Black people was in some ways expected. The old saying is, "Black people don't stick together. Sometimes a white person will treat you better than your own people." A lot of this belief is just a whole lot of generalization, but it's what most Black people believe.

When we arrived in Schenectady, I couldn't wait to show Iris her beautiful car. That night I told her what happened in Ft. Lauderdale with that white custom agent. She didn't feed the conversation. We made love and went to sleep.

A few weeks prior to getting our cars, I asked Iris what she would say if I said, "Let's go back to St. Croix." She put a big smile on her face and said, "I was waiting for you to say that." We made up our minds to return to St. Croix, and we were positive that it was the right decision.

Richard and I spent time together sharing our lives and matters of the church, the people in Schenectady and Albany. He talked about his past life and how he wasn't going to turn back to the world. I respected Richard because I always believed that he spoke from his heart what he truly believed was right. Even though he had that car accident, which crippled him slightly, he was talented with construction and was willing to help improve their condition. I especially appreciated how he encouraged and helped me at times.

The Church Fiasco

We had visitors who came by to see how we were doing: Sis. Dix, Richard, Jane, and Michael. Richard was frequently coming by because of his relationship with Jane. He did all of the interior work in Jane's house, and he was rightfully proud of his accomplishment. Jane, on the other hand, was close with Richard because he gave her attention from the time that she was in grade school. She was kind of "verbally adopted" by him, and it was not taken well by some people in the church because it was believed that Richard was spending too much time with her, considering he was married with his own children. In addition, a few people thought that it didn't look right, since he was involved in the church and was Sister Dix's son-in-law. Over the years, the whole situation got out of hand, and Richard and Jane were understandably resentful of the attention. Richard and Jane were both warned about their relationship and how it appeared, but they believed it was no one's business. I personally spoke with Richard about it, and he flat-out told me that he wasn't going to let anyone dictate to him who he could spend time with. I had an idea where he was coming from because I spent a lot of time-sharing with him intimate things, other than his relationship with Jane. I also spoke candidly with him a few times about his views, which concerned people and his position as an Elder in the church. I eventually gave up that issue with Richard until someone at the church, who was very close with Sis. Dix, spoke with me about my being in Schenectady. She told me when we first showed up at Refreshing Springs, she said, "I know Dr. Williams is here to take care of this mess with Richard and Jane." Well, the mess she was talking about was how their relationship was offensive to some people. Many people loved Jane, but they felt that she was old enough to understand Richard was denying his family time because he was giving it to her. I'm sure that wasn't the whole story because Richard's wife was upset about what she thought he was doing. I spoke with her. She had her own version about the situation, and I was shocked after listening to her. The fact was, no one had any concrete proof that there was anything more than a clean relationship going on between Richard and Jane. I was encouraged to speak with him by someone very close to him who I respected, and I did. I went to his house one Saturday and spoke frank to him, and he rebuked and rejected what I had to tell him. I told him it was a warning and he needed to do something that would change the opinions of others in the church. He said, "I don't care what anyone thinks."

After I spoke with Richard, he asked to be faced by his accusers. Sister Dix and some key people in the church arranged a meeting. Richard walked into the meeting with a number of stones in a brown paper bag. He was told that no one was saying that he had any intimate contact with Jane, but his and her relationship didn't look right. It was made clear to him that no one had proof of anything. When the meeting got too hot for him, he pulled the stones from the bag and slapped one in my hand. I was stunned. I don't even remember if he gave anyone else any. He said, "Let him or her who has not sinned cast the first stone." The meeting deteriorated; Richard rebuked us all and left.

After that meeting, which was wanted by a number of key people in the church, Richard hated me. He believed that I betrayed our friendship and put him on view to be humiliated. I don't feel that's what happened at the meeting, because that was the last thing any of us wanted to do, so we tried hard to fit him. He felt otherwise and decided to go on the warpath with me. I was in a vulnerable position since my family and I needed to stay in Jane's house because we were bound by a lease agreement.

The Richard and Jane episode broke whatever few bonds of glue that was holding me together. I felt alone and timid because although the situation appeared to be over, and it was business as usual at the church, Richard was mad as the hellish world he left when he became born again. He was still a born-again Christian, but one that was on fire and burning up in his own flames.

I came to understand that because we call ourselves Christians, Jews or Gentiles, doesn't within itself make us what we are supposed to be; it only gives us a label to hide behind. Doing right or wrong is a conscious affair, and is largely dependent on our character, which displays our strength and weakness. Our personality doesn't say a thing about us, but rather gets in the way of who we really are, and hides us from the world.

Submerged Hate

My job at the health center was just as challenging as Richard's hate for me. My boss, Dr. Bishop, was having a serious problem with alcohol and he was coming to work in less than a presentable manner. It wasn't until later that I understood how badly I failed him, and I would never forget it.

Dr. Bishop needed to go away and of all the doctors in the center, he asked me to be the acting Medical Director. I never held a position of that nature. I knew how to take care of patients, but supervising a bunch of people who had "much" complaints about their job environment and coworkers were a bit beyond my expertise. I told Dr. Bishop that I didn't have any experience in medical directing, and he said, "It's a breeze; don't worry, just keep things afloat." Well, that's what I tried to do. As far as I was concerned, the ship was sinking and I started throwing out life vests. I didn't know that they would all sink. The first thing that I did was call a meeting in order to find out what some of the problems were, and there were plenty.

Dr. Brown came to me one day and asked me what I thought about Dr. Bishop. I asked him what did he mean, and he said, "Tell me what you think about him."

"What do you mean?" I asked.

"Well, have you noticed him taking those Bishop pills?"

"What Bishop pills?" I replied.

"Those things he puts in his mouth every day."

"Are you talking about his drinking?"

"Yeah," he said.

"Well, I think he's an alcoholic."

"And a serious one at that," he said. The conversation never went beyond that. I called a number of meetings to follow up the first and made some changes in the way we were doing some things. There weren't any drastic changes to the infrastructure on the agenda; just some changes in some schedules, and one day I let people go home early because of snow. I thought that I was doing a good job, but when Dr. Bishop came back, he was angry as a wounded bear. He called me into his office and coldly asked me to sit. He had a difficult time looking at me. "Did you call me an alcoholic?"

"Dr. Bishop," I replied, "I didn't come to this health center to cause any problems."

"Yes, but did you call me an alcoholic?"

"Dr. Bishop, please."

"No, I want to know if you called me an alcoholic."

"Yes, Dr. Bishop, I called you an alcoholic, but I didn't me any harm to you when I said it. Who told you I called you an alcoholic?"

"That's not important," he timidly stated.

He leaned back in his chair and said, "I guess I do have a problem and I need to take care of it." His demeanor changed, and he looked at me. "I was told that you had meetings while I was gone and you made decisions that were not yours to make, and caused some problems in the health center."

"Who told you?"

"It doesn't matter."

His voice became strong and he said, "I'm going to cite you for insubordination for doing things you had no authority to do. I, for one, didn't tell you to do the things you did."

"Yeah, but you told me to be in charge."

He paused, looked away from me and said, "You're on one week suspension from the health center without pay."

"Dr. Bishop," I replied, "I need the money and can't afford to be suspended without pay."

"You should have thought about that before."

I left his office feeling sorry for him being an alcoholic, and sorry that I failed him. I could have talked to him about his problem earlier, but I thought that he would reject me, and I needed my job at the health center. I was deeper in debt. I do understand that it wasn't a good excuse for me to discuss his condition with anyone, but him. I know Dr. Brown did not tell him that I called him an alcoholic, but he may have mentioned it to someone, and it got back to Dr. Bishop. I asked Frank about it and he told me that it wasn't he, and I believed him.

The week that I was suspended I went to St. Croix with Iris in order to testify in the trial of my former associate, who shot Corcino. I was never called to the stand, but many others were. Corcino was convicted of manslaughter and sentenced to five years in prison. I didn't feel the trial was fair. It had turned into a Black and white issue. My former associate being white, and the victim, a dark Hispanic, set the stage for the fiasco. Post-hurricane stress was high and anything could have happened between people. I, myself, pulled a .38 revolver from my car glove compartment, and almost escalated a benign situation to possible physical harm resulting in death. I was sad about the results of the trial, sad that someone died, and their family would never see them again, and sad that someone went to jail, and was separated from their wife and children. Before leaving St. Croix, we went to our house to make sure that it was in order. We were not satisfied with what we found. We allowed a couple to stay there free if they agreed to maintain it. They turned it into a worst mess than it already was. They had horses and decided to build stables in the bush next to the house. They turned our nice yard that had green grass into dust because they were charging children in the neighborhood for horse rides. We decided that they had to go. We didn't say anything to them before we left for New York.

When I went back to work at Whitney Young Health Center, I was upset, because I thought about what Dr. Bishop did to me. I didn't believe that he had the right to suspend me and take money from my contract. I later found out from the administration that he was wrong doing what he did.

Dr. Bishop had some serious problems. One day he stayed at home because he wasn't in any condition to come to work. He called the health center and asked to speak with me. He was crying, and told me some things about his life. He said that his father was very stern when he was younger. Dr. Bishop was forced by his father to go to a racist school, where the Ku Klux Klan was active. According to him, they threatened his life. He was taunted and called a "nigger." He said that it hurt him terribly to be in a situation that threatened him, but he couldn't easily escape from it. I didn't know if it were he or the alcohol speaking. I listened. He told me that his life was messed up and he needed help. I offered to be supportive, but he was told to not trust me, and he turned me down.

I can't say that I blame him one bit, because the facts were, that I failed him. I was supposed to be his friend and I allowed gossip and fear of his position during my time of need to get in the way. The failure to be of help to someone rested not only in their wanting to be helped, but also in our ability to be strong and offer the help without gain for oneself. I may have missed a great friendship because I played the hand of cards that didn't belong to me.

I wasn't sure when we would leave for St. Croix. I wrote letters to pastors whom I took care of in St. Croix, asking them to help us financially. I got responses that were varied and one was particularly painful. One pastor told me she couldn't help me because she was going on the road, evangelizing in other islands. I spent a lot of time with her in my office ministering to her medically and sharing God's Word and all she could tell me was she couldn't help. The truth of the matter was she didn't want to. Some pastors were given free medical care for years in my office; I considered that Reverend Williams had enough problems to deal with in the ministry and didn't need to be burdened paying me. One pastor got upset when I asked him three times to help me. He sent me $500 and cut off communication with me. Rev. Walwyn from Grace Baptist Church, Rev. James from the Central Church of the Nazarene, and Rev. Lockhart from Assembly of God gave me sizable amounts of money. Rev. Brown and Dr. Law also contributed to our finances. Reverend Williams took care of some important affairs for me on St. Croix and saw to it that the Federal Emergency Agency assessed damages at my home. They helped us get $14,500. I thank God for him and all the pastors who helped me. I learned some important things asking for their help: First, because a person calls himself or herself a pastor doesn't mean that they're willing to help and lead others; second, pastors, being human, can and will show you their worst side if you catch them on a bad day.

Our lease at Jane's house was soon to end in a few months, and Iris and I decided to seriously start mentally packing our luggage. We told our friends that we were leaving and they were surprised. It was difficult for some to understand how we could be willing to face more hurricanes. No one except my friend Raymond understood. He told me long before I made the decision to return to St. Croix to not close the option of going back. When he said it, I wondered, how could someone who expressed so much love for me tell me to think about leaving them? The point was, Raymond was a real friend, and he was more interested in my happiness than his own.

Needing a Change

Iris and I decided to attend another church; we just needed a change. We went to a white Charismatic church on the other end of town. There were a couple of Blacks in the church. The people were very friendly and we enjoyed the services. On occasion, I went to Refreshing Springs at night and enjoyed their service.

John and Doris Belton were still stable friends with us and if it were not for them still attending Refreshing Springs, I would have been long gone. They represented what was decent in this life. Their honesty, love, and devotion to my concerns won me. They never ignored me, not even while I was going through problems with Richard. Richard was determined to make certain people pay for the "Rock Meeting" we had with him. The situation between us got worse when I told him that we were moving out of Jane's house. We had foolishly rented it with the option to buy. When we decided to leave, he took it personally. I told him about our finances being on the line and we couldn't afford to continue to pay $850 per month anymore, but we would continue to abide by the lease agreement.

One day a hot pot was placed on the Formica kitchen top and burned it. We decided to replace it, but Richard wanted to fix it and charge us. We replaced it and as a backlash, he and Jane decided that they would keep our security deposit, which was $850. I wrote Jane a series of letters stating that I wanted our money. She, under Richard's advice, refused to pay. Richard got as hot as hell is imagined to be, and started fuming. I was in a prayer meeting one evening, and someone poked me firmly on my shoulder. It was Richard. He made a hand motion for me to follow him. I did. When I got in the church lobby, he said, "Come on, let's go outside." I told him I wasn't going anywhere with him. He called me a "punk" because I wouldn't go with him. I could have kicked him down the stairs and injured him. I didn't want to hurt Richard. I loved him, and I told him so in the "Rock Meeting."

Twisted Values

On the day of our departure from the house, Richard and I had a prearranged meeting. I was to give him the keys to the doors, and he was to give me our money. After we cleaned the housecleaner than it was when we occupied it, he refused to look at it, and told me he wasn't going to give me any money. I told him he was wrong and I had not done anything to him. "You jive-time punk," he said, "you ain't gonna get nothing." Those were the last words I had with him. We left the apartment, moved into Iris's brother's house, and made it the best way we could. We took Jane to court for our $850 and won. She was mad, but she had to give back what did not belong to her, and she did. Even though Jane lost respect for me because I challenged her relationship with Richard, I never lost respect or love for her. I still love them both.

It Seemed Easy

On the day we left Schenectady for New York City, I had ambivalent feelings. In one way, I knew that I needed to get away from the confusion that surrounded everything, because once again I found myself in fire. On the other hand, I was going to miss my friends again, as I did before.

I made sure that I spent some time with Ephraim, Michael, Margie, Bro. and Sis. Belton and a few others. I was going to miss the many lunches I had with Michael, my talks with El-Wise, my intimate moments with Janet, and Dr. Brown's enjoyable smile. I would always miss refreshing Springs Church, because I had so many good times there.

When I drove my $74,000 car on the New York State Thruway, I knew that God was continuing to bless my family and me. I had obeyed His call again for the second time in my life, and I believe that He was with me.

We went to Queens, New York and stayed with my family for a couple of days. We had an enjoyable time. My mother was sad to know that we were returning to St. Croix. The day I told her I was leaving for the island, I said, "Ma, I'm going back home."

She replied, "You were born and raised in New York; this is your home."

I understood why she was offended, but what she didn't understand was my desperation to getaway from the raging fire of racism and racial prejudice in New York. She didn't understand my need to rid myself of Richard's hate, Dr. Bishop's hidden rage, and all the lies and deceit that some people who I met on my journey displayed. I thought that I was running for my life, but I was surrounded by fire and it was trying to consume me.

We drove to Ft. Lauderdale in our Mercedes Benz and we were able to appreciate our cars because the Mercedes Benz Company engineered their product well. We made a few stops, having the children. With nine people, we were destined to stop almost every hundred miles.

When we passed south of the Border, I got nervous. I was out of my environment and couldn't relax in the South. I still didn't feel safe there. The white customs agent at Port Everglades didn't help. I told Iris that I was concerned about going to the port again because I didn't want to meet up with that agent. I believed that he would give me a hard time. I didn't think that he would forget three Black guys picking up two Mercedes Benz. He represented a threat to me, my being Black. He had everything on his side, including race. When we finally arrived at the port, the agent wasn't there; instead, there was a white woman. She told me that we couldn't ship Iris's car because it lacked the certificate of origin. I said to myself, "Oh, not again." I told her the car was mine and we just shipped it from St. Croix a few months ago, and it was going back where it came from. She told me that she was sorry, but I needed the document. I stood motionless looking at her, and told her that the car was mine and I purchased it in St. Croix. She looked at me and said, "OK, I'm going to let you by this time, but if you come through here again without the certificate, you're going to have big problems." We took care of the necessary documents, and sighed with relief.

Chapter 30
Home Again

Out of the depths
have I cried unto Thee, O Lord.

Psalm 130:1

We boarded American Airlines at Miami International Airport. The flight back to St. Croix was refreshing, to say the least. Iris and I kept looking at each other smiling; we were going home, back to the place we loved and felt safe in. When the plane landed in St. Croix, my mind was relieved. Iris said, "We're back home."

"Yes," I replied, "we're back home again." The warm air filled my lungs the way it did when I first arrived in St. Croix seven years prior.

When we arrived home and saw our house, it looked terrible. The people who stayed there didn't take care of it; our daughter's cat died, my generator was destroyed, and our property looked like a bulldozer refaced it. I gave them thirty days to get out, and they got upset. I promised them when we left, that they could stay in our house for one year and I wanted to keep my word, even if they didn't keep theirs. For the rest of their stay, they wouldn't help me do a thing around the house. When they saw me cutting grass or digging a hole, they either watched or got busy wasting time. Iris and I were glad when they left. We had to clean up their mess after they were gone.

That night we all slept as if we were in a castle, and I felt complete, content and safe.

My first order of business was following up on my privileges at the hospital. I applied before my return. I went to the hospital in order to speak to Ms. Safe, the Medical Director's secretary, but she was not there. I saw her in the bank, and I asked her about it. "Oh Dr. Williams, you're not going to believe this. Your application was the only application out of all the doctors who applied for privileges that was lost."

"What," I said, "you lost my application for privileges?"

"Yes, Dr. Williams, I'm sorry." I couldn't believe they lost my application, and only mine. "Come by and fill out another one," she said. I did fill another one out and I told her to not lose that one. "Oh, we're not going to lose it, Dr. Williams. By the way, do you remember that nurse who gave you a hard time?"

"Who?" I asked.

"Nurse Duncan, she died." I was shocked when she told me about Nurse Duncan, but I wasn't surprised. Nurse Duncan had created hell in my life, but I felt sad that she died, like I felt when Ronald died.

I would have rather been her friend. The only difference between how I felt about her and how I felt about Ronald was, I hated Ronald for hurting me, but I loved Nurse Duncan in spite of the hurt. I knew I had grown.

I had $11,000 cash when I returned to the island; $4,000 was borrowed, almost $2,000 was given, and the rest we saved in New York. I told Iris in two weeks we would be broke. "How is that going to be possible, don't we have $11,000?"

"Yes," I replied, "God, revealed it to me." She didn't say anything else.

After we finished paying for another roof to go on our house, and building the interior of my office, which was housed in a mini mall, the money was gone. Iris called me on the telephone the second week of our return, and asked me for money to go shopping. I told her that I didn't have any and didn't know that I had one $100 cashier check in my wallet. "What happened to all the money, didn't we have $11,000?"

"I told you, Iris, in two weeks we wouldn't have any money."

A couple of hours later, Pastor Leomine went to my house and told Iris that she had $200 for us. She was one of the ministers (Reverend Leomine) I never let know that we needed money when I was in New York. I didn't have any particular reason not to ask her; I just didn't. I thanked God for her.

Iris and I were going to the Pueblo supermarket that evening, but before going, I told her to take me by Bro. Bell's house, who was a brother at St. Croix Community Fellowship Church. He, his wife, and daughter were living in a U.S. government trailer home because Hurricane Hugo devastated the house, which they were renting. He told me that he had some furniture to donate to my office. Iris stayed in the car and I went into his trailer. He invited me to sit. "Where is your wife? "She's in the car," I replied.

"Go get her, and bring her in."

"We have to get some food from the supermarket and I can't stay long. I told her that I would be right back," I replied.

He asked, "Does your family eat rice?" He pulled a bag of rice from his closet. "Do you have any sugar?" He pulled a bag of sugar from the top cabinet and put it into a brown paper bag.

I stopped him. "Bro. Bell," I said, "I didn't come here to get food from you."

He said, "For years you have helped people in need, let God do something for you."

His wife Jackie walked in, looking tired after a full day work. "Hi Liarian," she said, "What are you doing?"

"Jackie," I said, "I didn't ask Bro. Bell for anything; he just started pulling food from the closet and giving it to me."

"Honey," she said, "did you give him any cookies for the children?"

I couldn't believe them. They were displaced from their home and living in a trailer; their clothes were rotting in a basement of a friend's house. I stood up in their living room, and cried. I told them that I was supposed to help them; not them me. Bro. Bell told me to accept the help. A few days later, he took me to the place where the furniture was, which he and his wife wanted me to have. The furniture was very nice. I saw big rats running all over their soaked, mildewed clothes, and I felt terrible. He helped me get the furniture to my office in a truck, which I borrowed.

The first official day that I opened my office for business, no one came. The second day, two people came. As I was driving home, I was upset with God. "Lord," I said, "King David, said in your Word, 'I was young and now I'm old, and I've never seen the righteous forsaken or his seed begging for bread.' Lord, my children are about to beg, and feeding them is Your business, and I expect You to do something. I know You did not allow me to return to St. Croix to be a failure." From that day on my practice grew steadily, and we started satisfying our debts.

Our children were as happy as ever. I watched them run and play on our 7.5 acres of land, climb trees, and do whatever filled their time. I was happy for them. I saw a difference in Iris, she was relaxed and smiling. I knew St. Croix was the place where God wanted us to be without a doubt. I had decided to not deal with the Ob/Gyn department; it wasn't worth the hassle. My family had gone through enough and I didn't feel that it was fair to put them through anymore. I would have been entangled again with the midwives and Dr. De Chabert, the Chairman of Ob/Gyn; it would have taken time away from my family, and drained me of energy, which I needed in order to build my practice and enjoy my life.

I didn't have my airplane anymore; my cocoon was gone to the aircraft cemetery, and the money from the death insurance policy I had on it was all gone. It was my friend, and I dearly missed it. I didn't have it to protect me from the fire that continued to burn up the world. It played its role well when I had it, but like all things, it was vulnerable to the cares of this life.

I didn't have any money except for what I was making daily in the office, and it was just enough to get by. Many people didn't know that we had returned to the island, and as a result, many of my old patients continued to see other doctors. Some of those patients I never saw again in my office. Some of my patients asked me why I abandoned them, and I explained my horrible journey to them and they felt better about what I did. They understood that I had to do what was best for my entire family. One of my biggest worries was what people would think of me having left the island when times got rough. I think that it was my greatest fear; the fear of being rejected. I spoke with Iris about it many times before our return, and she said most people would understand. She was right. I loved the people of St. Croix. In many ways they were a part of my cocoon; the ones who told me how much they loved me, and the ones who adored me and couldn't stop talking about what I did for them through the years. They were life saving to me; they were my protection from the fire that couldn't burn me up. When I realized the role that they played in my life, it made me stronger and determined to do all that I could in order to keep them healthy and alive. I was determined to counsel and share with them what I believed God wanted them to have through me, and to give them my testimony, which was my journey. I knew that God put my life and the lives of other people together. Other people became a shield against the destructive raging fire of hate, anger, greed, malice, bigotry, racial prejudice, and anything that was not good or worthy to be a part of our lives. I was supposed to understand this at this point in my life. If I did, it would help me survive what was about to engulf me like a tiger, ripping and tearing at my soul, bringing me to a point of wanting to harm someone. However, if I remembered who I am, and relied on the Father of this universe, who created me and keeps me protected in His cocoon,

I would never become a victim to this world on fire, which is full of rage, seeking to destroy everything in its path; including it.

I didn't do much in the area of recreation. I didn't frequent the beach, scuba dive, ride a motorcycle or fly airplanes. I didn't spend time thinking about how to enjoy St. Croix again. I was so busy in my office and most of my energy was spent there.

My office was only 570 square feet of space. I had two exam rooms, a small office, reception area, and a small waiting room. I bought a small air conditioner to keep us cool in the blistering heat of daily 87-degree weather. If too many people came in and stayed, the air became warm and muggy. I didn't change my approach to patients; I talked to them a lot and took whatever time I needed to take care of their needs. Their problems were the usual ones that most family doctors see: high blood pressure, diabetes, asthma, bronchitis, sinus infection, and skin problems. I did what I knew best to do, and they were better afterward. We had a couple of people who wanted us to deliver them outside of the hospital. We scheduled them in our office and delivered three healthy babies whose parents were happy. I enjoyed those deliveries, but the first one was a mother who was having a baby for the first time. She literally begged me to deliver her. I told her that it wasn't my policy to deliver first pregnancies. I consented and did the delivery and Iris and I stayed with her for twenty-three hours while she tried to deliver her baby. We drove her home and she hemorrhaged from her womb when we got out of the car. When we entered her house, she fainted and fell on the kitchen floor and blood was coming out of her like a river. I stabilized her with medication and bed rest for a few days and she did well. I vowed after that to never deliver a first-time baby again, but I didn't keep my word.

The doctors at the hospital in Ob/Gyn knew that I was "back in town" well and healthy, doing what I did best. Comments started coming to me via patients how some people at the hospital felt that I was not a good doctor. Each time that I heard these comments, it angered me, and Iris had to calm me down. I wasn't doing a thing to any of them, and they were trying to disturb my life. I believed that I suffered enough. I was willing to let them be, and they needed to let me be. I wasn't asking them for anything except what belonged to me; my privileges in the hospital, which they were delaying. I continued to deliver babies and I tried to ignore the negative comments, but I couldn't. Therefore, I was constantly in battle with myself to keep my mouth shut. I knew as soon as I said anything to them that it would give them pleasure knowing that they got to me.

Wilbert Williams Jr., M.D.

Jewels in My Life

I needed Continuing Medical Education credit in order to renew my medical license. A conference was coming up in Chicago, Illinois, and I decided to go. It was a weeklong journey and I wasn't crazy about being in an ice-cold conference room for hours at a time all day, but going would have served two things, which I needed: one, to get the needed credit and second, to see Michael and Paula St. John, who lived in Wheeling, Illinois.

I missed Michael and Paula. They were the only white people in my life that I trusted 100 percent. I knew that they loved me with no regard to my color or race. I remembered Michael's kiss that Sunday at St. Croix Community Fellowship. When we spoke about race and color, I brought it up. I told Michael that I didn't understand what white people's problem is with racial prejudice. He said, "Buddy, do you know what the real problem is with people who hate someone because of their skin color or race? It's not fear, it's not money, it's not houses or land; its sin, and the sin in people's lives is a spiritual problem, and only God can help those people." I listened to Michael that day intently, and I knew he not only spoke his heart, but he spoke the truth. I wanted to see them.

When I arrived in Chicago, he picked me up and took me to his house. It was nice seeing Paula. Michael told their children to hug and kiss me, and they did, and it was exactly what I needed. I spoke with them my first evening there. I shared with them, my journey and how the hurricane turned our lives around for the worst, but God helped us through it. I talked to them about my battle with the medical establishment, and how tired I was. I talked to them about the church we went back to in St. Croix, St. Croix Community Fellowship. I told them that I believed the pastor's wife was prejudiced, but didn't feel the same way about the pastor. They, as usual, responded to me in a careful way by telling me that they felt that I should share my concerns with a minister we both knew who visited the church a few times and lived in Illinois. They called him over. When I saw him, we warmly greeted each other. It was about 7p.m., and he allowed me to share my concerns with him without interruption. We spent over three hours talking. He told me that he believed the races should not mix in terms of interracial dating and marriage. I told him that wasn't God's will, and he quoted "scripture" from the Holy Bible in order to justify his position. I told him that he needed to get on his knees and repent of his belief. He disagreed. He had spent way over the time that he intended to with me. He said his wife was waiting for him to return home, but if he left he guessed that I would classify him as I would any white man for getting up and leaving under such a conversation. I told him that he was right. He stayed a while longer, said his goodbye and left. I never saw him again. Michael, Paula and I sat in their living room for a few moments, not saying a word. I broke the ice, and told Michael that I was sorry for having that conversation in his house. I told them how much I respect and love them, and ask would they forgive me. They told me that there was nothing to forgive me for. They understood what I said, and they believed that it came from my heart. They knew that I wasn't a malicious person or one who got a charge out of hurting people or making someone look small. They fed my soul with love that night and told me that they loved me very much, and that God loved me. Every morning Michael asked me to take a walk with him. In the freezing cold weather, he was warm-hearted, kind and gentle. He talked to me about God, man and the universe. He told me every day in many ways that he loved me.

The conference went well and before I knew it, the week was gone. On the day of my departure, I got up early in the morning, went in the bathroom, looked in the mirror, broke down and cried. My heart was so heavy. I called for Michael and Paula. They came running to the bathroom, asking me what was wrong. I told them that I was very tired and I couldn't take it anymore. They prayed with me and shared more of their love that came from God. Michael asked me to promise him, when I had an encounter with a white person that was negative, to just pray for the deliverance of that person, and ask God to help me through it. I told him that I would. I hugged the children, kissed them and Paula and I said goodbye. I told them that I loved them very much, and they returned the same.

I Wanted to Smack Him

No sooner had I left Michael and Paula than I had my first challenge with an elderly white man whom I sat next to on the plane. He complained when I asked him to excuse me so I could sit. He told me to wait and don't be in such a hurry. I sat next to him, and put my Walkman headphones on. He told me to turn it down because it was disturbing him. He said some things after that with a tone, which I didn't appreciate. I got mad. I wanted to tell him to go to hell and caught myself; I remembered Michael's words to me. "Buddy, you're going to be challenged before you know it, call on

God, brother." I prayed for that man, as I looked at him. He was so pitiful and full of everything that is wrong with this world.

On the return flight to St. Croix, I decided to stop in New York in order to see my family. I had a good time with them. I couldn't stop thinking about my encounter with that minister at Michael and Paula's house. I felt sorry for him. He was convinced that he wasn't prejudiced against Black people; he thought what he told me was right before God. The tragedy was, he was very wrong and if he didn't allow God to work it out in him, the raging fire that is consuming the world would eat him up.

They Turned Up the Heat

When I arrived in St. Croix, it was business as usual. The children were happy doing what happy children do, and Iris was holding down the camp. I told her about my trip and I shared with her Michael and Paula's love for me, and how beautiful their children were. The following day I went to my office and saw a load of patients.

My privileges at the hospital came through and it was another factor in my life, which I had to deal with. Some attitudes had developed in the hospital concerning me. One nurse in particular, Nurse Nethersaul, was creating hell. She turned up the heat on me and fanned the flames, while waiting patiently to see me burn. One morning I went to the hospital in order to see a patient, who was my private patient, but she was admitted under another doctor. I was standing in the room reading the chart and a "student nurse" came in and asked me if she could talk to me for a moment. When I walked in her direction, she asked me to bring the chart. "Dr. Williams, I'm so embarrassed; Nurse Nethersaul told me to come get the chart from you."

"Why?" I asked.

"She didn't say."

I looked her straight in her eyes and told her I was a real doctor at that hospital with real privileges and it wasn't right for Nurse Nethersaul to ask me for it. I asked her where was Nurse Nethersaul? "I don't know," she replied. I was steaming. I called the operator in the hospital and asked her to page Nurse Nethersaul, but Nurse Nethersaul never answered. I said to my self, "She is hiding like a snake." I did not forget when she went to Dr. De Chabert, supposedly to help resolve what he called later a personality problem between us. She was rotten then, and still was. What she did to me hurt and I found it hard to pray for her. She wanted to destroy me.

No matter how hot she set the furnace, neither she nor anyone else would see me burn.

I had a couple more deliveries in my office and they went well. My patients were having their needs met, and I was content that I was able to help them.

I started getting tired of the routine of medicine. My pilot's license was not current. It was over two years since I flew an airplane, and I couldn't afford to buy one. I thought of things to do. Sometimes I rode my horse or planted vegetables. I never got much from it, but a small watermelon and a few tomatoes, squash or zucchini.

Farming

My in-laws came to visit us and my father-in-law discussed with me growing banana and plantain trees. I decided to go for it. We planted 1,600 trees on our property. It took two weeks to dig those holes, plant the trees, cover them with dirt and fertilize them. My father-in-law did most of the work by himself, because I had to work. I did help when I came home and on the weekend. I also hired a helper in order to assist him.

I also decided to become a poultry farmer. I purchased 500 baby chicks from the States and was raising them. I had a sign made up called "The Chicken Den," put it on my new red Datsun B2300 truck, built a cage to fit in the flat bed, went to my lawyer, and started a corporation. As far as I was concerned, I was moving ahead; far from the cares of this life. I did not realize what I was doing was trying to fix my cocoon, because the heat around me was getting hotter.

Every day I walked through the field where my mini plantation was and marveled at its beauty. I did not understand why the world was consuming itself with negative things because life to me in the setting of God's creation was beautiful.

I Didn't Start It

One day my son came home from school and told my wife that a boy in his school told him that his mother, who is the wife of a well-known obstetrician/gynecologist, said that I was a crazy doctor. My wife called her up on the telephone and she never denied it. Her husband developed a vicious streak in him concerning me. It may have had to do with the fact that I would not stop delivering babies out of the hospital. He had a good practice and some of my previous patients went to him for care. Many felt that he was very nice in the office and they liked his way. I only heard good things about him. He did not have any good reason to be threatened by me, except for the fact that I was cutting into the delivery business. However, not even that should have bothered him because he was making lots of money. After Iris spoke with his wife, we made the issue of Dr. Carr closed.

I was having a ball driving around the island in my truck with that sign. I was selling frozen Chickens, and became known as the "chicken man." It bothered my children to see me selling chickens, but it didn't faze me one bit. Iris was laughing at me in fun. When my children asked for money, I told them all I had was chicken money and they didn't want any of that stinking money because it was made selling those nasty chickens. Nine months later, the banana and plantain fruits were ready to pick and sell and that is exactly what I did. Almost every day I took them to my office, put them outside, put a sign on the window and sold them. I sold them on the honor system. I let people take what they wanted to buy and trusted them to pay me. I made a good penny between my two businesses.

I moved my office into a larger one because I needed more space to adapt to my patients. I moved to a shopping plaza, further east on the island.

I Couldn't Hold It Anymore

I confronted my pastor and his wife at the St. Croix Community Church and told them that I was concerned about racial prejudice coming from them. I told him that I didn't believe that he was prejudiced against Black people, but I was told by someone white in the church that was credible, that his wife felt the way the minister in Illinois feels. I told them of my encounter with the white pastor whom he exposed all of us to in the congregation. I didn't feel that he protected us if he knew that his friend and colleague of the faith felt the way that he did about Blacks. The church was interracial in make-up, and one family left, claiming the church was prejudiced and the pastor's wife exhibited negative racial behavior. Of course, they were shocked when I told them these things. My pastor looked very hurt, but his wife sat stone-faced. I asked her right face-to-face if she were prejudiced against Blacks and if she felt like the minister in Illinois. Her whole facial expression changed. She wanted to know who that white person was in the church who told me that she believed the same way. I told her who it was, and she was silent. She told me that she was not racially prejudiced toward Black people, but I didn't believe her. Iris sat with me while I spoke with them and she didn't have much to say.

I left St. Croix Community Fellowship after I visited the pastor one Saturday after work. I went to his house and told him that I didn't feel he handled problems that people had in the church well. After some time speaking with him the conversation went sour and he got a pencil and paper, dropped to his knees in front of me and asked me to tell him what to do. I asked him to get up. He yelled, "I don't want to get angry with you, what do you expect me to do?"

"What do you expect me to do?" I yelled back at him. "If you're going to act like this getting on your knees with a pencil and paper in your hand, I don't want to deal with it."

"Well, what do you want me to do?" he repeated.

"I don't want you to do anything, just get up," I replied.

At that point his wife walked by, but she didn't see him on his knees. The telephone rang and it was Iris. She asked me what I was doing at the pastor's house. I told her that I was speaking to him about the problems in the church. "Buddy, just leave him alone."

"Leave him alone," I responded, "he's aggravating me."

She begged me to leave and I did. I eventually left the church.

Who Cares?

My office was busy as ever, and a young woman about 21 years old came in for a postpartum check-up (a check-up after having a baby). I had never taken care of her before, but her sisters were patients of mine. She told me that she was a clinic patient of Dr. Carr. He took care of her during her pregnancy. She told me that she didn't want to see him as a patient because throughout her pregnancy he gave her aspirin, knowing she was allergic to it, and she had bled at that time because of it. I asked her why she didn't tell him she was allergic to it. She said that she did. It was hard for me to believe her story after that because it didn't sound like something a medical doctor would do; especially to a pregnant woman. I listened to her ramble on about her problem. I asked her if she had a pap smear (a sample from the tip of the womb to check for abnormality). She told me that she didn't. I asked her if she had anything else to say, and she said no. I had her completely undress and I examined her. The examination was unremarkable (no negative findings). I did the pap test and sent it to California for it to be examined. Within three weeks, it was returned to my office. It stated that she had a Class-4 pap smear, carcinoma in-situ-3, with severe dysplasia (a precancerous result). I immediately called her into the office and read the results to her. She took it well; in fact, too well. I made sure that she understood that it was a serious finding diagnosed by the pathologist in California. I told her that was all that they did at that company; they examine pap smear slides all day, and I trusted their diagnosis. I told her that she needed to go off the island and be examined by a specialist. The arrangement was made for her by Iris. Within a couple of weeks, she came back to my office, and told me that she couldn't afford to go to Puerto Rico. She went to the Frederiksted Health Center, where a visiting doctor looked at the pap smear results and examined her. He told her that she needed to go to Puerto Rico to see a specialist in Gynecology. He sent her to the head nurse, who in turn sent her to the social service department. The doctor in the clinic, the head nurse, and social service all signed a document, which gave her permission to go off the island. It needed a medical doctor's signature that was in the field of Gynecology. They sent her to another health facility on the island, and she ended up in the hands of Dr. Carr.

Dr. Carr examined her and told her that she had nothing wrong, and I was only upsetting her with the wrong diagnosis. He refused to sign the document, which would give her permission to go off the island. He sent her home with prescriptions for an antibiotic called erythromycin, birth control pills (a female hormone), estrace (a second female hormone), and Monistat vaginal cream (a medication to insert in the vagina for yeast infection). She came into my office a few weeks later, and told me that she didn't go to Puerto Rico, but she had taken the medication, and Dr. Carr told her that there was nothing wrong with her, and stop letting me upset her. I was furious with him. I told her that she had a serious problem, and I reminded her that I did not make the diagnosis, but a specialist made it. She left my office the same way she did the first time that I saw her, with a bewildered look. I was furious with Dr. Carr. I couldn't understand how he, being a well-respected Gynecologist, and knowing good medicine, could have done this to a 21-year-old Black female. Every physician in the world heard at some time that Black women suffer from cervical cancer at a much higher risk than their white female counterparts do. Cervical cancer can sometimes stay dormant for as much as five years before it expresses itself, and cause death. I pleaded with her to go off the island and get proper medical care. She told me that she didn't have the money. I took her to another Gynecologist on the island who was fresh in his practice, and asked him to examine her. I paid her bill, which was $50. The physician suggested putting her in the hospital to do a procedure called a "cone biopsy" (take a cone plug of tissue from the cervix for examination and cure). He wanted cash money for the procedure, and she didn't have it.

Iris called the pap smear company in California and told them that a doctor on St. Croix refused to accept their diagnosis. They responded, "Doesn't he know he can get sued?"

"I guess he does," Iris replied.

The company agreed to pull the pap smear slide and have it read again by two independent Pathologists. They wrote us a letter, which confirmed that the diagnosis was correct; as far as they were concerned, she had a precancerous pap smear and needed follow-up treatment by a specialist. I went to her house and told her what I knew and she didn't seem disturbed. I understood why later. Dr. Carr sent a nurse to her house in order to tell her that everything was OK and not to let me disturb her anymore. I went to the clinic where Dr. Carr worked when he wasn't in his private office or in the hospital. He wasn't there. I asked the head nurse to allow me to see her chart, and she refused. I told her if anything happened to the patient, she would have to answer for it. She asked me was I threatening her. I told her I was not.

By this time, I was fed up with Dr. Carr and his unprofessional treatment of this client. She didn't know any better than to believe him and not the test results, but her mistake was in not getting a second opinion. Dr. Carr put her life on the line; especially her being a Black female.

That week I went to the Medical Director's office, (Dr. Loyd Henry) and asked the Medical Director's secretary if we had a peer review committee. She told me that we didn't. I asked her whom do I speak with when there is a problem. She gave me the names of two well-known physicians. I went to one of them, who is an Endocrinologist (takes care of diseases related to the glands). He was upset with me and asked if I spoke with Dr. Carr. I told him that I didn't. He suggested that I speak with him. I asked the operator to page him. When he answered, I identified myself and told him that I wanted to speak with him. He told me to meet him at the operating room door. When we met, I asked him why he told a 21-year-old Black female who had a precancerous pap smear that there was nothing wrong with her. He replied, "Because there is nothing wrong with her." I asked him why he gave her antibiotics, anti-yeast vaginal cream, birth control pills and estrace, knowing that the estrogen hormone, which was in birth control pills and estrace, could enhance an already possible cancer of the cervix in the patient. "I didn't do anything wrong," he said. I asked him why he spoke poorly to the patient concerning me. "You spoke badly about me," he replied.

I said, "Don't you realize she could sue you?"

"She's not going to sue me, she's gonna sue the Department of Health." He told me that he didn't have any more time for me, and went inside the operating room. I was angry.

I wrote letters to a number of key physicians on boards: Commissioners of Health, the Chairman of Ob/Gyn, and the Medical Director of the hospital. For ten months, I sent certified return receipt letters to these people whom I thought cared about the quality of medical care in St. Croix. One well-known physician replied, asking me to take it up with Dr. De Chabert and the Dr. L. Henry, the Medical Director of the hospital. Dr. Gardene (ENT specialist) asked me, if I would be willing to volunteer to do breast exams in a private Radiologist's office. I agreed. "By the way," he said, "how did things work out for you with Dr. L. Henry, the Medical Director?" I told him that I wrote Dr. L. Henry and didn't get a reply to date. I told him to tell the Medical Director that I wanted that meeting or else I was going to take other steps in order to solve the problem pertaining to what Dr. Carr did. He asked me if I wanted him to tell the Medical Director exactly what I said because it sounded like a threat. I told him if the Medical Director wanted to take it that way it was OK with me, because I was fed up with the nonsense. The Medical Director sent me a letter asking to have all of my documents pertaining to Dr.Carr and the patient, and I did.

It took a month for Dr. Loyd. Henry to set up a meeting with me, Dr. De Chabert and Dr. Carr. I had to wait eleven months for that meeting. On the evening before the meeting, I was given a small tape recorder to record the meeting, if when I arrived they decided to record it.

I walked into the meeting and the Medical Director and the Ob/Gyn Chairman were sitting. I greeted them diplomatically and sat. Dr. Carr came in dressed in a nice island shirt, looking scared. The Medical Director, in a low tone, opened the meeting. Dr. Carr pulled a small Radio Shack tape recorder from his pocket and placed it on the table. I pulled mine out and he jumped in his seat and said, "see." "I told you, you can't trust this guy."

Dr. Henry wouldn't continue the meeting until the tape recorders were put away. The Medical Director looked at the folder of documents he had before him, which he asked me to send, and said, "Well, Dr. Williams, you seem to have something to say; what is the problem?"

Dr. Lloyd Henry sat there knowing exactly what the problem was. I painfully told him what he already knew. Dr. De Chabert sat in his seat and didn't speak a word. He asked me what I wanted them to do. "I want this young woman to be examined correctly," I replied. "I want her to have colposcopy [examination of the cervix with a high powered lens to look for abnormalities] and a possible biopsy."

"What is colposcopy?" the Medical Director asked.

It almost became a joke to me. There he was, moderating an important meeting, and had no idea what colposcopy was, even though it was the main diagnostic tool used in order to diagnose her case. He said that they wouldn't do the biopsy, and would have Dr. Carr do the colposcopy. I interrupted, and asked him how could he ask Dr. Carr to do it when Dr. Carr was the reason we were there in the first place? I asked Dr. De Chabert to do it, and he flatly refused. I reminded him that he took care of patients of mine with fewer problems, and asked him a second time to do it. He said that he wouldn't. Dr. Carr said, "Why don't you do the colposcopy, Dr. Williams?"

"I will, if you let me use the colposcope in the clinic."

"No, I won't," he replied.

The meeting degraded to who should do what. I looked at the Chairman and said, "If Dr. Carr did to your wife or daughter what he did to this young woman, would you like it?" He said nothing. He acted his same jellyfish self; spineless, the way that he did when he took my delivery privileges away after listening to a bunch of lying midwives. I looked at the Medical Director and said the same thing, and he said nothing; just like he did for eleven months while I awaited his response about Dr. Carr's unprofessional behavior. I looked at Dr. Carr, and started asking him the question. Before I finished, he jumped from his seat and said, "Don't you say anything about my wife." I still repeated the question. Dr. Carr was on fire as he tried to compose himself. Not only was he on fire, the flame of his own deceit, lies, bitterness, and hate was burning him up; he was being consumed. He made his own inferno. The two goons deciding Dr. Carr's fate told me that they would have another doctor in the clinic examine the patient. I told them that I wanted Dr. Carr to have nothing to do with the exam. The Medical Director would not agree.

I got up out of my seat and stormed out. Halfway through the executive office I realized that I left my briefcase. I stormed back into the office, looked at Dr. Carr, walked to him, put my finger in his face, and told him that he was one of the most dangerous doctors that I knew ever since I came to St. Croix and he was a liar. The Medical Director grabbed me and said, "Please, Dr. Williams, don't do this."

I looked at the Medical Director and said, "But what about what he did to this 21-year old Black female, he was wrong and he knew it."

"Please, Dr. Williams," he kept pleading. I picked up my briefcase and left.

After that meeting, I became an emotional wreck. I put out so much energy that there was none left for myself. I couldn't even practice medicine without pausing throughout the day to reflect on how everything turned out. I was mad as hell and full of fury. I wanted to hurt Dr. Carr, and make him pay for his treatment of that Black woman. Her life was now at further risk being Black and medically mismanaged, and in the next five years, she might develop cervical cancer. I told them all, if she did, I would make sure I personally walked into the courtroom with her by her side.

I didn't know what to do about my life. It was painful. I was discussing my journey with a woman I know and respect in a supermarket one day. I said to her, "These guys (the system) really did it to me."

She looked at me and seriously said, "You did it to yourself; you allowed them to do it to you." She didn't help to make my life any less painful, but she awakened me. I thought about her words, and I agreed. I left myself vulnerable to the system, and they took their best shots at me. I did what I believed I had to do. I stood up to them when I had to and told them I wouldn't accept their values or ride shotgun with them anywhere or any time, and it pissed them off. I told them in more than one way that they were not worth the sacrifice of my principles and my character. I let them know I was not just a doctor, but I was a real human being who loved people, and would shed emotional blood for them. I could have hurt Dr. Carr. I had it in me to do, but it wasn't what was right, and it would not have changed things. It would have made them worse.

Chapter 31

A Pastor Gone Bad

Except the Lord build the house,
They labor in vain that build it:
Except the Lord keep the city,
The watchman taketh but in vain.

Psalm 127:1

I attended a new church called "More Than Conquerors." It too ended up being a sad fiasco. A young Black man named Mc Kinney came to the island from California, saying God sent him here to do a work for Him, save souls, set the captive free and win the island of St. Croix for the Lord. He called himself a pastor and a servant of the Lord. A pastor he was; a good one he wasn't. He was full of his own kind of holy rage. He claimed to be pro- black, but not anti-white, and most of us Black people swallowed the bait, hook, line and sinker. Once he caught us with his lies, he began to fillet us. Many people were hurt by his actions and many lost whatever religion they had left, including me.

Pastor Mc Kinney at one time lived in New York City during the early part of his life. He attended one of the worst high schools in New York City, called Franklin K. Lane High School. The only other high school as bad as it was Boys High School, the one, which I attended. Therefore, Mc Kinney, being from New York and attending a rough high school, made it easy for us to strike a quick relationship even if it were on the shallow ground of our rough backgrounds.

He heard from a member in his congregation that some people at More Than Conquerors were speaking about me in a negative way concerning my practice of medicine. The venom that was spread about me even reached the churches, and Christians were just as brutal, if not more so, when it came to gossip. Brother Walker from the church invited me to meet him at his house (Bro. Walker's) and discuss what he heard. I don't know what his intentions were because it was never made clear as to how he was to help solve anything. The truth was, he was baiting me for his congregation. We had the meeting. I spoke my heart to him, and Bro. Walker listened. From my first meeting with him I believed that there was something not "kosher" about him, but I couldn't figure what. I visited "his" church and I took the family with me. His brother Dwane played the keyboard and the music was very uplifting. When Mc Kinney entered "his" spot to preach, at first he was calm and as he progressed in "his" message, the congregation was falling apart with the "Amens" and the hallelujahs. He first took off his jacket and someone took it from him. He didn't even ask anyone to take it; he just stuck it out as if he were selling it. He exposed his sweat-soaked designer shirt, and while his $75 tie swayed from side to side, he paced and hollered until people got up and danced in the aisles; he even danced himself. When "his" message was over, he gave an altar call, and the people responded. The collection plate never suffered for a lack of envelopes that were stuffed with money.

From my first visit to More Than Conquerors Church, the services were the same; high-spirited, and full of the charisma of Pastor Mc Kinney.

Mc Kinney told me he wanted to be my friend. I told him I wasn't crazy about the idea because pastors and I always seemed to tangle up in a friendship. There were the usual "I want to be your friend," and before I realized it, they wanted me to ride shotgun for them and overlook their behavior because we were friends. I didn't explain it to Mc Kinney this way, but I did let him know I wasn't easy with friendships.

Mc Kinney's wife was nice. They had three children, and he had a fourth daughter from before his marriage to her. The fourth daughter lived in the States. When her husband was ministering, she seemed to enjoy it. Most people in a congregation will, at some time watch the pastor's wife to get her response to the message. It's almost as if she puts a stamp of approval on it. Sometimes she sat in her seat still and silent.

During my friendship with him, I came to know some of his likes and dislikes about many things. I understood as well as others his stand on being Black. I do not know how many people accepted it, but I never heard anyone challenge it; not even the white pastor from Community Christian Fellowship. He eventually left his ministry and joined us at More Than Conquerors.

Mc Kinney so-called gave the pastor from St. Croix Community Fellowship an offer that he couldn't refuse. Mc Kinney met with him, and he told Mc Kinney that he just about wiped him out of members and his ministry was falling apart. The truth was, his ministry was coming apart long before Mc Kinney started "his" crusade. They struck a deal and Rev. Johnson came to "Mc Kinney's Church," and recommended that his congregation follow him. They also settled on property that Mc Kinney wanted, like folding chairs, PA system, and a Steinway piano worth, according to the pastor from Community Fellowship, $30,000. It was a done deal and the two of these people convinced some to go along with them. I didn't like it from the start and I told them so, but they went full-speed-ahead anyway.

After the deal was made, Mc Kinney told me about it. "Doc, I'm sharing this with you as a member and as a friend. I spoke with Pastor Johnson and he's coming over to our church to fellowship. He says that I've been a challenge to his ministry, and he's stepping down from his position at his church. We agreed to work together. What do you think? He won't be an associate minister; he'll be an elder like Walker." I told him that it sounded like a great idea, but I really didn't want to be under Johnson's ministry again. He told me that I wouldn't, and that Johnson would do what he told him to. According to him, Johnson put himself under Mc Kinney spiritually.

When Rev. Johnson came to the church, very few of his remaining congregation came with him. Most of those who did come didn't stay. Mc Kinney believed that the reason they didn't stay was due to the fact that they were white, and I agreed, but I didn't feel that was the total story later.

Mc Kinney had gone badly way before many people and I realized it. He channeled people in and out of relationships by talking down various ones and building others up.

His wife Carol was pregnant, and they asked Iris and me to be godparents. We reluctantly agreed. He prized himself as a friend of ours. We didn't know that he was setting us up to deal with some of his under-the-table operations.

He lined up a number of gospel artists to come to St. Croix. He came to my house one afternoon and asked my wife and me for $4,000, because he was short on a $12,000 commitment to sponsor a group called Commission. We lent him the money and he promised to pay it back in three months. The concert didn't go as well as he expected and he didn't make any money. He pawned it off as a church function, but told me it was a part of his new business. He convinced the church members that the profits from the "how" would go to the church, but he planned for it to go in his pocket. He did tell me that he would share some portion of it with the church. On top of the fraud, he wrote a bad check to Island Center Performing Arts and it bounced. Then, he wrote a number of bad checks; one to a local travel agent, and another to a commuter airline and they bounced. He then went to a local bank, wrote a bad check and tried to cover it with a check from a second bank and it bounced. With two bad checks written; one to cover the other from a second bank, put him into a bind. He was caught "kiting"(using a bad check to cover another bad check from a bank). He turned up the heat on himself; he made himself a criminal before the law. He was given 24 hours to show up at the first bank with $5,000 or he would be arrested.

He summoned a meeting with me and told me that he was in bad trouble. He had done something serious; he used money from More Than Conquerors church account to take care of some business, but he really did it for the church. He realized he turned up the heat on himself, allowing himself to fall prey to the cares of this life, instead of practicing what he was preaching and teaching in and out of the church. He asked me to take him to a number of places, and I did. He cashed a check and asked me to deliver some money to someone; then, I took him to a travel agency and he brought a ticket to Trinidad. I took him to the airport, hugged him and told him I would see him later. That was 10:50 a.m. By 8:30 p.m., he was back in St. Croix from the island of Trinidad with $8,000 cash in $20 bills, held together with rubber bands. He came into my office the following day and gave me $1,900 in old $20 bills. He thought that he was giving me $2,000, but it was short. I told him that he needed to tell the church board what he did and they would work it out.

On the night of the meeting, he cornered me in the main sanctuary and asked me if I were going to tell the board about the money that he gave me. He thought, being he was paying me my money, there was no need for them to know. I agreed with him. When we were into the meeting, he didn't tell them what he did, and as far as I was concerned, he refused to do so. I talked to him for about twenty minutes about his life, his family and his need to get a rest. He had the opportunity to tell the board what he did throughout the meeting, and they wanted him to speak to them. When the meeting was over, I walked over to him and told him that it was all going to work out, and hopefully the board would send him to California so he could work his life out. I didn't know it at the time, but he felt that I betrayed him, and made him look bad in the meeting.

We had a board meeting a few days later and some people of the board decided to send him away, and hush what he did. Though Mc Kinney was my friend, I believed that he was a liar and didn't have the church at heart. We had already polarized our emotions toward each other, and it was clear that he was going to continue to take advantage of the people at the church.

The following day I asked a police officer who attended the church, what did he think I should do. "Do you really want me to tell you what to do, Doc?"

I said, "Yes." He repeated his statement, and I responded, "Yes."

"Call the cops," he said.

"Call the cops?" I asked. He shook his head up and down. He dialed the chief of police at the main police headquarters. The chief of police asked me to come to the station and give my statement. I told them all I knew about Mc Kinney's fraud. I also gave them names of people in the church who could give them information about some of the things Mc Kinney did. Most of those people were upset with me; they believed I didn't have to do what I did. I was more devoted to God than to them. After an investigation by the police, more stuff turned up on Mc Kinney. He was writing checks on a closed church account from the previous church, which he ministered in California.

I was called, at my office, by a detective, who asked if I would be willing to go with the three detectives to Mc Kinney's house and have him arrested; I said yes. When I arrived at the police station, they were checking their weapons because Mc Kinney had a bodyguard from the island of St. Thomas. He claimed that he was afraid for his life and the safety of his family. When we got to McKinnney's house, McKinney wasn't there, but his bodyguard answered the door. The detective told him to tell Mc Kinney that they were looking for him and if he didn't want to be embarrassed, to turn himself in. Mc Kinney was on the run. He was apprehended at a major shopping plaza on St. Croix, the following Saturday morning. After his arrest, they locked him up in the juvenile detention center. Three people from the church bailed him out, and he was in their custody.

After "the Mc Kinney fiasco," all hell broke loose in the church, and I was cited for doing the unspeakable; having "a man of God" arrested. I was called "a Black Judas," and cited as needing to repent of my sin. A so-called "Bishop" from Trinidad called me out in church. He told the church what I did was wrong and they were going to see how they could help me. I was sitting in the front of the church. Instead, I got out of my seat and told the people boldly that Mc Kinney was a liar and a thief. Mc Kinney had come in with his bodyguard and was sitting in the back of the church. Someone said that they saw his bodyguard with a gun, but I never saw it. I disrupted the meeting by continuing to talk loudly. The congregation wanted to know what was going on. They had no idea that Mc Kinney tricked the whole church and was reckless with our money, our time and our lives.

The elders of the church got together and decided to cover up the fraud and send Mc Kinney away in order to recuperate. He didn't need rest and relaxation; he needed a change of heart.

My family and I left More Than Conquerors Church for all time. I vowed that I was not going to anyone's church again; I was fed up with church.

My life was twisted like a pretzel again and I couldn't tell myself that I was a good person or a bad one. I only knew that God loves me in spite of everything and everyone. I also knew that God loves Mc Kinney, and if he liked or disliked what Mc Kinney was or did, that was His business. I didn't feel that I was being offensive to God for standing up for the truth. Whether my part was right or wrong in having Mc Kinney arrested is for God to deal with me. However, I know regardless of what I did, I followed my heart, and if it were not for God, I would have walked away from it all.

More Than Conquerors Church continued on their journey, and I on mine. A remnant of the church ended up being in my house, because some sisters from More Than Conquerors asked if they could do so. I didn't want to thank God for it, because as far as I was concerned, as they say in the West Indies, "I done with you." I thought that I was finished with the church. I suffered in order for it to exist in my home with my wife and my children, and we eventually became a part of it.

My life at home was as imperfect as it always was. I still felt inadequate as a husband and a father. The same challenges, which I had for the past 46 years still faced me. I spent the last five years in midlife crisis and scored fair. I knew my life was nearing its half-decade, and I wondered if it had really been worth it to live in this world with all its problems. I wondered if I made a positive impact on this fiery earth. I couldn't confidently answer these questions and it only served to make me more anxious about my life.

I didn't cease searching myself, to find my purpose in this life, but I did stop trying to know things, which I believed were not mine to know.

I thought that at 47 years old I had my life under control. I was wrong. I allowed my emotions to play on me, and instead of me controlling them, they controlled me.

One of the most challenging situations that men face is dealing with our fears and faults as men, and being who we were created to be by God: Loving and considerate human beings. We need to love ourselves enough in order to admit our faults and see ourselves for whom we are. We can have victory over challenges. If we do not, our integrity will be on the line. We need to remember that one of our purposes on this earth is to prosper in all things, be healthy, and live a clean life as much as we are able to. We can overcome any problem in our life by drawing on the strength within ourselves, with God's help.

I love my wife with all God gave me to love her. She has been my friend and my partner on this long journey, and we will never part until death separates us. She has been my confidence in humankind, and she has helped me to see who I really am. I will always love her.

Chapter 32
Finding my Father

I cried unto the Lord with my voice;
With my voice unto the Lord, I make my supplication.

Psalm 142:1

I thought a great deal about my father. I missed him. I would have given almost anything to just see him and tell him that I loved him. It was too late to do any of those things so I grieved for him. I thought about my sister Janice when she told me once that she was depressed and called out to my father to help her. I felt that way a few times. He was always willing to help me when I asked although he was firm and sometimes harsh with me.

My father had taken the history of his family to the grave with him. I didn't know anything about them. I had no idea where to find them until I spoke with my mother and she helped me. I had a few leads that they were living in Connecticut. She told me about my father's brother, my uncle Louis. His wife, my Aunt Queen, lived in Montgomery, Alabama. My mother gave me Aunt Queen's address, so I wrote her. Aunt Queen responded quickly with a Christmas card. We corresponded a few years by letter. One day Aunt Queen's granddaughter, Angela, called me at work. I was shocked when she called me. She addressed me the way my father had been addressed. She called me "cousin Wilbert." Her voice was soft and relaxed. "Cousin Wilbert," she said, "I was speaking with my mother and she told me to give you a call. We just want to know you better." I told her that I wanted to see them and was thinking about coming to Alabama. She told me that they would love to see me. We had a wonderful conversation. I told her that I would get back with her about tentative dates. When I told Iris about my contact with my father's relatives, she had a smile on her face. She knew that I was excited. I shared the conversation with her and she said, "You really should plan to go to Alabama and visit your cousins." I didn't know until later that Iris believed that I needed to connect with my father's family for emotional reasons. She believed that some of my problems with restlessness were due to my search for my father's family and trying to fill a void.

I arranged to travel to Montgomery, on October 11, 1997. I was to stay five days with my father's sister in-law, my Aunt Queen Williams, and her children and Grandchildren. Iris took me to the airport to catch my flight at 7:15 a.m. She was in good spirits. I had never seen Iris looked that relaxed on any departure, which I made from the island without her. The ticket attendant was a patient from my practice. She greeted me with a warm smile. "So you're going to Alabama," she said.

"Yes", I replied, "I'm going to meet some of my father's relatives whom I've never seen."

"Oh, that's exciting; have a great time."

Iris kissed me at the customs entrance. I told her that I loved her and she said, "I love you too, honey."

Before I boarded the aircraft, my patient approached me, asked me for my ticket, and gave it to another agent. They had seated me in first class. I was shocked. A man was sitting in the seat next to me. He greeted me warmly and we mesh like bread and butter. I found out that he was a Christian businessman who lived in North Carolina. He was visiting his daughter in the island. We spoke about our lives and our past journeys the entire trip to Atlanta, Georgia. When we arrived in Atlanta, we planned to meet the next time that he was in St. Croix. I caught the next flight to Montgomery, Alabama. The Alabama landscape looked beautiful from the air. When we landed, I recognized the tower building from some old civil rights pictures. I thought about the racial prejudice I experienced in New Orleans, Florida and Washington, D.C. when I was younger. A fear filled me. When we landed, I thought, "Gee, no Klu Klux Klan's men to greet me." I expected a hostile attitude in the South but I didn't find it. The stories and the documentaries that I had been educated and indoctrinated by over the years were almost a thing of the past, and my Cousin Orlando would prove it to me.

I waited for my cousin Orlando, Aunt Queen's grandson, to meet me. I saw a well-built guy walking toward me and we greeted each other. We greeted each other cautiously because, he was looking for an older guy and

I had no idea what he looked like. He walked pass me; then, came back and looked at me. We pointed our fingers at each other and nodded our heads.

"Are you Cousin Wilbert?"

"Yes."

He helped me bring my luggage to the car. We hit it off well. I liked him from the start. He spoke with me about his job as a personal financial analyst with Primerica Financial Services. The knowledge that he had was what I needed in order to set my finances in order. He drove twenty-two miles to a place called Waugh in Montgomery County. Waugh was beautifully nestled in the country. I tried not to miss a thing. I scanned the countryside, and marveled at the woods. He stopped at a dirt road and said that he had to get the mail. There I saw four houses on top of a hill. The house directly facing me from the road was where my Aunt Queen lived. My father's brother, my Uncle Louis, built that house from the ground up with his own hands. To the right of it was a second house, which my cousin Louis, my deceased uncle's son lived in. Next door about one hundred yards was my Cousin Katie's home, Orlando's mother. My cousin Elmira and Katie were taking turns caring for my Aunt Queen who was suffering from congestive heart failure.

I got out of the car and took a picture of Orlando standing next to the road sign named Queen Williams Road, which led to the property. "My God," I thought. I didn't have a road named after me, but I also didn't own sixty acres of land either. I had not helped my children as much as she had or probably been on a journey as rough as hers. She deserved her name on a road and a sign and much more. Cousin Katie met me on the porch at Aunt Queen's house. She had a pleasant smile on her face and hugged me. It was a surprise to her that I looked younger than my stated age. When I entered the house, I felt warm all over. I couldn't believe that I was standing in the living room of my father's brother. On the piano, I spotted a picture of my Uncle Louis in his cap and gown taken when he graduated from high school. He and my father were spitting images of each other. Aunt Queen was lying in bed resting. She had not been well for more than a year. This was the reason why I decided to expedite my trip in order to see her. Cousin Katie guided me to her room as I looked at every inch of the house with such contentment. I had corresponded with Aunt Queen for seven years and felt wonderful finally seeing her. "Hi Baby," she said. "How you doing? You look so good and it's so nice to see you."

"It is great seeing you and I am so happy to be here."

"It's so nice having you here."

I hugged and kissed her and squeezed my face against hers.

Cousin Katie gave me the room next to Aunt Queen's room to sleep. "Cousin Wilbert," cousin Katie said, "This room is yours."

I noticed the broad smile on her face and the brightness in her eyes while she spoke those few words to me. I would realize later that my cousin Katy was loving, kind and compassionate and she never changed.

I looked around the room and marveled at the handiwork of my Uncle Louis. My uncle was a preacher and a builder. I sat on the edge of the bed and thought about my father and his ten brothers and his sister, Aunt Maggie who lived and died in Indiana. My father told me that he used to be a mason builder, but decided to become a barber. I figured that my father's family was all very interesting people; like a rainbow with different colors. Some were dark complexion like my Uncle Louis and my father and one was light complexion like my Aunt Maggie, who had Indian features like her mother, my Grandmother, Meg. I was determined to find out why my father didn't want to tell me anything about his family.

In the evening, my Cousin Elmira came home from work. She greeted me with warmth and love. She told me that it was so nice for me to visit. Later in the evening, I met Angie, Oscar, Mira, and Jackie. They were loving toward me, and of course, I soaked their love in. I stayed up early in the morning talking with Cousin Katie and her children Angie and Orlando. I just could not stop talking about how important it was for me to find them. I told them about my journey, the difficulties growing up in Red Hook Projects, and racism and racial prejudice. I told them that I was afraid of the South. They listened to me patiently while I rambled on about my life and my family. I told them that I loved them dearly. I tried to stop talking, but the words continued to flow from my dry mouth. It was not until 2:30 a.m. that Cousin Katie went to bed when I stopped talking.

The following day I hung out with Orlando. I was so glad to be with him. He took me to a credit loan business where he visited to copy documents. When we went into the establishment, Orlando and I started joking with them. I saw three white women behind the desk and Orlando started joking with them. I didn't think a black man could be out right friendly and assertive with white women in the South. He was respectful, but to the point and polite. They joked with him and I was shocked. I checked out their response to his joking and the fact that he was Black didn't seem to matter. I expected black people to be low key, find their place and shut up, but not my cousin, Orlando was bold. He took charge of his space and theirs also.

I enjoyed spending the day with Orlando. Unknowingly, he destroyed my first fear about the South, that a black man couldn't really be a man south of the Mason-Dixon Line. That evening I sat and spoke with Katie and Elmira about the South and my fears of being there. They assured me that the South had changed from the era of the civil rights movement. They let me know some areas were still holding on to the old ways, but Alabama had changed for the better. That evening I held them at bay again until early in the morning as I talked about my wife Iris and our children. We talked about their living in Connecticut before deciding to return to Alabama. On my third day, I spent a lot of time talking with Aunt Queen about my father. I wanted to know how she felt about him. I asked her if he were kind to her. She told m that he was kind and sweet and was particular about himself. I assumed that she told me everything she remembered about my father and it was all good. I was grateful and pleased that she shared some of my father's life with me. Her explanation helped me to understand some of the softer moments, which I had the opportunity to share with my father; especially the day that my father held a dead puppy in his arms and looked sad. She knew that I had written a biography of my life before going to Alabama, Beyond the Fire and the Rain. She made me promise that I would not write about my father's family. She didn't believe that it was right. She said, "Let it go honey, because the dead can't speak for themselves". I promised her that I would not write about my father's family in a book. I am grateful to my Aunt Queen Williams for her openness and kind words about my father and his family.

Later that afternoon I spent time with my cousin Louis, Jr. who lived a rock's throw from Aunt Queen. His features were more like my father's than anyone in the Williams' family was. I remember him coming to stay in our project apartment in 1972 for three months. I felt especially close to him because he reminded me of my father. He was just as interesting to spend time with as I spent with my father. He played the electric guitar for me and sang a blues song. I recorded the memorable moment with my 8mm Sony camera. As I watched him play the guitar, he seemed so content as if he had found his place of refuge in a comfortable "cocoon." When he finished playing, I didn't want to leave. Sitting with him was like being with my father. After, we sat for a while talking about my family in New York. He didn't smile at all that day. I wondered what had stolen the smile from his strong face. I thought that it was the cares of this life. That's what it was; the cares of this life stole his smile.

That evening I told my cousins Elmira and Katie how much I enjoyed being with Louis, Jr. They listened to me tell them how much he looked like my father. I'm sure that they were aware that he fascinated me. I wondered if they realized how much I loved him.

The following day I was with Orland again. We traveled around Montgomery taking care of his Primerica paperwork and visiting clients whom he recruited. I was shocked to see a white family across the street from his clients who were black. A white police officer was parked and speaking to the white neighbor. I asked Orlando if Alabama had many integrated neighborhoods. He told me that there were a few. Alabama didn't fit the picture that I had. I told Cousin Katie I couldn't figure Alabama out. She told me things had surely changed. That evening, Orlando took me to a black attorney's office in the city of Montgomery. She was a pretty black woman. She was with her daughter, who looked about seven years old, and sat quietly. I felt as though we had invaded her office and her space because she had no idea that we were coming. I said to myself, "My God I'm sure that she doesn't like this set up. At least Orlando should have called her first." I watched a beautiful black woman who was an attorney speak with authority in the state of Alabama.

Orlando told her who I was and she looked at me and smiled. "I want him to tell you his story," Orlando said. I sat thinking; she doesn't want to hear my story. She wants to continue her work, care for her daughter, and go home. It was dark outside, nearing late evening. She put her hand on her cheek, leaned back in her chair and listened. I told her where I grew up and how bad I was as a child. Her smile widened. I told her about my troubles academically and that medical school was very difficult. When I shared with her some racial things, which I encountered in medical school, she looked at me, tensed. I could tell that she was caught up with the things, which I told her. I spoke a bit about St. Croix and my family. She smiled again. Her smile was refreshing and clean; the kind of a smile that ministered to me.

It wasn't until I finished that she spoke to me. She shared her experience with me at the University of Alabama and Alabama Law School. She told me that the South's old racist boys' ways tried to mess her up. She didn't feel that they treated her fairly when she took her bar exam. "They unjustly failed me," she said. "I had to deal with them." She passed her bar and the state of Alabama had to do right. That she did. I was fascinated and captivated by her. She encouraged me. I was glad Orlando thought my journey was important enough to share with his friend. She wished me well. Orlando told her that I had written a book about my life. She said she was looking forward to reading it.

That evening I told Orlando I wanted to see Tuskegee University. He gladly consented. He was driving down route 80 on a two-lane road about seventy miles per hour. That road reminded me of the road in the movie, "Mississippi Burning." I thought, "Some cop is gonna pull us over, and my worst nightmare would begin. I told Orlando that he was driving fast. I thought that he would slow down, but he didn't. We turned into a dirt road. It was pitch black and a deer jumped in front of our headlights. It was beautiful. It reminded me of my hunting days in upstate New York. I thought again, "Some racist is gonna kill us up in these woods." I looked at Orlando. He told me to relax and not to worry because he had driven that road often. We stopped at a client's house. He was a doctor of veterinary Medicine who was not at home. "Okay," he said. "Let's go to Tuskegee." We flew down route 80 East to Tuskegee University. I was fascinated with the university. I asked Orlando to take me to the airfield where the Tuskegee Airmen trained. He started in the direction, but it was getting quite late. I told him to forget going. I was not up to anymore after dark driving in Alabama.

Sunday I went to Macedonia Miracle Kingdom and Worship Center under the leadership of Bishop Leo S. Lewis. Macedonia Miracle Kingdom was where Oscar, Orlando and Angela worshipped. I was ready for church. I was filled to the brim with deep emotions concerning my father and what I believed Alabama did to hurt him emotionally. I had emotional pain that I couldn't describe and I needed to bear my soul in music, prayer and song. I wanted to hear some good preaching down home style in the South. The church was beautifully decorated in bright colors and shadowed in gold trim. I felt a bit shy not knowing anyone, but Angela, Oscar and Orlando made me feel at home. I was in time for Sunday school. The class I was in was full of men of all ages with their bibles in hands as they listened attentively to the speaker. I was distracted in Sunday school. I kept thinking about my father in Alabama, calling white people, "No good low down dirty crackers." I was watching the black men who I believed were links to my father by way of slave ship. A feeling of intimate kinship was established, knowing the brutality our families suffered in the South. I was thinking about Martin Luther King, Jr. and the civil rights movement, the bombing in Birmingham, Alabama, the Selma Alabama march across the Edward Pettis Bridge, and the brutal attacks on Black people. Yet, I was no better off, in ways, living in New York. The North perhaps was worse;

although I believed that my living situation was better. I was less fortunate than these Southern gentlemen who probably had a greater sense of whom they were than I did. The distraction took up the better part of the Sunday school lesson. Perhaps I learned that my state of stability was not stable at all. After Sunday school, we gathered in the main sanctuary for the main service. People flooded the sanctuary while the choir took their seats at the front of the church.

Suddenly Pastor Lewis who was a handsome gentleman came out, grabbed the microphone and told the people to praise the Lord for their blessings. I sat looking at the beautiful people who waited patiently for the choir to sing while the band members tuned their instruments. Pastor Lewis prayed fervently and it was most dynamic. I was surprised when I heard him speak because I thought that I was going to hear moans and groans of a black preacher in the South full of Southern pain. I listened to every word, which he spoke wondering if he would avoid speaking on race issues. However, he cut deep into the subject. He spoke about Blacks bowing down to white people, but hating their own black skin color. He never held his tongue about the need for black people to be accountable for their actions. He told the congregation to get off their behinds and do positive things to help them and their race. I wondered how the pastor could speak directly to the issue of race and color and not be verbally crucified by some members. I think that I was the only one who was uncomfortable. Knowing that he spoke the truth, I settled in my seat, agreed with him, and gave the amens to the message. He told us that God was sick and tired of foolishness and our petty ways. He said, "If we are to be great and successful like God designed us, we better wake up and smell the coffee."

When he finished preaching, my ignorant view about Southern Black preachers was demolished. I felt as though I had missed a life of abundant positive values by living in the North. I believe that I would have been a stronger person, full of confidence and pride, if I had grown up in the South. I knew on my arrival at my Aunt Queens home that I had missed not only family, but also priceless love. My Aunt Queen, her children, and grandchildren confirmed their love for me by embracing me emotionally. I felt their depth of love each time words came from their mouths as they verbally said, "We love you cousin Wilbert." I must have told them a million times that I loved them. I couldn't help myself. In many ways, Bishop Lewis' message made me more confident that God can keep us even in the South. His message of Blacks being accountable and prosperous led me to believe that even in the deep South where racism raised its ugly head and destroyed many of our black brothers and sisters, we didn't have to be afraid because God was with us. I enjoyed the church service and the fellowship with other Christians. I got away from the crowd, went outside the sanctuary and found an isolated area to stand and think. I reflected on being in Alabama, not believing I made it a part of my journey. I continued to think about my father and what my life would have been if he had taken us back to Alabama to live. I remember him telling me a few times, if he had stayed in Alabama, he would have been killed or killed some no good low down cracker. If not for any other reason, I am grateful that we were raised and lived in the North. Everyone needs freedom from overt and covert racism. Racism primes ones for social war. We need to love each other and appreciate our differences. Although, with my energy, I'm sure, I would have been on many battlefields for justice. My cousins were doing well and they seemed comfortable and content living in beautiful Alabama.

Sunday afternoon we had a wonderful dinner of turkey, collard greens, vegetables, and cornbread. I did not tell my family that a highlight of my coming to Alabama was to eat their Southern food. That evening I went back to church with Angela and Orlando. The service was a blessing. Bishop Lewis spoke again about making an impact on the world by doing something for God with our lives. He spoke about Black people needing to be prosperous because God endowed us with everything we need to be prosperous and successful. I listened to him as intensely as I did the morning service.

At the end of the service my cousin Orlando told Bishop Lewis about my being his cousin from the Virgin Islands and that I had a wonderful testimony. I didn't want Orlando to spotlight me. Therefore, when Bishop Lewis called me to the front of the church, I was surprised. The Bishop spoke directly to me and told me that God had his hand on me. Bishop Lewis told me that he was going to pray for me. When he put his hand on my head and began the prayer, I fell to the floor. I didn't know what happened or why. He told someone to leave me on the floor and closed the service. While I lay on the floor, I was very relaxed as if I had been resting all day, feeling peace and being quiet. I must have lain there for five minutes before sitting in the same spot. I was self-conscious about what happened to me and wished everyone would go home or just vanish for the evening. After I composed myself, I wondered what Angela or Orlando would say to me about my experience. I didn't want to talk to anyone about what happened. Orlando mentioned how the spirit of God really moved in the service. He didn't have to tell me how it moved. I ended on the floor. He asked me how I felt and I told him well. I told him my being prayed for and dropping to the floor was my first experience. He asked me to tell Bishop Lewis about that being my first experience and I did. Bishop Lewis asked me to continue to trust in God. During the ride home, I was very quiet.

That evening I spoke with my cousins Angela, Katie, Elmira, and Jackie. Orlando was there. I just started talking and would not stop. They listened to me tell them again about my life. I spoke about Red Hook Projects, my family, my hurts, racism, and finding my father through them. I spoke for a long time. They never interrupted me. Cousin Angela said, "Let's pray." Well, she prayed and asked God to heal our family and release us from any generational curses, pain, hurts and wounds, which we encountered over the years. She prayed fervently. Everybody started praying. My cousins began to cry. Everyone was filled with joy. My cousins hugged me. I was refreshed and new almost like I did when I gave my heart to God. I apologized for keeping them up early in the morning. I knew that they all had to go to work. They didn't want me to apologize. They wanted me to know that they loved me. I felt their love to my innermost parts. I love them.

My trip to Alabama was wonderful. I will never forget it. I found my father through my loving family. I took pictures of them. I visited Lewis Jr. and told him that I loved him. He told me that he loved me also. I hugged him. I didn't want to leave him, but I had to go home to St. Croix.

On my last day it rained. I visited my cousin Oscar and his wife. He lived in a beautiful house that he and his wife furnished beautifully. Orlando drove me to the Montgomery airport in Oscar's new car. Their brotherly love encouraged me. I spoke with Orlando on the way to the airport. I told him how I loved him and how grateful I was for his love toward me. He was a bit reserved, but told me that he loved me also.

When the jet lifted from the runway, I thought, "I found him. I found my father in all of them." Thank God.

Chapter 33
The World is Beautiful

In the beginning God
Created the heaven and the earth.

Genesis 1:1

The crises in my life stood still for a moment, and I was able to see the world and some of its beauty. I took my family on a cruise, and we were launched into the deep ocean of the Caribbean. We boarded a cruise ship in San Juan, Puerto Rico called the Festival with Carnival cruise line. We had never been on a cruise before and we were all excited like little children. It was a nice ship, a nearly model of its fleet. As we cleared customs at the port, the children were going through their daily ritual of misbehaving, and Iris was doing what mothers usually do, telling them to shut up. I was my usual self, acting as nothing was going on. When we got on the ship, I couldn't believe how beautiful it was. It looked like a fancy hotel in some big city like New York or Dallas, Texas. There seemed to be tons of people on that ship. We were directed to our cabins, which were small but cozy. The children were going crazy talking about who was going to sleep where. Iris and I just looked at each other for a while, and then Iris took over. "OK, I'm going to tell you who sleeps where." The boys wanted me to sleep with them. She engineered the arrangement of sleep, and she and I ended up being in separate rooms. We didn't like sleeping apart, but the children won.

My first order of business was looking for all the food. I heard the food on cruises was fantastic and I was determined to find out if it were true. We went to the top deck of the ship and they were serving a small lunch of hamburgers, franks, French fries, fruit and drinks. I ate until my stomach burst; someone would have thought that I didn't have any food for days.

We enjoyed our first evening on the ship. It stayed in port until 10:00 p.m., at which time it departed for St. Thomas, Virgin Islands. We stayed up late that night and every night after. I ate food of all delights the whole day. They served us food 12 times per day every day. It was the highlight of the cruise for me. When we went to bed, we were all tired. I was up early at 7:00 a.m. and went to the main dining room to eat. I never saw so much food beautifully arranged in sections as it was.

They had a beautiful ice carving of an American Indian on the main table. I searched every fine line of its artistry, and I thought that the person who created this is full of talent and gifted. I knew many gifted people with great talent who added their gifts to this world, and never asked for anything in return, but to be recognized for what they offered and who they were. That carving represented to me some of the finer things in this life, and they are available to us all if we search for them. I was searching on my journey and finding riches. Everything the cruise had to give that would help me see another side of life I wanted.

The kids kept us busy, finding things for us to do. They either wanted us to go to the cinema, jump in the pool, or just clown around with them in the room. I had lots of fun with the boys during the evening. They never wanted to go to sleep and constantly did things in order to make sure that there was time spent in laughter.

I wanted to do more with the boys than I did, but I needed to spend time with Iris. Our time came at night when the children were told to stay in the rooms. We went up on the top deck where they always had food and music, or down to the main dining room for a 1:00 a.m. buffet. Sometimes we went on the outside deck and acted like newlyweds. I tried hard to give Iris some special time, but I never felt satisfied that I did, because in some ways I was trying to make up for the times I spent with her that weren't special; those times when I was engulfed in my problems, sulking and complaining how bad I felt. I was at least determined to not waste the precious time that we had together, even if I felt inadequate to give her all that she needed. I knew for sure, no matter what I felt, or how she received the time that I spent with her, there was no doubt that she was my love.

We met a friend in St. Thomas named Pastor Benjamin, who took us around the island in a flatbed truck. He wanted to show us a good time, and I wanted the family to see the island. They had not seen it in a long time. The island is so beautiful, but too small and too congested. We had a good time laughing and joking. I kept the children laughing, telling them we were like cattle being shipped to market in the back of that big truck. It was all in fun and by the time he took us back to the ship, we were tired and content. I thanked him for showing us a good time.

When we got on the ship and settled down, my first order of business was to find the food. If we missed food in one spot, they had it in another. I had a ball eating and my stomach was stretching on an hourly basis.

It was so nice and relaxing lying in the bed with the blanket tucked to my neck with the air conditioner blowing while the ship gently rolled from side to side. There was a gentle pressure on my body while the ship thrashed forward. I had never felt that relaxed before. I thanked God for His blessing in my life and I thanked Him for Iris and the children.

The island I enjoyed and loved the most was Dominica. It is so lush with vegetation. Banana trees were everywhere I looked. I purchased one of the largest pineapples I ever saw in my life and paid only $5 for it. It was funny standing before the owner of the business, which was nestled high up in the mountain, asking her how much it cost. She didn't know what to charge me. There was a kind of innocence in that woman, like the innocence of the forest that surrounded us all on that beautiful island. We stopped at another roadside stand; I tasted a new fruit, and my body enjoyed something brand new and fresh from God's precious earth. I delighted in all the things, which I saw and touched, and I felt a oneness with the earth and its innocence. We went to a waterfall in the midst of the forest. It was so beautiful, more beautiful than anything that I ever saw, flowing over rocks neatly fit together on a ridge. The water plunged to the pool below it and splashed, sending forms of pure water everywhere. I said to my self, "Oh God, You are so great and so wonderful, I love Your creation." I felt in my spiritual longing to become one with it, as if I were there alone having no responsibilities and no burdens. I felt free and clean, and I didn't want the feeling to flee from me, but I knew it would as soon as I left the serenity of it. We climbed up to the level we descended from, but we were on the backside of a hill, and I saw a mist so beautiful caressing the mountain before me. It was a remarkable sight.

I thought about the Black people living there and how rich they really are, but the cares of this life would prevent many of them from enjoying their riches from God. I was sure the pain of life's struggles to keep them well and protected was a daily exercise.

The island represented the pure side of life, the side that was distant from the fire, not burning up like the rest of the world, but it too was in danger of being consumed because man had taken charge of it.

When we left the island of Dominica, I prayed in my spirit that I would one-day return to greet it, and thank it, for showing me a purer side of this world.

I didn't like Martinique and Barbados because they seemed to me to be so caught up in the cares of this life. I didn't take well to the commercialism and what appeared to me to be an arrogance coming from the people. I am sure if I were to go back to the islands of Martinique and Barbados I would find a pure side to them. If not a pure side, I am sure I could find innocence in it. I would have to go where there is life that is new by the hour and untouched by man.

We thoroughly enjoyed the trip from Barbados to San Juan, Puerto Rico. We spent a day-and-a-half at sea. We went to shows, participated in fun times, filled our bellies to near-stretch capacity and enjoyed the Caribbean.

We never had so much fun as a family. The cruise was the best thing we could have ever done. I believe it served as a cocoon for us all, and protected us from some of the cares of this life. For me in a way it brought me a full circle to see myself without anger, without pain and without fear. I was better because of it.

The West Indies and all the worlds are the beauty of God's handiwork. It is meant to be enjoyed; not abused, not misused or destroyed. It was never meant to be taken for granted or ignored, but to be caressed and loved. It is one of God's gifts to us to enjoy and be blessed by. It is God's representative of what was made without a blemish and without scorn for man.

Chapter 34
Faith and Hope

Now Faith is the assurance (the confirmation, the title deed) of the things [we] hope for, being the proof of things [we] do not see and the conviction of their reality [faith perceiving as real fact what is not revealed to the senses].

Hebrews 11:1

When I think about the Juan Louis Hospital, I see a mind field of challenges. There is not a hospital in the world that is not challenged by its own record, but the Juan Louis Hospital has lagged behind the times and its slow progress is not acceptable. Now that we are in the new millennium, I wonder how we will meet the needs of our community. The Juan Louis Hospital today is not the St. Croix Community Hospital where I had privileges in more than ten years ago. In some ways, the Juan Louis hospital has improved concerning hospitality, which is due largely to a changing of the guards. Many health care staff from the old vanguard has left the health care system. This changing of the guards has been healthy because many health care providers have refused to change things for the betterment of our community. Much of the refusal to upgrade our system relates to hospital and community politics. There is a vast amount of favoritism and monopolized power by a few prominent people. The system has obviously worked for these people, but what about most of our community who belongs to the less fortunate.

There are things, we should be proud of like, our efforts to make the hospital a more suitable place to care for our sick neighbors. Even if our efforts have been dwarfed and we feel un appreciated and powerless to change some ills that plague us; at least we have tried to progress. There is still hope. The hope for a better tomorrow is in all of us. We need to continue to be strong and courageous and stand firm for what we believe.

There is always room to improve even upon excellence. Excellence is just a measure of where we are and how far we have come, not a final resting place. In the midst of the hard, trying times, which I have experienced I could have done some things differently and perhaps better. I was challenged to do my best. Still, the trying harder could not satisfy me, but I continued to have hope. It is in this hope that I speak to you that we all have to excel, so I stand with all who push toward the higher goals with integrity, justice, and truth in God. I pray that my family and I are making this world a better place because we are here. I pray that peace be upon us all in the name of God.

I will always seek what is beautiful no matter what prevails in this life. I know all that is good, perfect and beautiful comes from God, and the vicious fire that is raging, consuming mankind is not God's will for a creation He intended for it to be perfect, like the earth we came from.

The Core of the Fire

I stood in the core of the fire that was hotter than ever, and I refused to submit before the most influential images in my life. The system of this world faced me like a golden calf set high on a throne for me to worship as if it were my God. I saw the church before me, with its laws and bylaws, its do's and don'ts, its bigotry and hate, its scorn and pride and told it, "I won't bow before your images, even if you threaten to hurt me." I saw every negative incident in my life and every person who despised and hated me for being whom I am and standing firm with conviction, telling the system, telling the world that controls and destroy people's lives, "I won't bow down to you, even if you try to kill me." And I saw the many people who helped, loved and encouraged me, standing before me like faces in a mirror, and I said, "Thank you for your love and for not being ashamed of me, but reaching out to me, without gain for yourself on this earth."

My cocoon was made before I was born, before the foundation of the world, and God has protected me from the fiery furnace that this world is engulfed in. He promised me that he would never leave me, and I believe Him.

I understand like never before, like nothing else in my life, that it is more important to be willing to die for what is right, than to live for what is wrong.

I was Dancing in Fire but now I am "Beyond the Fire and the Rain."

Afterword

Therefore, I will not refrain my mouth;
I will speak in the anguish of my spirit;
I will complain in the bitterness of my soul.

Job 7:1

African Americans have faced racial prejudice, racism, and low self-esteem since slavery. As an African American, I have faced some racial, social and personal walls. If it were not for God, my parents and my wife, I don't believe that I would have become a medical doctor. Physicians are not born; they are made. The ingredients that make a medical doctor are faith, hope, perseverance, determination, and study. My faith in God has become my shield that protects me from the blazes of the cares of life. Hope has pointed me in the direction of a bright tomorrow. Perseverance has kept my doubting soul company, determination has been my staff on an unsure path, and study has quickened my mind. The success of my stormy passage across the dessert, over the rugged mountains, and across the choppy seas, has been the Creators grace. His grace is sufficient for me. God has never forsaken me.

I struggled against the odds to enter medical school, and become a successful physician. We will experience success if we stand on a foundation of love, truth, justice, forgiveness, and reconciliation. We can win every battle if we believe that we can with God who loves us, as He guides us.

Beyond the Fire and the Rain spoke to you about failure, triumph, and success. Failure, triumph, and success will prepare you to face your later years gracefully, humbly, and courageously. You will be blessed as you seek all that is just before God. We all need to be successful, and overcome challenges and prejudice from without and from within.

I pray that my journey has been inspirational for you, and you will soar like eagles, peering with your mental and spiritual eyes at the blazing challenges of your life. My hope and prayer is that you will gain strength and support from your parents, family, friends, and well-wishers, and that you will see obstacles as ridges to scale toward your dreams, goals, and aspirations. I sincerely desire that you will have a lifetime partner who will be as loving and as dedicated to you as my wife has been to me. Teach your children to face their challenges with hope, love, and courage with faith in God. Teach your children to fight the just battles against the enemy. Share with them the weapons of warfare that are not carnal, but spiritual. God will allow His grace to be sufficient for you and your children. I am living proof that one can make it Beyond the Fire and the Rain.

Special Acknowledgment

To my special friend, Dr. Robert V. Vaughn who spent eight years and countless hours incubating my work inside your humble, kind and gentle soul. I decided to combine your engineering labor on my two books, "*Dancing in Fire*" and "*Shouting at the Rain*" into one book. I am sure you would not make a fuss over my decision other than to tell me as you told me 20 years ago to not do it. You know I have always followed your advice. I know you will forgive me. It is going to be okay. I am never going to change another thing about these books except to put the names of some people who you suggested I not mention because I might loose allies in St. Croix.

Bob, it does not matter to me anymore if I have allies or enemies. I am at peace knowing that the precious hours and your careful care of my emotions by your tender and firm words has finally awakened me. You spent countless hours, afternoons and nights laboring over me. Why you allowed me more than 26 years in your company I will never know. I do know that your company and advice has made me a better man. You added to the foundation of my acceptance of me.

I know now that you set me up months before you left me to go home to be with God. You knew all along things that I as your friend and doctor did not know. You prepared me without telling me that you were going to die. I am still recovering from your departure.

I remember when you hand carried to my office an envelope with documents. You personally handed me everything I needed to know about your history and journey. You selected songs through others that you wanted sung at the celebration of your departure. I should have known.

You got the last one on me Bob. I should have never put it pass a B24 Bomber pilot to be prepared. You really laid it on me when after your departure; I was told that you wanted me to give your eulogy at your funeral. I am not sure but I believed you said the same thing to me one evening while we sat in your living room and had a beer.

So, Bob you prepared me for many things in this life. Some of it was forced but needed. Thank you. Thank you for loving me. Thank you for sharing your life with me.

Bob, I really think I had the last earthly word concerning you. I told a church filled with people who love you about some of our secret talks. When I see you, I will tell you all about it, if you do not already know.

By the way, the new title to your great work is, "Beyond the Fire and the Rain." Thank you for helping me get there.

Love, Buddy